M000236905

praise for seven

Leah Pump has delivered a candid coming of age narrative, recounting the innocence of youth, (with all of its emotional anxiety), and the joy of earned wisdom. It's a fun and compelling read.

– LaTanya Richardson Jackson

Leah is an inspiration to young girls everywhere, I'm so grateful she answered God's purpose for her, which has been a benefit to our community. *Seven* is Leah's written testimony, to help others get to a place of love, healing and completion.

– Cookie Johnson

The new book, *Seven* by Leah Pump, is a brave chronicle with a noble purpose. In this harrowing account of her true life suffering, Ms. Pump delivers a straightforward yet searingly brutal glimpse into the inner turmoil that keeps many victims of emotional domestic abuse tied to their abusers. Through this spellbinding memoir, Leah shares the gut wrenchingly raw *Seven* year emotional roller-coaster ride to learning the true meaning of love and self-worth. Ms. Pump vividly shares how she not only found the light at the end of a dark and tumultuous tunnel, but how she eventually became a beacon for herself and all the lives she touches. This compelling journey of transformation and self-discovery will surely inspire and serve as a helpful resource for those navigating their own path to self-love. Leah is a survivor of devastating abuse who was able to leverage her horrendous experiences and strong faith to become a powerful force for good in the lives of other young women through her creation of the LadyLike Foundation. Leah wholeheartedly devotes herself in all her philanthropic endeavors to ensure that no person will have to go through what she endured. This well written and frank retelling is a profoundly moving and inspirational must-read for those looking to bring meaning and purpose to themselves as well as to their romantic relationships. With all the chaos in our country right now, this message of perseverance and hope is beyond timely.

– Jami Morse Heidegger

Seven is an Intriguing read from the first page to the last page, which made it difficult to put down. I was thoroughly engaged with Leah's journey through her romances and compelled to learn the outcome of her Life experiences.

– Pauletta Washington

Seven by Leah Pump is a heart wrenching tell of personal pain and triumph. In what must have been a harrowing *Seven* years, Pump details her experience of excessive mental abuse at the hands of the man she thought loved her. Her spiral into the abyss of codependency and perceived love colored her ability to see the daily destruction to her otherwise sound decision making and exceptional drive. In *Seven* years Pump became a mere shadow of the person she once was, but through sheer strength, fortitude, and her undeniable faith, she was able to find herself again. The relatability of a first love is a familiar theme, but Pumps recount of a first love filled with manipulation, degradation, and abuse should serve as a warning to young women everywhere. In the most bold yet eloquent way, Pump has used her own experience to highlight the signs of predatory behavior for young women not yet out in the world, and has delivered a story of inspiration and triumph for those women experiencing a similar circumstance. *Seven* is definitely a must read for women everywhere.

– Lorna Kyles

We all have trials and tribulations in our lives. I respect Leah so much for being willing to share her journey, including her missteps, so that young women and men can learn from her story. Her book *Seven* is a transparent look at difficult times in her life, obstacles and relationships she had to overcome. The one thing that remains constant in her discovery is her faith. Her faith got her through to a better place. She now stands on solid ground.

As Michelle Obama says, 'We all have a story'. This is Leah's story.

– Debra L. Lee

Seven is a riveting, deeply personal portrayal of the many manifestations of falling in love for all the wrong reasons . . . and, ultimately, wondrous redemption through faith and complete obedience to God. Leah opens her heart and provides a brutally honest lens into the most intimate aspects of her life. Through these pages, our own faith is challenged. We witness the importance of having a strong, "prayed-up" mentor, with a commanding presence, who does not hesitate to let us know when we're veering away from God's path. Finally, we witness the Grace and Favor of God in all its splendidness. *Seven* is a must-read. Fasten your seatbelts for the ride.

– Vicki Palmer

Leah has dedicated her life to the enrichment and empowerment of young ladies. She teaches them the importance of self love and self respect using etiquette as a tool and education as a priority. Leah believes in the power of prayer and has been raised to have a relationship with God, which we have in common. I admire her devotion to The Lady Like Foundation. She has made a commitment to be the vehicle for change in the lives of so many young ladies. Leah is a true blessing to so many. I'm so proud to call Leah Pump a sister and friend. I love her!!

– Simone I. Smith

seven

A Story Of Love, Overcoming Challenges, Reinvention, And Being Complete

Leah Pump

with Ashley Williams

Seven. © 2021 by Leah Pump. All rights reserved. No part of this publication may be reproduced, distributed, or transmitted in any form or by any means, including photocopying, recording, or other electronic or mechanical methods, without the prior written permission of the publisher, except in the case of brief quotations embodiedd in critical reviews and certain other noncommercial uses permitted by copyright law. For permission requests, write to the publisher, addressed "Attention: Permissions Coordinator," 500 N. Michigan Avenue, Suite #600, Chicago, IL 60611.

13th & Joan books may be purchased for educational, business or sales promotional use. For information, please email the Sales Department at sales@13thandjoan.com.

Printed in the U.S. A.
First Printing, 2020
Library of Congress Cataloging-in-Publication Data has been applied for.

ISBN: 978-1-953156-28-0

letter from Leah...

I thought about this over and over and really searched my mind to see what lessons I wanted my readers to come out with after reading this book. I really didn't want this book to be just entertainment and enjoyment but to be an informative tutorial that might assist in this maze of love relationships.

In this maze you must discover who you are and your worth. You also have to know that God is directing your steps, and you have to be open. Throughout this maze you will discover self-love and finding the love that is meant and matched perfectly for you.

In your past you may have been treated as someone's trash, but what you have to realize is that someone, somewhere will treasure you.

Discovering who you are and your value is not an overnight process, but it is a tedious, challenging, heartbreaking effort that may take years. Whether your journey is one year or several, like mine, learning lessons is what makes it all worth it.

Be encouraged as you travel through my candid excursion. Enjoy the education!

The Best is Yet to Come!

Leah

forward

There is nothing more beautiful than the transition of a caterpillar to a beautiful monarch butterfly. The transition is not an easy one; it has struggles in its attempt to go from a darkened cocoon to the bright light of freedom.

This book takes us on an extraordinary journey of a young lady who goes from a fragile, insecure individual to a self-assured woman of distinction. She invites us to journey with her amid the many challenges she faces and allows us to grapple with consequences of her life-changing decisions. As we read this book, we find ourselves at times crying, at times laughing, at times shaking our heads, at times disappointed, and at times wanting to give a standing ovation.

I think all of us see ourselves in this book within our different relationships. It offers hope and real solutions if you are open to the lessons. It is so hard for many of us to listen to advice from the mentors in our lives or from people who mean well. We basically look for people who will agree with our thinking instead of adhering to real and authentic counsel that may not be what we are used to or agree with.

God gave me the job of being Leah's life coach throughout her journey. To see her real pain and then give advice that I knew at times she did not agree with, understand, or that seemed harsh, she would be obedient and follow. I never had a mentee to follow instructions to a "T" like Leah. However, when I see her end result, I am confident that although it was challenging, it was necessary.

May God bless you as you read this book and be better because of it.

Dr. Robert A. Williams Jr.
Pastor of McCoy Memorial Baptist Church
Los Angeles, California

dedications

I dedicate this book to the Lord, who carried me through this journey and blessed me beyond my wildest dreams. I also dedicate this book to my husband Dana, the one who taught me what real love feels and looks like. The one who always makes me shine and loves to see me succeed. You are my perfect match, my blessing, tailor-made just for me.

To my mother and grandmother Lillian Walker and Natha Lusk, where would I be without your constant care and support? You never gave up on me, you prayed for me, and you were there for me. I love you with all my heart. To my father, thank you for your patience and your love. I am so glad you got to see the finished product of me before you passed. How I miss you, and I hope I have made you proud.

To Ashley Williams, thank you for helping me put my story into words. Your encouragement and drive made this dream a reality.

Finally to my forever life coach and friends Dr. Robert Williams and Debbie Williams, thank you for your love, advice, and helping me to become who I am today.

This is for all of you!

negative six

A hundred and fifty pounds. I was a twelve-year-old girl carrying this much weight on me, and I wasn't even five feet yet. For as long as I could remember, I'd struggled with my weight. Diet and weight issues weren't the typical struggles of a young girl, but they were mine. Unlike other young children, I never had the luxury of going shopping in the children's department at any store. I was promoted without any hesitation from my parents and grandparents to the junior department at the tender age of seven.

I could never wear the cool, cute, trendy, fashion forward clothes that my peers wore. I had a deep desire to wear them, but with every dressing room visit, the horror would begin. I just could not fit them! They were either too tight or too short, and awkward to say the least. But I was driven, no matter what size I was, to wear the trendy clothes and fit in with my friends.

I remember one year shopping with my mother and grandmother. I was determined to purchase a Guess jean miniskirt that all the girls would be wearing at school that year. We went to the junior department, and I found it! I started pulling the miniskirts from the racks with excitement. I just knew I was going to be, as kids of today say, "lit" when I went back to school. As I pulled my final choices to try on in the dressing room, my mom came flying toward me saying, "Oh no, you have to put those back!"

Confused and a little frustrated, I said, "No, this is what I want to wear for school."

She looked again at my choices and in a calm voice said, "Leah, please put those back. Let's look at the flared jean skirts as opposed to the straight miniskirts."

By this time, I was really frustrated. With great determination, I kept the miniskirts in my hand, clutching them so tight even Superman could not have pried them out.

At this point, my grandmother rushed over to see what the commotion was all about. "What's going on over here?" she asked.

"I was explaining to Leah that she needs to put those tight miniskirts back, and we should focus on the flared denim skirts. They would be more flattering on her," my mother replied.

"Oh, just let her try them on. It's okay," my grandmother said, trying to defuse the situation. I assumed by the look on her face that she did not want me to have the miniskirt either. Perhaps she wanted me to see for myself how it would look on me, and then I would make the decision to proceed toward the flared skirts.

My mom became angry and told me with her strong, not playing expression and a voice that meant business, "Leah, put the skirts back now!"

"No, Mom!" I replied. "I want this one. Why can't I have one?"

"Because you are too fat!" she said with a loud voice, so loud that everyone in that section of the department store stopped and were all looking at me.

With that statement, there was no more discussion. I commenced putting the miniskirts back and began looking at the flared skirts.

Was I really that big? I was so embarrassed and so deflated. My feelings were so crushed I barely spoke for the rest of the day. I vowed to never to try on those types of clothes again and willingly shopped wherever my size permitted.

It never seemed to bother my dad so much because I guess it kept the boys off me, but with my mom it was different. She was very concerned about my weight. She worried so much about me because I would hoard food in my room under my bed. I would eat all night because this was the only time I didn't have restraints on me. Food was the first thing I would think about when I woke up and the lullaby that put me to sleep. The hoarding started to get out of control. It seemed like every time my parents would bring home delicious treats, as soon as the coast was clear, I would confiscate them and put them under my bed. My bed became a collection of snacks: chocolate chip cookies, licorice, M&Ms, potato chips, you name it, I had it! I had my own convenience store at my disposal under my bed.

Although my dad was lenient before, on one particular day he'd had enough. That day I came home from school, and it seemed like he had been awaiting my arrival because as soon as the door creaked open and he heard my footsteps, he began yelling, "Leah! Get in here now!"

I walked into the room, and there he was. He had removed the mattress and stripped everything from the bed to reveal what was under it. I was caught red-handed. He stood there with his face full of disgust and frustration. Then he began ranting.

"This is what you do all night? You hoard food under your bed! What is wrong with you? Leah, this is nasty! Not only do you have food, but you have bugs. Do you see the gnats flying in the air over your bed? This is unhealthy, and it has to stop. You have got to stop eating so much! You can't have any candy or sweets for the rest of the week, do you hear me?"

Just like being in the department store with my mother and the fiasco with the miniskirt, once again I was deflated and completely embarrassed. Why did I do that? Why did I hoard food? More importantly, why was I so hungry all the time? My parents were beyond frustrated with me, and they were at their wits' end with strategies to cease my eating habits, but nothing was working.

At school, I would eat my lunch early in the morning, so by the time lunch actually came, I didn't have any food. I'd beg all my friends for the lunch their moms packed them, so of course they would go home and tell their moms that I never had any food. The news always seemed to get back to my mom because she taught at the school I attended. So not only would she hear about me begging for food from the other parents, but she would see me sitting at the lunch benches with an empty lunch box while all the other kids were enjoying their lunches. She'd be so ashamed. Before I knew it, my mom signed me up for a Weight Watchers class, and here I was 12 years old weighing myself in front of all of these oversized adults. I even wore girdles, which were Spanks at the time, tummy wrappers, I mean all kinds of things. It didn't matter to me; food was still my comfort.

My weight led to me getting bullied by a group of boys at my school. But there was one boy in particular, Anthony, who made it his business to make sure he bullied me every single day. As soon as I would hear "Hey, blubber," I knew I was about to get socked and called all types of other names. I would always come home with bruises, and one day when I came home, my dad, fed up, told me, "The next time you come home with a bruise on your arm, I'm gonna put a bruise on you!" My dad's stern voice and strong eyes made my heart beat twice as fast when he was angry at me. I knew he meant business.

This meant I was going to have to stand up for myself to these bullies, and one day I did. We were all on the playground playing four square, and here came my personal bully, yelling, "You're so fat and you're so ugly!" Everyone was laughing hysterically until I got so annoyed that I threw the big red four square ball as hard as I could at his head, and it knocked him out. Clear as day! It felt so good to see Anthony lying on the ground like that. Needless to say, I never had a bruised arm again.

Ironically enough, years later, Anthony and I ended up going to the same high school. He kind of asked me to prom, and I kind of laughed right in his face and said, "Are you kidding me? You're the guy that used to bully me every day!"

I'll never forget what he said back to me: "Well, yeah, but you look so different now." And it was true, I did look different. I felt different too. When I turned thirteen, I decided to lose weight because I became interested in boys.

My mother recalls one day after coming home from school, I came into the kitchen where she was preparing dinner, and I said out of the blue, "Fat people are not even considered." She said that with that statement she knew that it was my critical point, and I was ready to take control over my weight. She did not know what triggered me to say something like that, and I never mentioned why I said it, but finally it seemed like this was the breakthrough she had been praying for.

I started taking care of my body and being mindful of what I ate. Instead of eating so many sweets, cookies, and breads, I would make healthier snack decisions like eating more fruits, proteins, trail mix, granola bars, and yogurt, and I drank a gallon of water a day. The weight slid right off of me. For the first time ever, I felt good about myself. I actually began to like the way I looked. I felt beautiful, confident, and proud that I actually was able to lose the weight on my own. It was so empowering. I felt like I'd done this for me and not for anyone else. I realized that if I wanted to change I had to do it; I had to make the decision and focus on making it happen, and I did.

Losing weight was such a dramatic life-changing event for me I even wrote about it in my personal statement when applying for college. Within the essay I wrote about how being overweight truly worked on my self-esteem and caused my confidence and grades to plummet. Yet with determination, making a decision to change the way I viewed food, making healthier choices, and introducing exercise into my daily routine, I was able to lose the weight. This resulted in me gaining confidence and my grades improving. I ran for student body president and won. I also graduated with honors from my high school. Everything seemed to be falling into place, and I was very content.

Fast forward to my college life. I entered college with a sense of confidence and accomplishment. Because of what I was able to accomplish with losing weight, conquering low self-esteem, and overcoming so many obstacles, I knew that there was nothing I could not do in college. This newfound confidence resulted in getting more attention than ever from guys on campus. I attended uc Berkeley. Just imagine. I went from being bullied with no guys liking me to having the intelligent, intellectual, and athletic guys all going out of their way to get my attention! I felt like the ugly duckling that grew into a swan and loved every moment of it. Although

I had this newfound self-image and my self-love was increasing, when you have been overweight for a long period of time, no matter how good you look, you still see yourself as overweight. At times when I looked in the mirror I would see the overweight little girl that I used to be. Every day I had to tell myself that I was not that overweight little girl anymore, and I never would be. I knew that it would be work to stay the way I was, and I was dedicated and determined to do so.

At UC Berkeley, I was doing great with school, friends, getting acclimated into my classes, my dorm, and the freedom that I was receiving. I enjoyed *every bit* of the freedom because my childhood was so conservative and structured. Honestly, conservative and structured parenting might have been an understatement. In essence, I had helicopter parents. In fact, when I got into UC Berkeley, my mom literally signed my name on the line and said, "You're going to Berkeley. No other school will do." I had gotten into a number of amazing schools including USC and a number of Historical Black Colleges, but UC Berkeley was number one on my mother's list, probably because she'd graduated from there as well. Needless to say, she was ecstatic when I got in. I remember when I got the acceptance letter in the mail she literally shouted. I mean screamed with excitement. My mother is very conservative and very reserved, so to see her shout and scream for excitement, you have to know she was extremely happy, to say the least.

My dad was an actor, a professor at Cal State Dominguez Hills, a deacon, and preacher at our church. He was extremely strict but very fun, if that makes sense. He and my mom created the most amazing balance like Yin and Yang. Whereas my mom was strict, reserved, almost rigid, with very high standards and a highly organized, neat, scheduled lifestyle, my father was a mixture of a strict, stern disciplinarian with someone who was fun, athletic, outgoing, spontaneous, loud, and crazy. There was never a dull moment in our household. My parents were very hands-on and always present. Almost too present, never missing a moment in our lives.

Education is a pillar of importance in my family. My mom was a teacher in LAUSD for over forty years, as well as an administrator. She graduated from UC Berkeley and received her master's degree in education from USC and her second master's degree in administration from California State University of Los Angeles. My dad came to Los Angeles from Chicago to further his acting career. After meeting my mother and marrying her, he quickly learned from my grandparents that acting should be considered a secondary job, and he needed to have the tools to have a more stable career. After being encouraged by my mother and grandparents to go back to school, he completed his bachelor's and master's from California State University of Los Angeles in the area of theater arts and communications. My father was the first in his family to graduate from college and obtain a post graduate degree. My uncle, my mother's brother, graduated from Stanford University and completed his medical school training at the Jules Stein Eye Institute at UCLA. He became an ophthalmologist.

My grandparents' idea of success was through education, so they too had college and post graduate degrees which they received after marriage and after having their children. My grandmother got her bachelor's and master's degrees from California State University of Los Angeles in education and administration, and my grandfather got his bachelor's degree from Prairie View A&M University and received double master's degrees in history and administration from USC.

My parents and grandparents raised my brother Chasen and me with uncompromising expectations of what we were to do. It wasn't a question of if we were going to college, but what college we were going to, and what our plans were after we graduated. Chasen was a super athlete, playing first string in basketball, baseball, and football. He was also an ultra-focused straight-A student, winning honor roll athletic awards every year. He was not only smart, but he had the drive of a Michael Jordan and Kobe Bryant. He had to be the best at anything he did, and he was. His schedule was packed with training, practice, tutoring, and church obligations. He wanted to become a pro athlete and had the grades and potential to become whatever he desired if his dream of going to the NBA, NFL, or MLB did not come to pass.

I was not a straight-A student because I struggled in math. As result I had a rigorous schedule of tutoring because I needed the grades and scores to meet the college admission requirements of the schools I wanted to get into. I engaged in tutoring twice a week and even on Saturdays, which was torturous. I hated it. I was also involved in performing arts, theater, singing, dance, leadership, church every Sunday, Sunday school, AND service. We were also heavily involved in our church's choir and participated in the youth activities at my church twice a week, every week. I was the president of the youth department, part of the Red Circle girls, which was the community service youth girl group at our church, attended Bible study, fed the homeless, and was involved in every aspect of the ministry. So let's just say by the time I reached college, I was churched out. So at Berkeley, I decided I wasn't going to go to church. I wanted to enjoy a less rigorous, rigid, and conservative lifestyle. I wanted to just be free to have fun and do exactly as I pleased. I felt like the caged bird that had been finally set free.

Absolutely nothing felt better than sleeping in every Sunday. My parents weren't there to wake me up early because we had to go to church, plus I didn't have a car as a freshman, which was the excuse I gave my parents. Yet my dad still called me every Sunday morning at 6:30 asking me, "What church are you going to today?"

I'd always say, "Dad, I'm not going to church. I don't have a car. How will I get there? Which church could I go to?"

He'd always reply with, "Well, you need to find one!" I'd hang up the phone and go right back to sleep.

He was relentless; he'd keep calling. Every single Sunday, he would call. "Leah, what church are you going to? Why don't you go to that church with that young guy who comes to visit our church in July? He seems young and energetic; it would be a fun church for you to go to. You should go! Plus, he knows our pastor so it would be perfect. They could look out for you and everything."

Sigh. "Okay, Dad, I'll think about it, okay?" Lord knows I was enjoying my new Sundays, but those 6:30 a.m. Sunday calls were getting on my last nerve. Maybe a part of me did feel bad too.

I had a friend at Berkeley that grew up with me at my church in LA named Tina. She was in her junior year of college, so she seemed to have the whole college thing down pat and taught me the ins and outs of Berkeley. Tina was one of my best friends; she looked out for me. It turns out that Tina's parents had been telling her to find a church in the Bay Area for years too. Just our luck, our parents talked after church about how proud they were of their Berkeley girls, and how we needed to find a church home. When my dad found out Tina had a car, I was all out of excuses. Our parents teamed up on us.

One day, Tina called my dorm room and said, "Okay. Let's just go to church to make our parents happy. We'll just go, and we won't have to go back." I agreed and kissed my sleep-filled Sundays goodbye.

The following Sunday, we woke up early and put on some decent clothes that were appropriate for church. Since I'd decided that I was not going to go to church, I didn't have any so-called "church clothes," but I put on the nicest dress I had. We looked up the location of the church my dad had been telling me about with this young preacher. It was in Oakland, so we got into Tina's Honda Civic and drove out. We got to the church a little late, sat in the back, and to our surprise, the service was amazing. The pastor's preaching was fresh and exciting. You could relate to his message, and it was very easy to comprehend. To be honest, he was remarkable! I held on to every word he said as if he were speaking just to me; it was something I had never felt before.

After church, it was tradition that if you are from a sister church, you are to go up to the pastor and introduce yourself, your church, and who your pastor is. So Tina and I sauntered up to the front where the pastor was greeting other members. We waited our turn, and when we got his attention, he introduced himself to us. "Hello! I'm James Jordan."

We told him our names, that we attended UC Berkeley, and that we were from Mt. Everlasting Baptist Church, where Dr. Michael Harris Sr. was the pastor. Immediately, his face lit up with excitement. "Oh my God, that's my pastor! I consider him a father." After he found out where we went to church and where we went to school, he was all in. It was like knowing that didn't make us strangers anymore. He continued the questions. "So you both are students at Berkeley? What year are you in? You guys must be pretty smart, huh?"

We just looked at each other and smiled to ourselves.

I told him I was a freshman, and Tina said she was a junior. "Well, if there's ANYTHING you guys need, I mean anything you need at all, we have computers you both can use. Even if you need ink, school supplies, items in your dorm room, or ANYTHING, just let us know and we will take care of it."

Tina and I were looking at each other with complete dismay that he was so welcoming to us. We were like, "Oh we're good! But thanks so much."

He told us, "Okay, but just in case you need anything at all, let me give you my number."

It was like I heard what he was saying, but at the same time, I was zoned out. The entire time he was speaking to us, the only thing I could think of was how fine this man was. I mean, have you ever seen a man so fine you have to ask God why he made him so fine? He had a chocolate brown complexion with capturing dark brown eyes and long eyelashes. Straight white teeth. His hair was very neat and cut close to his head, and he had a perfect build. He stood about 5'10 or 5'11, not too buff nor too skinny. From his mannerisms to his aroma to his immaculate style, the man was perfect. He reminded me of the actor Idris Elba. Same build, same look, and same swag. I was awestruck. To be honest, I'd had a small crush on him ever since he had started coming to our church in Los Angeles, and he had been coming for years. I never told anyone; it had been my little secret fantasy. He'd had an established day at Mt. Everlasting since I was about five or six years old: every first Sunday in July. I vividly recall being sixteen years old and sitting in one of his guest sermons. I remember praying, "Lord, please let him wait for me." So of course I knew exactly who my dad was talking about when he was trying to describe this "young and energetic" preacher. But for some reason, his attractiveness was even more apparent as he was speaking to me and Tina. I was mesmerized.

I finally snapped back into reality as he told us, "Well, if you need anything, you have my phone number. Just call us!"

We left the church and headed back to the car for our ride back to campus. As we got in the car, Tina said, "Gosh, he is really nice, don't you think?" She looked at me with wide eyes.

"Yes, he's so cool and he's SO fine!"

Tina was shocked. "Girl, what? You need to stop. He is old!"

"I know, I know! But he's FINE."

We both laughed together sitting in the car. Tina was probably thinking the same; she just couldn't believe I'd actually said it out loud. But I couldn't help myself. When we finally stopped laughing, we headed out of Oakland and started the drive to campus. I went to my dorm, completed some homework, then, of course, went back to sleep.

A few weeks later, Tina and I decided to go back to the church. This time, we made the decision on our own, without our parents forcing us. As we walked down the aisle, he stopped his sermon to say, "Oh! The Berkeley girls are here! The Mt. Everlasting Baptist Church girls who go to Berkeley are here!" Now everyone was greeting us, making us feel even more welcomed than last time. Inside, I was smiling so hard. As we sat down, he said, "Make sure you see me after service!"

Tina and I looked at each other, both wondering what he wanted to say to us. Throughout the entire service, during the sermon, the songs, and the offering, I was *only* thinking about seeing him after service and what he was going to say to us. I could hardly wait for service to end just to be in his presence again. I honestly couldn't even tell you what the sermon was about that day.

When we got out of church, Tina and I walked down the aisle again, waiting for him to finish talking to the members just like the last time. When he was done, he was so excited to see that we were waiting to speak to him, as if he wasn't the one that had told us to come see him after service. He asked us how classes were going and how we were adjusting to Oakland, but it was just small talk. Then he said, "You know what, why don't you guys come to my office?" Tina and I gave each other the look that friends give each other when they're trying to keep it cool but are kind of freaking out on the inside. So we walked to his office, and I was feeling really special because I didn't know any pastor who would take you to his office to continue talking.

We entered his office and almost immediately he began asking us all kinds of questions about our lives. Not in a weird way, though; it seemed like he wanted to know more about us to really be a mentor figure. He had this way about him that made us feel so comfortable that we could talk to him about anything. He was asking us about LA, how long we had been friends, which classes we were currently in, and if we liked the Bay Area. Then the questions got more and more personal.

"So do you two have boyfriends?"

We both laughed. "No."

"Are you virgins?"

Tina looked at me at the exact time I turned to look at her. This time we both showed the surprise on our faces and awkwardly said no. Now that question was awkward. I was wondering where he was going with this.

Unfazed, he continued on, "Okay, well, what's your relationship like with your fathers?"

I could tell Tina was over his questions, so I answered first. "My dad doesn't really understand me. We fight a lot. We're very up and down. He is very overprotective, and we don't see eye to eye on a lot of things." The truth was, my dad was very much a part of my life; in fact, he was there too much. He was just extremely strict and protective. I was definitely the apple of his eye, and he did not want me out of his sight, grasp, or control, so trying to get my way constantly led to arguments. But I didn't feel it was necessary to tell Pastor Jordan all of that. To be honest, I don't know why I didn't tell him the whole truth. When I was done answering that question, Tina replied, "My dad and I are fine."

Before he could even ask another question, I blurted out, "SO WHY ARE YOU SINGLE?" I wasn't even planning on asking him that. I noticed he did not have on a wedding ring, but I honestly don't even know where that question came from. Tina was eyeing me like she had seen a ghost. She mouthed to me, *What are you doing?*

I ignored her. "Is it just that you haven't met a nice young lady yet?"

"No, I haven't."

Surprised, I said, "Wow, how old are you?"

"Thirty-five."

In my head, I started calculating the difference between thirty-five and eighteen.

At this point Tina was on the other side of the office going crazy. She kept crossing her hand across her neck trying to signal me to shut up. By now, Tina was ready to leave, but I was too engaged in this conversation.

Then Pastor Jordan said, "So why do you ask that?"

"I mean, you're such a nice-looking man. Shame that you're single."

He just smiled. Tina's jaw dropped. She was looking at me like I had lost it. I really thought I had lost it too. Why did I say that? I had felt so comfortable asking him all of these questions that I didn't even think about how out of line I was.

Suddenly, Tina grabbed me by the hand and said to him, "Well, service today was amazing, thank you for everything!" And we walked out of his office.

When we got to the car, Tina slammed her door and yelled, "Why would you do that? You're doing too much, Leah! His questions were out of line! Are we virgins? What are our relationships like with our fathers? He sounds like a predator!"

"No he's not. It's fine!"

"It's *not* fine! And you were flirting with that guy! Like *really* flirting with him!"

I didn't say anything back to her. I mean, what could I say? She had been in the room and had heard everything for herself. Inside, I knew I liked him, I mean *really* liked him. But of course I'd never say that to anyone because he was way older than me. *Seventeen* years older than me. That was way too old, so I decided to just keep him as a secret little crush.

Back at Berkeley, I was enjoying my freshman year way more than I had ever expected. I never imagined I'd ever have this much fun, especially coming from a background like mine with constant restraints. There were parties every night, and so many handsome guys. There were all kinds of athletes: football players, basketball players, baseball players, and even Greek life. So of course every night all the girls would dress to impress. At least that was my plan. We were all dressed to kill. Since I had gone to summer bridge, I'd gotten to know most of the athletes and the other African Americans on campus. Summer bridge is a program that most colleges have where the incoming freshman class has a chance to stay on campus during the summer, take classes, and live in the dorms. It is a great way transition into college life, to become familiar with the campus and get to know the professors. It is also a way to get a jump start on earning units that will go toward graduation. Usually summer bridge programs are mainly composed of African American and minority students.

There were not many of us on campus, so the few African American students at Berkeley always seemed to come together. Not to mention, I was getting *a lot* of attention. Being an LA native, which has a lot of Hollywood influence, and going into any other state or city typically causes you to stand out because of your "Cali Girl" style or fashion. We have this certain vibe and style about us that is different from most states. I am a girly girl, from my hair to my nails to my toes, and I always made sure I looked good. So of course I was talking to guys, I was dating, I was meeting all types of diverse people on campus. I was having a BLAST. I was also doing amazingly well in my classes. It seemed like everything was coming together.

One day during summer bridge, my new friend Emily, who was also from Los Angeles, and I were walking to statistics class. When we met, we had an immediate connection and would be together every day. During our long walk to class, which was on the other side of campus, we would often have deep discussions about life, our parents, and shopping, which was our all-time favorite pastime.

Emily interrupted our conversation and asked me, "What type of man do you see yourself marrying one day?" I paused for a minute to think. As I was thinking, Emily said with great determination, "I want to marry an athlete. I can see myself as an athlete's wife. I would go to all the games to root him on and live in a big mansion. My life will be fabulous!"

I agreed with her. She seemed like she would be a great athlete's wife. She was a cheerleader in high school and had a great positive, supportive spirit. After quick deliberation, I said, "I want to marry a pastor. I want to be the first lady of a church."

Emily was shocked and amazed. "Why would you want to be that? I have never heard anyone say they wanted to marry a pastor."

My answer was very calculated and candid. "I have always wanted to marry a pastor. They are some of the most powerful people on the planet. I was raised in church, so celebrities to me were my pastor, first lady, and their families. I love the way they dress, their hats, how they smell, and how they carry themselves. First ladies are the epitome of class. All the women in church want to be just like them, and they are partners in ministry with their husbands."

I absolutely loved ministry. To be honest, although I was taking a break from church and wanted to experience life outside of it, I missed being in church. My heart is in ministry; it's my comfort zone. I'd loved all of the leadership positions I'd held at the church where I was raised, and I carried out my duties with passion and precision. So naturally when Emily asked me, I knew exactly what I wanted to say…I longed to be the first lady of a church.

After I explained to Emily why I wanted to marry a pastor, she had this grin on her face. "Okay, go on, first lady!"

"That's right!" I said, and we continued on to statistics class.

One morning, too early in the morning actually, I got a phone call. I slowly got out of bed to walk to the phone. I just knew it was one of my parents checking in. Nobody ever called me that early except for my parents, and they'd lose their minds if I didn't answer.

I drowsily yawned, "Hello?"

This slow, deep, raspy voice said, "Hello... May I speak to... Leah?"

"This is Leah; may I ask who's calling?" I said, puzzled.

"This is Reverend."

Oh my God. It was HIM calling me. I jumped up and snatched my sleepy voice away. "Hi!! How are you! So good to hear from you!" I exclaimed.

He began to say, "I just called to see how you were doing and if there was anything that you needed."

"Oh no, no, I'm good! I'm actually doing great, everything's going great!" I said.

"That's really good to hear. What time are your classes today?"

"Oh, they're not until later," I told him.

"Well, would you like to go to lunch?"

My heart stopped. The world stopped. *What should I say?* My head was spinning.

"Ummm, oh no, I have class and a ton of other things to do today. I can't have lunch today."

"Okay, well maybe some other time?"

"Yeah, maybe some other time," I rushed out.

In my head, I was thinking... *na uh.* NOPE. *I mean yes I have a crush on this guy and everything, but I definitely am not mentally prepared for lunch or anything like that. Nope!*

"Well, if you need anything, please, please call me," he said.

"Okay, I will, thank you!"

That one call began to be an everyday phone call. Every morning, very early, he would call me. I was so excited to talk to him that I didn't even mind being woken up. He was persistent. I felt like he was only calling to make sure that I was okay, and to see if I needed anything. No man had ever taken that much interest in my well-being. I began to wonder if he was calling Tina as well, so one day I casually asked if Pastor Jordan had given her a call.

"Yeah, he called," Tina said shortly.

I thought, *Okay, maybe he's really just checking in on us*. But as time went on, the more he called me and the less he called Tina. I suppose he could feel Tina's energy because she was not feeling that comfortable with him since he'd asked us those intimate questions. So I am sure she probably was not as accessible as I was when he called.

One Monday morning, Pastor Jordan and I were talking on the phone, and he completely caught me off guard when he asked, "Can I take you to breakfast?" Typically, he would ask if he could take me to lunch, so I was always able to use classes and studying as a reasonable excuse. I guess he had remembered me telling him I didn't really have class on Mondays, except for one in the evening.

"Leah, I know you don't have classes until later today. Let me take you to breakfast," he said.

"Ummmm, I-I-I, ummm…" I couldn't come up with an excuse quick enough. Once again, my mind was racing, and nothing would come out of my mouth. I tried to say something, but I could not utter a sound.

"You don't have anything to do. I will be there in an hour. Will you be ready in an hour?"

"Yes…" I said reluctantly.

"Okay, I'm on my way. What dorm do you stay in?"

"I stay in Unit 3."

"Okay. I'll see you in an hour," he said before hanging up the phone.

Let me just say, you have never felt panic until your crush tells you he will be outside in an hour. I mean, this man was always catching me off guard! All I could think to myself was, *What the hell did I just get myself into? What am I going to do? What am I going to say?* WHAT AM I GOING TO WEAR?! *Do I need to act more mature for him?* Panic. Complete panic. I started looking through my closet and drawers, throwing tons of outfits on the bed. I decided on jeans and a pretty purple blouse. Pastor Jordan *always* looked spiffy from head to toe, so I felt like I needed to look fantastic. My roommate LaToya sat up from her bed and gave me *the look.*

"Sooo where are you going?" she asked suspiciously.

"Oh nowhere, just going to meet my friends to study."

"Mm-hmmm," she said before lying back down.

Of course I wasn't going to tell her where I was going. I wasn't going to tell anyone, not even Tina. There's no way I was telling anybody I was going out with a man that much older than me. Nonetheless, I got dressed and was ready in an hour. He called to tell me he had arrived, and I met him downstairs. He drove a Buick. He was really a preacher who drove a preacher's car. I was like, "Oh wow, this is going to be interesting..."

When he got out of the car, he had on a green and black Adidas sweatsuit. It was just awkward to look at because I was so used to him being in a suit and tie. It looked like he was trying to be young, but it just didn't look right. It wasn't him.

I got in the car and thanked him for picking me up to take me to breakfast. We ended up taking a ride around Berkeley, and he was showing me all types of landmarks surrounding the campus. He showed me Berkeley pier, and I was so ecstatic to see it because it reminded me of being home in LA. The Berkeley pier wasn't as assembled as the LA pier; we have rides and restaurants and all kinds of fair-like activities, but it didn't matter to me. I was able to stand on the bridge and look over the water, and that made me happy. He began to tell me more about him.

"When I was younger, my father was very mean at times because I had a speech impediment; I could not express myself like my siblings could. He told me if I could not talk to him without stumbling on my words then not to talk to him at all. So I would run away a lot and stay at different places, sometimes shelters. I remember taking a liking to preachers because they were the only ones that took me in and accepted me for who I was," he said.

I was hanging on every word this man said to me. I felt sorry for him, and his words endeared me to him even more. My feminine nurturing side kicked in, and all I wanted to do was hug him and tell him that everything was going to be okay.

"You know when you asked me why I was single, and if I had anyone special in my life?" he asked.

"Yes," I said nervously.

"Well, there is this woman that I have been with for over fifteen years. I stay with her because I feel like I owe her. She has been with me and helped me anytime I needed it. She has a daughter that's not mine, but her daughter calls me Dad, and I feel obligated to be with her. But I don't love her, I'm not in love with her, and I want to leave. I just don't know what to do."

Once again, I empathized with him. He seemed like such a nice and happy person, but I could tell he was hurting. Besides, I was only 18, and I had never been in a relationship like that to understand the dynamics of something that deep.

"Well, if you're not happy, then you should leave! Everyone deserves to be happy," I replied.

"I know," he said as he sighed. He paused. "I really like you, Leah."

I blushed and shyly put my head down. I was a bit uncomfortable because there was so much that he had told me about his upbringing and background and this relationship that he was stuck in. I was feeling overwhelmed. I was too young to be someone's counselor; I didn't even feel like I had the correct words to console him. Besides, in my head I was thinking, *Whatever happened to breakfast?* I smiled and told him, "I think it's time that I head back to campus so that I can get ready for class." He agreed, and we headed back to the car.

As we got closer to campus, I began to think to myself, *I really hope nobody sees me with him...* So as he was talking about how appreciative he was of me going out with him, I quickly said, "Oh you can just drop me off right here!"

"Well, this isn't where you live, it's all the way down there. I'll drive you," he replied.

"Oh, I know, but you can just drop me off here. I could use the exercise!"

"Um, no, I'll take you to your dorm."

"No, no, right here is fine," I said hastily.

"Are you embarrassed to be with me?" he asked.

"Oh no, I can just use the walk, and I have a couple things I need to do before I go to my dorm."

He looked so confused, but luckily he let me out where I wanted him to. He gave me a hug and thanked me again for talking to him and listening to him. I got out of the car and started walking to my dorm. As I was walking, I began feeling emotions I had never felt before. Yes, this man had been my secret crush for years, yes, he was *fine,* but I felt confused and strange. I remember thinking *What am I getting myself into?* All I knew was I was too young to be dealing with all the vicissitudes of his life. *This isn't for me,* I said to myself. Yet I was having mixed feelings, so I walked to Emily's dorm. At this point, I just had to tell somebody. She was always easy to talk to and would be a great listener. I couldn't tell my parents, I couldn't tell my roommate, and I definitely couldn't tell Tina because it was obvious she wanted nothing to do with that situation.

I got to my girlfriend Emily's dorm room, and as soon as she opened the door, I said, "GIRL. You will never believe what just happened to me." I told her everything: that he was a preacher, he was older than me, and that he had just confessed his feelings to me.

"Well, how do you feel? Isn't this what you wanted, first lady?" she asked me.

"I don't really know," I replied.

"What do you think he wants?"

I have absolutely no idea, I thought to myself.

"Okay now, Leah, you got the older guys liking you too!"

We laughed, and I left her dorm before having to go to class.

The phone calls never stopped. Every morning, he would call me asking how my previous day was, if there was anything I needed, if I was available for lunch, and reminding me to come to church on Sunday. I never needed anything from him, and I didn't think I was ready to go out to lunch with him, but I felt comfortable going to church on Sundays. There were always people around, so I knew he wouldn't have the chance to get too personal with me again. At first I was still able to convince Tina to drive down to East Oakland every Sunday so that we could make it to service, but after a while she didn't want to go as much as I did. I guess she started to catch on, and she felt strongly about his predator vibes. But this meant that I didn't have a ride to church anymore, so one Sunday he called me asking why I'd missed service. I explained to him that I didn't have a ride anymore, so I would no longer be able to attend since it was so far from my school. "Oh, that won't be a problem," he said with ease. "I'll have one of my members pick you up every Sunday to bring you to church." So like he said, a member of his church picked me up the following Sunday and drove me back to campus after church. That routine became weekly. And that's when the relationship started.

Every time I would see James, I was constantly on a mission to look flawless, like I'd just stepped out of Vogue Magazine. He was the type of man who was very into fashion and well-groomed from head to toe—so well-groomed that he'd polish his shoes every single morning. He was very observant and meticulous when it came to his attire, which motivated me to be the same. I would spend my very last dime on a new dress, a blouse, or even a blazer just so that I could look good for him and look like I belonged with him. I knew I needed to find some sort of income if I was going to be able to keep up with his expensive lifestyle.

Not even a few days later, while I was in the nail shop, a woman kept admiring me from a few seats down. She eventually came up to me and told me that she admired my disposition and how I carried myself. She said that I'd make a great assistant. Her name was Pam.

"I own a hair salon in downtown Oakland, and I'd love for you to work for me. You can be my assistant; I'll teach you everything. Do you like doing hair?" she asked me.

"Yeah, I love doing hair!" I said quickly.

"Well, great. Here's my number. Give me a call, and we can arrange everything."

A couple days later, I met Pam downtown at her salon, and she gave me the job. I started working right away. She instructed me how to wash, perm, and set hair for her clients. Eventually, I got so good that I even started doing press and curls. In fact, I started doing hair in my dorm, mostly the hair of girls from Los Angeles. Most girls from Los Angeles love a flowy press and curl, and many stylists in the area did not specialize in press and curls. I learned how to master the technique and did almost all of the African American girls on the Berkeley campus. I would charge $20 a head, and $25 if they got a trim, and my appointments were always lined up! I made great money, plus I was able to get my hair done for free every week in the shop. It was a win-win. I loved it.

James and I began spending more time with each other, and after class he would always have me picked up and chauffeured to him, wherever he was. We spent many days visiting older people, going to various people's homes, or any preaching engagement he had to attend. I loved every second of being with him. He made me feel special and purposeful in his life. He would give me the best compliments, always reminding me that I was lovely and so smart and would often ask my opinion on various situations he had in his life. Being that he devoted his entire occupation to God, I trusted that God had sent him to me. Before I knew it, I was falling head over heels in love with him and throwing caution to the wind.

One night, he and I went to a lavish five-star restaurant by the lake. I had on a black blazer, black jeans, black heels, and soulful red lipstick, with my hair freshly done. He told me he liked it when my hair was done. He hated my hair pulled back or in a ponytail. He said my hair was beautiful and thick and looked best when it was down and classy. Because I wanted to please him so much, I made sure that my hair was always done to perfection, not one strand out of place. It was my goal to look as immaculate as he did, and I would do whatever it took to make sure I did so.

He had on a tailored gray suit and looked as if he had just finished a photo shoot with GQ Magazine. As I was ordering my food, I could see from the side of my eye that he was looking at me a certain type of way. When I was done ordering, he asked me, "Where are your earrings?" Usually, I would borrow my friends' or roommate's earrings, but that night I'd forgotten to put some on. I had never been a jewelry person, and I always misplaced my earrings, so I didn't bother to invest in any for myself. I just put on whatever I could borrow or whatever was closest in sight.

"I really don't have any," I said to him.

"Hm. Okay," he noted.

The next night, we ended up going out to dinner again. He was constantly on the go, so going to dinner became our norm. Just as our entrees were served, he placed a jewelry shopping bag on our table, right in front of me.

"I never want to see you without earrings again," he said as he pulled out multiple jewelry boxes. "I bought these for you." He opened all the boxes, and facing me were beautiful diamond earrings and gold hoop earrings. "Every time I see you, I want you to wear these, okay?" I was smitten and so surprised. No one had ever done anything like that for me. I thanked him for my gift and eagerly put on the diamond earrings with the biggest smile on my face. "Thank you so much, James, I love them!" I exclaimed to him. Unconsciously, I had just opened my Pandora's box, and he had the key.

One day while I was studying in my dorm room, I got a call from one of my friends whose hair I'd done the week before. She had always told me that the Lord spoke to her through dreams. She would tell me about times she would know that someone was about to die or things were going to happen before they happened. Anyway, I had a picture of James on my wall, and I guess she'd seen it while I did her hair.

"I had a dream about that guy you had a picture of," she said apprehensively.

"Really? Well, what did you see?" I asked curiously.

"Don't be scared, but I want to tell you that the Lord talked to me about you."

"Okay..." I replied.

"Well, I dreamt that the older man in the picture that you are dating, you are going to marry him. You are going to be a first lady. He's going to buy a green Ford Expedition for you and even propose to you with a 5 carat, pear-shaped diamond ring," she explained.

"Are you serious?! Wait, so are you sure you saw the ri—"

"But I also want you to know you are going to go through a rough time before everything gets better," she confessed.

"But are you sure you saw a ring?" I asked.

"Yes, Leah, I saw a ring," she giggled.

When I tell you that is all I needed to hear... that is *all* I needed to hear. The truth was, I had been looking for signs because at this point, I was still apprehensive to really be with James, even though I wanted to so badly. But after I heard my friend's prophecy, I was completely committed to making sure everything she said came true. God had spoken to me, and that was the only confirmation I needed.

A couple weeks later, it was winter break, which meant it was time for me to travel back to LA to be with my family. James insisted on taking me to the airport, so after I packed all of my bags and brought them downstairs in front of the dorm, he loaded them in his trunk. I had on my favorite Berkeley Cal sweatshirt, ripped jeans, and sandals. In my lap, I had my caboodle and my pillow, ready to get on the plane. As we were driving to the airport, he kept looking me up and down, kind of the same way he was eyeing me at the restaurant a couple weeks prior. Every time he gave me *that* look, it made me tense up a little and feel really insecure because I always put effort into making sure I looked good for him. Finally, he gave in and said, "What is that?" as he pointed to my caboodle case.

"Oh, this is my makeup case. I keep all of my eyeshadows and lipsticks and liners in here. I have been collecting makeup for years, and this helps to keep everything together," I confirmed.

"Oh, okay. And why are you carrying a pillow with you?" he asked.

"Because I love going to sleep on the plane!" I said as I laughed.

"Well, they have pillows on the plane…" he said with an odd expression.

"Oh, I know, but I like to bring my own pillow."

He gave me this strange look but continued driving. I thought nothing of it. When we got to the airport, he walked me as far as he could before we had to part ways. He told me that he would be waiting for me to get back and would pick me up from the airport as well. He hugged me and wished me a safe and blessed trip and told me to call him when I landed.

Back in LA, I felt more mature than ever. I had spent a lot of time getting to know myself and developing my own interests, dreams, and passions. Being at such a prestigious school, people seemed to respect me in a more elite way, and I loved it. I was completely different than the overweight young girl I had been and took pride in my self-growth and academic achievement. Even my family mentioned how much I had matured since leaving for Berkeley. We had a lovely winter break, but truthfully, I couldn't wait to get back to my own life in the Bay Area. All I could do over my break was think about James, apprehensive about fully committing to him, but honestly really wanting to. I wanted to be with him, but I was still a bit afraid.

James was blowing my phone up, calling and asking when I'd be back. He'd send me '444' on my pager every day, which meant *I love you.* If I didn't call him back immediately or in a timely fashion he would send '333' to my pager, which meant *divorce.* That made me nervous, and I would stop and call him immediately. When I figured out the date I'd be flying back to Oakland, I called James to let him know which terminal I'd be at, and what time I should be arriving. I was scheduled to arrive early Saturday morning. He told me he would be there, which made me even more ecstatic to get on that plane. My parents drove me to the airport and hugged me tightly before I walked inside. "Make good decisions!" my mom called out as I walked to the boarding gate.

When I landed, James was outside waiting for me just as he'd said he would be. It was the cutest thing to see how excited he was to see me. He screamed, "My Leah's back, my Leah's back!" He put all my luggage in the trunk and opened my door to help me inside the car.

"So how was it?" he asked.

"I enjoyed myself! I'm happy to be back, though."

He smiled. "I'm happy too."

As we were driving, he looked over to me and said, "You know, I really didn't like the way you looked in the airport when I dropped you off."

"What do you mean?" I asked. "I was just comfortable."

"Whenever I travel, I always dress nicely because I never know who I'm going to meet. You never know what opportunity may present itself, Leah, so you always want to make sure you look your best when you go to the airport, okay? From now on, I want you to look your best wherever you go."

"Okay," I mumbled quietly.

Every word he would speak to me I took seriously. He had a way of making me feel special, but he also made me feel like I had a lot to work on, and I was dedicated to working on myself in order to be the woman he wanted me to be. He made me challenge myself.

"Oh, and you know that pillow that you brought with you? That's tacky, don't bring that again. There are airplane pillows that you can use. Matter of fact, I'll buy you one," he exclaimed.

When we got closer to my school, he asked if I wanted to stop for food, but I insisted that I should get back to my dorm because I had to finish a couple assignments and prepare for the week. As we approached my dorm, he asked if I wanted help carrying my bags upstairs to my room. I insisted that I had it and it was okay.

"Are you ashamed to show me where you live?" he asked.

"Not at all. I just want to hurry upstairs so I can finish some assignments that are due tomorrow," I explained. I really didn't want him to come upstairs because our dorm room was a mess. My roommate and I were not good housekeepers. We were messy. God forbid anyone come to visit us; it would be embarrassing.

"No, I think you don't want me to see where you live. It's okay, I'll leave," he said like he was annoyed.

"I do want you to see where I live. I'm sorry, come up. I think my roommate is home," I said while taking his hand and leading him up the elevator to my dorm room.

As I turned the key to open my dorm room, I said loudly, "LaToya, I'm home" just in case she and her boyfriend were doing something inside. We had an agreement to do that every time we entered our dorm room so that neither one of us were surprised by what we saw on the other side of the door.

She screamed out, "Okay, cool, come in!"

We walked in, and the dorm room was a disaster. Clothes were everywhere: on the floor and draped over our beds. We had food open, and our trashcans were overflowing. So much so that gnats were flying above them. Our floor was covered with papers and shoes and snack droppings. In addition, it smelled. It was disgusting. It was a scene I was familiar with from when my dad found all of the food I had been hoarding under my bed. It was definitely a trigger from the past that I thought I had escaped.

James took one step in the room, dropped the bags, looked around, and was completely speechless. He looked like he had seen a ghost. He was shocked and disturbed.

He said, "Okay, Leah, I will see you later" and left.

I was so embarrassed. I knew what he was thinking. He thought I was nasty and dirty. How could he continue to date a girl like me? He talked all the time about how he hated nasty women who kept their homes and their cars dirty. Well, I fit the description, and now I knew how it felt. I now knew why my parents and grandparents always scolded me about keeping my room clean and organized. They taught me how to be clean, and I was just being rebellious. Now it was time to clean up my act, especially if I wanted to keep my man.

Back in my dorm, I unpacked and began to clean everything. LaToya felt the embarrassment and began cleaning her side as well. We promised each other to keep our room spotless and smelling beautiful. After hours of cleaning, I submitted my assignments and hung out with my friends for the rest of the day.

A few days later, I invited James to come back to see our room. I told him that the look on his face had gotten me together, and I knew he was disappointed with me. I'd cleaned and organized everything, and I wanted him to be proud of me. He came upstairs, and his face beamed. "That's my Leah!" he exclaimed. "This is how my perfect girl should live." I was so proud of myself and promised that no matter where I lived, it was going to be spotless and organized!

Later that week, all of my freshman friends got together because we had a lot to catch up on from the winter break since we were so used to being around each other 24/7. All of us agreed college life was way more fun than any break back home. After eating and talking with the girls, I headed back to my room to complete my studies before going to bed. As I was at my desk reading, I got a call from James.

"Come downstairs, I have a surprise for you," he instructed before hanging up the phone.

I grabbed my shoes, quickly brushed my hair, and put on some lip gloss before running downstairs. When I got to his car, he was sitting in the back with this huge box on the middle seat.

"I got something for you. Open it," he said calmly.

I opened the box, and inside was another box that said Saks Fifth Avenue. I looked at him in shock with wide eyes.

"Open it!" he exclaimed.

I ripped the box apart, and inside was this beautifully crafted alligator train case with a gold padlock on the front of it. *It was gorgeous!*

"*This* is what you should carry your makeup in. Something nice like this. You are classy and beautiful, and I want everything that you own to be classy and beautiful as well. Throw that plastic thing away and put all your items in here."

I hugged the case close to my chest and looked at him with soft eyes.

"For me?" I asked.

"Only the best for you, Leah."

The gifts never stopped.

In my heart, I knew I needed to tell someone about him. If I wasn't with James, I was thinking about him, which made me a little nervous because I had never felt so deeply about a man before. I knew I couldn't tell my parents, and I was still keeping this secret from Tina. I decided to tell my grandmother because I've always looked at her as a best friend, someone whom I could trust and confide in. I called her and told her I was dating someone older than me, so of course she wanted to know every detail. I ensured her that he was very mature and that he took care of me, and also that he was the pastor of my new church. She seemed to be very excited about him and even wanted to meet him. I knew that I couldn't bring him back to LA with me, at least not yet, so one day while James and I were together, I told him that my grandmother wanted to speak with him, and he agreed. I called her and handed him the phone so he could speak with her. They talked on the phone for a while, and before he passed the phone back, he told her that he would take care of me, and whatever I needed, he would make sure that I got. My grandma was very impressed, and that made me feel great because she's not the easiest woman to win over. She told me that she felt safe with me being with him and promised to keep James a secret between us.

"Is everything else okay with you, Ook? Is there anything you need?" My grandma has called me Ook since I was a little girl.

"Hmm. Let me think about that, Mama. Can I call you later and let you know?" I asked gratefully.

"Okay, hun. Call me later. Mama loves you!"

In the back of my mind, I knew exactly what I needed: a car. I wanted to be more independent and be able to get around on my own. I would ask different friends for rides, and I could tell they were getting frustrated with having to take me so many places because I never went anywhere close to campus. I'd completely ditched the whole college experience thing; I was entirely on another level striving to please my much older boyfriend. There weren't any Ubers yet, and I definitely wasn't riding the bus, so I *needed* a car. My grandparents had this agreement with me and my brother where we could get the car of our choice when we graduated from college. We had to show proof that we were walking across the stage with a diploma, and we could get the car we wanted; the only condition was that it had to be American made, specifically a Ford. But I was only a freshman at the time, so I wasn't sure if I could convince my grandmother to bend the rules for me a bit. I planned my explanation and gave my grandma a call back.

To my surprise, she wasn't against my request. I didn't even have to beg. She told me that I wouldn't be getting a new car immediately, but she had me find the nearest car rental establishment and rent a car for the meantime. So that's what I did. I found a cute silver Ford Focus that would allow me to get anywhere I needed without having to wait for someone to take me. My grandmother would pay the bill weekly, which was *extremely* expensive, but she was proud of me, so she allowed it. James thought the idea of my renting a car for such a long period of time was absolutely absurd. Honestly, it *was* pretty absurd, but how else was I going to be able to see him so often?

"This is crazy, Leah. Who rents a car for this long? What's your grandmother's number? I'm going to call her," he said firmly.

I gave him her number, knowing that he was going to tell her she didn't need to pay the weekly bill anymore because he was going to find a reasonably priced car for me. He was a man who never minded taking things in his own hands, and he'd promised my grandmother that he would take care of me. I never knew what was said on that phone call between James and my grandmother, but one week later, there was a white Ford Taurus outside of my room waiting for me. James handed me the keys, and I sprinted to the car faster than I'd ever run before. I was smiling from ear to ear, pressing every button in sight and adjusting my mirrors to see how cute I'd look while driving to my favorite songs. James was just smiling at me, watching me enjoy the moment.

"Well, do you like it?" he asked sarcastically.

"ARE YOU KIDDING? I LOVE IT!!!"

"You deserve only the best," he said. "Make sure to thank your grandmother too! And Leah, the next time you need something, please come to me first."

I hadn't slept with James at that point. We had been dating for months, yet I was still a bit uncomfortable and shy when it came to the thought of having sex with him. All I knew was I was an eighteen-year-old girl falling madly in love with a thirty-five-year-old man. I never felt like I needed anyone's existence to make me feel alive until I met him. He would constantly tell me how perfect I was and that I was created just for him, which I started to believe. He was treating me so nicely, with the nice hotels, restaurants, and gifts, that I felt like I owed him something. But what could I give a person who had the world at their fingertips? Giving myself to him seemed to be the only thing worthy for a person that vast.

I contemplated sleeping with him, but I thought if I had sex with him, I would lose myself completely... but I almost felt like I should lose myself because he was worthy of losing myself to. So when we were out of town at these five-star restaurants for his preaching engagements, I would contemplate if I was going to sleep with him or not. I never got the feeling that he wanted to rush me into sex; honestly, sleeping with him was something I wanted to do. I just wasn't ready. Every single thing about him was so out of my league, but I wanted to prove to him that I was capable of being the woman he could choose. I wanted him to want me, crave me the way I craved him. I decided to wait a little while longer before I would sleep with him, but I did want to be able to spend more time with James alone, without having to wait to be in hotels.

One weekend I decided to take a trip back to Los Angeles to see my family. It had been some time since I'd seen everyone from back home. When I got back, it was a cold, rainy night in Oakland. As I walked out of the airport, the air smelled moist and felt crisp on my skin. James was already waiting outside the airport and rushed over to grab my bags and cover me with an umbrella to the car. He drove me back to his office. As I sat down, there was a black jewelry box with a red bow on the top on the glass table in front of us. I looked at James, and he sat up, smirking at me.

"Well, are you going to open it, or keep looking at it?"

"James, you didn't have to get this!"

"I know. Just open it."

I opened the jewelry box, and inside was a white and yellow gold watch with diamonds encrusted around the bezel. The light reflecting off the diamonds made it shine in that box like no other. It was the most beautiful watch I had ever seen. It was absolutely stunning. In that moment, I said to myself, *I've got to do it tonight. I have to.* I looked at James and said, "I want to have sex with you."

He was a bit lost for words, but finally managed to get out, "Are... are you sure?"

"I'm sure. I really want to," I said passionately.

"Leah, please don't sleep with me because I gave you a gift. I don't give you gifts so that you will sleep with me, I give you gifts so you will look professional and elegant when you're out."

"No, I want to. I love you."

And so we did. I finally gave in to myself. I made the decision to have sex with James, a man who was seventeen years older than me, because I wanted to give myself to him being that he was giving me so much. Besides the gifts, he took my way of thinking, my maturity, and my overall appearance to a different caliber. He made me feel special, and I felt that he deserved me. All of me.

That night was unbelievable. I felt like I was a woman, a grown, mature, sexy woman. No one could tell me anything, and everything was going just the way I wanted. Between us, he was definitely more experienced sexually, so there was a lot that he taught me so that I could please him in the way he wanted to be pleased. As the months went by, I learned an array of things, from lingerie to looking beautiful before bed, and even how to make my sheets crisp and smell perfect every night. He taught me the exact way he wanted me to be presented for him. James was a teacher and taught me all that I needed to know about being intimate. I had been intimate before, but this was the first time that I had been with a man. He had standards.

James and I got to the point where we were so sexually involved that I was afraid to get pregnant. That would completely disappoint my parents and grandparents, and I still had so much respect for them. Yes, I was living my best life, still in my freshman year at Berkeley with my man, but I still had parents in LA that would be on the first flight to me if I was to get pregnant. So that was just not an option. I insisted on using condoms, but he never wanted to because he said they were really uncomfortable for him. Anytime I'd bring one out, he'd just laugh and take it out of my hand. I was always too afraid to push for protection, so I had to take matters into my own hands. I decided to go to the campus clinic where my parents paid for my healthcare, so I was completely covered. I got on birth control so that I could feel more comfortable about being sexually active and not getting pregnant. So I was set. I was living my life like it was golden, looking forward to every encounter, and I was covered, not going to get pregnant.

One Saturday morning after leaving a beautiful hotel, James packed up the town car with our suitcases from the weekend of attending a convention. We both liked to dress exquisitely, so we had a plethora of items each time we traveled. Even though we were only driving back to Oakland and it was very early, I still looked polished and sleek. I had on a black pantsuit with black pumps. My hair was neatly done in a soft flip, and my makeup was clean and elegant. I looked immaculate at all times. You'd never catch me lacking. James finished with the bags, and we began the drive back.

He looked over at me and just kept staring at me with the cutest smirk ever. This man was just sooo fine to me. I mean if looks could kill, I would have been dead for a while now.

"Why do you keep looking at me like that?" I said innocently.

"You know you look good, right?" he asked me.

"You think so?"

He smirked a bit, and just kept looking at me.

"What?" I laughed.

"Leah, I'm going to marry you when you graduate."

My. Heart. Stopped. Did the man of my dreams really just say he was going to marry me?

"Are you serious?" I asked quickly.

"I am," he confirmed.

Well, that's all I needed to hear. That was a confirmation from my friend's prophecy. She wasn't lying. When I got back to my dorm, the first thing I did when I walked through the door was search through my drawers for a college catalog. I needed to figure out how to organize my classes so that I could graduate in three years instead of four. I wanted to marry the man of my dreams as soon as possible. It was possible, but there was one class I knew would give me problems. I'd ended up getting a C+ in Mass Communications 10, and we needed a B+ or better. I was with James so much that I didn't spend the necessary time studying in order to pass. They only offered the course once a year, so I would have had to wait a whole year to take it again. I didn't have the time, so I decided to switch my major. At the time, I was a journalism and communications major, but I chose to switch to sociology with a minor in education. My dream was to be an anchor woman, but I figured I could just be a teacher since everyone else in my family was. I mapped out my classes: twenty units per semester and thirteen units in the summer, as well as work study: that was my plan.

By now, you might be wondering where my girl Tina was as my life got more hectic. We saw each other at school pretty often, but she made it clear she didn't want anything to do with me and James, which I respected. I didn't push her. So I wouldn't talk to her about him. I would talk to her aunt about James, though, because she was all for it. Tina's aunt had a beautiful house in West Oakland. Tina lived there, and I would stay there on the weekends. In fact, I lived with her right after I moved out of the dorms while I was looking for an apartment. She'd always make home-cooked meals, and even gave me some tips on how to cook better. I loved being there; she was a little older, so she reminded me of my grandmother. She had a lot of spunk and sass, which I loved so much. I absolutely adored Tina's aunt. We affectionately called her "Auntie." I loved talking to her and asking her opinion about this and that. I would often come home from being out with James and find her in bed watching TV. Almost every time I would find her in that position, I would get in the bed with her and talk to her for hours. One Sunday after church, I drove back to Tina's aunt's house for Sunday dinner. Tina had one of those answering machines that would play the voicemails out loud.

When I got to her house, she said there was a message for me on the machine with a strange look on her face. I walked into her room where the machine was and pressed play.

"Leah. Call me immediately."

It was my dad. He must have been looking for me and knew he could find me at Tina's aunt's house. I knew something was wrong; I could just hear it in his voice that he was angry at me. I instantly called him back out of nervousness.

"Hey, Dad, what's going on?" I asked innocently.

"Did you think I wasn't going to find out?" he asked.

"Find out about what, Daddy...?"

"THAT YOU WERE DATING THE PASTOR?!" he yelled.

"What? No, I'm—"

"DO NOT LIE! DO NOT LIE TO ME, LEAH WALKER."

"Dad, what are you talking about?" I pleaded.

"I was at church. I happened to run into Angie McKinley, and you know she's very involved in conventions and the church world. I was telling her how concerned I was about my daughter turning into a woman so fast, wearing suits and talking about how a gentleman should treat her, how they should open her car door before she gets out of the car, and what real men do. I'm just wondering what's gotten into her since she went to school, and who was she dating? And you know what that woman told me, Leah? She said, 'Oh you don't know who she's dating? It's all over the church world. She's dating the pastor at her church! She's been on trips with him, to conventions, and has been with him at his revivals. Everyone knows.'"

"Dad, I—"

"I AM NOT DONE. DO NOT CUT ME OFF. Angie told me he's a womanizer, he's known for having countless women! He's known for being a hoe! And if he's a hoe, you're a hoe!" he yelled furiously.

"I'm not a hoe! How could you say that?!" I questioned.

"Are you dating him, Leah?"

"Yes! But he isn't that type of—"

"I DEMAND YOU STOP DATING HIM RIGHT NOW! IT'S OVER! I didn't send you up there to be dating a hoe! I sent you to go to school. THAT'S IT! End it right now, Leah!"

"Dad, I can't end it! I love him!" I said.

He went silent.

"You make me sick," he said softly and hung up the phone.

I. Was. Horrified. I sat there in Tina's bedroom for minutes just wondering if that conversation had really just happened. I had never heard my dad sound that furious, ever. But I did love James. I loved him, and that was that. In my mind, it was us against the world. I didn't care who knew, and I wasn't going to end our relationship on my dad's command.

Immediately, I wanted to call James and tell him what happened. I must have called him twenty times, but he was just not answering me. I called the church office, his cell phone—nothing. I couldn't call his house phone because I didn't have it, which really bothered me. I was blowing his phone up, but I couldn't get a hold of him. Later that evening, he finally answered one of my calls.

"Leah, what's wrong?" he asked curiously.

"Oh my God, my dad found out!" I exclaimed.

"Found out about what?"

"He found out about us!"

"Us? What do you mean he found out about us?"

"Angie McKinley told him everything! That we're dating and that I've been to conventions with you and travel with you, and she said it's all over the church world," I explained.

"Well, what did you say?"

"I said it's true! And that I love you!"

"What? You told your father that...?"

"Yes!"

"Why would you tell your father that? Why didn't you just lie? Why didn't you protect me?!" he howled.

"Protect...*you?*" I said, confused.

"Now it's out! Now you have ruined *everything!*"

"How did I ruin everything? All I said was—"

"You shouldn't have said a word. You should have lied. You're not a private person like I thought. You ruined everything! Let me call you back."

Before I could even get another word in, I heard the phone disconnect. He didn't call back for the rest of the night. My heart sank to the pit of my stomach. I felt so small and insignificant to a person I thought the world of. I'd anticipated that he'd be ecstatic to hear how I'd defended his name to my father. I mean, that's a *big* deal. Why did he want me to lie about our relationship? Did he lie about our relationship? The entire night my mind was flooded with questions. I lay in the dark at Tina's aunt's house pondering what I'd done that could have made him that upset. My thoughts led me to sleep.

The following day, I woke up and got ready for class. As I was driving to campus from Tina's aunt's house, I got a call from James. It was the weirdest thing. When I answered the phone, he acted like nothing had happened the night prior. He seemed completely fine, which was very weird. He mentioned how he was just a little upset that I didn't protect him, but everything was going to be okay and not to worry. It did ease my mind to know that he wasn't mad at me, but I was still confused why he kept saying I didn't *protect* him. The truth is that I'd lost my power. From having sex with him, to being depressed, to confessing my love for him to my parents, the ball was no longer in my court. My emotions, my physical and mental state all depended on the status of where our relationship lay at the moment. I was giving my absolute all, yet receiving mediocrity disguised by sex and material items. The more he pulled away, the more I pushed myself to become the woman he wanted.

About a month later, I found myself waking up very early to catch a sale at Macy's. Remember, I always wanted to look *perfect*. Every event, church service, or convention, I'd buy a new outfit. I had an event to go to with James that day, so I had to wake up very early to catch the sale. The night before, I'd slept at Tina's aunt's house, and her aunt asked me to take her grandson with me because she was out of town. She told me that I could take her car. So I took her grandson with me to Macy's, got my outfit and shoes, and rushed back to the car so I wouldn't be late to the event. He hated when I was late or if he had to wait for me, so I was nervous to get back in time. On our way back, the traffic was heavy. As I veered into the fast lane on the freeway, a huge truck honked loudly at me. The truck was in my blind spot, so I couldn't see it as I was merging. Out of frantic reaction, I switched quickly back to the lane I was in, and as I tried to switch, the front tire on the passenger's side came off, and the car spun out of control.

"Leah, leah! Get control of the car before we crash! Get control!" Auntie's grandson yelled.

"I Can't!" I yelled frantically.

The car spun through two lanes almost as if it was hydroplaning and quickly came to a halt as it slammed into the center divider on the freeway. My head hit the steering wheel, and I blacked out.

When I came to, I looked over at Auntie's grandson, making sure he was okay.

"Are you all right?" I asked.

"I'm fine. Are you okay?"

Before I could answer, another car pulled up to the side of us.

"Get out of the car! The car is on fire, get out!" the man yelled.

I managed to reach my purse with my personal belongings and my cell phone. We got out of the car and stood as far away from the flames as we could in the fast lane by the center divider. As I was looking back, the entire car blasted into flames. Instead of thinking how blessed we were for not being seriously injured, all I could think about was how I wasn't going to make it in time to attend the event with James. Minutes later, the police and fire department arrived, put the fire out, and towed the car. The ambulance came with paramedics to assess us, and they took us to the hospital to get further assessed. While I was standing on the freeway looking at the destroyed car, something in my spirit kept telling me to go home for the summer and not stay in the Bay area. *Go home. Go home, Leah...* It almost felt like God was talking to me and trying to protect me, but I couldn't figure out what He was trying to protect me from. I chose to ignore the sign. I didn't know what my spirit was trying to tell me, but I didn't listen.

Although the car accident made the start of my summer a bit rocky, I persevered and decided to stay in Oakland so I could complete my summer classes. My parents really wanted me to come home so they could take care of me, and sort of give me a break, but I didn't have the time. They were so worried about me, especially when they heard about the accident. I still needed to complete thirteen units that summer if I wanted to graduate in three years. Summer sessions began, and my classes were fairly easy, which I appreciated because I wasn't straining myself too much while still recovering from the accident. James would stop by sometimes to keep me company, but still not as much time as I would have liked. My mom flew in the day after the accident. She demanded to see the car, which was demolished. I took her to the body shop where the car was being evaluated by the insurance company. They thought there must have been a malfunction with it because of how the wheel just came off. It not only came off, but the whole wheel came off of the counsel. If it wasn't for the grace of God I would have been dead. It's funny how I couldn't see that when the accident occurred; I was too occupied. But after the accident it became clearer that God had really saved us.

When my mother looked at the car in the body shop, tears welled up in her eyes. She hugged me tightly and said, "Thank you, Lord, you spared my baby's life! Thank you, Lord, thank you, Lord!"

The car was completely burned, and the front was crushed in. The wheel was severed, and I only had a little cut on my forehead and experienced a little whiplash. God had truly spared me! I could not stop thinking about the words I'd heard on the freeway: *Go home, Leah, go home.* What was the Lord trying to tell me? What was the lesson I was to learn from this accident? Was I headed for destruction if I did not go home? Was this a foreshadow of what was to come? Needless to say, I did ignore all of the signs and continued my quest of graduating in three years. Nothing was going to stop me.

I decided to ignore the signs and stay in the Bay Area for summer school. Since I had to take classes over the summer, I didn't get the chance to go home. By that point, I knew for a fact I wanted to live by myself in an apartment. The summer following my freshman year, I conveniently forgot to submit my dorm application on time to secure my spot in the dorms. I told my grandmother that I wanted to live by myself, and she told me I could start looking for places. I found an area that was close to where I knew he lived, even though I had never been to his house. He would never let me go to his house. But he would always say he lived close to the water, so I knew that much.

negative five

The apartments by the water were absolutely beautiful, so rent was kind of high, but it was a safe and exclusive place that I knew my grandmother would approve of. I found a studio apartment right off the water, called my grandmother, and she gave me the security deposit for the first and last month so that I could move in. My studio was absolutely beautiful. There were huge bay windows that overlooked the city from one side and the water from the other. They'd recently renovated the place with polished brown wooden floors, eggshell paint on the walls, crown molding, and high ceilings. I loved it, and I knew James would love it too. Of course I invited him over the first night I moved in. I wanted him to see how responsible and mature I was for moving off campus just after my freshman year. When he came over that night, he was blown away at how nice my studio was.

"Now this is how my girl should live," he said as he wrapped his arms around me.

"Right. I love it so much. You're welcome any time," I said.

The next step of my apartment was getting it furnished. James made sure that I got everything I needed. Within a couple days, he singlehandedly furnished my apartment. He set up everything: my bed, desk, dressers, large TV, and a kitchen dining set together for me. He made sure that everything looked beautiful and classy. My studio was stunning before, but he made it a place that was breathtaking to walk into every day. He even picked out the bedding for the cherrywood sleigh bed he chose for me. I felt like the luckiest girl in the world. I couldn't thank God enough for putting James in my life.

A couple months later, I began my sophomore year of college. It was an adjustment transitioning from the dorms to apartment life, but it was a transition I loved making. I was still doing well in my classes, and I loved my new major, sociology. A regular day for me included driving to campus, taking classes all day, then staying at the library until James would tell me he was going to come over. I'd rush to submit my assignments, drive home, freshen up, and tidy up the house before he came over. I'd light candles, sweep the floors, and make sure all of the counters were spotless. He'd never comment on my place if everything was in order, but he would make me feel a bit embarrassed if even the smallest thing was off, like a dish being in the sink. So I made sure *everything* was perfect. We'd lie together at night, and he'd tell me how happy he was that I was his. I belonged to him, and I wouldn't have it any other way. Little did I know with each encounter, slowly but surely, I was losing my power and his interest. I was always available for him. He never had to wonder where I was or what I was doing. I wanted to be available so that I could be with him whenever he beckoned me. Many people said that I should have pulled back, and that absence makes the heart grow fonder, and I believed that, but I did not want to miss any moments of being with him. I was consumed with him, but was he consumed with me? Was this all a game to get me and then dump me? I wondered all the time if he thought he had won his quest to win me and now the thrill was gone. Only time would tell.

Before there was text messaging, there was a text messaging service. You would call an operator and dictate what you wanted sent to the recipient's cell phone. I began to use the text messaging service every morning, telling him to have a great day and that I loved him. I never missed a morning; it was the first thing I did when I woke up. I'd go to all my classes, simultaneously checking my cell phone frantically to see if he had replied. Sometimes he'd call me while I was in lectures and I'd run out of class just so I could speak to him. He was the only distraction I allowed myself to have while I was on campus. I was taking four to five classes daily, knocking out units like I was crazy. I was focused; I had a plan. I had to be very diligent with school because I knew I wouldn't have time to take classes over if I needed to be done in three years. I didn't have time for campus functions, events, or sororities. I was so determined to get as many units as possible that sometimes I'd take two classes at the same time. I'd spend thirty minutes in one class, then run across campus to catch the last thirty minutes of the next class. I decided to get a job on campus, because it was getting expensive trying to keep up with this lifestyle. I was getting my hair done all the time, always trying to buy new clothes and makeup, while only having the allowance my parents and grandparents gave me. I got a job in the office of Student Affairs, which was perfect because it worked with my class schedule. I continued to do hair on the side but stopped working at the hair salon because James said that he did not want me to work there anymore and that it wasn't a good look for me. I loved working there, so instead of quitting I just worked sporadically or when he was out of town.

I began to notice that James would go all day before calling me back sometimes. It was completely different than when we'd first met, when he was calling me every morning to wish me a good day and ask when he could take me out to lunch or dinner. As the months went by, his calls became less and less frequent, and I wasn't seeing him as often as I was accustomed to. I'd call, leave voicemails, use the text messaging service... nothing. The only time I knew I'd be able to see him for sure was during Bible study and church. Since I had my car now, I made sure to attend Bible study every Wednesday and both services every Sunday.

One odd thing about James was that he had a lot of female friends. He would tell me that he got along better with women than men. He'd hang out with two women from the church that he called Chipmunk 1 and Chipmunk 2. Chipmunk 1 was really cool with me; in fact, when I didn't have a car, he would often send her to pick me up from the dorms and take me to different places and to meet him at different churches. She was really nice and sweet. But Chipmunk 2 was a little different. We didn't spend that much time together, and he kind of kept her away from me, but I didn't really know why. It just seemed like she wasn't too happy that I was around at times. And she never picked me up and never took me places when I didn't have a car. Only Chipmunk 1 would take me places. He spent a lot of time with Chipmunk 1 and Chipmunk 2, but I assumed they were just friends and chalked it up to that. Still, he did hang around a lot of women. I would even see different women coming to church, and I mean beautiful women, different sizes and colors. You'd see them once, and you wouldn't see them again, so I began to wonder if he was inviting these women to his church to hear him preach. I always tried not to think too much of it, but every time I'd see a new, beautiful woman sitting by herself, I couldn't help but wonder.

One particular Sunday after service, I sat in the first row and waited for James to be done speaking to his members so that I could talk to him. I always would keep myself occupied with talking to the older women who reminded me of my grandma. About forty-five minutes later, James walked over to me and sat to the left of me.

"Stop hanging around after church. I want you to go home, and I will call you and tell you where to meet me," he said aggressively.

"But why?" I asked.

"Well, I don't want people to think you're chasing me or that you're my hoe or my bitch. I always want you to be a lady. So go home," he said. He patted my knee and walked away.

That was the most embarrassing thing a guy had ever said to me. I packed up my things and walked to my car. On my way home, I was just so confused. Had I done something? Did he not like me anymore? Was I annoying him? Then I thought to myself, *He is probably right!* It did look thirsty waiting almost an hour for him. It wasn't ladylike. So the following Sunday, I left immediately after service, just as he'd told me to do. I went home, worked on some assignments, and set my phone right beside me so I wouldn't miss his call. I worked all night, cleaned up around my apartment, cooked and prepared food for the week. I figured I should have the house and his food ready in case he called me and wanted to come over.

No call, no pager text, nothing. I decided to call him to make sure he was okay, but he didn't answer, and I must have called about eight different times. When I accepted that he wasn't going to come, I put all the food away, showered, and went to bed.

I eventually ended up hearing from James the following night. He apologized for not reaching out to me because he was piled with work, so I couldn't be mad at him. I wished I had known that throughout the day, because I had been paranoid to the point that I couldn't focus on my work, and I didn't have an appetite all day. I was a nervous wreck because I didn't hear from him. I was feeling emotions I had never felt before and didn't know anything about. I was in a race for a competition I'd never been trained for. When I talked to James that night, I told him how worried I was that he hadn't called me. I guess he could hear the tremor in my voice, because he quickly began to try and make me calm down. I remember him telling me things like:

"Leah, you know if you can't ever reach me, I'm just taking care of business. That doesn't change the fact that you are mine. You are perfect for me, Leah. You know that, right?"

Sigh. "I know, I just miss you, that's all," I said.

"Well, let me fix that for you. I'm on my way."

"Oh, it's fine. I have class really early and I have a few things I need to compl—"

"I'll be there in 15 minutes," he said before hanging up the phone.

I wanted to call him back and insist he not come by, but who was I fooling? Truthfully, I wanted him to come over anyway. I was just *trying* to make him miss me like I missed him.

Oh well! I thought to myself.

I let out a quick burst of excitement in the mirror, then proceeded to freshen up. He hated to be waiting downstairs for me, so I got ready quickly. I showered, brushed my hair into a high ponytail, put on the diamond earrings he'd gotten me, and put on fresh clothes that were comfy enough for me, but still pleasing to the eye. I lit all my candles, made my bed, and made sure there were no dishes in the sink. In 15 minutes he was at my front door buzzing my apartment, and I let him up. I warmed up a plate of food for him that I'd cooked earlier—chicken and Alfredo pasta with a side of spinach—and sat next to him. He looked at me as he was eating and kept giving me those looks he always gave me. It was one of those looks that yell a million words through the eyes with no words needed. It was a smirk, but a subtle, sexy smirk.

"This food is good. Where'd you learn to cook like this?" he laughed.

"Taught myself!" I chuckled.

When he was finished eating, I took his plate from the table to wash it. He came behind me, and I felt his warmth and strength on the back of my neck and the blades of my shoulders. Whenever he stood close to me I would get chills in my body. It was like a spell he would put over me when we were together. He knew exactly how to have me in his control, and that was the position I wanted to remain in. As nights like these became more and more frequent, his calls became less and less frequent. If I didn't hear from him during the day, I'd go back into those anxious fits, yet our sexual life still existed. Even if I wouldn't hear from him for days at a time, I'd still give myself to him when he was available. He became my pain and my remedy. Like the song by Daniel Ceaser and Her, he was my coffee that I needed in the morning, and my Tylenol that I took when my head hurt. No one could make me upset in the way he could, and no one could heal the wounds he created other than him. The days James would disappear became frequent, to the point where I started to become depressed. I would barely be able to focus on my classes, and I definitely couldn't eat. I was losing my appetite frequently, to the point where I lost twenty-five pounds in two months. I became completely lovesick. I wasn't Leah.

Around mid-October, my mom flew into Oakland to see how I was doing. She stayed with me, of course. Immediately when she saw me, the first thing she said was, "Oh my gosh, Leah, you've lost so much weight!"

"No, I haven't, Mom," I said quickly.

"Yes, you have! Are you sick? Look at your hair!"

My hair had been thinning out. I was constantly putting heat on it so that I'd always look presentable for him. My quest for perfection was weighing on me. Every week, I would have my hair in different styles because I wanted to be this perfect first lady, this perfect princess for him, from head to toe. My mom immediately picked up on my changes.

That Sunday, I took my mom to James' church with me. After the sermon, I walked her to the front of the altar so she could meet my pastor. That is how I introduced him to her, of course. My pastor.

"Reverend Jordan, this is my mom. She's visiting for the weekend from back home."

"Mrs. Walker! We're so happy to have you! You have raised an amazing, God-fearing young lady. She comes to church every Sunday, and she is so smart!" he ranted.

"Umm hmm," my mom said in her stern side-eye way. It was like she knew something.

"Please allow me to take you both to a nice dinner tonight! It's only right we show you an amazing time while you're in the city. How does that sound?" he asked her.

I quickly intervened. "Oh, that won't be necessary, I'm sure she's very exhaust—"

"That would be nice, Leah, don't you think?" my mom asked.

Sigh. "Yeah! Sure, okay!" I said reluctantly.

Dinner? With my pastor and my mom? Let alone my pastor/boyfriend and my mom? This was not part of the plan. In fact, the plan was to take my mom to the altar, quickly introduce her, and leave. Why would James want to take me *and* my mom to dinner? I mean, this man was just all over the place! He barely had time for me but wanted to make time to take my mom out. TO SAY WHAT?! So many thoughts were racing through my mind. I was hoping and praying that James would keep our dinner strictly professional so that my mom didn't get suspicious. She could absolutely not find out about us because I could not bear the thought of hearing my dad call me a hoe and have James tell me that I did not protect him. All of that was too overwhelming. But my mom is precise. She picks up on the smallest of things; there's nothing anyone can get past her.

My mom and I went home after service and got ready for dinner. He told us the name of the restaurant, and what time to be there. When we got to the restaurant, the waitresses were waiting on our arrival. They led us to an exclusive section where James was already waiting. He quickly stood up to greet my mom, pulled out her seat, and then pulled out mine.

"Please help yourselves! The entire menu is excellent. Order what you want!" he insisted.

My mom looked at me with an impressed expression. I smiled back at her and continued to look down at the menu. I wasn't giving any clues. My mom and James began conversing for quite some time, which I liked because it kept him from interacting with me. I chimed in here and there, but for the most part, I kept quiet and ate my dinner.

"Please excuse me as I go to the men's room..." he said before getting up from the table. Not even a second passed after he walked away before my mom leaned over and said, "Does he like you or something?"

"Oh, no, he's just nice!" I confirmed.

"Mmm. *Extremely* nice…" she said.

After James came back to the table, he and my mom continued talking for a little before the check came. He paid for our meals, and my mom gave me that *look*. I smiled and looked away. I knew I was going to hear about it the whole way home…

Then out of the blue he said, "You know, your daughter and I spend a lot of time together."

My mom looked up with a stare as if to say, "I knew it!" She replied, "You do? Does she have time for this? I know her school schedule is rigorous."

He replied, "It is, but I make sure she has everything she needs."

My mom, being the direct Virgo that she is, pursed her lips as if she was getting ready to say something she had been dying to ask the whole night. "Well, are you dating my daughter?"

He said, "I wouldn't say that, but we really like each other."

This conversation was a bit intense; in fact, I could not hold my tongue any longer. I burst out, "Yes, Mom, we are dating, and I love him!"

At that she burst into tears and left the table.

"Why would you do that? You ruined a perfect evening," James said.

In shock, I said, "I ruined it? You were insinuating too much, so I decided to just tell her! She knew anyway. She just wanted you to admit it!"

My mom came back to the table and said, "I am very disappointed. I think you are a nice man, and you take good care of my daughter. However, she is too young, and her father and I did not send her up here for this. We sent her up here for school. I can't tell her who to love because matters of the heart are complicated, but I will say this is not what we intended or planned for her."

James respectfully told my mother that he understood, and he would ensure that I would focus on school and do what they intended. We all left the restaurant in confusion, especially me. What was he trying to do or say? He often confused me. I could never put my finger on what he was up to. He was like a maze or a puzzle that only the skilled could figure out. Later that night, my mom packed her things, and I drove her back to the airport so that she could be at work the following morning. As we drove to the airport, she began to talk about the dinner with James. "Leah, I know that James is very impressive to you. He is older and established. I can see why you would like him. However, there are many things that older men deal with or have in their lives that you may not be ready for or able to handle. I know you are very mature, but dealing with him can be a lot, especially with all that you have to do going to school."

Of course I had an answer for her and replied, "I know, Mom, but he tells me everything, and I know I can handle it. I would not let anything get in the way of finishing school, so you don't have to worry about that."

My mom gave me a stern look as if she was not playing and said, "Leah, I want you to be careful and think with your head and not your heart." She kissed me, got out of the car, and headed to her boarding gate.

One particular weekend, I didn't hear from him at all, and I was just really going crazy. I was calling him, texting through the service, and I just couldn't reach him ALL weekend. This time I was determined to find out where he was at. There was an older couple in the church that I had become really, really close to. I would call them Gigi and Papi. They were an older couple who didn't have children of their own, and James introduced me to them as his parent figures, but I fell in love with them. She was easy to talk to, fun, and would tell it like it is. I loved older people so much, getting close to them was like second nature to me. Gigi and Papi went to James' church and would always keep me in the know of what was going on and what I needed to pay attention to. On this particular weekend when I couldn't find him, I called Gigi.

"Hey! Sorry to bother you, but I haven't been able to reach James all weekend. I just want to make sure he's okay. Do you know where he is?" I asked.

"Oh baby, he's in Vegas with Dianne," she said calmly.

"Dianne?" I asked. "I didn't know that he was still talking to Dianne."

The only other time I'd heard about Dianne was the time we went to the pier. Dianne was the woman he felt like he owed because they'd been together for so long.

"You know what, I really need to tell you something, and please don't breathe a word of this to anyone," she said.

"Okay…"

"He lives with Dianne. He, her, and her daughter all live together in his condo by the water. That's why you can't go to his house, because she's there."

"What? Well, why doesn't she come to church?" I asked.

"Because he told her that she could never come to his church. She goes to another church," she said.

"Wait a minute, so are you sure they live together?"

"Oh yes, they live together. They *are* together," she confirmed.

"You know what, I'm going to call you back, okay?" I said before hanging up.

I was shocked. I was hurt, upset, and embarrassed; I just couldn't believe it. I was dating a man that was living with another woman? After everything he'd told me about them not being happy, they still lived under the same roof? Was I going to continue to date him or was I going to end it? I debated it in my mind for days, the entire time he was in Vegas.

I figured there must be some reason he hadn't married Dianne yet. From what I could tell, they had been in each other's lives for years, yet he told me he was going to marry me. *I must be the one he really wants,* I thought to myself. I did want to ask James if he was living with this woman, but I didn't want to break the trust of Gigi, because I wanted her to be able to tell me anything. I knew she wouldn't lie to me, but I just needed him to tell me himself. So I planned in my head how I was going to ask when he got back from Vegas.

When he got back, he picked me up the following day, and we drove to dinner in downtown Oakland. On the way was my perfect time to ask. He did not know that I knew he was in Vegas at all, so I had to ask him in a way that was not incriminating or would divulge my sources of information. So I just asked, "Do you live with Dianne? Does she live there?" I asked.

He looked at me quickly. "What do you mean?"

"Exactly what I said… Does she live there?"

"Why would you ask me a question like that?"

"Well, I've never been to your house. I can't call your house… so I don't get it," I said.

"No, she doesn't live there, she just stays there sometimes. Her brother is on drugs and stole all her money and clothes when she lived with her mom. Her daughter, mom, and brother all lived in the same house, and her brother would steal all her stuff, and so that's why I said she could live with me. So she brought stuff over to my house, and she goes back and forth," he explained.

"She goes back and forth?" I asked, irritated.

"Yes, she doesn't live permanently with me."

"Mmm. Does her daughter go back and forth?"

"Yes, but she stays mostly with her grandmother. The only reason I don't want you to come over to the house is because I never know when she's coming or leaving. I just don't want you to be exposed to that. I'm trying to protect you and respect you," he assured me.

I believed him. It didn't seem that bad, and I was still pretty young and naïve, so I was just feeding into all this information. So I kept dating him, loving him, and spending time with him. The girl in the house wasn't a factor to me because I never saw her, she didn't go to our church, and I never had any encounters with her. My only mission was to marry him, and I wasn't going to let that dream go because of a house guest. Plus he was always blowing my mind, treating me to amazing experiences and showing me a fabulous lifestyle.

There were so many times that James would be out of town at a convention or revival and would want to see me right away. So he would call and tell me that a train or a plane ticket was waiting for me after I got out of school. I would rush home, pack an overnight bag, and be on my way. I loved getaways like this; they were spontaneous and fun. It was like he was my Prince Charming and

I was his princess that he would sweep away with him every now and again. How could I even be worried about Dianne when he treated me like this?

I did not have to want for anything or ask for anything. He would have a sixth sense of what I needed and made sure I had it. For example, one night I was on campus really late typing a paper in the computer center because I did not have a computer or a printer. He was calling me over and over again because I had not made it home, and it was late. When I got home I finally called him back.

"Where have you been?" he asked.

"I was typing a paper in the computer center. It's due tomorrow, and I needed to make sure it was done," I said.

"I don't like you being out on campus that late. It's not safe," he said.

"I know, but I had no choice. I don't have a computer and I had to get it done. I'm sorry," I said.

He was serious about me not being on campus late, and he was definitely going to do something about it. That Christmas he said that he had a gift for me, but I had to wait to get it when I got back to Oakland. When I arrived back in Oakland in my apartment as soon as I walked in I was surprised to see a brand new computer with a printer all hooked up with internet and an email! I had given James a key to my apartment, and he came in to hook all of this up. He had a big red bow on it. I was so happy and so surprised. Now I never had to stay on campus late again, and I had email so I could email James and instant message him whenever I wanted. I was in love, and I wasn't going to worry about anyone else he might be involved with.

negative four

When James wanted to spend a lot of time with me, we would hang out in my apartment. He also loved introducing me to important people in his life. When it was someone he wanted to impress, or any place of class and elegance, he would always want to bring me. I felt like this was a good thing because it made me feel like he thought I made him look good. And we did look good together. Everywhere we would go, people couldn't stop staring at us—in restaurants, at stores, at churches, everywhere! We always looked immaculate, and together we were impeccable.

Although we looked good together and loved being with each other, while getting to know one another we would have our disagreements. It would usually be over the smallest things or it would be over something he was trying to control or make me do. When we would get into little spats I would do my normal—give him the silent treatment—which he hated. I would turn my phone ringer off so that I would not be tempted to answer. I did have caller ID, so I would know when it was him calling, and I would let it go straight to voicemail and answer all of the other calls. This would go on for at least three days, and at that point he would break down, come over, and have make-up sex to make me forget how mad I really was. And I would forget and go right back to where I was before the argument, madly in love with him.

One morning, during one of our fights when I was not speaking to him, he called me very early.

"I know you are mad at me, and we will talk about that, but I need you to go with me today. I'm meeting with this really famous pastor and his new wife. He is going to be preaching the Oakland City Wide Revival this week. They're from Los Angeles. You'll like them," he said.

"Oh, I don't think I'll be able to go. I have class all day. That won't work," I replied.

"No, I really want you to go with me, I really want you to meet them. He is very, very powerful, and he's an amazing pastor. I really like him a lot, and I need you to go with me today."

I hesitated because I wanted him to know that I was not letting him off the hook and said, "I will go, but I am still angry with you."

I dropped everything for the day and went with him. He picked me up from my apartment. I decided to look like a sexy first lady to make him see what he was missing those days we were not talking. I wore a long, tight pencil skirt with a black turtleneck sweater, black high heel boots, and a black velvet hat that had a big black flower on the side. I would cock the hat to the side to make myself look chic and sophisticated. I also wore the "Russian Red" lipstick from MAC that he adored. He would go crazy every time I wore this hat. He thought it was elegant, and the way I wore it was so sexy. I wanted to give it to him that day!

We picked the couple up from their hotel, and immediately, I liked them. The pastor, Dr. Tigner, was pretty shy and quiet, but very on point and sharp. His wife, Varie, was a little younger than him, but like a big sister to me. We hit it off right away. I sat with her in the back while James and Dr. Tigner sat in the front. She was complimenting me on my makeup and my hair, and just saying all these nice things about me. I told her that I could show her everything from where I shopped to where I got my hair done, and she was all for it. That day, we all drove up to San Francisco to go shopping. Varie and I went to Nordstrom to look around. The first thing I wanted to do was go to the MAC counter.

"Wow, all of these shades are so pretty! What is this line?" Varie asked.

"Wait, what? It's MAC, like THE MAC. Have you never heard of it?"

"No! Never. But I like what I see!" she said as she tested out the lipsticks.

"GIRL! Where have you been? You MUST try this Russian Red lipstick. It brings out any outfit, and it would look so gorgeous on you! It's what I have on right now," I exclaimed.

She ended up buying so much from MAC and was so happy about her findings and was excited that we had met so I could tell her about all the latest trends and fashion. That day was the beginning of an amazing friendship with not only Varie, but her husband too. Varie and I instantly stuck like glue. I was so ecstatic that I finally had a friend that was with a pastor as well, a big sister who could show me the ropes, someone I could talk to about all my problems. It was perfect. Dr. Tigner also gave me great advice. He was rooted in the

Lord and always kept it real. He was a very wise man who didn't speak too much, but when he did, everything was important and useful to me. Even when Dr. and Mrs. Tigner went back to their home in Los Angeles, I would still talk to Varie almost every day and still kept close with Dr. Tigner. One night I called them after James and I were having an argument, because I wanted mature advice. I wanted to know their opinion on James.

I asked Dr. Tigner, "So what do you think about James?"

"He's not for you," he said firmly.

"Really? Why do you think that?" I asked curiously.

"You're too innocent. You're perfect! He's a dog! I love him dearly, and he's a great preacher. But he's a dog, and he is no damn good..."

Even though Dr. Tigner told me this, I didn't really listen. I would appreciate my conversations with him dearly, but I still felt like I was the one James wanted at the end of the day. One night after a long conversation with Varie and Dr. Tigner, I told them about Dianne, and they already knew all about her. They had both met her before and knew that James had been dealing with her for years. They knew it was a very sticky situation and that I would probably get hurt. Dr. Tigner said to me, "There is a Scripture I want you to read and meditate on; it is Psalms 119:71. Read it to me."

I got the Scripture and read it. "Psalms 119:71, It was good for me to be afflicted, that I might learn your statues."

I asked Dr. Tigner what that meant in my situation. He said, "It is good that you go through pain and trouble so that you can learn more about God and yourself. You need this for your development."

I was like, "Okay, thank you, talk to you guys later. Love you!" I had no idea what he was trying to say, but that Scripture haunted me. It was like the Lord wanted me to know something. It plagued my mind day and night.

Eventually, James didn't want me to be with Dr. and Mrs. Tigner at all. He would put these restrictions on me and tell me I shouldn't laugh and talk with them as much when they were around. Maybe he began to realize that Dr. Tigner knew about some other women James was interested in and was afraid the news would get back to me by way of Varie. There would be times where James would randomly tell me not to trust them because he didn't know what their intentions were and things like that. To keep James happy, when they would come around for conventions, I wouldn't speak, but when we were all away from James, I kept in close contact with them. They became my family away from home. However, as time passed it became hard to keep my relationship close with Dr. Tigner and Varie because of James' restrictions, so I eventually stopped talking to them. This was very hurtful, but I thought it was necessary to keep my relationship good with James.

One Saturday morning, I needed to replenish my fridge. I went to the store closest to my apartment, by the water. I got all of my groceries and was standing in line, looking in my purse for some coupons, when I saw this older woman in the line next to me who looked familiar. Then it clicked: *That's the lady Gigi pointed out to me in church a couple weeks ago. That's Dianne's mom!* The mom was allowed to attend the church, but Dianne wasn't.

"Oh, hi, Leah," said the older woman.

Our church was fairly small, so most of the members knew me by name.

"Hi! So nice to see you! How are you doing?" I asked.

Suddenly, a woman walked up to us and stood right next to the older woman. She was beautiful: long hair, rich chocolate skin tone, and fairly thin. Immediately, I knew that was her. That was Dianne. I was speechless. She was like a chocolate Barbie doll. Drop dead gorgeous. And her mother just ate it up. She looked at her daughter and then back at me with a sly smile as if she was saying: *Yes. This is my daughter. This is who he's involved with...*

I felt a little intimidated because I didn't look like her. At that point, I knew why he was attracted to her.

It was interesting because I'd asked Chipmunk 1 what Dianne looked like a while back while we were in the car one day.

"She's gorgeous, just like you," she'd said. "Except you guys have two different looks."

I never asked her what Dianne's look was. But standing there in the store with her, I *knew* that was Dianne. She didn't even have to tell me her name. I *knew* that was Dianne. And she was gorgeous.

"Well, it was so good to see you," I said before walking away.

I decided to go shop for more groceries to give them time to be in line and get out of the store before I had to stand in line again. It was just so awkward, and I didn't want to end up having to stand right behind them again. I waited about ten minutes, checked out my groceries, and put all of my bags in the cart. As I was walking to my car, I felt like there was something behind me. I turned around, and it was Dianne and her mother following me in their car. I tried to act like I didn't see them. I kept walking to my car and stopped when I reached it. I still didn't turn around. I saw them stop and stare, then speed quickly past me. *What did I get myself into, Lord?* It was so strange for them to do that, especially because Dianne was driving James' car. I tried to act like the incident didn't happen, and I never told James about it. I chose to never bring Dianne up, actually, because every time I would bring her up to James, he became very hostile. All I knew was nothing seemed to be getting easier.

A couple weeks later, James picked me up from my apartment around noon. When I got to the car, there was a little girl in the backseat just smiling at me. She looked to be about four or five years old.

"Um, James… Whose kid do you have in the backseat?" I joked.

"Oh, that's Aamira. I'm going to adopt her. Isn't she beautiful?" he said, smiling. "Come on, get in, I'll tell you all about it."

So I got in the car, and he was telling me how her foster mom was new to the church, and he felt like the foster mother had too many children on her hands. James loved kids, and Aamira had stolen his heart; he felt that the Lord had told him to adopt her. It never really sat well with me; it just seemed so forced and rushed. We spent the whole day with Aamira, and I could tell she really made him happy. That day turned into many days throughout the summer that James, Aamira, and I would be together. We would do all these cute things with her, and I felt like James wanted me to get this sense of family with him. I would go out of my way to buy her things to make him feel like I was supporting him. I wanted him to see me as not only a great girlfriend but a great mother figure. I loved kids, and I wanted him to see I could love the little girl that he chose to adopt. He eventually ended up telling me that he and Dianne were going to have to adopt Aamira together, because there needed to be a mother and father figure. I didn't understand how it was going to work out, because how could they just adopt a child and not be married? Every time I'd try to ask him questions about it, he'd brush the conversation off and tell me that I couldn't get in the way of his plan to better Aamira's life. I did want the best for her, but I just couldn't understand how the dynamic of the relationship was going to play out.

A couple weeks before the adoption was final, everything did a complete 360. Aamira told a lie about James that could have damaged his character forever. Knowing that he did not commit the act that he was accused of, he turned himself into jail with all of his deacons and preachers there to support him. He only spent a day in jail, and I was there to pick him up when he made bail.

He took all sorts of lie detector tests. This process was a lot for me and truly devastating to him. I didn't have any words to say, and I felt a darkness in my stomach and in my mind by even trying to process what Aamira had said he did. He never seemed to me like the type of person to do what she claimed. I knew he didn't do it.

Aamira's story changed over and over and over. It turned out that her foster mom told her to say that because she didn't want to give her up. "Who raises these people?" he shouted. The case was dropped, and he was back to living his life normally again as best as he could. God had truly delivered him, and it was definitely a testimony.

Going through all of this was really overwhelming. I wanted to be there for him, and I wanted him to see me as a "ride or die chick." Although I appeared to be super strong on the outside, I was really struggling on the inside. Was I supposed to go through this being only nineteen?

I remember praying to God that things would just get easier. It seemed like all I wanted to do was graduate so I could marry him, yet I kept having all these distractions that would really take me into some low points in my life. It was nearly impossible to focus on school while going through so much. Jail, the little girl, dealing with him and Dianne… not to mention all the other women I suspected him to be with. I was only nineteen. I wasn't raised nor prepared to understand and handle these situations he put me in. The words from my friend's prophecy kept ringing in my ear. "It is going to get worse before it gets better." I held on to those words hoping, wishing, and praying that things would in fact get better. Many nights were a constant inner battle trying to defeat these demons while still striving to succeed academically. That summer was brutal. I thought I could make everything work. I thought I would be the thread to hold him together. I believed I could fix everything, but I was starting to feel like it was too much for me to handle. Maybe this was why the Lord kept telling me to go home after the accident. This was clearly too much for me.

negative three

I n order to deal with all these issues, I decided I was going to start having more fun on campus. I figured since he was still involved with other people that I needed to be involved with other people as well. This was my last year in college, and I was on track to graduate. I wanted to make up for the first two years where I had totally ditched the college life that I'd enjoyed so much in the beginning. I needed to have fun too! So between work, school, theater, and doing hair, I told myself I was going to start dating some guys on campus. And that's what I did. I would go out to parties and meet all types of athletes. I'd actually notice there were handsome guys in my classes, and I was giving people chances instead of turning every guy down that approached me. The days that I wouldn't hear from James, I would really have fun, and I was living my best life so that I wasn't in my apartment being miserable without his presence. I was really enjoying myself and loved the social life I was involved in, but in the back of my mind, I would still be thinking about James sometimes. But I'd try to get myself to not think about it and have fun, just like he was. I was hearing about different types of women he was involved with because now I knew people that would see him out with different women at restaurants and church outings. It seemed like everyone really wanted the best for me and would tell me everything he was doing so that I'd get away from him.

I was going out to different events on campus, to movies, parties, and step shows, and it really helped to take my mind off of James. It made me feel a little better about myself as well because I didn't feel as down and miserable while wondering where he was and why he wasn't calling me. It wasn't until I was having fun on campus that I realized what I had been missing. When I would come around, people would always say how happy they were that I was finally going out with them. Yes, I had fun, and yes, I was going out more, but I still didn't let up on my classes. At the end of the day, I still wanted to become his wife after all of my hard work. Going out more and dating younger guys was only so that I wasn't driving myself crazy and enjoying college before I graduated and got married.

There were two guys that really caught my interest. One was a very smart gentleman I met in one of my classes over the summer. He was ultra-intelligent, super stimulating, and super cool. He'd studied abroad and had more than enough units to graduate. He was also a part of the Kappa Alpha Psi Fraternity, which made him super attractive. There was something about those Kappa men. They were sexy, with a brilliant side to them that was intriguing. He was truly my match intellectually but super challenging. I loved conversing with him and asking him about everything. Sometimes I think he thought I was annoying, but I did not care. He was a challenge, and I loved it. Anything to get my mind off of James was great for me.

The other was a football player who was a year older than me. He was in the Omega Psi Phi Fraternity, so he had that sexy, manly, rough vibe that I loved. He was also very aggressive. I would be honest and tell him that I had someone, but he didn't care. He would say, "Call me when your man is not around." He would often call when James was over and say, "Green light or red light?" If James was over I would say, "Red light." If James was not there I would say, "Green light," and he would be over in the next fifteen minutes.

These two acquaintances made life easier to handle. They would fill up my lonely time, and I could be myself around them, sexy, cool, and smart. I was very grateful for them both. I was able to focus on studies and have the fun that I deserved. It was a great balance.

As it pertained to my parents, they began to be less on my bumper about my relationship. I guess they understood I was only going to push against them, which they didn't want. My parents and I were really close growing up, and I knew they still loved me and only wanted the best for me. My mom would always tell me to please focus on school before committing myself to James, which I had promised her I would do. My dad, specifically, was hard to convince because of our age difference, but he ended up meeting James one weekend when he came to visit me and was satisfied. He would always tell me, "Leah, I really think he likes you. I really do." Which was great, because nothing meant more to me than having my parents on my side. However, I could still see the concern on his face whenever he mentioned James. It was like he was trying to be okay with it for my sake, but he really wasn't. I knew deep down he wasn't.

Through my last year of college, things were running a bit smoother. Everything fell into place, and I was scheduled to graduate that May. I was having fun on campus, talking to my parents, and I was still dating James. I ended up renewing my lease on the same apartment, and I was starting to see James more often. I'd cook his favorite meals like macaroni and cheese, red beans and rice, pork chops, greens, banana pudding, and of course pancakes. Anything he said he liked I would cook for him. I mastered all of his favorites and some of mine, like pound cake and sweet potato pie. I was a little Betty Crocker. The reason I wanted to cook so well and have him enjoy my food is because he always bragged about how good Dianne could cook and how she would get out of her bed at any time of the night and make him whatever he wanted. I wanted to be the same way. I was in a constant competition, never knowing if I was winning or losing.

He would also brag about what a great love-maker she was and how her body was perfect. He would often say that my body was not—my boobs weren't perky enough, and my butt was flat. I wanted so bad for him to approve of me and brag on my cooking and my body, so whatever it took, I did it. I was in a rivalry with Dianne in my head because I wanted him to love me more than he loved her. I wanted him to pick me. I wanted him to be with me and only me.

Constantly trying to be perfect for him would cause me to be up super late because I had to finish my assignments. My workload was very rigorous. It was my junior/senior year, so I had 22 units to complete, and I had to do well. I would sometimes stay up all night, drinking different coffee and energy drinks to keep me awake so that I could finish all my papers and assignments. I was driven. It was nothing for me to go out with James, come home after midnight, stay up all night to complete a paper, sleep for an hour, and drive to campus in my pajamas to turn it in. This became routine. I was burning the candle at both ends, but it was worth it. I had to graduate.

It was the Christmas before my graduation. My grandfather had promised to buy me the car of my choice, as long as it was a Ford, if

I proved to him that I was graduating. That holiday break I brought a copy of my transcripts home for my grandfather to see that I was really graduating. He did not believe me. It was a whole year early, so he needed to see proof. He looked at my transcripts and saw my completed units and the units I was scheduled to complete in the spring, which totaled 120 units: enough to graduate. He looked up from my transcripts and said, "I guess we are going car shopping!" I was so excited. I'd done it, and I was so proud of myself.

We went car shopping that next week at Galpin Ford in the San Fernando Valley. I wanted a green Ford Explorer Sport. It had to be green because it had to fit the prophecy that my friend gave me my freshman year. It would not be a Ford Expedition that she said James would buy me, but a green Ford Explorer would suffice. I thought that as long as it was green it would fit the prophecy that I had held on to so tightly. My grandfather took one look at my choice and said, "This is it, let's pay for it and be done." I drove home that day with my grandfather in the passenger seat and my grandmother following behind us. My grandfather fell asleep as I drove, which was a good sign. He was proud of me, and I was so grateful to him.

One of the things I loved most about my family that is a true deal breaker to all of us is the importance of keeping your word. If you can't follow through with what you say, if you can't keep your word, then you don't have good character. Our family stood firmly on the motto, "Your word is your bond." My grandparents and parents stood by this principle. If they said it, they were going to do it. You could trust their word, and you knew they would keep their end of the bargain. My grandparents promised to buy me a car, and they really did it.

And so the time came for me to graduate. Every day I would look for a proposal. When we would be at church, or anytime we'd go to dinner, I knew he was going to ask the question at any moment. He knew I was graduating soon, and he'd promised to marry me. I knew like my family he was going to keep his word. Days went by. Weeks went by. And no proposal yet. I kept eagerly waiting.

The weekend of graduation finally came, and it was magical. My parents and grandparents flew out to Oakland, and James treated them like royalty. He had them driven to my campus in a stretch limousine, he made reservations at a beautiful restaurant overlooking the water, and he booked them hotel rooms at this upscale boutique hotel overlooking the water. He did everything for my family and paid for everything the entire weekend. My family was very impressed and happy. I had done it! I'd finished UC Berkeley in three years and was set to marry the man of my dreams. All I was waiting for now was the proposal. I graduated Saturday at Black Graduation, which is an exclusive graduation for African Americans on campus. It's a time where all of the African Americans who are graduating that year from their various majors can graduate together on one stage. It's a huge cultural event where there is dancing, singing, and a grand celebration for what we accomplished.

That Sunday, we all woke up early. James had the limousine pick me and my family up and escorted us to church, where he told us he would meet us. We got into the church and took our seats as we listened to the praise and worship. I sat in between my mom and my dad, with my grandparents to the right of us.

In the middle of the service, my dad leaned over to me and whispered, "Leah, did you read the bulletin?"

In the bulletin, he had an entire page dedicated to me. He was saying how proud he was of me for graduating in three years, and for carrying myself like a lady and keeping God first in everything I did. The bulletin was beautifully written, and I could tell he'd put a lot of effort into making it special. I kept reading, blushing at how happy he was that I did well in all my classes. I got to the end of the bulletin, and it read: "Leah, you are an amazing girl ready to take on this world. It's going to be so hard to say goodbye to you."

Goodbye...? What did he mean goodbye?

"Leah, did you read it? Wasn't that beautiful?" my dad asked.

"Uhh, yeah! Yes. It was great," I said hastily.

Okay... I thought. *He wants to surprise me... He's going to get on his knees at the end of his sermon and ask for my hand in front of the church at any minute.*

My dad preached at church on this day as a guest speaker. My dad always loved me to sing before he preached, so I went to the altar and sang "Speak to My Heart." After my dad preached, we had offering and did the benediction... no proposal. *Okay, I have one more graduation next weekend. He'll ask me then...* I said to myself.

So the next weekend came, and it was time for my final graduation. This time, it was a culmination for my major that only my parents came to. My family had driven back to Los Angeles after church the prior Sunday, and only my parents drove back for my major graduation. It was an amazing graduation, yet the only thing I was thinking about was when James was going to propose.

My graduation day came—no proposal.

James called himself being helpful by ordering a U-Haul to come pack up all of my things so my dad and I could drive it back down to LA, with my mom following behind us in my new car. So that's what I did. James and I packed up my apartment, loaded countless amounts of clothes and all of my furniture into the U-Haul, and prepared to head back to Los Angeles. James came by to say his goodbyes to me and my family, and when he hugged me, he whispered to me, "Don't worry. I'm still going to marry you; I'm going to come get you from Los Angeles."

I was absolutely distraught... I'd done everything: busted my ass, worked my fingers to the bone, took on an insane class schedule, went through all the drama of court cases, women... only to find myself driving back to LA in a U-Haul with my degree and my dad. What a waste! How embarrassing this was! How could I do this to myself? How could I manage to work so hard for nothing? More importantly, why didn't I say something to him or hold him accountable? I'd seen all of the signs—why did I not pay attention to them? Why did I think something magical was going to happen? Why would I believe him? He devastated me, and I was so disappointed. This was one of the hardest lessons I had to ever learn: never do anything hoping that someone else is going to hold up their end of the bargain. Do it for yourself, let it be a personal accomplishment.

Wallowing in despair and defeat, I went home to Los Angeles. My family was so happy to have me back. Everyone was over the moon that I was back in Los Angeles, except me. I was sad every minute of every day, wondering how long it would be before he would marry me. You have to understand, I never envisioned myself going back home after I graduated. The absolute *only* thing that kept me motivated and so determined over my three college years was the proposal I was expecting after graduation. Week after week, I just knew he was going to come down and get me. I didn't want to make any quick changes in my life because I still wanted to believe, so badly, that James was going to keep his word and come to Los Angeles to get me. My grandmother ended up calling me a couple weeks after I got home.

"Hey, Ook... now you know your family doesn't sit around and do nothing after getting their degrees. You got a degree to work. You *will* get a job! So you have three teacher interviews next week. Get yourself together so you can be ready for your interviews, baby!" she said excitedly.

The entire time I was just looking at the phone like... *huh?* None of this was a part of the plan. I never saw myself actually being a teacher, even though I minored in education. But because I loved and respected my grandmother so much, I ended up going to all three of my teacher interviews.

I ended up landing a job at a private Lutheran school. I was a first grade teacher at a predominately Korean school, and I absolutely loved it. I started working at the age of 21, so I was the youngest teacher at the school, but I connected so well to all of the children. All the teachers respected me because I graduated early from UC Berkeley, so my credentials held power, despite my age. My parents furnished my classrooms with all types of supplies and decorations, and the first graders touched my heart in a way I wasn't expecting. I felt a true calling to children and educating them, and I ended up thanking my grandmother so much for forcing me to get out and get a job. My passion started to become children, and this job helped the time pass faster for my first year back in Los Angeles.

I still kept in close contact with Gigi and Papi. Every Sunday, Gigi would call and tell me about all the various women he would be with at church and different conventions, and how much time he was spending with Chipmunk 2. Chipmunk 2 was the one that he kept away from me, and she never seemed to like me. So after constantly hearing about all these women, and him hurting me so badly for sending me back to Los Angeles after graduation, I began to resent him. Even though I still loved him, the thought of us actually getting married became a thought that seemed so close, but impossible to grasp.

I flew out to see James a lot on weekends throughout the year, but he began only flying me out Friday evening and Saturday and would send me home before church Sunday morning. It was like he didn't want people to know when I was back.

I flew up to Oakland for New Year's Eve, and I was so excited because I thought it was a sign that he wanted to spend that holiday with me. I wanted to think he was going to propose, but I eventually stopped getting my hopes up so that he couldn't crush them.

The weekend was nice. We went to the movies, shopping, out to eat, and had a great time together. When I'd come, he'd get us beautiful, lavish hotels to stay in for the weekend. I never stayed at his condo, which was a sign that Dianne still lived there and things had not changed.

As we were leaving the mall, he got a call from one of the members and put the call on speaker.

"Pastor, watch meeting is tonight. What would you like to do?" the member said.

"Watch meeting? Tonight? Wait—tonight is New Year's Eve?"

"Yeah! You don't know what date it is? Did you forget?" he joked.

"Wow. I'm going to have to call you back," he said.

I looked at him and started laughing. "Wait, you really didn't know it was New Year's Eve today?" I asked curiously.

He looked at me and said, "You're going to have to go home. I didn't know it was New Year's Eve. I have things to do. You need to go home."

I was heartbroken. He drove me to the airport, and I spent the beginning of New Year's Eve on a plane back to Los Angeles, again with no ring and no signs of a proposal. *Leah, you've gotta get yourself together. You have got to...* I said to myself. I had *had* it!

I got back home and continued teaching my first graders. I wanted to get my mind away from James so badly, so I really was investing time into my students, my family, and girlfriends from high school and college. They were taking me out to clubs, and I really felt like I was getting my life back as I was starting my second year of being a teacher.

My next educational step was to get my master's in education. I didn't know when, or even if James was going to propose, so I needed to go on with my life. When you're a teacher, the only way to get a pay raise is to get a master's degree or become some sort of administrator, and that's when you can start making good money in the field. So I started applying to graduate schools like USC, UCLA, and UC Berkeley for their education programs and got accepted into all three. I really wanted to go to USC, but I decided to wait it out to see where life would take me in the next couple months before I committed to a school.

One day while I was at work I decided to call my grandmother to tell her what I wanted for dinner that night. I would spend every Wednesday night with her because I would attend a Bible study at a church near her house. So instead of coming all the way home after Bible study, I would just go over to her house, and she would always have something special for me to eat. This week I had a taste for a chicken pot pie from KFC. I called my grandmother, but she did not pick up. I called her house phone, then called her on her cell phone until she picked up.

"Hi, Mama! Where are you?"

"Oh, I am at the hospital with Dada [that is what we called my grandfather]. He is not feeling that good and they are going to keep him for the night," she said.

In shock I said, "In the hospital, what hospital? Dada is sick?"

"Oh, he is just not feeling good today, Ook. He will be okay, just needs to be in the hospital." She tried to sound calm, but I knew she wasn't. No one in our family had ever been in the hospital or ever sick, so this was something new for all of us.

"What hospital is he in, Mama?" I asked.

"He is in Cedars-Sinai. I am going home to get some things for him, and I will be going back to the hospital."

I said, "Okay, well, call me later."

"Okay, love you." And she hung up. Immediately I started calling my mom and dad telling them that Dada was in the hospital and that we needed to get there as soon as possible.

Every one of us was in a true panic. We fled to the hospital and found my grandfather looking really bad and barely eating. We were scared and afraid. As my mother stood trying to feed him the dinner the hospital provided, a middle-aged White male came into the room wearing a doctor's coat. We all looked at him.

My dad was the first to speak up. "Hello, may we help you?"

"Yes," the doctor exclaimed. "My name is Dr. Stein, and I am your father and grandfather's oncologist."

"Oncologist!" my dad exclaimed. "He doesn't have cancer."

"Yes, he does," Dr. Stein said. "In fact, he has had cancer for the past 15 years."

We were all speechless and looked at my grandfather, who could not respond at all or hear the conversation that was going on because he was hard of hearing. Immediately I started tearing up.

Just then, my grandmother walked in. "Hey, everyone, is everyone all right?" she said.

"Mama, why didn't you tell us?" I was so angry! "Why didn't you tell us Dada had cancer?"

"Well, Dada didn't want me to tell anyone. He wanted us to fight this together. He did not want to worry any of you."

"I know, but Mama, this is terrible. You should have said something," I said.

"I know, but I had to respect his wishes," she said calmly.

For the next month we were at the hospital every day. My grandfather had experienced complications with his cancer that caused him to have stomach ulcers and ultimately landed him in the ICU for the month. I was with him every day, staying with her at the house and going to the hospital with her. We even spent some nights in the hospital putting chairs together to make a bed so we could get some rest. I remember stealing covers for her from the nurses' stations just to keep her warm. Our bond, which was already tighter than ever, became unbreakable. I knew she needed me, and I was there for her.

Because James had a fond respect and admiration for my grandparents, he became very concerned about my grandfather. Our phone conversations were still frequent but would be interrupted with all that we were going through. My grandfather had to get several surgeries and stayed in the ICU on a respirator for the duration of the month.

James wanted to come and see him. There was an event that he needed to attend there, so he decided to couple that with coming to see my grandfather. He wanted me to pick him up from Burbank Airport when he landed that Friday night. I was so excited he was coming in, but I was also nervous about my grandfather's state. On my way to the airport I totally got lost. James hated to wait on people to pick him up from the airport and would be furious about it, so I frantically tried my best, but I totally forgot how to get there. I had driven an hour out of the way before I finally arrived.

He was so angry. "What happened to you? You know I don't like waiting on people at the airport. You are so inconsiderate. I have been sitting here for over an hour and now I have totally missed the event! How do you think I feel? How could you do this?" he yelled.

"I did not do this on purpose. I got turned around. I got lost. I am so sorry. I've been going through a whole lot. Please forgive me," I pleaded.

"There is no excuse for this. This is terrible! I can't believe you did this. Just take me to the hospital."

I drove to the hospital in silence. Did he understand what my family and I had been going through? I did not purposely pick him up late, couldn't he understand that? When we got to the hospital and into my grandfather's room, James saw my grandfather on the respirator and puffed up big because of all the medicine.

He looked at me with the saddest face and said, "I am so sorry for yelling at you. I had no idea this is what you were going through. I am so sorry." He hugged me, prayed for my grandfather, held his hand, and we left the hospital together hand in hand. I was so relieved he saw what I was dealing with, and his remorse for his attitude made me feel so much better. I was so happy he was in town, so happy.

One night while my grandmother and I were asleep we got a phone call. "Mrs. Lusk, Mr. Lusk is going to pass within the hour. Please come to the hospital." A few days prior they'd told us that there was nothing else they could do. His body was not responding to the surgeries, and we had to make a decision whether to take him off of all the machines or just leave him on the respirator for oxygen until he passed. We decided to do that.

We rushed to the hospital, and he had already passed. It was the first time I had experienced the death of a loved one. I had mixed emotions. I did not like watching him go through so much pain, but I also did not want to lose him. My grandmother's life was tied to his. She had married him when she was only 17 years old. She had come out to Los Angeles with her father from Texas on a free train ticket that he'd received for his exceptional work at his job. They were coming to visit relatives when my grandmother decided to call her friend from school, Dorothy, who'd moved out to Los Angeles, to see if she could come to visit her. Dorothy was so excited she had her brother bring her to see my grandmother. When Dorothy's brother brought her to see my grandmother, something happened, because the next day he came by himself. Needless to say, that one train visit ended up being a one-way trip because my grandmother never went back to Texas. Dorothy's brother was my grandfather. Two months later they were married.

Now my grandmother had to lay to rest the love of her life of 53 years. They had worked so hard together. They had taken turns putting themselves through college and graduate programs while having children and working day and night shift jobs. They had managed to save enough money to purchase property, build apartment buildings, pay the property off, and put two children through school. They put my uncle through Stanford University, where he graduated cum laude, then went to UCLA Jules Stein Eye Institute and became an ophthalmologist. My mother graduated from UC Berkeley with her undergrad, USC with her master's degree and was an educator for over 30 years. They had done an amazing job.

They both came from very meager beginnings, but what they had accomplished was something worth being proud of.

My grandfather's funeral was one for the history books. I sang his favorite song, "In the Garden," and to everyone's surprise, James spoke on the program. His speech was outstanding and heartfelt. He spoke about how he wished he'd been raised by a man like my grandfather who had standards, worked hard, and was an excellent provider for his family. He spoke about how he was jealous of my uncle and my father for having such a polished role model in their lives and that all he wanted to do was to live a life that emulated the character, respect, and standards of my grandfather. He received a standing ovation by the 500 people in attendance that day. He made me so proud to be with him. This day solidified in my mind that he was going to be my husband, and my grandfather would be proud. I hoped.

negative two

One day I got a call from the pastor whose church I had been raised in, Dr. Michael Harris Sr., and he said, "Leah, there's a young pastor coming out here for our revival from San Antonio. I want you to be his host. His name is Terry Patrick. He wants to go to all the hip places, and you're young, so I know you'd be a perfect fit for it. Would you mind doing that for me?"

"Okay..." I said.

My pastor knew for a fact I was still involved with James, so I knew it was a plan to get me away from him. Everyone questioned James' intentions with me, and so any chance they got to introduce me to someone else they would take. This pastor, Terry, came from a nationally known family, and they were very much admired through the whole church community. His parents were a very well respected and established pastor and pastor's wife, so it was a pretty good match, actually. Besides, I was still feeling some type of way about James sending me home so easily like I didn't matter to him. He had made no moves toward marriage, and I wanted to get my mind off of him, so I agreed to host Terry for the week. My parents ended up hearing about it, and they were *ecstatic* because, even though they didn't say it, they did want me to get away from James. Not to mention, they loved Terry's parents and knew that the match was perfect.

The Monday came where I was scheduled to meet Terry, to begin hosting him and show him around LA. My pastor and his wife told me to meet them in his office before service so that I could meet Terry. I walked into the office, saw Terry sitting next to my pastor, and instantly walked out before he could turn around and see me. The pastor's wife rushed out behind me.

"Leah! Where are you going? Why did you walk out?" she said as she called after me.

"Hmm. He's not my type," I said.

He was on the shorter side, thin, fair skinned, wore Armani-type glasses, and had short dreadlocks, and I just wasn't here for it. He seemed to be an 'earthy' type of person, and he was the complete opposite of James. I immediately knew I wasn't interested.

"Baby, it's not always about the looks," she said. "I want you to go inside. Just meet him first. And then I want you to hear him preach. After you hear him, then talk to me."

So I did. I sucked it up and went inside the office to introduce myself to Terry. We talked briefly, and I told him I would see him after he preached. I left the office and went to take my seat.

When I say Terry might have delivered one of the best sermons I had ever heard in my life, I really mean that. He was funny, he was well-read, and he was hip, making all types of modern, hip examples and connections to the real world that I could relate to. He had intelligence beyond measure. He was everything my pastor's wife had said he would be. I was in awe. All the negative opinions

I had of him when I first walked into the office instantly vanished after his sermon.

So I decided to give him a chance. I showed him around LA, took him to Melrose, took him to all the hot spots in LA, all of the hole in the wall eateries like Roscoe's Chicken and Waffles, and we really had a great time that week. He was so nice to me, and really seemed to be into me. We went to a breakfast restaurant called Jack and Jill's, and he kept staring at me.

"Why do you wear all that makeup?" he asked. "I can't even see your freckles; it looks like you have freckles. Do you?"

"Yeah... I do, actually." I blushed.

"Why do you cover them? You'd be even more beautiful if you let your natural features show," he commented.

I couldn't help but compare his opinions to James'. James didn't even want me to leave the house without makeup. If my lipstick would even smudge while we were at dinner, he'd signal me to go to the restroom so I could re-apply it.

"And why do you dress like that? Do you wear a suit everywhere you go? You should wear one of those Juicy Couture velour sweat suits; they seem so comfortable and it would look so nice on you!"

I absolutely loved being around Terry. We were inseparable the whole week. I felt like God had sent me a breath of fresh air. He seemed to really like me for me, and I didn't have to put any effort into being a girl he liked. He didn't try to mold me to be any woman except Leah. He relaxed me. He was my catalyst into finding myself and falling in love with myself again. We'd play Lauryn Hill and Maxwell and just vibe together in the car. I felt so free and at ease when we were together. He was the first person to totally take my mind off James, and it felt *so* good. I was happy, and I wasn't bending over backwards and driving myself insane to please a person that was never pleased. I was never enough with James. With Terry, I was everything, and more, all by being my authentic self. He liked when my hair wasn't done and traced my freckles like constellations in the sky.

Through Terry, I began to get closer to the Lord. He encouraged me to really immerse myself into the Word and to find life within myself. And so I did.

I'd go to church, Bible studies, and things like that, but it wasn't like I had done it back in Oakland. There, I can honestly say I was only going to get and keep the attention of James, instead of truly going to get closer to the Lord. Without a clear mind, one can't fully process the depths of the Lord and listen to what God is really trying to express. One day, I had a revelation within myself. I told the Lord that I was no longer going to have sex with any man other than the one I married. I maintained my stance.

I will admit, James would still fly me back out to Oakland, but I did not have sex with him. He couldn't understand why I was doing this, since we had been so sexually involved before. It gave me a sense of power to have something he wanted so badly but couldn't get. I was so determined not to give my power away again, since I knew how low I could get, mentally and emotionally, when the ball wasn't in my court. Yet my dream was *still* to marry James. I figured if I could regain control of myself mentally, James would never be able to have that control over me again, so our relationship would be healthier.

The confidence I gained through the Lord really was pivotal in my growth as a woman in Christ. My mind was clear, and I was able to understand things for what they were, instead of what I wanted them to be. But I don't think I could have grown without the encouragement of Terry. He believed in me in a way that made me see myself in a different light.

It only took a couple of months for James to find out that I was seeing Terry. I don't know how he found out, but when he did, he was furious.

"So you are dating Terry from San Antonio?"

"What do you mean? What are you talking about, James?" I said.

He replied, "You know who I am talking about. I know everything! How you hosted him while he was preaching the revival at Mt. Everlasting Baptist Church. How could you betray me?"

I was thinking to myself, *Betray you? After all the women I have caught you with? The least I could do, or the only sane thing to do was to date!* But I did not say anything. I just listened silently and took everything he said in without denying anything.

"I talked to him on the phone, Leah. We talked! He knows about me."

All I could do was gasp and be in shock. I did not know what to say. Honestly he made me feel guilty, but then all of a sudden he said, "I want to come to LA to see you."

At that moment I was confused because I thought he was mad at me and was going to call it quits with me. How in the world did he talk to Terry? Did someone tell Terry about him? The church world is very small, so I was sure someone had told James. I was outdone. The moment I finally started liking someone else, the moment I got my head together and started thinking clearly, the moment my mind began to open up to more possibilities, James found out!

The day that James called me about Terry, I had no idea how he'd found out, and he never told me. Much later, I found out that Terry had called James. When he found out who I was dating, when I told him I was dating someone, and it was really difficult—I didn't know where it was leading—he found out who that person was. Being in the church world, especially both being pastors, it's kind of like a brotherhood where, if you're dating someone, and you know the pastor of who you're dating, I believe it's standard that you tell that person. I couldn't believe it. Never in my wildest dreams would I think that Terry would call James and tell him that we were dating or that we were talking. I don't even know exactly what he told him, but all I know is that Terry called him to let him know. This actually saddened me because I was confused as to what it meant. Did he tell him because he wanted James to stop pursuing me? Did Terry think that by telling James, that would stop everything, and that I would be all his? I really just couldn't understand. Instead, it made James want me even more. It pushed James to want to marry me faster than anything that had evolved over the five years we had been together. Whatever plans Terry had by telling James completely backfired. He became more aggressive than ever about marrying me.

That weekend he flew to Los Angeles. While he was in town, he really was determined to win me back over. He was super nice, took me to the movies and out to eat, but it just wasn't doing it for me. And he could tell. But he was not easing up.

One night at dinner, he looked at me with deep eyes and said, "Leah. Marry me. I don't want to wait anymore."

I almost choked on my water. I never actually thought the words were going to come out of his mouth. This was still my only wish, even though I debated it in my mind, and I really still wanted to marry this man. I believed that I had matured enough over these two years and thought that God wanted me to marry him. I figured

I could pray the other women away, or that he had finally decided for himself that I was the only one he wanted. So I agreed.

"You will have to get the blessing of my parents first," I instructed.

James and I completed a marriage counseling course, and now it was time for him to ask my parents if he could marry me. The marriage counseling was James' idea, and I think he did it to buy time, to make me think we were getting closer to marriage even if we weren't. The counselors we had were renowned for counseling even the most tumultuous marriages. They would get people back together and get people married. I absolutely loved them. They were real and authentic, transparent, and called James out on many things. They would also keep him accountable, which was very uncomfortable for him. There were many times where they would pull me to the side and tell me that they really did not think he was ready to get married and that I might need to rethink things. They kept me accountable as well, which was good because it kept everything very balanced. I would always be determined to continue with our counseling, hoping that he would finally be at the point where he was ready.

In addition to the counseling, our marriage counselors required us to take classes with other married couples to learn our roles as husband and wife the way God created marriage to be. I would meet with her married women's class weekly, where she would teach us how to cook delicious meals and then give us a lesson on how to be an amazing wife. She would teach us about being clean and organized in our homes, how to effectively communicate with our spouses, marital intimacy, etc. He would meet with the husband and the men monthly because he lived in the Bay Area. He would fly down for his classes, which were to encourage him and teach him how to be a loving husband. We loved these classes and completed them with ease. I truly thought we were finally on the path to marriage.

I set up the meeting at my parents' home, and James came over to meet with them. I was very scared because my parents had their doubts, but I had to do it if I wanted to get married. James delivered his case and said that he loved me and wanted to marry me. My dad explained his reservations and concerns about our age differences and also what he'd heard about the type of man James was—and rightfully so. I could tell my dad was really trying to be open for me, because he did love me, and the last thing he wanted was to lose me. Maybe my parents thought I would flee Los Angeles and secretly marry James anyway if they disagreed. He ended up winning my parents over, convincing them that he would be a great husband to me and take care of me as well as he could. They reluctantly said yes, even though I knew they didn't want to. With my parents' blessing, everything was set to go. I was finally getting married.

One day, as it got closer to my birthday, James flew out to Los Angeles again. The time he was away, we talked every day, and things seemed to be flowing easily. Before he got on his flight, he told me he had a nice dinner planned for me. When he finally landed, I got a message from him saying that I was to go to the Beverly Center and meet him at PF Chang's. As I walked in the restaurant at the Beverly Center, I saw one of my friends.

"Hey, Necole, what are you doing here?" I asked excitedly.

She handed me a single rose. "The man who loves you told me to give you this and tell you to go to the furniture store Z Gallerie upstairs," she said calmly.

"What?" I asked.

"Don't ask any questions. Just go upstairs," she prompted.

And so I went. When I got to the door of Z Gallerie, I saw another one of my best friends from high school named Tia. She handed me another single rose.

"The man who loves you told me to give you this and tell you to go to the shoe store next door," she said.

"What is going on? I was just downstairs and—"

"Don't ask any questions, just go next door," she prompted.

And so I went. When I got to Steve Madden, Emily, one of my best friends from college, was standing there with a single rose.

As soon as she saw me, she began crying and could barely get out what she was trying to say.

"The man who... loves... you... told me to... give you this...."

She handed me the rose as she kept crying frantically.

"Emily, what's wrong? What are you trying to tell me?" I asked.

"I-I-I can't tell you... Just go to Ann Taylor," she managed to get out through the tears. She hugged me and sent me off to Ann Taylor.

And so I went. When I got to Ann Taylor, I walked in, but this time I didn't see any of my friends waiting for me at the door. One of the saleswomen came up to me and said, "Hello, is your name Leah?"

"Yes..." I said cautiously.

"The man who loves you told me to bring you over here. Can you follow me?" she asked.

I followed her into the dressing room, and she swung the door open and guided me inside, smiling. When I walked in, there were about six different elegant outfits surrounding the walls. All of them were absolutely stunning.

"The man who loves you has bought all of these for you. He wants you to pick one outfit of your choice and wear it for tonight," she said.

I went into the dressing room and looked up at the dresses and outfits as they shone in the lights. In my heart, I just *knew* that I was picking the outfit I was going to be proposed to in. I felt like a princess in a fairy tale and this was a magical treasure hunt leading to my proposal! This was it! This was the nicest thing anyone had ever done for me. I picked out a sky blue silk pantsuit that had a blazer, slacks, and a cashmere shell to match.

"Great choice," the saleswoman confirmed.

As she packed up the rest of the dresses in a bag for me, I realized I didn't have any shoes to match my pantsuit.

"Oh gosh! I need to go downstairs and get some heels for this," I said out loud.

"You better hurry! Your chariot awaits at seven o'clock!" she said as she handed me my bags.

So I rushed downstairs, while trying not to mess up my new outfit, ran into Charles David, picked out heels, and quickly put them on. I looked at the clock on the wall, and it read seven o'clock. I walked quickly to the parking lot, where there was a stretch limousine, and out walked James in a black tailored suit. I just knew this was the moment he was going to get on one knee and ask for my hand in marriage.

He got out of the limo and yelled, "HAPPY BIRTHDAY! SURPRISE!" as he handed me a bouquet of roses.

"Ohhh…. Thanks… this was… amazing!" I said, trying to sound appreciative.

And it was amazing. It was *great*, actually. It just wasn't the proposal. *Again.* I had no idea what was happening, so I just decided to go with the moment. No one had ever done anything that nice for me before, so I just decided to be grateful.

We got into in the limo and headed to G. Garvin's. At the time, it was one of the trendiest restaurants by the Beverly Center, on 3rd Street. As I walked in, James opened the door, and to my surprise, all my friends and family were inside waiting for me. My parents, my grandma, our marriage counselors, each one of my friends who passed out roses during the magical treasure hunt, and some of our closest friends. They filled the entire restaurant.

"SURPRISE!" everyone yelled.

It was such a special moment for me. The fact that James had gone through all of that for my birthday made my heart grow even fonder. I walked around and thanked everyone so much for surprising me on my birthday. It meant the world to me that I got to spend that night with all of my loved ones. Everyone ate, the food was absolutely delicious, and I was just smiling from ear to ear the entire night. When the check came around, James paid for everyone's dinner. He liked doing things like that; he wanted people to see him as this big spender type of guy.

Everyone started singing, in unison...

"Happy birthday to you... Happy birthday to youuuuu. Happy birthdayyy dear Leah, happppppppy birthday to you!"

As everyone was singing, the whole staff of the restaurant walked out of the kitchen with a huge platter with a silver cover on it. As they placed the silver platter on the table in front of me, they took off the cover. On the platter was a 5.1 carat pear-shaped diamond ring in the middle of chocolate sauce that read, "Will you marry me?"

I yelled so loud. I couldn't believe the moment was here! Everyone actually surprised me, because I really thought they were there for my birthday! None of the moments when I'd suspected he would propose compared to the actual moment. It was beautiful. It was absolutely stunning and perfect.

"You didn't answer, Leah. Will you marry me?" James asked as he grabbed my hand.

"OF COURSE! OF COURSE I WILL!" I yelled.

Everyone around me yelled in excitement, and I held my ring up like a trophy. This was all I had wanted, all I had worked for. I was finally going to marry the man of my dreams. All the ups and downs and everything I'd endured was finally coming to fruition. I was FINALLY getting married, and everything was going as my friend had prophesied. The ring, the green car, things getting worse before they got better—everything seemed to be in alignment. Or so I thought.

So now it was time for the engagement. In my mind, I decided that it made the most sense for me to go to Berkeley since I was getting married, and that's where James lived. One of the requirements for grad school is that you have to take the GRE as well as the MSAT, which is for educators. If I passed the MSAT, I'd be able to start school in August, which was perfect because that's when I wanted to get married. This meant we had three months to prepare for the wedding as I'd simultaneously study for and pass the MSAT. I had it all figured out, per usual.

When I told James that we were setting the date for August, he didn't seem as enthusiastic about getting married so promptly as I was. A couple days after he proposed, I told him when I'd like the wedding to be.

"What do you mean we're setting the date for August? We're not going to get married this fast," he said.

"Oh, *yes* we are!" I affirmed.

Like wait a minute. He put me through all of that, went through everything with my family, and he thought we weren't getting married quickly? *Tuh!*

"Are you sure?" he asked me.

"I'm sure," I said.

"Well, I'll have to think about it."

That threw me completely off. I mean, weren't we supposed to be equally excited to marry each other? Did he give me the ring just to shut me up? He'd always randomly throw these quick jabs that would make my gut turn inside out. I didn't want to bug him, though, so I didn't push for the date so much, even though I did want to get married as soon as possible. I figured he'd come around and become as excited as I was to have our beautiful wedding. And he did. Finally, a couple weeks later, he called me one day.

"You know what. Let's do it. Let's get married in August."

"Really?!" I yelled.

"Yes!" he said. "But I don't want to have anything to do with the wedding," he insisted.

"What…what do you mean you don't want anything to do with the wedding?" I asked.

"Exactly what I said. I don't want to have anything to do with it. I'm just gonna show up."

"But… you have to. I mean, you have to help me pick colors, pick your groomsmen—"

"Yeah, I'll get around to it. Just handle everything. I've got to go, though, bye!"

And he hung up the phone. *Well… it sounds like I have a wedding to plan,* I said to myself.

Back in the Bay Area, James was starting to make a room in his office, inside the church, which was just a two-room space. He was planning to implement a bed, a small bathroom with a shower, and a little space for a closet. We'd talk on the phone and he would keep telling me he was "fixing it up for us."

I thought it was so sweet that he was turning his office into a double office so that I'd have my own workstation. Out of curiosity, I finally asked him, "What made you decide to fix your office space for me?"

"Well, I don't have enough money to buy us a house right now, so this is where we're going to live until I can figure it out."

"Live?" I asked. "Like in... your office?"

"Yeah, and Dianne and her child are going to live in the condo," he said.

"Well, isn't it *your* condo? Why can't we stay there?" I pleaded.

"I wouldn't make them move out of the condo to find somewhere to live. That's not fair. I'm marrying you, I'm not marrying her, so I want to start fresh with you and just give her the condo," he insisted.

"Okay..." I said.

So that was strange... We'd be living in the small studio in his church until we saved enough money to get a place? I couldn't tell my parents that because all my life they'd kept me in a beautiful home and would be offended to know I was going to be crammed into a place like that. Matter of fact, I wasn't going to tell anyone because it was a bit embarrassing, to be quite honest. Honestly, I was just happy to get married, so onward with the wedding! He didn't want to plan anything? Fine, I'd plan everything myself. That way I could make sure it was everything that I'd dreamt it would be.

I wanted to get married in Beverly Hills, so for days I was researching and going to look at different churches in Beverly Hills. I wanted the reception at the Beverly Hills Hotel, my favorite hotel ever. I went and got a date, then made sure that it was available for our day, and it was. My mom helped me create our invitations, which were absolutely gorgeous. Honestly, I was having so much fun planning my dream wedding that I began to not even care that James wasn't active in my planning. All I knew was that I could have every single thing the exact way I had been envisioning this day all of my life.

From a little girl, while everyone else was playing with dolls and dollhouses, I was reading and collecting bridal magazines. I had a whole collection of them and already knew the type of dress I wanted, how the church was going to be decorated, how the brides-maids' dresses were going to look, and how the reception would be flooded with flowers. I had been planning my wedding since I was a child.

While planning for our wedding, I still had to be on top of my studies for the MSAT if I planned to take and pass the exam by August. I wanted to have something to do while being in Oakland, because I've never known not working or going to school. I didn't want to only be at home doing nothing; I still wanted a life for myself. I took the practice MSAT a couple times throughout the course of those three months, but every time I'd take it, there were certain sections that I just *couldn't* pass. You have to pass all the sections in order to pass the test as a whole. I knew it was because I wasn't completely focused with everything else I had going on. I had to make the decision to forfeit the year, take the test after I got married, and then go back to school. That way, I could just plan for the wedding, since I had to hold up James' end as well.

One of the hardest parts about that was trying to find grooms-men. I was trying to think of any men I could incorporate because James wasn't picking anyone at all. Little did he know, there was no challenge that was too big for me. You better believe I found men to be in my wedding, as well as tuxedos for them all.

By now you all may or may not be curious as to what happened to Terry. The truth is, we never really fell off. Although our rela-tionship was long distance, we kept in touch with each other. I was a little disappointed about his call to James. I still did not under-stand why he did that, and we never addressed it. However, I felt he, at least, deserved to know about my new commitment from me personally. I really did care about Terry and felt an indescribable connection with him, but I had wanted to marry James for years. Terry already knew that I was dating him because the whole church world knew, and I was very honest with him, even though it was complicated. I felt horrible, but I also felt obligated to tell him. So one night I had to suck it up and call.

"Leah?"

"Hey... Terry... How are you?" I hesitated.

"I'm good, you?" he asked.

I guess he could hear in my voice that something was wrong.

"Oh, I'm fine... Hey, do you remember that guy that I told you about that I'd been dating?" I asked.

"Yeah."

"Well, he asked me to marry him..." I said softly.

"And what did you say?"

"I said yes," I confessed.

There was dead silence on the phone. He didn't say anything for what felt like forever.

"Hello?" I said.

"Hello?" he responded.

"Well, are you going to say anything?"

"What is there to say? You've made your decision... I'm not very happy about it, but you made your decision."

"I really didn't know where our relationship was after you left LA and—"

"You didn't know what our relationship was? Leah, I like you, I really like you. Was that not clear? Did I not show you that?"

"I really like you too. But we never solidified what we were or if we were committed to each other. I know we are still getting to know one another, but this is something I have been waiting for over five years. I am so sorry, but I have to do this."

There were no words that could fully express how heart-wrenching it felt to be having that conversation with Terry in that moment. He was wonderful to me and deserved nothing but the best in return, yet I still felt like I had to marry James because of how much energy and time I'd already invested. It hurt me so much having to accept the fact that I lost a genuine friend, but it hurt me even more to know he was hurting, and I was the reason. He didn't deserve that. The connection we had was undeniable, but I had to make a choice. We stayed on the phone for a little while longer before hanging up. Our conversation was filled with silence; only our emotions could be felt through the phone. Would've, could've, and should've questions filled my head. Was I losing him forever? Could I handle never talking to him again? Although it hurt, I still had to get myself together and continue planning the wedding.

There was enough planning to go around for everyone. My grandmother and my mother helped me with every single thing since James wasn't involved and wasn't even asking how the planning was going. Not to mention my parents funded the entire operation.

The day came when it was time to get my dress. I wanted a beautiful A-line princess dress because I knew James loved those types of dresses. My mom, grandmother, and I drove to Beverly Hills for our appointment in Barney's bridal department, where I tried on all kinds of dresses, but I wasn't satisfied until I found *the* dress. After hours of trying on different dresses and showing my mom and grandmother, I finally found my dream dress. It was absolutely gorgeous. My mom loved it until she saw that it was five thousand dollars. But my grandmother said to me, "You're my grandbaby. If this is what you want, I'm paying for it," and she bought me the dress.

When we left the store, I was more than ecstatic with my dress. It was stunning, but I couldn't help but feel bad about how much my grandmother spent on it. When I got home, my mom asked, "Do you really like the dress like that? You know that is a very expensive dress, right?"

"I really do like it," I replied.

"I think you should think about that. That's a bit much to pay for a bridal gown, don't you think? I don't think you should allow Mama to buy you that. You should be more considerate."

She was right. I called my grandmother and explained to her how much I appreciated and loved the dress, but I insisted on finding something cheaper. We returned the dress, went downtown, and found another dress that I ended up loving even more. It was a two-piece, crystal trimmed corset bustier with a separate tulle skirt with crystals on the veil. It was absolutely beautiful. This dress was only $800.00. It was a steal! And it was gorgeous. My grandmother was pleased, and I felt better about my decision.

About two months into the engagement, we had a family reunion. It was in the midst of planning so I didn't want to go, but my grandma really wanted my mom and me to go with her, so we went. We were to fly into San Antonio and drive to Palestine, Texas, where the reunion was to be. When we got to San Antonio, we checked into our hotel (we were only going to stay for the night, rent a car the following morning, and head to the reunion). When we arrived in our room, I asked my mom what she wanted to do for the night.

"Maybe you could call Terry and see what he's doing," my mom suggested.

Why would she tell me to call Terry?! I'm getting married in a few weeks!

"What?" I said, confused.

"You're in his city. You should call him. I'm sure he wants to hear from you," she urged.

Okay... Yes. I had been thinking about him since that phone call. Yes, I knew I was coming to his city. But no, my plan was not to go see him. In fact, that was the last thing I wanted to do! ... But was it? Did I really not want to see him? Would he even want to see me? Undoubtedly, I had all kinds of different thoughts running through my mind. *Maybe it wouldn't hurt to see him,* I thought to myself. I decided to call him. He answered the phone right before I was about to change my mind and hang up.

"Leah?" he asked.

"Yes!" I said awkwardly, at a loss for words.

"You okay?"

"Yes! I'm in your town," I said.

"You are?"

"Yeah, I have a family reunion in Palestine, so we flew into San Antonio."

"Come see me."

My heart dropped. I didn't know what to say.

"Come see me," he insisted.

He gave me the address, and we hung up the phone. My mom looked like she was going to burst.

"Well, what did he say?" she asked.

"He said that I should come and see him," I replied.

"You should go!"

My grandmother didn't say anything.

So I mapped the address and drove to his condo. As I got to the door I was just so nervous to be face to face with Terry that I almost considered leaving. I took a deep breath and rang the doorbell. He opened the door and just stood there and smiled. Instantly, I felt everything I'd felt when we first hung out. Every emotion I'd pushed away came back ten times stronger instantly. I had never felt anything like it.

"Leah," he said. "You are beautiful." I blushed and smiled. I thought to myself, *Why is he doing this to me?*

I walked into his condo, and he started to show me around his place and got me a glass of cold water. I thought the conversation would be awkward, but it wasn't. It felt natural and genuine as if nothing had changed and we'd picked up right where we left off.

We were laughing and catching up on each other's lives, when out of nowhere he cut me off mid-sentence and said, "*Why* are you doing this?"

"I-I... I have to. I said yes, I gave him my word," I said as I put my head down.

"You don't have to do this, Leah. Why won't you just be with me?"

"I can't..."

"You can! Yes, you can. You know what we have. I'll be good to you. I'll take care of you."

I've never heard anyone speak more believable words than Terry in that moment. I looked at him, and he looked back at me passionately and with purpose. Our souls were speaking to each other. He leaned over and kissed me.

I melted.

It felt so wrong, yet so right. So right... And so for hours, that's what we did. We talked, cuddled, and kissed.

I don't know what hit me, but out of nowhere I felt a heavy sense of guilt on my chest.

"I should be leaving now. I shouldn't have done this," I said as I gathered my things.

"Please don't—"

"I have to go!" I said as I rushed out the door. "I'm so sorry!"

On my way back to the hotel I drove in silence. Why did I still have such strong emotions for another man when my wedding was weeks away? Was I in love with Terry and not James? Was I making the right decision? I prayed on it and asked for clear guidance and direction because I felt so lost on the way back. *All these emotions will go away soon*, I told myself.

I thought my mom and grandmother would be asleep by the time I got back because it was already around twelve a.m. But of course they weren't.

"Well, how was it?" my mom said, sitting up in bed.

"It was really nice! We talked and had a nice night," I said.

"Did he say anything?"

"Yeah, he asked me why I am marrying James…" I mumbled.

"And what did you say?"

"I said because I had to."

"Well, what are you going to do?"

"Mom! I'm marrying James!" I yelled. "You know I'm getting married in a few weeks!"

She and my grandmother lowered their heads like they had just been let down. I started to wonder if they had even wanted to attend the family reunion, or just wanted to use that as an excuse so I could see Terry in hopes that he could stop me from marrying James. I eventually got ready for bed and lay down thinking about everything that had just happened. My mind was racing like crazy. Just as I finally started to drift into sleep, I got a call from James.

"Leah, how is your trip?" he asked.

"Oh, it's really nice. We are driving to the reunion in the morning," I said casually.

"You know I miss you, right? I can't wait to see you, beautiful. I was just calling to say I love you."

"I love you too," I replied.

I hung up the phone and looked up at the ceiling. *Sigh.* What had I gotten myself into?

We ended up having a wonderful time at our family reunion. It was the perfect getaway during the rigorous planning I was doing.

We said our goodbyes to our family and headed out back to San Antonio so that we could catch our fight back to Los Angeles. When we got back to San Antonio, I had the urge to call Terry one last time before I left for LA.

"Hey, Terry!" I said.

"Leah, how was the reunion?" Terry replied.

"Great. We are back in San Antonio now. We fly back to LA in the morning," I said.

"Come see me," he said.

"Okay," I replied. I wanted nothing more than to see him one more time before I got back to LA.

When I got to his condo, he insisted that we go to the grocery store and that I make him dinner. I agreed because I loved to cook. We went to the grocery store and bought pork chops, salad, macaroni and cheese, corn bread, and yams to make candied yams. When we got back to his condo, I cooked, and he watched. Every chance that he got he would grab me and kiss me. It felt so natural and so right. Our chemistry was everything, and we both acted as if we never wanted to let go.

I stayed there longer than I thought, so long my mom called me to tell me to come back so that I could get enough sleep to make our flight in the morning. I told Terry that I had to go, and he understood. This time when I left we hugged goodbye as if that was the last time we would see each other.

We kissed one last time, and as I left, he said, "You know you don't have to do this."

I said, "I know, but I have to." I took one last look at his face and walked away.

My wedding date was approaching faster than ever. The countdown was on. Before I knew it, we were two weeks away from the wedding. At this point, we had to get a marriage license. James told me he was going to come down to LA so that we could take care of all our business because he had been in Oakland for the past months building the studio in his church.

He came down to LA, and we headed right over to the Beverly Hills courthouse. Upon arrival, James told me that he wanted to apply for a confidential marriage license.

"What does that mean?" I asked.

"I don't want anyone to know about it or be able to get any records of it. I want it to be confidential."

"Oh…"

"Yeah, a lot of celebrities get confidential marriage licenses. It's very common for elite people."

Well, that's what we got. I went along with getting a confidential marriage license because I believed every word he told me. Whatever he thought was best, I did too. Now, not only did James request a private license, but he kept the overall news of our marriage even more discreet. He didn't tell anyone we were getting married. One day when I asked him for the addresses of his friends and family members to send their invitations, he got VERY mad at me. I mean, the anger came out of nowhere! He was saying things like, "What part of private do you not understand?" "I want this to be private!" and "I'm not inviting *anyone! Unless I change my mind, don't ask me again!*"

Now hold up... With the amount of money my parents were investing into this wedding, it should have been the furthest thing away from private. We were spending thousands of dollars for the church, Beverly Hills Presbyterian Church, followed by the reception in the ballroom of the Beverly Hills Hotel, as well as paying per guest for a candlelight dinner of four hundred and fifty people. It was an entire celebration that was planned to a T. I wanted the entire *world* to see how beautiful this wedding could be! I spent countless days and long nights making sure it was a fairy tale, and he didn't want to tell *anyone?*

I had to talk about it with someone. Pretty much everything else I kept very private between family and friends because I didn't want anyone judging me even more for marrying James. I'd take his jabs and internalize them to the core, but I couldn't hold it anymore. I didn't want to tell my grandmother, nor my mother, nor anyone in my family. I decided to talk to one of my best friends, Tia, about what he had just told me. We had been friends since the tenth grade, so she knew me very well.

I went over to her house and told her *everything.* Everything came running out like an open faucet. It felt so good to be getting everything off my chest that I couldn't stop venting about how inactive

James had been for our wedding. I even told her about my time in San Antonio with Terry.

I asked her to be very honest with me. "Should I marry James?" I sighed.

"Of course you shouldn't marry James. Don't you know nobody wants you to marry him?" she said unapologetically. "Can't you see that the fact that you just saw Terry in Texas was a sign you're choosing the wrong man? It's God's divine will that you should be with Terry, you shouldn't be with James. I mean, you do know that, right?"

"Really?"

"Yes, Leah. Really. This marriage is not a good thing. Nothing good will come of it," she roared.

Sigh.

"But I've got to marry him. I have to. I said yes."

She put her head down in silence. "Leah. I know you're an adult. But I want the best for you. I just wish you'd at least think about it."

Conversations like these happened more than often. They'd be so awkward sometimes because I felt like the whole world was against me, and James was never there to back me up. I'd walk into rooms and overhear my family wondering what was wrong with me, and why I was making this mistake. I'd hear them bashing him for not putting any effort into the planning of the wedding... I heard everything, yet I acted like I heard nothing and kept pushing forward.

The day for the rehearsal dinner finally arrived. It is standard that the groom pays for the rehearsal dinner, so James decided he would. Our dinner was at Reign, a popular, upscale soul food restaurant in Beverly Hills. Everyone was there: all of my bridesmaids, his groomsmen (which I had to pick for him), flower girls, ring bearers, and my family. James didn't speak to anyone. He stayed at our table the entire time, not once getting up to thank people for coming, or even thanking my parents and grandmother for paying for everything for us. He had our marriage counselor speak for him and make all of his announcements. Everything was very awkward. I looked at my dad and saw the discomfort raging through his body. I could tell he was furious James wasn't speaking to him, because after all I was his daughter. My dad is always loud and full of light and personality, but that night he was completely quiet. I could tell tension was festering between my family and James. The whole ordeal made me very unhappy. This was supposed to be the happiest time of my life, but I wasn't happy. I was anxious and sad. Why couldn't James just acknowledge my parents? Were they that bad? For them to refrain from saying anything was very admirable because they were literally not standing in the way of my desire. However, not having peace between my parents and James was torturous. Why was I continuing with this wedding? I kept thinking to myself that this couldn't be how it was supposed to be.

After the rehearsal dinner, things took a turn for the worse. I got home after feeling weird and nervous at the dinner. As I pulled in the driveway, my headlights shined over the front door and I saw my dad rushing outside. I could see he was yelling but didn't hear what he was saying until I got out of the car.

"WHAT ARE YOU DOING?" he yelled.

"What do you mean what am I doing?" I said, confused.

"HOW COULD YOU MARRY THIS PERSON?! HE'S CRAZY! I'VE BEEN TRYING TO HOLD IT AND HOLD IT, BUT I CAN'T HOLD IT ANYMORE! WHAT ARE YOU DOING?! ARE YOU TRYING TO RUIN YOUR LIFE? HOW

DARE YOU JUST SIT THERE AS HE BLATANTLY IGNORES US AND DIS-
RESPECTS US?! ARE YOU STUPID?! ARE YOU DUMB?!"

"I know what I'm doing! I'm marrying the person that I love!
And nobody is going to stop me! Not you, not anybody! I'm going
to marry him!" I yelled back. He was expressing my exact feelings,
but I couldn't agree with him. I had to defend my love for James
and our marriage; I just had to.

So here I was, yelling back and forth with my dad in our driveway the night before my wedding. It was the worst feeling to know
everything was collapsing as I was about to make one of the biggest
commitments of my life. I truly felt like I could fix everything and
prove everyone wrong. It seemed like I wanted to prove everyone
wrong more than pay attention to my feelings and what I was going
through. The idea of marrying James consumed me and was more
important than what was going on in reality. My parents were in
real pain, and I was not doing anything to stop it.

We eventually stopped yelling at each other, and my dad told
me, "Leah, I just love you so much, and I don't have a good feeling
about this. But you are my daughter, and I love you regardless of
what choice you make."

We hugged and went into the house.

By that point, I was completely over the day. I took a shower and
got ready for bed. A little later that night, I got a call from James.

"Hey! Tonight was nice!" he said.

"Yeah, it was great," I said, trying to sound convincing.

I didn't want to tell him about the argument I had just had with
my dad because I was afraid that would make him act even worse.

"Well, there's something I'd like to run by you before tomorrow," he said.

"Okay, what's that?" I asked.

"I'm going to be taking care of Dianne and her child for the rest of her life, whether it be in the condo or wherever; I'm going to be taking care of them financially. Can you handle that?"

Dianne? She hasn't been brought up through our whole engagement... In my mind, I was thinking to myself, *Is he crazy?* But out of my mouth, I said, "Okay..."

"Also, one more thing. I am not going to tell anyone that I am married to you until I am ready. Can you handle that?"

I thought he must really have cold feet. Was he really saying this to me? So I said, "Umm... okay."

"Great! Well, that's all I wanted to talk to you about. I'll see you tomorrow!"

I could not sleep. I mean, could you imagine? I was tossing and turning all night. On what was supposed to be one of the happiest and exciting nights of my life, I was completely torn and conflicted over everything that had just happened. I was still distraught about the fight with my dad, and then left to deal with my fiancé telling me he was going to be taking care of another woman and her daughter for the rest of their lives, and he wouldn't own up to being married to me while we were going to be crammed at the top of his church?

Somehow I convinced myself that everything was going to be okay and that things would smooth out and get easier with time. I kept repeating to myself, "Things are going to get worse before they get better" over and over, then I went to sleep.

The next morning was a Friday. I woke up still conflicted but trying to stay in good spirits because it was my wedding day. This was the day I had been waiting for since I was a little girl. My dad ended up coming to my room and apologizing again for being so emotional the night before. I appreciated his apology, but in my heart of hearts I knew he was right to feel the way he felt. It was heartbreaking to see my dad like this, but I had to push forward.

Tia and my friend Sophie from Oakland had spent the night with me that night, and when we woke up, they were there to take me to get my nails and hair done for my "special" day.

Everything was prepared and spectacular; I was so proud of how wonderfully everything had turned out. Our wedding took place on a Friday night, lit by candles. Our colors were cream satin and black, very classy as I knew James would like, and so did I. I had each bridesmaid's dress custom made. They wore strapless, cream, satin straight dresses that accentuated their waists and curves. Each of them had simple satin shoes. All of my ladies had beautiful shapes. One of my bridesmaids was pregnant, and James was adamant about having her and her husband in the wedding. They were the only ones he had a hand in choosing. He left the rest of his bridal party to me. We had just met them; they had gone through the marriage counseling classes with us.

All of my bridesmaids were absolutely gorgeous. It was the prettiest wedding party that you've ever seen. Every girl was *beautiful* in her own right. They ranged in skin tone from chocolate to Caucasian to biracial... it was diverse and absolutely gorgeous.

The flowers were white roses and Casablanca lilies. Casablanca lilies were my favorite flower—every time James would buy me flowers, that's what he would get. Just imagine Casablanca lilies and white roses everywhere. Going down the aisle of the Beverly Hills Presbyterian Church, I wanted satin fabric to swag from each pew to the next, to distinguish the aisle that the bride was coming down. On every pew was a lit candle with Casablanca lilies and roses draping from each candle. The flowers were simply exquisite.

My dress was princess style. It was a strapless bustier with crystals all across the top. The skirt was A-line, and the top was a bustier that laced up my back like a corset. It was off-white, and I had a cathedral train complemented with a crystal headpiece that matched my crystal bodice. The veil was as long, if not longer than the train of the dress. The whole train and veil draped down flawlessly when I was to walk down the aisle. It was a fairy tale, absolutely exquisite. It was stunning.

The reception was even more magnificent at the Beverly Hills Hotel. As soon as people got out of the valet, everything was covered in red carpet, even the stairs and the entrance. Inside, the whole hotel was pink. It was my favorite color, which was exactly why I wanted it to be there. When you walked into the reception, each table had a huge candelabra in the center that you couldn't see over. There were four long-stemmed white candles, and in the middle of the candelabra was a huge Casablanca lily and white rose arrangement. It was just flawless. We had a full band that played R&B and jazz. We danced all night. It was definitely a classy, elegant wedding. Our cake was from the famous Hansen's Bakery in Los Angeles, my favorite bakery. I have had a Hansen's cake every year for my birthday, so I absolutely had to have a Hansen's cake for my wedding. It was a 5-tier chocolate wedding cake covered with elegant cream swirls and delicate white roses covering the top tier. The cake was like nothing I had ever seen at anyone else's wedding. It was unique, classy, and one of a kind—just like James and me.

Though I was still thrown off, I was trying to tell myself to be happy the entire day. Altogether, my parents and grandmother had spent about one hundred thousand dollars on the wedding, and I didn't want their money to go to waste. There were candles and flowers all over the floors. Cream silk drapes were everywhere, radiating elegance. The flowers alone came up to around ten thousand dollars, so as you can imagine, my family went all out for me.

As I arrived at the venue, my marriage counselor told me that my pastor, who was supposed to be marrying us, was getting out of the hospital. I didn't want anyone else to marry me except for my pastor, Dr. Michael Harris Sr. Luckily, about an hour later, we got a call saying Dr. Harris was very sick but was going to come do the wedding because he loved me so much. I will say, if my pastor wasn't able to marry me, that would have been the ultimate sign for me that I wasn't making the right decision. But since he pushed through, I truly felt like my calling was to marry James. I just had to grit and bear it and get through this. It was time for the wedding.

The ceremony was to start at 7 p.m., and although we started late, everything else came out exactly how I wanted it. For our song, I had a remix of the song *Beauty and the Beast* from the acclaimed Disney movie instead of the traditional *Here Comes the Bride* sung for me by our marriage counselor's youngest daughter as I walked down the aisle. Instead of Beauty and the Beast lyrics, they were switched to *Leaah and Jaamess*.

I had four beautiful flower girls. Three of them were students from my school, and the other was my little cousin. They performed a beautiful dance for me and James, throwing rose petals down the aisle in a coordinated flower girl march that I choreographed. Each of my bridesmaids looked absolutely stunning, and the groomsmen that I picked looked immaculate. Candles lit the entire room; it was a dream night.

After my bridesmaids walked down the aisle, it was my turn. Everyone turned around, admiring how beautiful my dress was. My dad was standing at the door as I heard the horns begin their call for me.

"Okay, Leah, it's time," my dad whispered to me.

"It's time, Dad! Let's go!" I said.

As I began to walk, I didn't feel my dad's weight move with me. Our arms were locked, so it was almost a tug back. I looked at my dad with slight confusion, trying not to cause any attention.

"I can't move! I can't move my feet, I can't pick them up. I don't know what's wrong!" he whispered.

"Dad! We gotta start walking!"

I don't know what that was about, and I don't know if I ever will. Maybe his nerves were bad, or maybe he just psychologically did not want to give me away. Luckily, he was able to get his feet off the ground and walk me down the aisle to Pastor Harris and James.

"Who gives this bride to be married?" said my pastor.

"Lillian and I, Charles Walker, do," said my dad.

He shook James' hand and proceeded to his seat. I will never forget what Pastor Harris said as we took each other's right arms getting ready to recite our vows.

"I come with great reservation in joining this man and this woman to be married in holy matrimony."

I thought to myself, *Did he say what I think he said? He comes with great reservation? Maybe he is still not feeling well. He couldn't mean that.*

Pastor Harris continued the marriage ceremony, and James and I exchanged vows, kissed, and were graced with my pastor's blessing.

After the ceremony, everyone headed to the Beverly Hills Hotel for our reception. All night James had been telling me how beautiful I looked and how amazing the wedding was. He couldn't believe how nice and well put together it was. Even though I was only 23, I did an amazing job, and he noticed.

I even sang a song to James that I had written myself. I had been rehearsing for days with the head musician of the band.

You're my blessing, the answer to my prayers. My blessing, only God could prepare, My one and precious gift... oh how my spirit lives for my blessing. You're my love, my friend... my blessing...

James loved the song. Everyone loved the song. In fact, everyone kept complimenting us on how nice the ceremony and reception was. Yet as we ate, James still did not once get up to greet any of our guests or speak with anyone in my family. I went around to everyone and thanked them for coming by myself. He didn't bother to make a toast... nothing. My mom took it upon herself to greet the guests, which was her right especially after she, my dad, and my grandmother had spent so much money. With every greeting she said, "Thank you so much for coming. I don't know about this." She literally was telling everyone that she had reservations still about our marriage and that she did not know how things were going to work out. People told me what she said, and all I could say was, "Wow, I can't believe she told everyone that!"

I didn't let that stop me from having a nice night. I had put a ton of effort into making the night special, and I let nothing get in the way of that. I was completely oblivious to anything that could have altered my mood. All I knew was I was finally and officially married to James Jordan.

That night we stayed in the presidential suite of the hotel. It was gorgeous! James was blown away by everything. He said that it was the most beautiful wedding he had ever seen. It seemed as though all of his apprehension about getting married had gone out of the window. He seemed to think he had made the right decision. We consummated the marriage, and finally, I had what I had always wanted: James as my beloved husband. I could finally breathe a sigh of relief.

That Sunday, we were on a flight to Oakland so that he could be at his church that morning. He didn't want any of his members to suspect anything. He didn't invite any of them, just his head deacon, one of his sisters, and not even Gigi and Papi, who had been through the whole journey with us. I don't know why he didn't want to include them; he knew how much I loved them. He just didn't want them there for some strange reason. I remember packing my best church outfit so that I could look immaculate, as it would be my first time attending the church as a first lady. Right before the wedding, Dr. Harris' wife and her best friend Gail loaded me down with St. John Knits. They said that only the classiest first ladies wore St. John Knits, and I had to have a plethora of them so that I could fit the mold. They gave me the most gorgeous St. Johns and had them tailored to fit me perfectly. I was ready to assume my role as James Jordan's wife and the first lady of his church.

As we walked into the church, James showed no attachment toward me in front of his members. His demeanor changed instantly. As he did his sermon, I was waiting in the pew, wondering if he was going to introduce me as his new wife. I didn't want to get my hopes up too high because of how adamant he was on being private and not wanting to tell anyone he was married to me. I wondered if he really was going to do this, especially after the beautiful wedding we'd just had two days ago. Right after praise and worship, James asked me to stand up. *He's about to introduce me as his wife,* I thought to myself. I got up smiling ear to ear, and everyone started clapping.

"Leah is back, everyone. She's back to do her masters at Berkeley! We are so proud of you, Leah! Give her a hand," he exclaimed.

No introduction… I tried my best to look happy and thank everyone for acknowledging me. But why was he telling his church that? I was not there to do my masters, and he knew that. We'd had many conversations where I'd told him I was going to forfeit the year of going back to school to marry him. I wasn't there for school; I was there because we had just gotten married. Let's not forget, I had a 5.1 carat diamond ring on my finger! How was he going to explain that to people? Was I supposed to hide that too? Plus he had a new diamond encrusted wedding band on his left hand. Was he going to deny that as well? All of this was so strange and completely confusing.

After church, everyone was telling me how proud they were of me for coming back to finish my education, but the energy was off. I could just feel it. Certain people were looking at me from the corner of their eye, and I could see them whispering to each other. I didn't know if people knew, but I didn't mention it to anyone either.

When everyone left, I went upstairs to his office. To get to the office, you had to walk up about one hundred steps. The church was an old theater, so the office was really just a light-room.

When I walked in, James was sitting at his desk.

"Hey, you did really good today!" I said as he turned around.

"You made me marry you," he replied.

"What?"

"You know I married you to save my ministry."

I couldn't even say anything back. I didn't know what to say, nor where to begin. I walked to the bathroom, changed my clothes, and washed my face. I looked at myself in the mirror for a long time wondering where Leah had gone. I knew I had lost her, but I didn't know where along the process she had slipped from my fingertips.

I lay down in the bed as I waited for James to finish working. There was absolute silence. I kept wondering was all of this worth it? Was marrying James worth this feeling that I had in the pit of my stomach? A cloud of depression quickly enveloped me, and for the first time I did not know what to do.

A couple hours later, we packed our overnight bag to head back to Los Angeles so that we could get our things to head out for our honeymoon. When we got to the airport, my grandma was there waiting for us in the white Ford Ranger truck that had belonged to my grandfather, which she now drove and adored.

As we got into the truck, James couldn't stop talking to my grandmother. It was so weird because he never had a problem with her but couldn't stand my parents.

My grandmother randomly said, "We should stop by Leah's parents' house before Leah leaves for the honeymoon. You guys owe them a thank you for the wedding."

"Oh, it's fine, we don't have to do that. I'll call them and thank them!" I said hastily.

"I'm not going over there! I don't owe them anything! They don't like me, I don't like them. I don't owe them a damn thing," he said.

My grandmother's eyes were almost bulging out of her head.

"But you do. This is their daughter! You married their *daughter*; you owe them THAT. At least that! Let them see her one last time before she leaves! You know when she gets back from Atlantis, she goes straight to Oakland! You owe them that!" she pleaded.

"I'm not going to that house!" he yelled.

There was silence. My grandmother gave me a disgusted look. I looked out the window quickly to try and avoid eye contact. But she knew I saw her.

My grandmother proceeded to drive to my parents' house anyway. I was in a complete panic; I had no idea what was going to happen.

When we arrived, my grandmother told me to go inside and tell my parents I was leaving. I knew I did owe them a thank you, at the least. After all the money they'd spent on my wedding, it was only right that I went to see them before leaving. I needed to say goodbye.

I walked into the house.

"Mom! Dad! I'm here!" I called out.

"Leah! We're so glad you came before you went to the airport!" my mom said.

"Well, where's James?" asked my dad. "Is he in the car?"

"Umm, yeah!"

"Oh cool! Let's go out and talk to him!"

Lord, please don't let this be bad, I said to myself.

So my dad went outside to the car and walked up to James sitting in the passenger seat.

"James, you're not going to get out of the car?" my dad asked.

"I have nothing to say to you."

"Wait a minute, you have nothing to say to me? What are you talking about? What have we done to you?" my dad scolded.

"I know what you say about me to people!" James screamed.

"What have I said about you, man? You just married my daughter! How could I have said anything about you when you just married my daughter? I didn't say anything about you, man! You can't speak to me like a man and get out of the car? Come on now!" My dad was outraged.

"There's nothing I have to say. Nothing!" James said.

My dad broke down in tears and got on his knees.

"James, look, man... This is my baby... my daughter... if there's anything I've done to you, I'm sorry... I just don't want her out of my life. Please, just forgive me if there's anything I've said that offended you," my dad said with tears and pain in his eyes.

"I don't want anything to do with you. Ever. And you're never invited to our house."

My dad looked at me... I looked at my dad... I looked at my new husband... I looked at my grandmother...

I could literally feel the pain coming from each of my family members. Everyone was speechless.

"Leah, let's go. We're going to miss our flight," he said.

I kissed my parents and got in the car. My grandmother didn't say anything to us the whole time we drove to the airport. Her heart was broken, and I knew it. All along she had tried to understand James and really liked him. After this episode I could tell she was done. I don't think there was anything James could do at this point to regain her trust. It was over. It was in this car ride when I realized I had just married a monster.

The ride to the airport seemed like it took a lifetime. My heart was filled with hurt, disappointment, and pain. How could James talk to my father like that? My dad had gotten on his knees and begged for James' forgiveness, and James did not budge. How could James be so disrespectful, mean, and heartless to my parents? And how did I get in the car with such a monster? Why didn't I say anything? Why did I keep condoning James' bad behavior? I had completely lost myself and my sense of reality. Why was I so scared that I could not stand up to him and demand respect for my parents? Something deep inside was wrong. This was not right, and for the first time I was scared. Scared of how my life was unfolding and scared that I had no way out. What had I done?

negative one

I know what you're thinking... Why did I still get in the car with this man after what he said to my dad? And honestly, I don't have an answer for you. I actually tried to not think about it while I attempted to enjoy my trip. So there I was on a first class flight with my new husband on what was supposed to be one of the most joyful flights a woman should ever experience. Yet James and I barely said a word to each other. He had nothing to say, and neither did I. I reclined my seat and went to sleep until we arrived at our honeymoon destination: Atlantis.

We got off the plane and arrived at one of the most beautiful sights I'd ever seen. I could see the clear, blue water and greenery before we even landed. At the hotel, we were greeted by two butlers holding a sign that read THE JORDANS. They took our luggage upstairs, and we were escorted to a beautiful, luxurious room. I told myself while I was there, I was going to enjoy myself and this beautiful place. I had never been out of the country before, and I was determined to make it the best experience, regardless of everything that had just transpired. I prayed that everything would work out with James and my dad and left it in God's hands.

I started unpacking my bags and looking at all the activities that were available for us. I wanted to go to the spa, ride jet skis, and parasail. I wanted to do any and everything that was available to us at this amazing resort.

As I was sitting on the bed looking at the pamphlets, I looked up and saw James feverishly trying to call someone. He was pacing back and forth across our room like a madman trying to get his phone to work, which was only making him more furious by the second. I could tell he kept trying to make calls, but he couldn't get any reception, nor hear his voicemail. At the time, telephone companies didn't have international phone packages, and if you were to use your cell phone, it was an absolutely astronomical price. So he had to resort to using the hotel phone to make phone calls, but it seemed as if he didn't want me to hear the calls, so he left to go to the lobby and told me he'd be right back.

But of course, he didn't come right back. It took him a while. As soon as he opened the door, out of worry, I asked him, "What's wrong? Who are you trying to call?"

He looked at me and replied, "You made me do this… You made me marry you!"

"Wait a minute… what?" *Not this again,* I thought to myself.

"I can't even call Dianne, or anyone for that matter, to see if they know about the wedding! How am I supposed to find out if anyone knows we got married or not, Leah? No one can find out! This is all your fault!"

"How is this my fault? You asked me to marry you, James!"

He stormed out the door, slamming it behind him. Once again, I was crushed. I was afraid because here I was out of the country with this man who was showing his anger more and more by the day. He became unrecognizable. I couldn't believe our honeymoon was starting like that. I was miserable.

For five days, all James wanted to do was eat and go back to the room immediately. At dinner, he'd barely talk, and it was just awkward and uncomfortable. The most I'd hear from him was him ordering my food for me, and most times he didn't even get what I wanted.

We weren't intimate with each other at all, we didn't sleep with each other, and we didn't do any activities. I knew that nothing would make him feel better until he was able to hear from someone back in the States to let him know that everything was okay, and no one knew what was going on. Could you imagine how heartbreaking it was to see how much energy he was investing into ensuring no one knew he had married me? There are no words to describe the feelings that gave me.

So I had to keep myself busy. I'd go down and walk to the different boutiques alongside the beach and even go out to eat by myself sometimes to try and find the foods that I wanted.

One day, I finally convinced him to go to the beach with me. It took some begging, but he did come. He put his swimming trunks on, and I put on my bathing suit. As we were walking down to the beach, he looked at me and kind of chuckled to himself.

"What's so funny?" I asked.

"Oh, I just didn't know you had all that cellulite."

"Ohh... well yeah... Hold on. I left something in the room. I'll be right down."

I rushed up to the room and got a coverup. From that point on, I knew I was always going to wear wraps with my bikinis because I didn't want anyone to *see* me and my so-called cellulite, which had never bothered me until James mentioned it.

If that wasn't embarrassing enough, my hair had been getting frizzier and frizzier since the day we arrived. I decided to wear my natural hair because I thought we were going to do a lot of water activities, which we didn't even end up doing. But the mist from the water and air was making my hair swell up like a blowfish. Each day he'd just stare at my hair and say something like, "Your hair looks terrible…"

But I didn't have many options. I didn't bring a flat iron, and if I had it in a ponytail, he'd say, "You know I don't like when you wear your hair like that. It's tacky. You need to go get it done."

So I went back to the spa area and luckily found a hair salon with native women from Nassau pressing and styling hair. *Sigh.* Thank God! So I was able to get my hair done, and I finally felt pretty. I went back up to the room to show him.

"Oh, that looks much better," he said. "You look beautiful!"

"Thank you! Well, it seems like you're feeling better. Are you?" I asked.

"Oh yes! I talked to Dianne and the Chipmunks, and everything's okay! You want to do some activities?"

In my head, I was thinking, *Did he really wait five days until he heard from someone?* But I didn't want to pass up on the opportunity to enjoy my trip, so I agreed.

So finally we were having an actual honeymoon. We went horseback riding on the beach, parasailing, we went into the city for a tour, and he even took me shopping. I finally felt like I was experiencing how a honeymoon should be. We were doing exactly what we should have been doing from the beginning: enjoying each other and enjoying Atlantis, which was a beautiful place. He seemed like he was happy.

What I couldn't stomach was the fact that his happiness didn't stem from me; it stemmed from the fact that he was able to have peace in knowing nobody had found out about our marriage. Marriage is a milestone in one's life, and it really confused me that he put so much effort into keeping us lowkey. Was he ashamed of me? Had he had second thoughts about asking for my hand? I had a million and one questions running through my head during our honeymoon, but I hoped and prayed with everything in me that I would end up being happily and openly married to the man I so loved.

The last couple of days, we had a magical time, and also finally made love.

Before I knew it, it was time to head back to Oakland where my new life as James Jordan's wife awaited.

We landed on a Sunday morning, so before getting on the plane, I was dressed and ready for church.

Remember Papi? The husband of Gigi who always told me about James' whereabouts? He was there to pick us up from the airport and drove us straight to service.

When we arrived at the church, James pulled back the van door and began to fix his collar by looking at the window. As I began to get out the car, he quickly put his arm in front of me.

"Oh, no. You're not going to church today."

"Why wouldn't I go to church? I'm already dressed," I asked.

"Do you not remember me telling you no one is to find out that we're married until I'm ready?" he said firmly.

Papi intervened. "Just let her go to church, James! It's church!"

"I said no!" James yelled. "Take her home with you, and I'll come get her after church! And that's that!"

He slammed the door shut in front of my face and walked off to preach to his church.

I put my head in my lap and just began to cry. I felt worthless, inadequate, inferior...

Papi turned around and patted me on the back as he said, "Baby... you just don't know what you got yourself into."

I looked up at him with tear-filled eyes. "What do you mean, Papi?"

"There's so much going on that you don't even want to know."

"No, Papi, you have to tell me! Please!"

"Baby, it's a whole world of mess going on since y'all got married. He ain't tellin' you nothin! I mean nothin'!"

"What is he not telling me?"

"For one, Dianne found out about your marriage while you guys were away."

"She did? Wait, he didn't tell her?"

"Of course he didn't tell her!"

I instantly understood why he was so frantic on our honeymoon. He didn't want Dianne to find out.

"But why wouldn't he tell her?" I asked.

"Leah, Dianne was pregnant..."

"What?!"

"Yes, Leah! She was crying so frantically that she lost the baby," he said softly. "That's why he didn't want anyone to find out about your marriage because he's still involved with Dianne—and other women."

"Other women?" I asked.

"Oh yes! Like Chipmunk 2! He's involved with her too!"

"WHAT?!"

"This is why he doesn't want you to come to church, Leah. He's trying to fix this mess before you come back, then act like nothing happened. I'm sick of this. I'm sick of how he's treating these women. You don't deserve this, Leah," he said as he looked at me in the rearview mirror.

Papi made me swear that I would never speak of what he had just confided to me.

The ride back to Papi's house felt empty and silent. I knew something in my spirit wasn't settling right, but I never thought it was *this* bad. I couldn't believe I was even in this situation. Mentally and emotionally, it was a mess!

I stayed at Papi's house while James was at church. I had about three hours to sit and ponder about the life I'd started since I put that ring on my finger. I was full of outrage, yet still struck by confusion. I had more on my plate than I knew I could handle.

When James picked me up, he was silent most of the car ride, as was I. It almost felt like I was riding with a complete stranger. I mean, he had this whole life that I knew nothing about, yet he was my husband. After a while, he finally broke the awkward silence.

"You can come to church next week."

"Okay," I agreed.

"I want you to know that later this week I'm going to meet with Dianne and her daughter to have a meeting about everything. They found out about us getting married, but I need them to know I'm still going to support them."

I nodded in agreement as I continued to look out the window. I didn't have the strength to look at him.

I was still quiet. I was upset and angry, yet I felt like I'd brought all of this on myself. I was the one that said yes to this. The night before our wedding, he'd said he wasn't going to own up to me and tell anyone that we were married until he was ready, and I'd said okay. He'd told me he was going to be taking care of Dianne and her daughter for the rest of their lives, and I'd said okay to that too. Everything that he said he was going to do, he did. He didn't lie to me; I'd agreed to this. So yes, I was upset and hurt, but I'd agreed. So I went along with it. I felt like I had no other choice, and it was what I deserved. Once again, I found myself praying and hoping that things would get better.

We got back to the church, which was also our home. We walked up the hundred steps to reach the lighthouse where we slept. I went into the cramped bathroom to remove my makeup, and as I was looking in the mirror, I saw a rat run quickly behind me next to our bed. Sometimes at night, I thought I would hear a slight chattering that sounded like small animals running across the ceiling, but never knew what it was. But now it was certain: I was living in a rat-infested, run-down lighthouse that was as big as my bedroom used to be in my parents' house.

No one knew where we lived. I was embarrassed and ashamed to tell any of my friends or family where I was staying. The sad part about it is, I thought it was okay to live in this place because I loved him. I thought it would only be temporary until we could save enough money to live someplace else, but every night felt like forever. I got in the bed and prayed to God that He'd change our circumstances as soon as possible. During my prayer, I could hear the rats running behind the walls and snacking on the food on the shelves in our room.

When James would go on his revivals, he wouldn't take me, which left me too much time to be alone. I didn't want to stay by myself because the church was in the worst part of Oakland, and I'd be all the way at the top overlooking everyone. So I began staying at his deacon's home with his wife, or at Gigi and Papi's.

When he got back, he would go into these weird fits of needing space from me. One specific time, he picked me up from Gigi and Papi, and on the way home he told me he was going to take Chipmunk 2 to the movies, and I couldn't come because married couples need to have their space so they don't burn out their flame.

So when he went to the movies, I had to figure out what I was going to do to kill time. The hardest part about that was there wasn't much I could do because we didn't have any money. I found myself being alone with no money more times than I could count since I had been married. I was absolutely miserable. He'd promised me that we would never have to worry about money and that he would always provide for me. That was a stretch because now although living in his church was free, he was taking care of a whole other household. In addition, the way he got paid from the church is he would receive a stipend for his living expenses and he would receive an offering from members in a specific envelope that was called "Love Offering." Love Offering was an offering that members gave to support the pastor. Pastors who don't take a salary live by faith through these envelopes. Whatever is in those envelopes is what they trust God has given them to live on. Usually when pastors opt for Love Offering, they do not take a salary at all from the church; they totally live on those envelopes and their stipend.

These envelopes are what we lived on. Before he married me, his Love Offering was very good. In fact, he would let me count it and deposit it into his bank account if he was going out of town. Now that we were married, his Love Offering dwindled. I assumed it was low because his supporters knew he was lying about our marriage.

All they wanted was for him to tell the truth. I know they knew something based on all the side-eye looks from the members, all of the whispers, and many people trying to get a look at the ring I had on my finger. It was like they felt betrayed and were not going to budge until he told the truth. So while they did not budge we had to live off of a tight budget; we shared plates when we went out and only spent money on the necessities. We were the brokest, best-dressed couple anyone had ever seen. No one knew how much we were struggling, and I could not ask my parents for anything. As far as they knew, we were fine.

While he was out with Chipmunk 2, I chose to stay home and rest, because I couldn't find anything to do. James got home much later, but I was already asleep by then. I could hear him walking up the steps, which woke me up.

"I didn't mean to wake you. Go back to sleep," he said.

"It's fine. I want to pray, will you pray with me?" I asked.

"No. Stop asking me that. I'll never pray with you," he said.

That was such a mystery to me. Why would he not pray with me if he was a pastor? Why could he not share his spiritual life with me? How much more could he hurt me? I went into the bathroom so that I could pray alone. I kneeled down next to the toilet stall.

Lord, please protect me and my family while I am away from them. Please forgive me of all my sins, known and unknown. I am confused, Lord, but I trust you that you will make things better...

As I was praying, I could hear James trying to whisper on the phone, outside the bathroom. I tried to keep praying out loud so he wouldn't think I was listening to his conversation.

God, I love you. Thank you for all you have done and are doing for me...

Simultaneously, I heard James say, "How many times did you cum today in the movie theater?"

My heart sank. Tears began to run down my face as I tried my hardest to keep praying out loud.

Lord, I trust you, and I know the best is yet to come. In Jesus' name, Amen.

I got back in the bed and James kissed my cheek before I rolled over to stare at the wall to fall asleep. James began breathing heavier, so I knew he fell asleep. But I couldn't. I couldn't stop thinking about my life. The pain was so loud in such a quiet room that I couldn't even hear the rats moving around, like I usually do every night. My nightmares were becoming my reality.

Still not being able to sleep, I began to ponder on how I could make the man sleeping with his arms around me love me again. How I could make my husband want to tell the whole world that I was his wife? I figured if I could alter myself to become his dream woman, he wouldn't even want the other women anymore. So that's what I decided I was going to do. I was on a mission to make him love me, and only me. I closed my eyes and fell asleep in James' arms.

As time passed, I found myself altering almost everything about myself to become the perfect woman for my husband. I was getting my hair done *every* Saturday, perfecting my makeup, and looked impeccably professional and clean every single day. I wanted to look better than the best and become someone James would be honored to behold. I wanted to be the best-looking woman in the church, from head to toe. I wanted to look the best so that he did not focus on anyone but me. Yet it still seemed the more I pulled, the more I tried, the more he pushed me away. Making him love me like he used to love me became more and more of a fantastic feat because he never wanted to spend time with me. I think the reality of being married had sunk in with him, and he just didn't want to be married. Or at least not to me. What I began to slowly realize is that I can't make somebody commit, or make a man marry me if he's not ready. There's nothing that can make a man be ready unless he is ready. So I suffered the consequences of him marrying me when he wasn't ready because he didn't want anyone to know about us, and he made *sure* of that.

On Sunday mornings, all we had to do was go downstairs to access the church to start worship. He would make me wait a while after he went downstairs before I could go downstairs. He didn't want anyone to think that I lived there. From outside of the light-house where we stayed, I could see when everyone had made it inside service, and then I would go downstairs so I could blend in effortlessly.

There were even times where I would go with him to various outings to other churches, and he would make sure to not announce me. It is common practice that when a preacher introduces himself, and he is married, he asks his wife to stand and be recognized. I was never asked to stand, because no one knew who I was. I looked like a regular member sitting in the pew.

When it would be time to introduce me to his preacher friends, he'd always say, "This is my friend, Leah." It hurt so bad to not be valued enough for someone to acknowledge your union. You have no idea how damaging that was to my psyche and self-esteem.

It was really a melancholic feeling that he gave me. It's almost impossible to verbalize the internal conflict and neglect that began to consume me. But I was still determined to make him love me again, whether it was sexually making him love me or praying that he would. Nothing was working. I mean *nothing*.

One particular Sunday, we began our regular routine. We both woke up in the same bed, got dressed, he went downstairs, and then I waited my turn to come down. As I was walking down the aisle to my usual seat, I looked to the left, and in the center of the aisle was my mother and grandmother. I couldn't believe it. I was only one month into my marriage, and my mother and grandmother were already flying to Oakland, unannounced. Of course, I still had to play it cool.

I walked over, sat next to them, and aggressively said, "What are you guys doing here?"

They looked stunned and sad. My mom replied, "What do you mean? I am your mother, you're my daughter. I have the right to come check on you!"

So I sucked it up, and we sat through the service.

Not one time did he ask my family to stand or acknowledge them for coming. I know he saw them; the church was only so big. We were all supposed to be family, but not once did he show thanks to my mom and grandmother for coming from out of town. They were so embarrassed and sad, but I didn't say anything to them because I didn't want them to know what was going on. Or how miserable I was. I was very secretive about the whole ordeal. I never even brought them upstairs because I didn't want them to know how I was living.

After service, James finally did come up to us. He didn't say much to my family, but he did make small talk. My grandmother barely looked at him. And my mom insisted on all of us going out to lunch to catch up. I could tell James wasn't amused by the idea, so before he could say anything, I did.

"Oh, James has a ton of work to do! How about we just have a ladies' brunch?"

"That would be great. Have fun!" James said as he kissed me on the cheek before walking away.

My grandmother looked at me in disgust.

My mom let me pick out the restaurant, and I chose one of my favorites, by the lake. Before the waiter could even bring our waters, my mom began telling me how she was feeling.

"We just want to talk to you, Leah, and see how you're doing. I've been having a strange feeling in my heart that something isn't right. He didn't even acknowledge us in service, baby."

"What kind of life are you living?" my grandma asked.

"This is my husband. This is the life we're living, and if you don't like it, just don't come here anymore."

The looks on their faces still haunt me until this day. I knew I had just hurt them, bone deep, and although I'd said that, I didn't mean it. Especially to my grandmother. I love her with every ounce in my veins. But I had to say that to save face. I had to make them believe that I was okay because I'd pushed so hard for this marriage.

"Leah, don't you want to come home with us? You don't have to stay."

"No, I want to stay here."

"You want to stay and live in a church? This is the life you want to live?"

"Yes. It's going to be okay. We're going to get a house soon."

I never figured out how my mom knew I was living in the church, but news always seemed to get back to them quicker than the speed of light.

The rest of the afternoon was quiet. We are a very intimate family, and that day, I never felt further away from them, even though they were inches away. A part of me wanted to tell them the truth, but a part of me felt like I had to stay and fight for my marriage. Before I knew it, it was time for me to take them back to the airport so they could fly back home. I could feel their sadness as they hugged me before getting on the plane.

After I dropped them off, I went back to the church. As soon as I saw James, he asked, "Why didn't you tell me your mom and grandma were coming?"

"I didn't know they were coming. Do you really think I knew that? Why would I want them to come and see me like this?"

"They were coming to spy on us," he said angrily.

"NO, they weren't coming to spy on us!" I said. "They're worried about me!"

So of course the rest of the night was very awkward. I just felt sad and alone and was angry at myself for not leaving when I had the opportunity to right in front of me. I didn't know what to do. I was losing parts of myself so quickly, I didn't even know where to look to pick my pieces up.

The following months were the same for me. Going through the motions, feeling unhappy, yet masking it all, and being the perfect woman for my husband. My depression began to worsen, and I became desperate in looking for answers. I decided to begin fasting, which is sacrificing something for days while praying heavily, so that in turn, God blesses you tremendously. My spiritual fast was with food. While I fasted, I prayed heavily for the Lord to allow James to love me again, like how he loved me before. When I thought I had an answer, or felt any glimpse of light that things were getting better, I'd stop fasting.

One Saturday morning, I woke up with a missed call on my cell phone from my mom. I had one cell phone from James, and another one that my grandmother had paid for. My family didn't know about my other phone, though, so they would only be able to reach me on the phone my grandmother gave me. And of course, I never gave them the phone number to the church, where we were staying. When I called my mom back, I could hear something was wrong, just from the tone in her voice.

"What's wrong, Mommy? Is everything okay?" I asked, concerned.

"Leah, your acting coach, Tony Conely, passed away," she sighed.

"What?!" I yelled.

Tony Conely was my acting and voice coach from back at home. He taught me everything I know, alongside my other acting coaches in which I attended their performing arts school in Los Angeles: Amazing Grace Conservatory. From middle school to high school, I took acting and singing classes with Tony, and we'd put on theatrical shows for the city to come and see. Once I was nominated for an Image Award for best actress in a play called "Annie May and Asbury." I would have never been nominated if it weren't for Tony.

Hearing the news crushed me. He had just MC'd my wedding a couple months ago, so it was so confusing to hear that he had passed.

"Leah, I think you should come back home for the funeral. He was such a good person to you," my mom exclaimed.

Not knowing if James would allow that, I reluctantly replied, "Mom, I don't know how I'm going to do that."

"What do you mean? Tell him you're coming down to the funeral, and that's it!" she yelled.

"You're right, Mom. I'll figure it out."

I hung up the phone and thought about how I was going to tell James. He was very controlling about where I went without him.

But I figured it would be great to go home for a couple days and be around my family that loved me. Honestly, I needed that break.

When James got home later that day, I told him that my voice coach, whom I had been close to as a child, had just passed away, and that I needed to go home in order to attend his funeral. Surprisingly, he agreed, with no hesitation.

So the next week, I flew down to Los Angeles to attend the funeral. I was so happy that I was able to get away and be around people I'd grown up with. I got to rekindle relationships I had with longtime friends from my performing arts school and was able to feel genuine love from people that really missed me. Everyone, of course, wanted to know how married life was, and I'd always reply with something like, "Oh, it's a lot of work. But it's great!" It was hard to keep an authentic smile on my face, but I needed to. Something in me wanted people to be happy and proud of me, even though I was never happy and proud of myself. I found myself always changing the conversation before someone could ask me too many questions.

After the funeral, I spent the night at my grandmother's house. I just loved being with her, and I felt like I needed to spend time with her since I was back home.

The next day was Sunday. I decided not to go to my home church because I just didn't want anyone to be able to ask me questions about James. Instead, I wanted to go to a church around my grandmother's house that I liked just as much. Before leaving for church, my grandma made me a big breakfast, and told me to sit down and eat before leaving. When I sat down, there was a huge file of papers behind the orange juice.

"Mama, what's this?" I asked.

"Leah, you know I never like to get in your business or try to persuade you to do something you don't want to do, but I really need to talk to you," she said as she sat down next to me.

"Okay..." I said apprehensively.

"The weekend of your wedding, when you married James, something really strange happened."

"What?" I asked.

"This strange woman, I can't recall her name, but she dropped this file on my porch. And she said there's some things we as a family need to know about James."

"Well, what is it?" I said as I started opening the folder.

"This file has every single court case that he's ever been involved in. Leah, baby, he changes his name for fraud cases, he was involved in a court case of a little girl who said some things about him, financial situations. I mean, she even—"

"Stop, stop, stop, stop, stop."

I just needed a second to catch my breath and flip through all of the pages. The file was a mile high. Everything he had ever been involved with was there.

"Leah, *this* is the monster you're married to. *This* is the person! Leah, baby, you can't stay married to him! You can't do that! I love you dearly, but this person is going to hurt you! Can't you see?"

I was traumatized. It had only been two months, and everything was simply out of control.

"I don't know why he wants to be involved with you, or if he wants to take everything our family has. But this person doesn't care about anybody but himself! You've got to make a decision."

I didn't know what to do. I couldn't figure out why my grandmother had been hiding this information from me for two months, but I guess she just wanted me to be happy. I trusted my grandmother from the bottom of my heart, yet I still needed a second opinion. I drove to my marriage counselor's house with the file. I wanted to ask him for his opinion.

He took a minute to look through a few papers before crossing his legs and taking off his glasses. "Leah, this is very disappointing. This man is dangerous, and you're not safe. You need to leave," he demanded.

"I do?" I sighed.

"YES. *YOU NEED TO LEAVE*. This man needs to get himself together. I hate you're in this position, but you need to separate yourself from him, and fast."

"You're right."

The truth was, I knew I needed to leave. Everyone knew it. In my mind, I'd made the decision to leave him, but how was I going to do it? James was crazy! I thanked my marriage counselor for his time and left his house, in a frenzy, thinking of ways to escape this marriage.

I must have pondered on it all night. I knew I needed to get my things without James seeing me because I honestly didn't know what backlash that would come with it. Finally, I thought of a plan.

I was going to drive in the middle of the night to get all my stuff, but I didn't want to go by myself, so I needed to bring one of my girls with me.

Tia! Tia was one of those girls you could call that was down for any and everything.

The next morning, I called her when she was at work and explained to her everything my grandmother had told me. She didn't even need all the details before asking me when I wanted to do this. She was more than ready to see me leave James, too.

"I knew he was a bad person. I'm just glad you found your proof. So when do you want to do this? And how?"

"Well, I was thinking I could rent a Suburban, and we could drive up in the middle of the night, get all my stuff, and head back before he even knew I was there. He's a heavy sleeper."

"Okay. Let's go tonight," Tia said with no hesitation.

So that was the plan. I rented a truck, told my parents I was going to get my things, and Tia and I headed out to Oakland around 10 p.m. so that we could get there around 3 a.m. In and out.

On the way there, all my nerves were nonexistent. I felt empowered and knew we could pull this off. I'd found the answer I was waiting for, and I was ready.

The fog was thicker and powerful than usual on our way to Oakland. We could barely see the car in front of us, and the ground was even icy. Tia asked me if I thought we should turn around, but my mind was set. My purpose was intentional. I wanted to do this.

As we got about halfway to our destination, I did begin to feel a little scared about how James would react to my leaving. Would he be angry or sad? I honestly didn't know. But I was about to find out.

It took us about five to six hours to get to Oakland. When we were getting off the freeway, I realized that I didn't have a key to the gate to get to the church. There was a gate that needed to be open in order to access the parking lot. After a quick thought, I directed Tia on how to get to a member's house. I knew he was the only one that had a spare key to the gate.

I knew exactly where the member stayed because this was one of the houses that James would make me stay at over the weekends when he wouldn't want me to go with him to his various preaching revivals.

The clock struck 4 a.m. when we pulled into the member's driveway. I knew it was way too late to be coming to his home, but I felt like this was my only way. I walked to the door, rang the doorbell, and waited in the brisk wind.

"Leah? What's going on? Do you know what time it is?" said his wife with scrunched, sleepy eyes.

"Yes, I'm so sorry to bother you both so late. But I really need to use your gate key to the church," I explained.

I could see the confusion in their faces.

"I'm leaving Oakland. Well, James... I'm leaving James. I appreciate all that you two have done for me but... I can't stay here any longer. I can't deal with James treating me like this anymore."

"Oh, baby..." said his wife.

I knew it was no surprise for them to hear me say this. They knew the troubles that I faced within my marriage and often witnessed firsthand what I was going through.

She smiled. "It's about time," she said peacefully.

I knew she would give me the keys easily if she could, but it was her husband that got in our way. I could feel his apprehension with giving me the keys without James' consent.

"Ah, I don't know, Leah. Why don't you just give him a call? I don't really feel—"

"Please. I need to do this. I need to save my life. Please."

He looked at me sternly. Without saying anything, he left the door and came back with the keys.

Now that I had everything I needed, it was time to escape.

Tia and I left the member's house and headed to the church, through the high-crime city of that part of Oakland. Tia couldn't believe what she saw on the streets, and I knew deep down she was thinking why on earth was I living in this area? We come from a nice upbringing; this was the complete opposite.

We finally arrived at the church, and I got out the car to unlock the gate with shivering hands. My fear was present, but there was no turning back. We were in.

We walked quietly to the door, and I used my personal key to unlock the squeaky door. I pushed softly, trying not to make a peep, with Tia close behind me. The church was cold, and its age was evident in the smell.

At last we walked up the long flight of stairs to get to the lighthouse at the top of the church. When I put the key into his office door, we were startled by a voice.

"Hello?!... Cher?" That was the nickname he called me.

The office separated the bedroom from the entrance, so he couldn't see me yet.

"Yeah?"

"You're... here?"

"Yes!"

"What are you doing here?"

When I got through the office and opened the bedroom door, there he was, in bed with another woman. I turned the light on, and the woman yelled as she covered herself.

Tia and I looked at each other with disbelief. I mean, I was gone because I was attending a funeral, and there was my *husband* in our bed with another lady. I was disgusted. I wasn't shocked, though, nor was I mad. I had almost known that he was going to be with someone else; I had just never caught him in the act before.

"I came to get my stuff." I laughed.

"Leah, we didn't do anything! I swear. We have clothes on!" he exclaimed.

"Yeah, we just met today!" the woman added.

"Well, did he tell you that he was married?" I asked.

"Well, no. He didn't tell me that..."

"Of course he didn't tell you he was married. He doesn't tell anyone, actually. Matter of fact, did he wear his ring today?"

"No..."

"Yeah. Of course he didn't." I smiled. "He doesn't want people to think he's married. He does what he wants."

The lady was so confused. Tia was standing there looking like she was watching a live screen performance.

I looked at James and smiled obnoxiously before proceeding to throw all of my clothes, shoes, and personal items in large black trash bags. Tia came from around the bed to help me.

"You're married? That's horrible of you!" the woman yelled. "Here, let me help you," she said to me as she picked up some of my clothes.

Tia yanked the clothes out of her hand. "Um, no. We got this. The woman who was in the bed with your husband is not going to help us pack!"

"Leah, please give me a chance to explain, baby! Please! It's not what you think. I did not sleep with her!" He got out of bed and tried to grab my hands in an effort to caress me.

"Baby, please don't leave me!"

"Let me get my stuff. Please!" I said firmly, pulling my hands away from his.

Tia and I were on a mission. His pleading was so irrelevant compared to the task at hand. We were grabbing everything of mine and putting it away in those bags. We got to a point where we weren't even putting things in bags anymore, we would just remove clothes from the hangers and put them straight in the car. We were done in less than an hour, while James just sat in the bed acting like he was going to cry.

As I came up the stairs for the last time to get my last bit of clothes, a gun suddenly appeared by his bed. I knew for a fact it wasn't there when I had walked out. My body tensed.

"Leah, if you leave me, I will kill myself."

"Please don't do this, James. Look what you've done to me."

"Baby, I know I've been a horrible husband to you. I promise I'll be better! I'll own up to you! I love you, baby, you know that!"

I felt so sorry for him in this moment. He was such a lost soul. I felt bad for him, but I felt worse for myself. I grabbed my last bag and picked it up in my arms.

"I'm so sorry, but I have to do this." I walked past him and never turned my head to say goodbye.

Tia was in the car with the engine running, already waiting on me to come downstairs so that we could leave. I looked at that church while driving away, in the rearview mirror, looking at God's temple, yet feeling that the man of God inside was the furthest away from God. He really needed help.

As we were driving, me in my car that was parked at the church and Tia in the Suburban, Tia could not stop thinking about everything that we had just witnessed, and she called me from her cell phone.

"I told you not to marry that man! We really just caught him in the bed with another woman! And look at where he had you living! Leah, what were you thinking?!"

I had no answer for her. In fact, the only thing I could think about was the fact that I had finally left my husband. I almost couldn't believe it. *Did I make the right choice? Has he killed himself to relieve the agony I caused from leaving? Should I go back to make sure he doesn't shoot himself?* I mean, I had a million thoughts consuming me.

I finally came to. Tia was still going off, but after a while, I wasn't even listening to her. I had to cut her off.

"Hey, I'm pretty exhausted, and I know you are too. Let's sleep at Emily's house, then we can head back to LA after we sleep. Turn right at the light."

Emily graduated from Berkeley a year after I did but still lived in Oakland. I called her and explained that I had just left James and needed a place to stay.

"Girllll! Come over!" she exclaimed.

When we got to Emily's, Tia could barely park the Suburban straight before getting out and telling Emily everything we'd just experienced. As late as it was, Emily was wide awake, at the edge of her bed, hanging on to every word that she said.

"Yes, girl, then she had the nerve to try to help us pack!" Tia blurted.

"No way! Leah, forreal?!.... Leah???"

I barely heard them talking. My phone was ringing off the hook. James, of course.

"You're not going to answer that, I just know you're not!" Tia urged.

"I'll be right back. I'll make it quick."

Yes, I answered the phone. I mean, how couldn't I? Besides anything else, I was honestly worried.

"JAMES! What do you want?!"

"Leah, please come back. I'm about to kill myself."

"No you're not! I'm not coming back."

"I need you! Please come back so we can talk and pray. We need to pray together!"

"No, James. Look how much you've hurt me! Plus you never wanted to pray with me, remember? NO!"

Somewhere between my anger and James' pleading began an entire conversation on the phone. He always had this agency over me that made me do things I didn't want to do. The entire time, Tia and Emily were looking at me so disgusted and annoyed, but I kept talking. Before I knew it, they went to sleep, and I was still on the phone talking to my husband, who I'd just found in bed with another woman.

The next morning, Tia didn't really say much to me before getting in the car. She drove the Suburban, and I drove my car that I had left in Oakland back to Los Angeles. I knew she was furious that I'd talked to him all night after we had just spent the night getting all my things. I didn't push the conversation because I would have been annoyed with me too.

The entire five-hour drive back to Los Angeles, I was talking to James. He couldn't stop telling me how sorry he was and admitting to all of his mistakes. He felt like he knew I was the one for him and insisted that he would allow me to have a position in the ministry.

James knew that one of the stipulations that really hurt me was the fact that he didn't want me to do anything in the church, since he didn't want people to have any idea of our marriage. I couldn't talk, sing, dance, I mean he didn't even allow me to participate in ministry at all. *That* really hurt me because my second nature was church. I love the Lord. I sang in the choir all of my life, I praise danced for years, I was the president of the youth at my church, as well as president of my choir, president of the Red Circle Girls, which was responsible for missionary work. So for me to not be able to do anything within the ministry, and just be a pew member was very strange for me. It never settled well with me having to constantly sit in the pew.

"I promise if you come back, you can be in the ministry. You can sing, you can dance, you can lead the youth, you can do whatever you want, Leah. I was wrong for that. That's your gift, I'm so sorry!" he exclaimed.

I was still angry on one hand, but on the other, I was slightly intrigued because it seemed like he was finally changing. I was apprehensive, but he did sound completely different.

I stayed with my parents for three weeks. While I was spending time in LA, I still talked to James constantly, the whole time. Within those three weeks, he convinced me to come back.

So there I was, repacking my car with everything Tia and I had packed up that early morning in Oakland. I put everything back in my two-door Explorer sport and was ready to drive back all by myself.

My dad happened to come outside while I was packing my car, and he softly asked, "What... what are you doing?"

"I'm going back," I confessed.

He put his head down in shame. The pain was evident on his face.

Then my mom came outside. "Leah, what are you doing?"

"I'm going back to my husband."

There was nothing they could do or say, and we all knew it. At the end of the day, I was still married to James.

I finished packing all of my things and hugged my parents goodbye, though I knew it hurt for them to see me go again. I got back in my green Explorer and headed back to Oakland.

As I was driving back, the phone rang. It was my marriage counselor. The wife.

"Hey, Leah! I haven't heard from you. What are you doing?" she asked eagerly.

"Hey! Oh, nothing. I'm just driving back to Oakland."

"What?" She paused.

"I'm driving back to Oakland," I confirmed.

"And... why would you do something like that?"

"Well, he said that he was going to buy me a house and get me out of the church and inflict some boundaries with Dianne, and he said that he was going to let me operate in the ministry. He apologized, and he changed."

She took a long sigh. "Leah. How could somebody change in three weeks? You didn't give him enough time apart to even get his act together. Those are just words, and his actions have spoken louder than his words! You haven't held him accountable for *anything*. Do you remember he was just in the bed with another woman? Do you remember all the things he's put you through? Did you not believe all of the evidence in the file that was left on your grandmother's porch? How do you know he's going to buy you a house? What's changed in *three weeks*? I'm very disappointed in you. You are making a terrible decision, and I promise you it is going to be 100 times worse when you go back this time."

I was silent. What could I say? Everything she said made sense, but I didn't want to believe the evidence. I wanted to believe that he'd changed, and he was going to do everything he said.

"Well, I'll talk to you later," she said before hanging up the phone.

On the rest of the drive back, I convinced myself that my marriage counselor wasn't right. I could hear it in James that he had changed. She didn't know what she was talking about.

I finally got back to Oakland. Back in the church—back in the same room.

There he was crying to me, ecstatic that I had come back to him.

"I'm going to tell the whole church that I'm married to you on Sunday. I promise you. I owe you that!" he pleaded.

We had a wonderful night together. We got everything off our chests and spent all night interacting like old times. I felt nostalgic. Things felt back to normal, and in a couple days, we weren't going to have to hide our love for one another anymore. I couldn't wait for him to make his announcement come Sunday.

We had more days full of love, and genuine time spent, before Sunday morning had arrived. I put on my prettiest suit, a St. John knit of course, did my hair and makeup to perfection, and couldn't stop smiling in the mirror at what he was going to announce to the church. I finally felt like a first lady, and I was finally getting the recognition I felt I had *earned*. I went downstairs and blended in with the rest of the members walking into the pew.

Service began, and he didn't make the announcement before the sermon, so I figured he was going to wait until the end. I anxiously waited through his great sermon, and upon service finishing, I knew it was almost time. During invitation, where people walk down the aisle, I saw him take a seat in the pulpit. Suddenly, he began urgently motioning for Chipmunk 2 to come up to him. I don't know what he said to her, but she walked back to the pew, picked up her purse, and left the service.

That's odd... I thought to myself. I specifically wanted Chipmunk 2 to be there so that she could hear that we were married.

Finally, he told everyone to stand, and he was about to do the benediction before everyone left. I quickly got uptight. Was he not going to tell the church, like he'd promised?

As everyone was getting their things ready to go, he quickly said, "I just want to let everyone know that I am married to... Leah, and yeah... we're married."

The silence was so loud.

Thankfully, someone started clapping slowly, followed by a few more shallow and slow claps until finally there was a unison clap... *Barely.*

That was it?

Instantly, I understood that he'd told Chipmunk to leave because he didn't want her to hear that he was married to me, so that he could still do things with her. *Wow,* I said to myself.

I also noticed that Dianne's daughter that always attends the church wasn't present that Sunday.

He was still playing games.

Once again, I was left devastated. Once again, everyone was right. In that moment, I understood the position I had put myself in. My marriage counselor was right, my parents were right, my grandmother, in her silence, was even right. She was the only one that didn't say anything to me when I left.

Here we go again, I thought.

After church, I grabbed my stuff and walked up to our room. I was trying to up my body language, so that I could fix myself up enough to thank him for announcing me. He was sitting at his desk, working, with one hand on his head.

"You made me do that... I didn't want to do that," he said sloppily. "You made me announce you to everybody." His tone was slow and flushed.

"Wait a minute! You said you were going to do that! That's what *you* said you were going to do. You owed that to me!"

"But you made me do that. It was forced," he growled. "Because you left, I was forced to do that."

Just like my marriage counselor had warned... *nothing* had changed. Nothing.

So now, I was officially back in Oakland, still living in the church. But, as he promised, he was going to buy me a house.

He actively began trying to find a house for us to move into. He'd often ask me where I wanted to live, and I gave him various places I liked. I think I liked them so much because they reminded me of Los Angeles. After he looked around the places I had suggested, we narrowed our search to the neighborhood of Montclair. It was a hilly area that had the vibe of Laurel Canyon, which I loved, because I love driving up the canyons. The area was absolutely beautiful, and I couldn't wait to find our new home.

To my surprise, Chipmunk 2 had just recently gotten her real estate license—which I thought was a major coincidence. James had her look for our home in Montclair, which I found really strange. First of all, it felt weird because I knew for a fact that they had a relationship, but I didn't know if she knew we were married, since she'd left before he announced it to the church. Besides that, though, I just didn't want *her* to find my house. I mean, why would I want someone who was actively involved with my husband to be finding the house he and I would soon be living in? It was completely contradictory in my head, and it was an insult. Yet I stayed quiet because I wanted to get out of that church and for James to do as he'd said.

Sometimes she'd pick us up from the church or other places to look at houses, and I'd just stay quiet because I didn't like the fact that he'd made her a part of this deal. Anyone in real estate knows that when an agent sells a house, they get a percentage of the profit.

Meaning the woman who my husband had made cum in the movie theatre was about to get a commission off our new home, which she was going to help us find. I absolutely couldn't stand the thought of it.

One day in particular, we planned to go house hunting again. James let me know he was close, and to start heading down so he could pick me up. When I got downstairs, James was driving Chipmunk 2's car, and she was just sitting in the passenger seat smiling at me. *You guys are that familiar that you can drive her car?* She gave me no indication that she was going to move, so I finally had to sit in the backseat. She did not respect me at all, and I was getting really tired of her.

We began driving around the Montclair area looking for houses that impressed me. James was very sincere in me liking where we lived. I saw beautiful houses, and I desperately tried to see myself living in them, but something never felt right about them. It never felt like it was the right thing to be doing, yet we kept looking.

We finally found one that I actually liked. It was a two-story home with the bedrooms below the entrance level. It was on a cliff with vivid views of the mountains and canyons on a quiet, private street. I really tried to envision myself in it because it was a stunning house in an exclusive location.

James and I made a decision to buy that specific house. In order to purchase it, James said that he first had to liquidate a couple of his assets in order to make a sizeable down payment. Since I wasn't working, didn't have any money of my own, and couldn't ask my parents or grandmother for money, I just allowed him to do what he needed to do to purchase the home.

In order to qualify for a house, the buyer needs to do a credit check. Being only 23 at the time, I didn't have any credit. I had only one credit card to my name, up to that point. When you're a freshman in college, the credit cards are lined up at your door because it's the first time you're out on your own. They know college students have no money yet the most expensive taste. I got a Discover card that had a $1,000 balance, and I blew that in a few months easily. One year my grandmother asked me what I wanted for Christmas, and I asked if she could pay my credit card off, which she did. She told me to never use it again after that, so that was the end of my credit history. Credit cards weren't allowed in the family unless it was a dire emergency.

Knowing this, James insisted that we apply for the house using my credit, since it was so good. He had different properties around California that he liquidated cash from for the down payment, and when he'd finally liquidated enough, we were ready to sign the escrow papers. Upon signing, I noticed that there was only my name on the papers—not his. *Just mine.* I asked him why only my name was there, and he told me that it was because we would get the best deal for the house if it was under my name, being that my credit was impeccable. He told me not to worry, as he would be the one paying for everything.

The whole situation made me feel so eerie. I constantly had a mental battle in my head... *Should I put my name on something this big? Well, he is my husband, and he is buying it, so I should sign.*

Before I knew it, the papers were signed. We had just closed our first deal together as a married couple. James had a couple more business engagements to handle, so I headed down to the car before him. When I got to the car, I sat down, took a deep breath, and exhaled a painful, uncontrollable cry. I had no idea why I was crying, but I couldn't stop.

James quickly came back to the car before I had time to get myself together.

"*What* are you crying about?" He scowled.

"I... I don't know!" I sobbed.

I had no answer for him as to why I was crying. The house was perfect. Yet I just got this feeling that it wasn't right. Have you ever had that feeling where you can't put your finger on it, but you just feel something isn't right?

The escrow papers were signed, and at this point we were just waiting for the papers to go through. As we waited, I would pray that if this was the house for us, that God would bless us with it, but if it wasn't, to reveal that. I was really afraid to make a move like that and put my name on something so big.

The escrow papers quickly went through. *I guess the Lord said this house is for us*, I said to myself. The house was ours!

Next thing we needed was furniture. James said that he had furniture at different properties that we could go get, which we ended up doing. But he wanted to buy a new bedroom set because he didn't want me on a bedroom set that he had been in with someone else, along with him still wanting to buy a few more pieces of furniture. We went to a furniture store named Levits, where I found a beautiful, serene bed set. I was more than pleased with my decision.

When we got to the register, he told the cashier that we were going to apply for credit.

"Leah, you're going to apply for it because your credit is better," he said hastily.

I did the credit check, and of course I qualified. So now the house and the furniture were in my name.

Moving on next was the utilities and the phone bill and everything else that came with having and maintaining a house. The water, the lights, cable, the gas.... Since my credit was better, like he said, all the utility bills were in my name. Everything was in my name.

In a matter of days, I signed my name on more dotted lines than I had ever done in my entire life. I was overwhelmed at how many large commodities I was now tied to. It was so much, so fast. It should have been a highlight in my life, but I found myself crying every day through the process. It was like someone was telling me not to do this. Something in me, every single day, was yelling *Don't do this!!!* Yet I still tracked on. There I was with my first house, now hundreds of thousands of dollars in debt.

So what was I going to do now that I had just signed my name on all these bills? I felt that if I had done all of that, I should at least try to enjoy the beautiful house that he bought me. I really did try to enjoy it. I tried to decorate and get really fine china to make the house a home... but for some odd reason, I couldn't unpack. I would unpack everything else, like things for the kitchen and for the bathroom, but for some odd reason, I couldn't unpack my things. Every time I would walk into my closet, I would hear the words in my head: *This is not your home... this is not your home!* I would wonder what that meant. It was my house; I just had to make it a home for me and my husband. I was trying my hardest to be happy, but I kept feeling like I was just miserable.

I kept feeling like nothing I would do, nor could do, would make James love me. I could tell he was still wondering about Dianne, and he was *still* hanging out with Chipmunk 2. It just didn't stop. Thus, me being miserable didn't stop. It seemed like it was just an ongoing rotation, that no matter what happened, I was still miserable. Yes, I had the house, but I still didn't have his heart.

There was a couple that lived near us that happened to be a pastor and his wife. James loved them, and I began to love them too. They'd come over almost every night with their beautiful son. He had the cutest blue eyes, curly blond hair, he was the cutest little boy in the world.

Together we'd go to the movies, we'd go to restaurants, and the wife, Erin, and I got along so well. This couple was my saving grace; it was like I could be down, and the doorbell would ring, and things would just be better for a while.

Erin and I seemed to share mutual feelings about our husbands. It was never something we'd talk about; I just felt like she got me and maybe was going through something similar, even though her husband was extremely nice and super funny. When we'd go out to dinner, her husband would say the funniest things, and I'd just be laughing so hard along with them. I would notice that out the corner of my eye, James would be looking at me in an odd way, but I couldn't figure out why, because he knew why I was laughing. It was hard to care about that. At the moment it finally felt like the world was lifted off my shoulders.

We'd say our goodbyes and would plan for the next time we would all hang out. One particular night, as soon as James and I got in the house, he looked at me sternly and said, "You laugh too much when he talks."

"What?" I said, confused. "He's funny!"

"You don't need to laugh that much. It's not that funny. You're doing too much."

It was just like all of the joy I would have he would try to take away. So I'd try to find joy in everything. He was sucking the life out of me little by little every day.

I didn't have a job, so I thought it would be a good idea to start looking for one. But looking for a job in the Oakland educational system was difficult. I needed Oakland credentials in order to work. Not to mention, I didn't really know much about how the private schools operated in Oakland. I wasn't having much luck, so I continued just trying to be happy and make things work at home.

Dianne's daughter, Sammy, who called James "Dad," would come over to the house sometimes, and even bring some of her friends to spend the night. Sammy and I began to have a really good relationship. She had beautiful long hair, and since I knew how to do hair, I started doing hers all the time. We would talk and laugh, and she'd tell me about different boys that she was interested in. Sometimes James would have me pick her up from school or take her to her basketball games and different afterschool activities.

I really liked that we were getting close because I never wanted to get in the middle of her and her dad's relationship. No matter what Dianne thought, I wanted her to know that I would never hurt her daughter. It was important to me that my intentions were clear.

One day while Sammy and I were in the car, I looked at her and told her, "I just want you to know something."

"Yeah?" she said with wide eyes.

"You know I would never be involved with your dad if I knew the extent of how much he was involved with your mother."

She looked at me deeply.

"And I'm so sorry, Sammy."

"I know. I know you wouldn't."

I was so relieved that she understood that. From that moment, we had a great understanding bond. I knew where she came from, and she knew I would never disrespect her mom, and I knew she wouldn't disrespect me. I really loved her for that. James appreciated the way I took care of her. I think it gave him a little bit of peace about his and Dianne's relationship.

Months into living in the house, nothing had changed. I still didn't have a job, and I still felt the same. I'd hang out with Erin, and my friend Sophie that used to live in the apartment complex with me by the lake when I was in college. We kept in contact and created a close friendship. Every time I felt like I needed an escape, I'd call Sophie, and we'd drive up to Walnut Creek, walk in and out of stores, and eat at our favorite restaurant: CPK. I found myself trying to be as happy as I possibly could.

One day, while I was with her, I got a call from my pastor from Los Angeles, Dr. Michael Harris Sr.'s wife. "Leah, I hate to tell you this, but Pastor Harris is in the hospital."

"The hospital?" I responded quickly.

"Yeah, he's really sick."

Since I had just had that previous experience with my grandfather, I asked, "Is he on a respirator?"

Usually when you're on a respirator, it's not good.

There was a long pause.

"Yes..."

Instantly, I knew I had to go back to LA.

James and I made arrangements to get back to LA as soon as we could. As soon as we landed, we went to Cedars-Sinai, where he was located. As soon as I saw my pastor hooked up to the machines, I fell to the floor. All these emotions started rushing toward me, along with all that he'd taught me. Instantly, I remembered that I hadn't done what he asked me.

A few months before we moved into our house, while James was gone doing God knows what, Pastor Harris had called me on the phone and said, "Hello, what are you doing?"

"I'm at the church," I replied.

"Oh, you're in your little apartment upstairs, in his office?"

"Yes."

"Well, where is James?"

"I don't know," I said.

"Now is the perfect time."

"Now is the perfect time for what, Pastor?"

"The perfect time to leave."

"Leave? What do you mean, leave?" I asked.

"Pack your stuff and come home."

"Why, Pastor?" I said, puzzled. "Why do you think I should come home?"

"Leah, all of us know how he's treating you. He has disrespected me in the way that he's treated you. He is not my son in the ministry anymore. He has totally disappointed me by not saying that he's married to you and introducing you as his friend. I mean, Leah, pastors from all over the country are calling me and telling me how he's treating you. It's time for you to go. He is not worth being with. He does not have your best interest at heart. He is not the one for you! You should pack up your stuff *right now*, and leave," he urged.

"Pastor, I know. But I made a vow, and I'm gonna stick to it."

"Leah, the door is always open for you to come home."

"I know, Pastor… But I'm gonna stay."

That was one of the last conversations I had with him before he got sick. And so when I saw him hooked up to the respirator, I was devastated. So was James, because in his own way, he loved him so much like a father.

We stayed with Pastor Harris, prayed with him, kissed him, and said our goodbyes.

That night, Pastor Harris passed away. This was the pastor I'd been baptized under, who'd prayed for me when I was born, and who'd even married my parents. I'd participated in his church since I was a baby, but even when I went to college, he supported me in all of my collegiate endeavors.

When he found out that I was graduating from Berkeley in three years, he made sure everyone knew. He was so proud of me. He would call me up to the front of the church every Sunday to announce my graduation. I would be a bit embarrassed, but he was just so proud.

Then, when I was getting married to the man who he thought was this great guy, he introduced it to the church, and had me show off my ring... I mean, he acted as if he was my own dad. My hero, my pastor, the shepherd of my soul here on earth had passed away, and it was the saddest day ever. We made it just in time to say our goodbyes, and then flew back to Oakland.

A few weeks later was the funeral. Pastor Harris' wife asked that I'd sing the song called "In the Garden." It was a song that I sang at my grandfather's funeral, and that I'd sing at different programs.

There were two services. One was at our church where he pastored for over 45 years, and the other service was at The Cathedral in West Los Angeles, which would house way more people.

Of course I said that I'd definitely sing. When the time came for the funeral, we flew down to Los Angeles and attended the funeral. Everyone was there. It was like a reunion for everyone who was born and raised at our church.

When I walked into the building, the first person I saw was Terry. He was with his family. When we made eye contact, he quickly looked down to avoid me. But his parents saw me and asked how I was doing. His brother and sister were also there, and I gave them hugs as well.

We gathered into the main sanctuary, and everyone took their seats. My heart was in my stomach because Terry was there, and we had so much unfinished business. On top of that, James was acting like a fool because he felt like he should have preached Pastor Harris' funeral. I don't know what made him think that, but he felt very strongly that he should have done the eulogy.

He was acting completely out of character, pacing back and forth outside like he wanted to fight. It was so embarrassing and awful, but I had to sing, so I could not focus on that.

Everyone saw it. They were looking at me like *Gosh, how do you deal with this?* I could see the hundreds of people just staring at me as if they were asking me why would I do that to myself. It was very clear what everyone was thinking.

When it was my time to sing, my uncle played the piano for me, and I sang my little heart out. After I sang, everyone stood up and gave a standing ovation. My dad, my mom, and my grandmother's faces were so proud, a look I had missed seeing from them. I felt that I really gave my pastor my last and final gift.

After I sang, the rest of the program continued. Jessie Jackson gave the eulogy that night, and we were off to our hotel.

The next day, we went to the big funeral, which was at The Cathedral in West Los Angeles. It was pretty amazing. Pastor Harris actually preached his own service. They played an old video of him preaching on the screens, and there was not a dry eye in the room. That was one of the most beautiful services I have ever been to. We said our goodbyes and headed home.

As we left the service, in the hallway I saw Dr. Tigner and Varie. I was so happy to see them. I said, "Hi, Doc and Varie!"

They both smiled, but Varie looked a little sad. She said, "I heard you guys got married." When she said that, I immediately realized why they were sad. It was because I did not invite them to the wedding. They were so kind to me and so supportive, and I knew they were crushed that they hadn't been invited.

I felt horrible and said, "Yes, we did."

Our exchange was so awkward, and she said, "Well, congratulations. See you later." And we left.

I hated that things had gotten so bad between us. I truly loved them, but James had demanded that I stop talking to them. I did that to make him happy, but inside I was deeply saddened.

We flew back to Oakland that night so that James could preach that Sunday morning. After church on Sunday, I got a call from Pastor Harris' widow. I was amazed and confused that she was calling me right after the funeral.

She said, "Leah, you looked beautiful at the funeral."

"You did, too," I said. "I can't believe you're calling me!"

"Well, I just wanted to thank you guys so much for everything, especially our relationship, and the love that you showed to me and my husband. I just want to thank you. And you sang your butt off!" She paused. "And, by the way, I have a message for you."

"Yeah?" I asked.

"From Terry. He told me to tell you to call him. These are his exact words: 'Tell my Leah to call me.'"

I was flabbergasted. He wanted me to call him? Wow! The crazy part was... I wanted to call him.

And I did.

Of course I was apprehensive, because James could not find out! I had to sneak and call him when I wasn't around James, which wasn't too hard since James wasn't around that much. But he would pop up sometimes. I finally got a chance to call him, and before I could double back and hang up the phone, he answered.

"Leah..." he said, like always.

"Hey, how are you doing?" I replied.

"How are *you*?"

"I'm doing great!" I answered quickly.

"No, really. How are you doing?"

"I'm great!" I repeated.

"No... tell me how you're doing, Leah."

Sigh. "I'm okay... Why do you ask?"

"Everyone is talking about what you're going through. All over the country, people know that he's not owning up to you and all the drama, Leah. Are you okay?"

"No, I'm not okay, I'm really miserable... I don't know what to do. I want to leave, but I don't know how to leave... I just don't know what to do," I confessed.

"Leah, you're so beautiful. You're so amazing and so valuable. Why are you taking this? Why are you putting yourself through this? Your parents have invested so much into you, your grandmother, Pastor Harris... everyone loves you! Why are you doing this to yourself when you have all these people that love you?"

"I know. You're right..."

"You're too good of a person to go through this."

Terry was right... He was absolutely right, in fact. He was telling me everything that I had known about myself but had forgotten over time. He gave me the emotional and motivational support that I needed, at the right time.

Every chance he got, he'd call me on my other phone. The connection was rekindled instantly. I would tell him what was going on, and he'd help me through it. He'd listen to me express my feelings, talk me through my pain, and would always tell me that he was praying for me. He was exactly what I needed.

I became more and more depressed every day. Nothing was making me happy. I would be so depressed that when I woke up in the morning, when I opened my eyes, I would be so upset that I was alive. It was bad. Can you imagine being so depressed that you didn't want to wake up? That's how miserable I was.

Several times a week I would wake up crying uncontrollably. James would ask what was wrong, but I would never say. I was just so sad and so unhappy. One morning when I woke up I started praying.

"Lord, I am so sorry. I repent for disobeying You and marrying this man I know You didn't want me to marry. I want to leave but I don't know how or if that is what You want for me. I need You to show me what the rest of my life would be like with him. In Jesus name, Amen."

The Lord did not answer my prayer for three weeks. Then finally I had a dream of me being on a roller coaster, going up and down, around and around, and I was screaming my head off. The Lord spoke to me and said, "The rest of your life with James will be like a roller coaster, out of control, up and down all the time, always in circles, never stable." After the Lord told me that, I said, "I want to get off! But not until You show me what my life would be like without him. All I know is dysfunction and confusion. Please show me what the rest of my life would be like without him."

The Lord did not answer me for another three weeks. Finally, I heard the Lord speak, and He said, "Relief. Without James you will have relief, and I will restore everything that you lost."

I said, "Thank you Lord! Now it is time for me to leave!"

I no longer cared about the prophecy from the girl back when I was a freshman in college when she told me I was going to marry James, and he was going to get me a green Expedition and a pear-shaped diamond ring, and that things were going to get worse before they got better. I no longer tried to make this prophecy come to pass. I was done with that prophecy! It was not for me; it was a trick to curse me into a lifetime of depression. I got my answer from the Lord, and I made my decision. Now the only problem was I did not know how I was going to leave. I definitely needed a plan.

I planned that since we did not go to church in one car, when he left for church on Sunday morning, I would just wait until he left, then pack my car and drive back to LA. That seemed like a great idea, but every Sunday when I would plan to leave it seemed like he knew. Before he left for church, he would say, "Cher, Sister So-and-So needs you to pick them up and bring them to church." When he would do that it would be impossible for me to leave because I had to pick that person up for church. Then some Sundays he would say, "Sammy wants to ride to church with you." Now I definitely could not leave because Sammy was depending on me for a ride.

It became ridiculous! I could not leave. Every time I tried, he would throw a monkey wrench in my plans. I felt like I was stuck. It seems like the moment I decided to leave, he knew it or he knew something was up. It was amazing!

One day, while James and I were at one of the church members' son's basketball game, I kept feeling this horrible feeling in my chest. Intense pains.

For some odd reason, the pain made me think about my period. I thought that was a sign that I was cramping, and my period was finally coming. *But* why hadn't I got my period yet?

On the way home from the game, I asked James if we could stop by Walgreens.

"Sure. What do you want to get?"

"I think I want to get a pregnancy test because my period hasn't come yet, and I know I'm not pregnant, but I just want a test to see what's going on."

So we went to Walgreens, and I got a pregnancy test and headed home.

His daughter Sammy was home with some of her friends, watching TV and eating pizza that I ordered for them.

I went downstairs to the bathroom to do the pregnancy test. I was at ease because I had taken many before. I used to want to be pregnant, thinking that a baby would make him love me and give me the attention I longed for. So I'd take pregnancy tests all the time. Anxiously.

I did the test and put it by the toilet as I washed my hands and confronted myself in the mirror. I put my hands on the sink and stared long and hard at myself, noticing how much I'd changed. I began to trust my feelings of not being happy. I could see it all over my face… I missed who I used to be. I wasn't myself.

I snapped back into reality just as the results on the test appeared. I saw two lines.

No, no, no, no, no. There was no way.

The pregnancy test pack comes with two tests. So I took another test and waited for the results.

Two lines again…

I was pregnant.

I sat on the toilet, breathless. Silent. I was lost.

How??? How could this be? It had been seven months and I had not gotten pregnant before How could I get pregnant now? Just as I was gaining my strength to speak up for myself… just as I was curating the power inside of me to leave and get my life back… I was pregnant.

The feelings of confusion instantly began. I was now carrying his child… How was I going to leave when I was pregnant? All of my plans to leave had to go down the drain. Then I thought, *Do I have to have this baby?*

Suddenly, the door opened. There he was standing in the doorway, wondering what the results of the pregnancy test were.

"Well, what does it say?"

I sat on the toilet and immediately burst into tears.

"I'm pregnant…. I'm pregnant… I'm…. I'm pregnant," I confessed with dismay.

"Really?! That's great!!! This is great!" he rejoiced.

"It's not great! How could we bring a baby into this situation? How could you say this is great?! We're not good!"

"Well, kill it then!" he said sternly before walking out of the bathroom.

I continued to sit there in the silence that was yelling at me. My confusion was screaming at me while anxiety and fear took over my entire body. Out of anytime this could happen, now it was happening? After all the times I had tried in the past, I was pregnant *now?* I really thought that a baby would make him love me again. I thought if we had a family he'd forget about Dianne and just be with me. As the pain got stronger, those thoughts had begun to go away. I had stopped trying, and now I was pregnant. I just couldn't understand why. It was horrible!

The first thing that came to my mind was calling Terry. When I finally got out of the bathroom, it just so happened that he had called me. I couldn't answer, though, because James' daughter and everyone was there, and the nervous energy of James was so intrusive. He kept trying to force me to eat while trying to be mad at me at the same time. I finally couldn't take it. I went downstairs, closed the door, and ended up calling Terry.

I was crying by the time he answered the phone.

"What's wrong, Leah?" he asked.

"I'm … I'm pregnant."

"It's okay.… It's okay, it's going to be okay. Just because you're pregnant doesn't mean you have to stay. It does *not* mean that. You can still go home! You can still be cared for and loved by your family. It doesn't mean anything."

I looked at the phone and couldn't even believe that in this state, he still cared about me. He was still giving me hope when I thought there was none.

Later that night, I showered, wanting to go to bed early. James held me the entire night. It was the funniest, weirdest feeling. *Now that I'm pregnant, he wants to be around me?* Strange… Really, really strange.

The next day was Sunday, so I made an appointment for Monday to go see a doctor. I just wanted to see how far along I was and figure out what it was that I was going to do.

Lo and behold, he wanted to go with me.

*But not too long ago, he didn't want me around, he didn't want me to do ministry, nor be at the church. I couldn't sing, have relationships with anyone… He didn't want me to be involved with my family, never wanted to take me anywhere, didn't want to tell anyone I was his wife, but **now** he wants to go to doctor's appointments with me?*

Nonetheless, James started going to every doctor's appointment with me. In fact, he didn't let me out of his sight. Everywhere I wanted to go, or even places he had to attend, he wanted me to go with him. It was like he had this feeling that I was going to try and do something. It weirdly went from him not wanting anything to do with me to needing me around all the time.

All of these new emotions and the anxiety that I felt began causing me to bleed every single day. I couldn't stop bleeding! I began going to the doctor often, trying to figure out why this was happening.

After a few weeks of being so disappointed and upset with myself for getting pregnant just when I wanted to leave, I asked him if I could go see my parents. I really needed to go.

He agreed.

I was bleeding, but I still got on a plane to Los Angeles. My parents had already known about the pregnancy; in fact, I told my mom soon after I found out.

My mom assured me that it was completely up to me if I wanted to keep the baby or if I decided not to. She said that she was not going to tell me to keep it, and she was not going to tell me to get rid of it.

"It is your decision, and we will stand by you whatever you decide," she told me.

My grandmother was very quiet about it but felt the same.

"Leah, I'm upset that this is the situation, but whatever you decide I'm fine with."

It meant everything to me that I had family by my side through every obstacle I was faced with. During my time in LA, they took great care of me and made sure that I was resting often. I was still bleeding a lot, and I was in a lot of pain, excruciating pain. I really believe that I lost the baby during that week. Which gave me feelings of relief, because I honestly didn't want it.

It didn't feel right bringing an innocent life into this situation where my husband didn't love me and didn't value me. It just wasn't a world I would want to bring a child into. I really feel like I wished the baby away.

I was reluctant to leave my family, but I knew I had to. When I got back to Oakland, James kept asking me if I was still bleeding. He was extremely nervous.

"Do you think you're losing the baby?"

"I don't know..."

He'd ask, and ask, and ask! "Do you think you're losing the baby?"

"I DON'T KNOW, JAMES!"

He was so concerned about this baby! I didn't even know if he loved me or wanted me, but he was so concerned. He insisted that we go to the doctor immediately.

That Monday, we went to the doctor as planned. The doctor put the sonogram inside of me to monitor the baby.

"I'm going to just check around and see what's going on, I know you've still been bleeding."

He kept looking and looking, but was silent before leaving the room.

"I think we lost it," James muttered.

We waited in silence.

The doctor walked back in the room. "Mr. and Mrs. Jordan, I'm so sorry to inform you, but you have lost the baby. I am so sorry."

James immediately lost it! HE WAS LIVID. He threw his keys to the ground and hit the wall. "Why would God do this to us?! Why?!"

All I could think was... *Thank. You. God.*

Now I could finally, finally leave.

After we left the doctor's office, I was feeling a sense of relief. I felt like I could finally get out of here. James was definitely mad. As we walked to the car, a sense of strength came over me.

"I need to go home," I confessed.

"What?" he asked.

"I need to go home to see my parents."

For the first time, he actually looked at me with a sense of compassion.

"You've been through a lot. I've put you through a lot... I understand... How long do you think you're going to be there?"

"I have no idea... but I *know* I need to go home. I want to see my parents and be in an environment of people who love me... I need to go home."

Later that evening when we went to bed, he again expressed how he understood that I wanted to go home. He admitted to being a terrible husband, and how he wasn't there for me the way he should have been. I couldn't believe he was admitting how much he had put me through. He apologized for all the women, everything at the church, making me unhappy... everything!

"When do you want to leave?" he asked reluctantly.

"I want to leave next week," I decided.

So for the next few days, every day he'd be so nice to me. He'd keep saying, "I understand… I understand…"

While he was consistently apologizing, he was having different friends call me to encourage me to stay and not give up on our marriage. I had so many calls from friends telling me that James would try harder.

But I was so firm in my head, and I was so firm in what I believed about going home. Nothing swayed me, nothing changed me. No matter how nice he was, no matter how many people would call me, I just knew that it was time for me to leave.

That Sunday before we went to church, he was taking an extra-long time to arrive. When he finally did, I could visibly see in his face that he was sad. All night prior, he had been crying and begging for my forgiveness. To be honest, I was crying too, because I still did love him so much. But I just knew… I knew that this was not the destiny God had for me, and I needed to get out of there.

Right before he went into church, he sat on this chair right before the entrance. I saw him sitting there with his head down. He saw me looking at him and said, "Come sit with me for a minute."

I did, and as we sat there, we hugged for what seemed an eternity. Tears flowed from his eyes. "I'm so sorry, Leah. Is there anything I can do to make you change your mind?"

"There really isn't."

"Let me take you on a trip. We can go to Vegas, I can take you to a couple shows, you can get massages from the spa. Then when we come back, I'll help you pack all of your stuff, and you can leave."

I felt like I owed him that.

"Okay." I sighed.

After opening the doors of the church, he proceeded to tell everyone how we never really had a trip since we'd been married. He told everyone how I had been through so much, and that he wanted to take me on a trip for a couple days as a getaway because that's what I deserved. All of a sudden, all of the members started coming up to the pulpit, bringing money for the trip. It was very endearing and very loving. I felt special. I knew that the church loved me, especially the older women. I *knew* that they cared for me and saw my pain. They saw how he treated me. So for them to bring money for the trip, that did make me feel accepted and loved. But it didn't make me happy about our situation. In addition, after he made the announcement that we were married, his Love Offering increased. It was as if all his members wanted him to tell the truth and own up to me. After that they wholeheartedly supported us. Our finances went up, as well as their love and acceptance for me. It was so sad that after all of this I was leaving.

The next day, like he promised, we went to Vegas. We went to shows, spas, concerts... It was really fun. It really was. But every time he'd look at me and ask, "Are you still going?" I'd say, "Yes."

I didn't want to have sex with him because I didn't want to get pregnant. Even though we would get intimate, I still was very leery. I didn't want anything to stop me from leaving. I was so determined to leave once we got back home.

Once we got back to Oakland, we had a church service the next day. He was so sad and so quiet, yet so affectionate. It's like he knew this was the end. I was just as sad, but I feel I did a better job at hiding it. You have to remember, I *still* loved this man with all my heart. I hated that things weren't working out. But I knew that if I wanted my life back, I had to get out of there. That service was really difficult. It was like I was saying bye to all of my friends, and especially the older people I had gotten close to that looked at me like a daughter. I even got close to a lot of the teenagers in the ministry, including James' daughter. I got really close to her, actually. That last service was really sad. I was literally saying goodbye, but I couldn't *say* goodbye, if that makes sense. I knew it was goodbye, but they didn't. So I had to act very normal. But at the same time, I was very sad.

There was a secret entryway into the choir stand and the pool pit on the side of the church that he could access through from his study before he entered the church. This particular Sunday, I was walking with him in that secret entryway into the church—almost together. It was just so weird because we never did that. Usually, I would enter the church coming from the back office, where we used to live. It seemed like the moment that I decided I was going to leave, everything that I'd ever wanted him to do he was doing. There was nothing more that I wanted than to be together in the ministry. There was nothing more that I wanted than to walk into church hand in hand so that people could see our love for one another. But it was happening when I was leaving. *Crazy!* I don't know if it was the devil trying to entice me to stay, like he had *often* done with him. Acting so good when I was getting ready to leave. Was it the devil? Or was he really changing?

I had to finally realize that he wasn't changing. He had done this before—"changed"—and then went right back to his old ways.

There he was, sitting on this chair on the side of the church. He was just looking at me.

"Can you just come sit with me?"

I sat with him on his lap, and we hugged for what felt like an eternity.

His eyes swelled up with tears, and so did mine, honestly. And then we walked in to church.

That last service was sad. But I still knew in my heart that I was doing the right thing.

When I got back to our house, I immediately started packing my things. I'd never fully unpacked, so the boxes were fairly ready in my closet. I began putting the boxes in the back of my Ford Explorer. I put the seats down and started putting every item of clothing and shoes in the car. Anything I could fit into the car, I did. James helped me pack every single item.

"Are you taking all your clothes?"

"Yes, I'm taking all my clothes"

As he packed my clothes in the car, he'd cry and cry, and I'll admit I did feel so bad... but I was so determined to leave.

The last box was packed, and it was time for me to go. Knowing the type of person he was, he was always trying to out-think me. He's a thinker... always thinking.

He invited that couple that I love so much that had that little boy to come over before I left. Basically to stop me from leaving. As we were waiting for them on the couch because I didn't want to be rude, we started to get intimate... and started making love.

What am I doing? I'm never going to get out of here if I continue to do this!

I was sending the wrong messages.

I don't know if it was the height of emotions... I don't know if we both thought that we were losing each other. I don't know... all I could keep saying to myself was... *Leah, you're leaving today. You are leaving today, Leah.*

I stopped the intimacy. He understood.

Then the doorbell rang. It was the couple and their son.

They were looking so sad, especially the wife. She was looking at me as if she was sad that I was leaving, but also, it seemed like she understood. I loved her so much for all the times she and her husband came over, because when they came, it was a time of relief for me. It was a time of laughter. We could go to the movies together, eat together, and I did her hair. I loved her. Saying goodbye to her was really sad. Even saying goodbye to her son and her husband was sad.

But I had to keep reminding myself: *Leah, stay focused.*

We said our goodbyes as they realized they couldn't talk me out of leaving.

It was the two of us, again, by ourselves. Not for long, though.

His secretary came next, who I loved as well. She had been there for me. I knew she loved me, and I knew she saw everything that was going on. I knew she couldn't fault me for leaving, but yet, she didn't want me to leave.

She tried to talk me into staying as well while simultaneously telling James how she understood why I needed to go home. I loved her for that.

We said our goodbyes, and it was just us two alone again.

"I have to leave now," I said to him.

"I know."

We walked outside to my car, and immediately he broke down… and so did I.

"Please don't leave… Please don't leave me. I'm so sorry. I'll be a better husband, I'll be a better person! You are a blessing to me, Leah. You're a blessing to my ministry. Please don't leave."

I broke down. I couldn't stop crying. "I *have* to," I whimpered. "I have to go."

We hugged. Gave each other a final kiss... I got in my car, and I drove away.

As I drove, it was pouring rain. I remember driving down the 510 freeway to the 5 South, coming to Los Angeles.

As soon as I got on the freeway, I called my mom and dad and told them I was coming home.

"We'll see you when you get here!"

They asked no questions. They sounded so overjoyed and happy. A sigh of relief came over me like never before. I called my grandmother and told her the news as well.

"Praise the Lord, praise the Lord!!" she shouted.

Right then, I knew I'd made the right decision.

Next, I called Terry.

"I'm coming home!"

"Oh my God, that's so great! I'm so proud of you. Call me at every point. You made the right decision."

There I was driving in the rain... I could barely see, but I kept driving. I was scared about what the next chapter was going to be, but I kept driving home. I was crying tears of joy and praising the Lord. I was glorifying God because I really felt like that chapter was over.

I'd learned my lessons. I'd learned not to get into a relationship with someone who was still tangled up with someone else. I learned that a person is who they are! They're not going to change. I learned that you can't change a person no matter how much you love them, no matter how much you make love to them, no matter how much good you do for them; you can't change them. They are who they are. What's not for you is just not for you! That was not my life, that was not my destiny. As I thought about all of these things, I was praising God, shouting at the top of my lungs, crying to the Lord, telling Him how grateful and thankful I was for Him getting me out of my misery and depression. I felt like I saw the light at the end of the tunnel. I didn't know what was next, but I knew *that* part was over... and the best was yet to come.

zero

finally got to the half point of LA. At every point, I was calling Terry. I felt excited about coming home. What was really great was that I had something to look forward to, since Terry still loved me. He didn't hold it against me that I had gotten married, and I really appreciated that. He happened to be preaching a revival in Los Angeles the day that I came back.

As soon as I got back, after that long five-hour drive by myself in the rain, I was finally home. I hugged my parents so tightly. They were so overjoyed to have me back.

I got settled in my room and changed from my old clothes. By that time, Terry told me that he was done preaching and to meet him for dinner.

I rushed at the opportunity. I wanted to meet him.

James had been calling me, too, on my way back. Of course I was answering the phone, but keeping the conversation short. I didn't want to go back, and I didn't want to feel bad about my decision. So I talked to him, but I made it very short.

That night, I went to see Terry. I felt like Leah again. I felt like this amazing, spontaneous, fun Leah. I missed her. We talked, we laughed. He didn't mention anything about James, my marriage, anything like that. We just caught back up right where we left off. I was so happy to see him.

We hugged, we kissed, we talked, we laughed.

He went back home to San Antonio not too long after we met. We were still talking every day, and it really felt like I was in a new chapter of my life. However, I didn't want to jump into anything too quickly. I was still fresh out of a marriage, and I wasn't even divorced yet. There was no paperwork that was signed yet, or anything. I was really in a place of getting my bearings and figuring out what the next step was.

While figuring out my next step, though, I found myself in a state of deep depression. Walking out of marriage, it's kind of a phase of mourning or grieving. It is as if you are mourning the loss of a loved one. Every day, I was waking up contemplating if I'd made the right decision. What was I supposed to do next? Should I get a job? Should I stay in bed and sleep all day long? Figuring out your next steps in life can be fearful. I also would have these dreams and visions of me sharing my story to hundreds of women. I saw myself encouraging women and telling them my testimony. These visions were real, so real that I knew they came from God. I just was not in the position to do it now; I was too depressed. I needed more time to heal.

Day after day, I'd be in bed. In the mornings, James would call me and ask about my prior day, and what I had planned for the day at hand. He was being *so* nice to me.

Of course, this was what happened the last time I left. I went right back. So I was trying to keep rushing off the phone, yet I would still answer when he called.

Yet Terry was still calling me, encouraging me, and talking to me. We were becoming friends again. I was feeling all kinds of mixed emotions of what to do next. What was I doing?

Our family reunion was once again coming up in Texas. My grandmother wanted me to go with her, and I agreed to. But before that, she had been calling me every morning.

One specific morning, she called with a different tone in her voice.

I answered the phone.

"Leah, what are you doing?".

"In the bed," I said dully.

"In the bed doing what?"

"I'm just... in the bed."

"Hmm. Are you depressed?"

"No... not really," I replied.

"'Cause I know you not depressed over that man!"

I was speechless. My grandmother never swears.

"Let me tell you something. Me and your parents have been through a lot with you in and out of this marriage. We spent a *lot* of money. I just want you to know that if you go back to that nigga, you will lose all of your inheritance. I won't give you shit! Nothing! I'm sick of you being with him... I am sick of him! I'm sick of you being whatever you're being! I'm just saying you need to get your ass up and get out of that bed and stop being depressed!"

"I'm trying, Mama!"

"No, you're not trying hard enough. You're not trying hard enough, Leah! So this is what you're going to do. In order for you to keep your inheritance and *not* go back to Oakland to that nigga, I have set up a job for you down the street at Childkeepers Preschool. I'm supposed to be working there, being their supervisor, but I'm going to give it to you instead because you need a job. You need to make some money, and you need to get your mind off of that nigga up north! You are going to get a job, and you are going to work. Meet me there in an hour."

"Yes, Mama," I said.

I immediately got off the phone and proceeded to get dressed as my grandmother *demanded*. I met her at Childkeepers Preschool.

Thank God for my grandmother; if it wasn't for her, I would probably still be in bed to this day.

I started working immediately. I was finally back doing what I loved—teaching children. Working with preschoolers is a little different. You have to do potty changes, cook food, facilitate nap time... But it was so good for me. The kids were so loving and adorable. I can still remember some of them... Carlos, Natasia... They were so cute! They loved on me every day. They told me the cutest stories and had the most joyous, sweetest laughs. It was exactly what I needed to build myself back up, and it gave me something to look forward to. I looked forward to seeing their cute little faces every day. They hugged me, kissed me, and even put their snotty noses on me. I didn't care. I loved them to pieces.

During the weeks while I was in LA getting myself together and working the preschool job, James called me and told me that he couldn't take it anymore, and that he was coming to LA to see me. Of course I was really afraid to see him, and I didn't really know what to expect. I just didn't want to get to a point where I was so weak that I'd go back.

"I'm flying into town only for a couple hours. I just need to see you. You don't have to be scared," he said.

"Okay," I agreed. "I get off work at 3."

"I'm going to fly into the Burbank Airport. Meet me at the Hilton right across the street from the airport."

I drove over to the hotel. We embraced, but slightly. He got a room for us.

"I just want to talk to you," he said.

I went to the room, and he had a massage table laid out.

"I know you love massages. Can I just massage you?"

I'm a sucker for massages. I absolutely love them. *Nothing will happen,* I thought to myself.

I climbed on the table, and he proceeded to give me a massage. It was a really great massage, actually. I could tell he was trying really hard. When he was finished, I got off the massage table and began to put my clothes back on. Then he proceeded to take his clothes off.

"What are you doing?" I asked.

"Don't you want to take a nap?"

I shook my head, signaling my disinterest.

He still proceeded to take his pants off.

"James, what are you doing?"

"I thought... we would—"

"Oh... you thought we would... have sex?" I laughed.

"Yeah, I mean, I flew all the way down here. I thought we could—"

"Oh no.... No, no no. I don't want to do that with you."

The way he looked at me after I said those words was a look I'll never forget. It was a look of utter disappointment.

"You're really done with me."

"Yeah," I confirmed.

I could not believe how strong I had become in a matter of weeks. I resisted the man who used to make me weak in the knees. I said no to the man whose soft caress and sensual kiss would cause me to slip into amnesia and forget about all the turmoil he had put me through. I said no to the man whom I had loved for so long. I could not believe that I was strong enough to say no and mean it. I had my power back, and it felt oh so good. I put my clothes back on and gave him a hug. He walked me down to my car. The look on his face was of defeat, as if what he had planned did not unfold as he thought. As he walked away from the car, I knew in my heart that might be the last time we saw each other ever again.

As I drove out of the hotel parking lot, I checked my phone and had a million missed calls. I'd completely forgotten all about my phone. It was like my parents and grandmother had a sixth sense that I was with him or that he was in town.

As I headed down the highway, my grandmother called me. "Leah, where are you?" she yelled.

"Oh, I'm just out with some friends."

If I told her where I really was, that wouldn't sit well with her at all. It would be a complete firestorm, actually.

"Okay. You're on your way home, right?"

"Yes! I'm on my way home."

I knew she didn't believe me. But I stuck to my story.

The reunion was coming up, and it was time for me and my grandmother to go to Texas. My mother couldn't make it this time because she had a prior engagement. My grandmother wanted me to make all of the arrangements and book the tickets.

"But we have one thing you need to do before we go."

"What is it, Mama?"

"You need to get your divorce papers together. We're not going to Texas, you're not seeing Terry until these divorce papers are signed and sent to this man up north."

I remembered seeing a place called "We The People" on Wilshire Blvd. "We The People" is a place where you can do legal documents and legal filings, but you're doing it yourself, so it's half the cost. I realized that my grandmother was serious, so on one of my lunch breaks from the preschool, I went there. It wasn't too far from the school. I met with one of the advisors and told him that I wanted to get a divorce. He asked me several things like:

"Do you have any kids?"

"No."

"Do you own any property together?"

"Yes. But it's only in my name."

"Why do you want to get a divorce?"

"Irreconcilable differences... we just have differences..." I said. I wasn't going to say infidelity, or any of the other things I had experienced.

They got the paperwork started.

"Okay. That will be two hundred dollars."

Remember, I came back with absolutely nothing. I just began working, so I didn't even have two hundred dollars to file for this divorce.

So I had to go to my grandmother. I told her I found a place to get the divorce papers all written up. She wanted to go with me to "We The People," so I drove her, and she paid the two hundred dollars and got the paperwork in motion.

Now I had to serve him. But how was I going to do that from Los Angeles? When you serve someone, that means that you have to place the documents in their actual hands.

I thought about his secretary, Jasmine. We had a good relationship and respect for each other, and she knew why I'd left him. I knew she'd be the perfect person to serve him. Plus, she called me every day while I was home just to check on me and see if I was okay. So I gave her a call.

"Jasmine, do you think that you'd be able to serve James the divorce papers for me?"

"Leah, you're moving that fast?"

"Yeah. I'm moving fast. I've got to get my life back together and start over. I need this chapter finished."

"I don't want to do this," she said. "But I know what you've been through. I'll do it for you. Fedex them to me, and I will hand them to him."

"Perfect," I exclaimed.

As I proceeded to get the papers together, it was going on three weeks that I had been home. In those three weeks, my grandmother had gotten me a job and had me start my process of divorce. During these three weeks, every single day, James would send me flowers or candy. He would send me roses or Casablanca lilies—and a huge bouquet of them, at that. He is not cheap at all. Each gift would have a note of him expressing how much he loved me and missed me.

I was still talking to him every day. I would keep the conversation short, but I *would* answer the phone every single day. He would be so strategic with his gifts, like he had always been. He would send me jelly beans, but he knew I only liked certain colors: red, pink, white, and purple. So he would send me the jelly beans separated and placed in containers in order for me to just have the colors that I liked. He'd even send me typed letters explaining how much of a bad husband he was and how much he missed me. He claimed that he'd realized his wrongs and was practically begging for me to give him another chance. Some letters even expressed how depressed he was since I was gone.

My friend Sophie from Oakland called one day, and she seemed worried. "Leah, are you okay?" she asked.

"Yes, I am fine," I replied.

"You are not in Oakland anymore, are you?" she said in a concerned voice.

"No, I left James. I am back in LA trying to get my life together. I just couldn't take it anymore," I said.

"I am so glad! I had a strange feeling about you, and I have been calling you and you have not been calling me back. So I went to your house in Montclair and knocked on the door."

"You did!" I exclaimed.

"Yes, I was worried! I thought something happened to you. When I knocked on the door James answered, and he looked terrible. He said you were gone, and he did not know if you were coming back. It was really eerie. The house had a strange spirit. I knew you were gone," she said.

"I had to go. It was awful," I said.

"I know, and I am so glad you are at home with your family who loves you. Stay in touch and know I love you."

I told her I loved her too, and we both hung up the phone.

It was so good to know that my friends still loved and supported me even through making the hardest decision of my life.

One day, the letter that I opened was shocking. There were pictures. The pictures were of me conducting sexual acts on James that I had no idea even existed. In the letter, he said, "Remember, I have these."

When I saw those pictures, I immediately knew he was trying to scare me and blackmail me. That was it for me. Jasmine had to serve him those papers and serve him immediately. This marriage had to be over.

Seeing my grandmother's seriousness about me moving on and also talking to Terry and dealing with his seriousness for us to become an item put a lot of pressure on me. Terry really wanted me to commit to him, which caused a little bit of stress because I was dealing with a lot already with leaving James. How was I supposed to commit to someone so quickly? He was very adamant about it, yet patient with me at the same time. Every time I'd say, "I can't do this right now, I'm going through a lot." He'd seem to understand but was still persistent with pursuing me.

Not too long after I sent Jasmine the papers, she called to let me know that she had received them and had served him.

"He opened up the papers and told me he couldn't believe I served him," Jasmine told me. "He became furious at the fact that I served him."

"How could you not know that this was coming? The way you treated that girl, of course this was coming," she told James.

"I feel really bad that I had to do that to him, Leah. I feel guilty. But I understand," she said to me.

"Don't feel guilty. This is what needed to happen. I have to be done with this."

The divorce papers were in his hands. Now all he had to do was sign, and we'd be good. We had nothing to exchange. I didn't want any alimony—like Tina Turner, I just wanted my last name and we were good! But, of course, being the person that he was, he did not sign right away. My part was signed; I was done. I could head to Texas with my grandmother.

As soon as I got to Texas, we landed in San Antonio and I saw Terry, of course. We went to dinner and did all types of fun engagements together. That Sunday, my grandmother and I went to his church, and he did a wonderful sermon. After church, we said we'd go out to dinner, and we did. We were back to old times. I really was happy, but at the same time, I did not want to jump into another serious relationship. Although it felt so good and uplifting to be with Terry, I still didn't want to commit right away. I wanted to get myself together (emotionally) before jumping into another relationship. He should have understood that, but he didn't completely. Although he encouraged me, I wasn't afraid to tell him no and go on with getting my life together.

I was still working at Childkeepers for a while, but I began looking for another job. I needed to make more money so that I could be more secure. I needed to find a place to stay because although I was staying with my parents, it was getting a little bit claustrophobic. Of course they were going back and forth in their heads, wondering if I was okay. They complained that I kept asking them for money and were on me about getting a real job. You know how it is when you move back in with your parents. I couldn't even be on the phone or leave the house without them wondering who I was talking to or where I was going. I had already been married, and owned my own home, so coming home and trying to be grown while living under their roof wasn't something that I wanted to deal with. Thus, I began looking for an apartment. I wanted to live in the Beverly Hills adjacent area, which is close to Robertson.

My mom would tell me that wherever I wanted to live, to drive around those areas and see what they had to offer. So I looked online on Westside Rentals to try and find an apartment. I would also drive around, like my mom said. I was on a mission to find an apartment. I received my tax return, which was enough money for a security deposit and my first month's rent. I was set.

After a week of searching, I finally found an apartment, and it was perfect. I had enough for the down payment, as well as the first and last month's rent, which was $1,650. The apartment was on Wooster and Olympic, right around the corner from Robertson, so it was a beautiful area! Not quite Beverly Hills, yet still a really nice area. I always wanted to live in nice areas.

Even though this apartment was a little bit more than I was expecting to pay, I was fine with that. I wanted to live there, and it was perfect for my new beginning. It was a new start for me.

The apartment building was managed by this older Jewish lady, and she seemed to really like me. She was from Russia and had a very strong Russian accent. She showed me the apartment, and I instantly loved it. She told me it would take about a month to get cleaned, and I told her that was fine.

"Are you sure you want it?" she asked me.

"I'm sure! I want it," I insisted.

"Great! Well, I'm going to check your credit and make sure everything is squared away.

I'll give you a call in a couple days."

When she told me she was going to check my credit, of course I was worried because, remember, James had put all of these items in my name. The furniture, the light bill, the water bill, was all in my name. Not to mention the house was in my name. My credit was not that great, and I know he was not that great at paying bills on time. In fact, I would know every time he was late with paying the bills in my name because they would contact me with late notice curtesy calls. I could just imagine what my credit score was, and I was only 24.

A few days went by, and I got a call from her, as she promised.

"Leah?"

"Yes!"

"I don't know what it is, but there's something about you that I like. I'm not going to check your credit."

"Really?!" I couldn't believe it.

"Yes! But I'm not going to give you the apartment that you saw. There's a better apartment that's downstairs, it's right across from my apartment. It's beautiful, it's clean, it's one bedroom, one huge living room, one bathroom, a huge kitchen with a nook for eating… It's perfect for you. It's going to be ready in a few weeks, is that okay?"

"Absolutely!" I said, amazed.

"Do you want to come see it?"

"Sure! I'd love to."

"Great! When you come see it, you can sign the lease, and then it's all yours!"

I couldn't believe it… I was praising the Lord! She didn't even check my credit?! Was this a sign that I was moving in the right direction?

God did say that he'd restore everything that I've lost… I was so excited.

I went and saw the apartment. She was right; it was even more beautiful than the one that I had seen. There were beautiful white floors. Everything was beautiful. The kitchen and bathroom even had brand new tile floors.

So I signed the lease, and I thanked her so much.

"It's something about you that I like… Maybe it's because of your name, you have Hebrew name. Maybe that's why."

"Maybe so!" I said reluctantly.

And that was it! I got my apartment.

Now it was time to furnish it. All my furniture was up north with James. In my storage, I only had a bed and a dresser. I didn't have anything else. My next challenge was getting enough money to furnish the apartment. I didn't have much money at all; I was only getting a couple hundred bucks from working at my job.

I happened to be driving by when I saw a garage sale down the street from my new place. My parents were garage sale lovers; they absolutely loved them. So I was used to going to them and finding hidden treasures at these sales. This garage sale had all of this beautiful wood furniture. There was a desk, a bookcase, a shelf area, and a trunk. There were so many pieces.

I asked the lady how much everything was. "These are beautiful pieces! Why are you getting rid of them?" I asked.

"Well, we're moving back east. We just bought all of this from Pottery Barn."

Pottery Barn? I thought to myself how expensive it was going to be. "Oh, I love it!"

"I can give you everything for a good price."

"How much?" I asked.

"One hundred dollars."

"One hundred dollars?" I gasped. "All of these pieces for a hundred dollars?"

"Everything! The trunk, the desk, the bookshelf, the table, you can have it!"

"I'll take it!" I said quickly.

So now I had that furniture. Then my mom said that she'd buy me a couch. She took me to Melrose and Western, which has many Korean furniture stores. You can get beautiful furniture for really cheap in that area. So I went there, and she bought me a couch.

Not even a week later, I happened to be driving near my parents' house down Redondo, in the mid-Wilshire area, and there was *another* garage sale. I saw this glass coffee table with iron work on the bottom holding it up, with an end table to match. I got out of my car to inquire about it. I wasn't turning my nose up at anything because I barely had any money.

"How much is this table, ma'am?" I asked.

"Hmm. Seventy-five for both."

"Seventy-five for both?!"

"Yes."

"I'll take it!"

I put down the seats in my Ford Explorer and put the new furniture in the back seat. I was so excited. My apartment was coming together. It seemed like my life was getting on the right path, and God was working things out in my favor.

Now it was time for me to find a church.

Trying to find a church was a bit difficult, especially because my roots were at Mt. Everlasting Baptist Church, but as I mentioned, our pastor had passed away. They were in the midst of finding a new pastor, but I was in a deep state of brokenness, I needed a pastor to build me back up. Well, I had met a friend and her daughter before I got married to James, and they were very good for me, ministry wise. The mother was Cynthia, and her daughter was Serenity. They were both very instrumental in my life. Serenity and I were so much alike, as far as getting married to the wrong person and being married for less than a year, then having to leave and start our lives again. Her mother, Cynthia, was a good mentor to me. She really helped me break ties between James. I would go over to their house every day, and they'd feed me and talk to me, encouraging me on what I should be doing, and I really enjoyed the friendship. In fact, one day when I was over there, James had been calling me. Cynthia asked me if that was James, and I said yes.

"Leah, I know you don't want to do this, but you have to stop answering his phone calls. Remember, if you keep answering, you're going to go back, just like you did the last time. It's going to be worse than ever."

"You're right," I admitted.

"You really need to change your number."

"You're right," I said again.

At this point, James hadn't signed the divorce papers yet. So it was really like playing with fire that I was still talking to him, but he had not signed. We were still in limbo.

I took the mentorship I received from them seriously. For so long, the relationship was great. However, something that she told me didn't really sit well with me.

She wanted me to go to her church, but it just didn't feel right in my spirit to join her church. It didn't feel right. It almost felt like Cynthia was really trying to control me. She would tell me what to do with Terry as well, and it would just leave me in a state of confusion sometimes. I felt really down if I didn't please her, and I felt depressed a lot after she criticized me. She'd tell me of my intentions that actually weren't my intentions at all.

One day, one of her friends happened to be over, and I really liked her friend. This friend also had the gift of wisdom and speaking into my spirit. I asked her friend, Sister Sheila, about some of the ways I was feeling.

She comforted me and told me, "Leah, the Lord speaks to you."

"Yes, He does," I confirmed.

"The Lord has told you exactly what to do."

"Yes, he has."

"And don't let anybody else tell you what the Lord is telling you what to do. You know what to do."

It was in that instant that I knew what church I needed to go to. I *knew* I had to be out of Cynthia's control. So I stopped going over to her house, and I began feeling very relieved. I knew that my next step was finding a church. I knew that the church that the Lord was sending me to was the pastor that did the revival in Oakland: Dr. Tigner. I had been going to this big church in Gardena, The City of Deliverance, but the church was really huge, and I just couldn't find my place in it. So even though James had told me to not be involved with Dr. Tigner, I knew in my spirit that was where I was supposed to be. Every time I would go, I felt at home. I felt like it was the place that the Lord wanted me to be. I felt like this was the pastor that I needed in my life to build me back up. I felt that his wife was the big sister that I needed to encourage me, uplift me, and help me. I needed to join, but I needed to be sure that was the church that I wanted to be in.

I prayed about it, and I talked to a lot of people about it. I talked to Dr. Harris' son, Michael Harris the second, about what church I should join. I told him about Dr. Tigner.

"He's an awesome pastor. He's very studious, so if you're planning on learning a lot, then you should go."

"I do want to learn a lot. I really feel comfortable there."

He gave me the okay. But then I felt like my allegiance was to Dr. Harris' son and his wife, Tamara, because his father had been so instrumental in my life, and I loved him so much. Out of loyalty, I decided to join his son's church.

He had a church in the valley. Even though it was far from my apartment, I said that it was okay, I would make the drive.

One night, I drove out there, and I committed that would be the night I was going to join. He preached an awesome sermon. The spirit was high, the praise and worship was on point. It was now time for the doors of the church to open, the time when people who want to join the church or dedicate their lives to the Lord would walk down the aisle. I began getting out of my seat to walk down the aisle.

Right before I could, he closed the aisle and said, "Grab hands with the person next to you for the benediction."

I couldn't help but wonder if this was a sign. Did God not want me to join the church? As soon as I was going to walk down the aisle, it was closed right in front of me? *Hmm.*

It was at that point I knew that even though Pastor Harris the 2nd loved me, and so did his wife, Tamara, it was my destiny to be with Dr. Tigner and his wife, Varie.

Rev. Michael Harris the 2nd, and his wife Tamara were very supportive of my decision to join Dr. Tigner's church.

The next day, I called Dr. Tigner and Varie, and I met with them at their house. Dr. Tigner told me that he was waiting for me, and even had a job for me.

"You have to hurry up and make your decision. Are you going to be with us? Don't wait too long. Remember, I have a job for you!"

I don't know why, but one Sunday morning in 2004, I made my decision. I walked down the aisle of the Memorial Baptist Church, and I became a member. Dr. Tigner became my pastor.

positive one

It seemed as if my life was changing the moment after I joined Pastor Tigner's church. He knew that I had been praise dancing for years and dancing in productions all throughout high school and college. He had also seen me dance at a banquet that he had, and he was so excited and overwhelmed.

"I want you to do that with some of the ladies at our church!" he told me.

So right away, he put me in touch with another girl at the church who was a praise dancer. He asked us to start a praise dance ministry, which we did. It was very successful. God really blessed us when we danced, and I felt that we were very anointed. My whole life was changing, honestly.

I was already ahead of the ministry, and then I ended up getting another job at the Samuel Goldwin Children's Preschool in West LA. I got the position for a preschool teacher, I had a new apartment, this new life, new job, a new church home... I was just really excited.

One day, Tamara, Rev. Michael Harris the second's wife, called me out of the blue and told me that she wanted me to be their Women's Day Speaker.

"I think you'd be great. I want you to speak from the heart and tell your testimony."

I was stunned. I knew the Lord had shown me that what I had gone through was to be a vessel to help other women. However, I didn't know that it would be this fast that I would be sharing my story, because it had just happened. It was still fresh. It hadn't even been a year, only a few months.

Yet I prepared a speech. It was called *What is Your Fragrance?*

My speech was to talk to the women about fragrance. I told them that a fragrance is something that goes through a terrible process. In fact, it's the result of not so good smelling items that are crushed together—like manure, for example. When they're put together, they make a beautiful smelling fragrance. In the Bible, there's a Scripture that says, "We are the fragrance of Christ." (2 Corinthians 2:15)

I encouraged the women by telling them that all the things that we go through create a beautiful fragrance that follows us wherever we go. That smell is our testimony. When people smell the fragrance on us, we must tell them about the journey that we went through in order for that scent to be so beautiful. We must tell about the horrible, crushing, not so good smelling incidents and situations in our lives that created the beautiful fragrance that they smelled today. That was my intro for my speech. I told them that my fragrance was made with disobedience. I did what the Lord did not want me to do, which was marry a man that He did not want me to marry. Through that, I told them the story of what it was like to be with him, leaving him, and then currently being on a path of restoration, reinvention, and where the Lord was restoring everything that I had lost.

My testimony touched so many women in the room that they were crying… they were cheering… they were standing on their feet. This was a confirmation that this was exactly what the Lord had wanted me to do.

My new life was taking on a rare form, and I was really excited. I was very happy.

But dating was very difficult.

Dating was… disappointing. I was going through a divorce, and James still had not signed the papers. So I had to file some more paperwork in order for the divorce to go through, because he was not signing.

I went back to "We The People," and they told me there was something else I could file which could force the divorce with or without his signature. Going through that was frustrating because he was still sending me letters, flowers, and candy in hopes that I would finally come back.

He even sent an anniversary card a year after our marriage. August 23rd. *Happy Anniversary? We're not even together,* I thought to myself. I think he was living in a different world as to what was really happening. He really didn't believe that I had made my decision. I guess he was right because the last time I'd gone back. But this particular time was longer, and I still hadn't gone back. So I didn't understand why he just wouldn't sign.

I had Terry in San Antonio, and even though we were going back and forth, like I said, I didn't really want to commit. I wanted to see what was out there, and I really wanted to give myself some time to heal. I would meet different people, and as soon as I would tell them that I was going through a divorce, they wouldn't be interested in me anymore. They would like me, we would have chemistry, things would be going great, but it wouldn't matter after I told them. It was a devastating situation to be in at the age of 24 going through a divorce. It seemed like no one my age was going through what I was going through. I had no one I could relate to or anyone who really understood my position. I was *trying* to move on, but it was so hard to do.

Terry would come into town, and we would hang out and have fun, but then he would go back to San Antonio, and he traveled a lot. All over the country, actually. So it was really hard to establish a relationship. Although he wanted me to commit, I just didn't understand how I would do that if he was traveling so much. I wouldn't hear from him for months at a time, and then out of the blue, I would get a letter in the mail, or he would send me a book that he wanted me to read or a postcard from where he was preaching. It was just weird. I didn't understand him at all. I also could not understand the vicissitudes of his hot and cold behavior. He would be upset with me one minute, and then tell me how much he loved me the next. It just was really, really awkward. Therefore, I thought I had room to see other people.

I would date, and I would feel like I was getting my groove back, but like I said, every time I brought up my divorce, it would be ruined. Especially for the younger guys. Younger guys didn't have kids, they had never even been married before. They didn't understand going through a divorce. Older guys, though, they understood going through a divorce, because they'd probably gone through it themselves. They had kids and had lived more. But it was the younger guys, the ones that were more my age, that were the most disappointing to date.

Another thing that would turn them off is that since I was trying to start my life on a better foot, I'd promised the Lord that I would not have sex with anyone until I got married again. I felt like all of the crazy and irrational decisions that I made with James were mostly because I was sexually and emotionally tied to him. I thought that if I didn't sexually tie myself to another man, then I could be mentally strong and able to make sound decisions. So when I would date guys, that would be the first thing I said.

"I'm not having sex with anyone until I get married..."

At first, they would think that was so honorable and great, but then after a while of not having sex, they would all become disinterested. They'd just stop liking me. Their interest would come to a halt, and their calls would fade into oblivion.

Finally, one day in the mail, I got a letter from James, and he signed off on the divorce. I finally could file the papers. This was almost eight months after leaving him. I sent them in, and now it was just a matter of waiting for the divorce to be final. I was in a predicament where I wanted to date and move forward, but I couldn't because I wasn't officially divorced yet. I felt like I couldn't fully move forward until that was behind me.

During the time where I was heavily hanging out with Serenity, she introduced me to this guy named Donnie. Donnie was very, very attractive. I mean, so fine. He was in the marketing field and had graduated from UCLA. I felt like he wasn't just a great catch, but he was also a great friend. He was a great person to bounce ideas off of, to hang out with and have intellectual conversations with. He loved the Lord, he loved church... so I thought it was a great connection. We'd go out to dinner, we'd go to the movies... but I had to be honest and tell him that I was going through a divorce. It seemed like as soon as I told him, he no longer wanted to pursue a romantic relationship with me, so we became just friends. *Really* good friends, but of course my feelings were hurt that he never wanted to pursue the romantic side because of my divorce that was pending. But it was okay; I was happy just being his friend. He was the type of friend where we'd both go out on dates and come back and tell each other all about them. Even if we heard something funny on the news, we'd call each other and laugh about it. I really enjoyed our friendship.

Donnie ended up meeting someone and eventually living with them and later marrying them. Although things did not work out for us, we stayed really good friends.

There was another guy that was at my church who was a musician. Keith. He wasn't really my type. But he had been divorced himself, with two kids. He didn't care about my divorce at all. He lived with his grandparents off of Slauson, north of Crenshaw. He persistently pursued me, but I just couldn't find it in myself to like him. I talked to Dr. Tigner about it. I would always talk to him about the different guys I dated. He encouraged me to date, but always reminded me to never take it too seriously.

I started going on dates with Keith, and he began getting serious with me quickly. Almost stalker serious. It was to the point where I'd be at a place, and he'd follow me. He'd go through these crying spells, and he'd pop up at my house—I mean all kinds of things. It was just too much. It was a little frightening because I felt myself starting to like this guy. We had great chemistry and conversation, but it just wasn't for me. We'd hang out almost every day, but I'd never put a title on it.

One day, Dr. Tigner explained, "You need to stop hanging out with this guy because he really likes you. He's taking it seriously, and I know this isn't for you."

You know it's bad when your mother chimes in to tell you what your conscience is telling you. My mom mentioned to me it was going to fall into fatal attraction category if I didn't let him go, since

I didn't feel the same way that he felt about me. How was I supposed to get out of this relationship that I wasn't even supposed to be in?

I did like him. He was so sweet. He was very thoughtful and generous, he'd take me to concerts, the movies, bowling—I mean all sorts of really fun things. He did not make a lot of money, but he would go out of his way to impress me, which was sweet. He'd bring his kids around me, and I loved kids. He was a great guy, but I knew I needed to get out of it.

It took me a long time to get out of it. I can't really explain it, but I began falling even deeper for him. Have you ever been in a relationship that you know you shouldn't be in? You try to tell yourself you're not in the relationship, but you really are. That was what was happening.

On the other side, my job situation was a little weird. Being a preschool teacher just wasn't working out. I really hated working there. My hours were from 10 a.m. to 7 p.m., and dealing with little kids was really tough. But I made the best of it. I would make a lot of friends out of the parents, and sometimes the parents would hire me to be their kids' nanny for different weeknights or weekends. I made a nice amount of money on the side doing that.

Eventually Pastor Tigner put me over the youth department of the church. I was really busy with the youth, doing the dance ministry, and I would also teach Bible study every Tuesday night. I'd teach the girls, and then another young minister would teach the boys. I had about 30 girls every Tuesday night, and I really got into my teaching groove. I would teach the girls about the Lord, and I loved that. I'd teach them the right way to worship and the importance of church, about people, their character, and even the way they should live. It was actually really fun. I made a lot of great relationships where the youth began to really look up to me. I really appreciated that.

Being a leader for the youth while being a new member in the church was challenging. People did not take to me very well, because I have always been a very "take charge" kind of person. Especially when someone gives something to me. I was already accustomed to being in leadership positions. So when Pastor Tigner put me over the dance ministry, I was ready. I was setting schedules, doing rehearsals, figuring out costumes. It was really successful. We even had Friday night live services once a month where we'd do dance, singing, and a testimony. We had a young preacher for those nights, and it was becoming a big deal. Even though things were successful, people did not take to my leadership. I had a lot of conflicts between the ladies telling me that I was taking over and that I was bossy, or that I needed to take a class on how leaders should conduct themselves. It was really challenging, and much different than the pastor I grew up with. It seemed that I always had challenges with women because I was always misunderstood. The pastor I grew up with would always stand up for me or call people in for talking about me. Dr. Tigner was different; he made me stand on my own two feet and face the criticism without his help. I would cry often to him, and he would just look at me and say, "So what are you going to do about it?" He was going to make me a strong leader even if it killed me.

I never saw myself as bossy. I saw myself as getting the job done. I followed instruction to a T, so whatever Dr. Tigner wanted to see within the Youth Department, I wanted to get it done, and I wanted him to be pleased with my leadership. Although I was taking over and organizing, administrating, I knew that was my gift. A lot of people were intimated by that or felt the need to try to be better. It caused a lot of problems. I'd find myself being alone a lot, or just being with older people, because they understood me better than young people. It was really awkward, but I was used to it. To be honest, I needed this because it was making me stronger.

One particular day, Dr. Tigner had a teaching conference. In the conference, he teaches pastors from all over the world how to preach expositorily, which means interpreting the Greek and the Hebrew of the verse and making it palatable and simple for people to understand. He had been doing the conference for over twenty years.

Because the youth department was growing at an amazing rate, Pastor Tigner decided to do a youth conference in Palm Springs. He wanted me to teach the girls' class. He called it the Ladylike Class, where we would talk about women in the Bible, but we'd make it practical and on their level where they could understand it, and even do some projects and activities that would bring it down to where they were in life at that moment.

I talked to them about Ruth and how she lost her husband and had to pick up wheat in Boaz's field. As a result, Boaz fell in love with her, and they got married. She went from working in the field to owning the field.

I also did a piece on the Song of Solomon. It was about being single and relationships and how you know that a man loves you. This lesson was about how King Solomon loved this sheep herder, Abishag. She was invited to the kingdom to minister to King David, who was sick. Historically, in those days, when an older king was sick, they would search the land for a beautiful young woman to come to the kingdom and minister to the king so he would feel better.

Abishag lived on the outskirts of Israel. Solomon, King David's son, saw Abishag and fell deeply in love with her. She wasn't royalty, she was a sheep herder, yet still King Solomon dropped everything to fall in love with her and have her as his wife. It is one of the most beautiful stories that you will ever hear.

As I was telling the young girls about Solomon and Abishag, of course I was so into it because of how into love I am. I really wanted these young girls to know how far a man will go to prove his love for the one he loves. In the story, Solomon put a banner over Abishag's head, which means that she was his. He openly displayed his love for her in front of the entire kingdom. He wanted everyone to know. Solomon would have leaped over valleys and jumped over mountains to get to her, meaning that even though she was far away, it didn't matter. Whatever it took, he was going to win her love, and no matter how far she was he would go through leaps and bounds to get her. I was so involved in this story because I love love. It was reminding me of all the things that James did do, yet all the things he didn't do.

As I was telling this story to the girls, with all of my theatrics and different tones in my voice, really trying to reach the girls, out of the blue, one of the girls raised her hand and said, "Excuse me, I have a question."

"Yes?"

"I just want to know is this true?" she asked.

"Yes! It's absolutely true. It's in the Bible! Anything in the Bible is true."

"No, I know that. But is it for real? Does this really happen in life?"

"Yes. It definitely happens in life," I confirmed.

"Well, how do you know that? How do you know so much about love? I mean you're telling all these stories, but how do you know that all this stuff is real? Because I've never seen this before."

"It's real…"

"But how do you know? You don't seem that much older than us. You can't possibly know about this kind of love!"

"Well… let me tell you my story," I sighed.

So I just began to transparently tell my story. The story of James and me. I explained to them how he blew my mind at 18 years old by buying me gifts, taking me to five-star restaurants and hotels, buying me anything that he could get his hands on. I told them the story of how I didn't have a car, and he figured out with my grandmother how to get me a car. I told them how I didn't have a computer, and I'd be up late at the library writing papers and came home to a computer with a printer, and access to the internet. How I didn't have a cell phone, so he bought me one. I even told them how he showered me in jewelry that I didn't have. My point for the stories was to tell them how he blew my mind. I explained to the girls how the only thing I could give James in return was my body. And how I gave myself to him over, and over, and over again, until I began to lose myself. I told them how he said that when I graduated, he would marry me. I loved him so much that I figured out how to graduate in three years so that he would marry me. Twenty-one units per semester, 13 units in the summer, all for him to still not marry me right after graduation, like he promised.

I told the girls how after two years of being at home, he finally married me, but when he did he didn't own up to our marriage and hid me from the world—the complete opposite of what Solomon did for his lover. I had no banner over my head. He told people that he wasn't my lover, that he was my friend.

I told them how I lived in a rat-infested studio apartment on top of the church so that he could still take care of his girlfriend that lived in his condo. I told them how depressed I became, and how much weight I lost from not being able to eat. I told them how I had no self-esteem left and felt inferior to James. Because the person I loved so much did not love me.

I continued to tell them how I eventually left and got my life back. That the woman in front of them was currently building her life back up. I told them the story so that they wouldn't fall into the same trap that I did. I told them that if I could spend the rest of my life making sure they didn't fall into the traps that I did, then I would do just that. I began getting so emotional that tears were rolling down my face.

I turned to the young girl that had asked me the question. "That's why I'm so passionate about this. About love, and how somebody is supposed to love you. Solomon's love is how it's supposed to be. Not how I had it."

After I told my story, there was not a dry eye in the room. I had those young girls in the palm of my hand. Anything I would tell them, they listened. I couldn't get rid of them; they were hanging on to me from that point on. They were going back to my hotel room, sleeping on my floor, asking me all kinds of questions. I heard about abuse, I heard about parents, I heard about dating older men… They were telling me everything.

When I got back from Palm Springs, the stories of these girls were pounding on my heart. I decided to start the LadyLike class in my apartment. I would have them over, and we'd have slumber parties. We would do makeup classes and talk about Eve, the first woman, and how beautiful she was. I made sure they knew how beautiful God designed them each to be, with all their assets and God-given talents. I taught them how we should use our gifts to the fullest to serve the Lord. We talked about Martha, and how Martha's gift was cooking. After the lesson, I would teach them how to cook. I taught them about Dorcas, whose gift was sewing. She sewed for the poor. After teaching them about Dorcas, I taught them how to sew.

It just became this amazing group. The LadyLike Class. We kept it going. The girls would bring their friends, and their friends began bringing their friends. And it grew and grew. I felt like this was what the Lord wanted me to do. This was why I'd gone through all of this... This was what I was dreaming about when I left James. These were the visions I was having. This was the testimony that I was supposed to share with all these girls. I absolutely loved it.

Of course, when something is receiving a lot of attention and popularity, other people feel like they can do it too, and do it better. There were other groups at the church popping up, of people wanting to do girl groups in competition with mine. I was really deflated about it, but I just kept pushing and focusing on my LadyLike Class.

So I had my LadyLike Class and my preschool job. But I decided that I wanted to go back to teaching elementary school. I wanted to be on a regular schedule, not a night schedule.

I called back to my first teaching job, when I was teaching first grade before I married James. I asked if they had any teaching positions open, and they did. They had a third grade teaching position open. I interviewed with the principal, and he hired me right away.

I was literally coming into my own and loving my newfound strength and purpose. I started teaching third grade at First Lutheran Elementary School in Koreatown. I was feeling good, a feeling I hadn't felt in a long time. I felt like I was where I was supposed to be. So I was over the youth at my church, teaching the LadyLike Class, and teaching third graders. Even though dating gave me challenges, I was okay... I felt that I was on a good path and things were really working out in my favor.

positive two

inally, after a year and a half, the divorce was final. All of the papers were in, and I was feeling confident about my decision to divorce James and my new life that was unfolding. I felt that I could actually move forward now. I was still teaching at First Lutheran Elementary School, and I began having the desire to complete my master's in education like I had started out before I married James. I knew I couldn't go to UCLA, UC Berkeley, or USC anymore because I would have to re-apply, which was a rigorous process.

My mom and dad were telling me that if I wanted to further my education, I was on my own. I needed to go to a school that I could afford, somewhere that would give me some sort of financial assistance because my parents were completely over with paying for my schooling.

I applied to Pepperdine University, and I got in for the Master's Program in Education. It worked really well with my schedule because I could work full time and go to class on the weekends, as well as Friday nights. So it would take about two and a half years for me to complete the master's program, which would be great because then I could earn more money and be more independent. My grandmother was actually helping me out with my rent, because even though I was teaching full time, a couple months of living taught me that I would be completely broke after paying my rent each month. So I would pay part of my rent, and my grandmother would supplement the rest. I was really blessed to have her; she continuously had my back and supported me through everything.

My apartment was fully furnished and absolutely gorgeous. I had Ultrasuede couches that were a cream color, with bedazzled throw pillows from one of my favorite Indian stores. I even had hints of pink, turquoise, light blue, and lavender. It was so beautiful! I put flower arrangements everywhere, and my bathroom was all white, with a white shower curtain and beautiful white rugs. I put together my own shelves for my bathroom, utilizing different items from Target. I was very frugal, but it was beautiful. I knew how to be resourceful. I had my bedroom set from Oakland, so I still had my sleigh bed and my detailed cherrywood dresser. Full closet and mirrored doors. My kitchen was all white with cream-tiled floors. I decorated my kitchen table with exquisite china, silk napkins—even the napkin clips matched the décor of the whole place. Everything was neat, organized, and matched beautifully. I loved being able to make a place reflect my eye for beauty, and also loved having my own sacred space. I kept it super clean, because James taught me to always keep my space organized and clean. I never forgot that.

One day, when I stopped by my parents' house after work, my mom told me that I had a certified letter in the mail.

Certified letter? Okay...

I opened the letter, and it was a letter from a lawyer. James' lawyer. It said that he was ready to assume the loan on the house that he had purchased when I was in Oakland. Remember, the house was in my name.

The letter expressed that he was ready to put the house in his name, on one condition: that I'd send back my wedding ring.

That was disturbing to me. When I came back from Oakland, he would write me letters every day. Every single day.

I was in so much debt from all the furniture, utilities, and insurance bills being in my name. All the credit card debt was in my name. It was my grandmother that helped me and paid all my bills off. So literally, he was pretty much living debt-free. All he had to pay as it pertained to me was the mortgage on the home that we'd lived in.

After I left him, I didn't want to get a lawyer to sue him for the house because he paid for it. He made over $100,000 down payment on the house, so I really felt bad taking the house from him. He deserved it—he could have it. As long as he was making the payments, I was fine. Like I said, I would get calls informing me that he was late, but he'd always end up paying it. I just kept it in my name and went about my life.

But that was a lesson that I learned: to never assume that someone is going to be nice to you after you leave them. When you get a divorce, it is all about business. It is not about emotions or feelings; it is simply and only business. You must take care of business and take care of yourself because they will not. Put your heart aside and navigate with your brain. I hate to be so cold, but this is how it is. No one is thinking about the other person or the other spouse. They are hurt, so they are operating in hurt, not in fairness or in love.

So I was worried, to say the least. I had seen how he was with lawyers and suing people. I remember while we were dating, he sued his cleaners for ruining one of his shirts! He was very vindictive, and to be honest, I was frightened. The lawyer said that if I didn't send the wedding ring back, then I'd have the house in my name forever. I couldn't believe it. As nice as I was to him? I'd tried to do the divorce nicely. I didn't tell anybody in his church that I was leaving, I didn't make a big ruckus about how he treated me… I could have done so many things to him that would have ruined his career and the church. But I didn't. I left silently. And now he was going to send me a letter saying that if I didn't send back my wedding ring, that I would have the house in my name forever? A house that he knew I couldn't afford?

The problem was I didn't have the ring anymore. My grandmother paid off my credit cards, and my parents paid off my bills, but it was so much that I was in over $50,000 worth of debt. I had to get the money from somewhere to help her. I pawned that ring… I had to get myself out of debt. I needed to be in a position where I could live.

Interestingly enough, in the process of pawning the ring, I found out that he'd lied about its worth. When he gave it to me, he told me that he'd saved up a large amount of money for it. Remember it was a 5.1 carat, pear-shaped diamond ring. He told me it was worth $50,000. He showed me insurance papers and the diamond certification confirming that price.

I was shopping around to sell the ring, to find the best price for it. I went to pawn shop after pawn shop. For awhile, every shop that I went to, I heard the same price over and over: $3,000.

I finally asked a nice lady at a pawn shop how it could be only worth three thousand dollars. She told me that it had many flaws. She took her specialized diamond magnifying glass and showed me there was a feather in it, and there were black carbon spots inside of the diamond—I mean all kinds of things. It was ridiculous! I even showed them the paperwork that James gave me, yet it still didn't prove what I thought it to be worth.

I kept shopping. One shop told me it was worth $4,000, another shop told me $5,000. Finally, one particular pawn shop in Beverly Hills, on Beverly Drive, gave me the most for it. $8,000. That was the highest price that I was offered. Can you imagine how devastated I was? But still, I didn't make a big deal about it. I took that $8,000 and used it to pay off what I could. I tithed off it as well. And that was it. I was done with the ring and really upset about the lies. The more I thought about the pear-shaped ring, the more I thought about the prophecy. The only reason I wanted that particular ring was because of the prophecy. I wanted everything to fall in line with what my friend said would happen. That is not how prophecies from God come to pass. You don't have to do anything or make anything happen; it happens because it is supposed to, just as God said it. This was a hard lesson to learn, but I learned it the hard way.

So when I got that letter asking me to give the ring back, I was completely shocked and overwhelmed. What was I going to give him if I didn't have the ring anymore?

I had to get a lawyer. It's so funny; he didn't want to get a lawyer involved when it came down to the divorce, but he was willing to get a lawyer involved to get the ring back. Something was very fishy because, if I knew him like I thought, there was something that he wanted to do with this house. Did he want to put Dianne in it? I wasn't really sure, but knowing him, he wanted to do something with the house and get my name off of it. Which was fine, because I didn't want the house anyway. But to ask me for the ring back, I felt that was very insulting and devastating. Especially because I didn't want to take the house from him, and knowing that he put all the bills in my name, I still never asked him about it. Now he wanted the ring back so that he could assume the loan? I was not going to let him off easy; this was going to be a fight.

There was a particular woman at Dr. Tigner's church who was into real estate. She was very savvy about the logistics and the laws of it. Her name was Denise. She was responsible for finding and helping my pastor and his wife, Varie, get their home. They bought Ray Charles' mansion in View Park. Denise was the key person responsible for making the deal happen. Even though it was rundown at the time they bought it, they renovated it, and it's stunning to this day.

So I called her and told her what my situation was. I told her that my ex-husband was trying to make me assume the loan on the house unless I sent my wedding ring back. She told me that I was going to have to get a real estate lawyer.

I was 25 years old at the time. Get a real estate lawyer? I'd already been through enough with the divorce, now a real estate lawyer? I just had to tell her I didn't have the money for that.

"Don't worry. I have the perfect person that can help you," she assured me.

She gave me this person's information in the Brentwood area. He was a real estate lawyer who specialized in these types of cases, especially divorce, property, etc.

I went to meet him that day, and I told him my story.

"Well... he has every right to keep this house in your name."

"Yeah, but I can't afford it! I just started working as a third grade teacher. I don't make that much money! I only make about $35K annually, if that! I do a couple tutoring gigs on the side to make some cash, but I don't have any money to pay a house note."

"Well. I need $2,000 for a retainer fee, and then we can figure out what we're going to do with this house."

Great. Now I had to figure out how I was going to get the money to pay for this lawyer.

Of course, the first person I thought to call was my grandmother. I told her and my parents about the situation. My parents didn't feel that sorry for me because they felt that I'd done this to myself, involving myself with this man. Which I had, so I couldn't be upset about that. My grandmother was honestly the only option I had. I felt bad, but I had to ask her.

"Mama, can you please let me borrow this money so I can get this lawyer and just be done with this man?"

"Of course," she said without hesitation.

She wrote the check to the lawyer, and even went with me to meet him. She just wanted me out of it. Everybody at this point was sick of James and didn't even want to hear his name anymore. Including me!

When my grandmother and I met with the lawyer, he had more questions.

"Why did you get rid of the ring?" he asked.

Why did I get rid of the ring?

Well, I'd gotten rid of it because he put me in so much debt. Furniture debt, credit card debt. Then he'd told me to pawn it so that I could get myself out of the debt he'd put me in.

"Well, how did he tell you?"

And all of a sudden, I had an epiphany.

Remember when I left, he would send me jelly beans and he would only send me certain colors that I liked? Sometimes flowers too? Along with those gifts, he would send letters. In those letters, he would say how sorry he was, and that if I came back he'd be a better husband. He kept telling me how good I was to him and all the things he loved about me. I was getting a letter every single day. Every single day. I kept all of them. In one of the letters he told me to pawn the ring to get myself out of the debt that he put me in.

I told the lawyer.

"Do you have that exact letter?" he asked me.

"Yes!"

I'd kept every single letter. I don't know why, but I kept every single letter James wrote me in an envelope. Even in order. Each letter was on his business letterhead, with his name, church address, and his phone number.

I rushed home after the meeting, went to the place in my room where I'd hidden them, and I found the letter. Just like I had thought, it said: *Please pawn the ring to get yourself out of the debt that I put you in.*

Immediately I called the lawyer and told him I'd found the letter.

"Great. Please bring me a copy ASAP."

Without hesitation, I got back in the car and took him the copy.

"This is all we need," he said with a smile.

He highlighted the words that said, "pawn the ring," sent it back to James' lawyer, and that's all she wrote! I did not have to assume the loan. James had to assume the loan and pay for the house.

I was free from James, and free from that house.

As you could probably imagine, I wasn't hearing from James anymore. No more letters, no more phone calls. He couldn't call me anyway, because I changed my number. I knew he was pissed off. I was dead to him, and that was completely fine, because I needed to move on.

So I was divorced, finally, and had no ties to that house—thank God! He could move in whoever he wanted to move in, and do whatever he wanted to do, whether it was with Chipmunk 2 or Dianne or whoever! I didn't care. I was just so happy to be free.

I was still teaching, I was going to school on nights and weekends, and I was finally putting my life back together again. I was still over the youth, and I was just having a great time.

I was still pretty insecure when it came to myself and dating. I continued dating the divorced musician who had two kids and was living with his grandparents. Keith.

Dr. Tigner was not very happy with my dating him. He thought that it was a dead-end street, and that I was going down from James, not going up. It was the weirdest thing—every time I'd be hanging out with Keith, Dr. Tigner would happen to call me. He never hesitated to tell me I shouldn't be with him.

But, when you think about it, when you're getting out of a bad relationship and you are hurting, it's almost as if you want to be with whoever is giving you attention.

Even though I knew Keith wasn't for me, he was good for me at the time. Or so I thought.

He would pick me up on Sundays, and we'd go bowling, or to the movies, and he'd listen to me. He'd let me say whatever I needed. He'd even email me these beautiful letters every morning saying how grateful he was that I had given him a chance. It was very nice for me at the time. I needed to be lifted up a bit. I had been kicked down so much that it felt good to be lifted up. When I would take him around my family, I would introduce him as my friend. My grandmother would look at him kind of crazy, as if she was looking past him and not at him. I would find it so funny. I just knew that she knew he wasn't my type. He was a little overweight, and just wasn't the kind of handsome and charismatic guy I was used to dating. My dad would just play it off and didn't take it too seriously at all.

Tia would try to set me up with different people because she knew what I had been through and knew that I needed some psychological and emotional uplifting. She knew that I needed to be around people who were for me and wanted the best for me, instead of people that didn't. So she set me up with a guy who owned a barbershop in the valley. Kevin. He was a little younger than me, but very sweet and nice. We had seen him on several occasions, and Tia was really close to him. She asked me one day if I would ever give him a chance.

"No, I don't really like younger guys," I said.

You have to remember James was 17 years older than me. Keith was 7 years older than me. Terry was 12 years older than me. I liked older guys and just felt better with them.

But the barbershop owner was very persistent. He kept bothering Tia about me, but I just couldn't wrap my head around it. I tried getting coffee with him, but I felt like I was dating my little brother. Older sisters always take care of younger brothers like a mother. That's how I felt with Kevin. He was sweet and very mature, even business minded. I just did not want to date a younger guy.

One night, Kevin invited me out to his First Friday Service. On First Fridays of every month he'd turn his barbershop into a spiritual club, where people would do spoken word about the Lord, and bands would come and play gospel songs. It was a young, hip, and fun crowd, and I enjoyed myself so much that I began going to the service on occasion. It was very flattering that he liked me, and I did try to entertain the idea of dating him, so I would go to these events to see if dating him would work. At the First Friday services, he would also have clean comedians do a set. On one particular night, a comedian was doing a set with an illustration using his keys. For some strange reason he threw his keys in the audience, and they hit me smack dab in the head! Out of all the people in the crowd, why would they hit me? I called Dr. Tigner and asked him why the keys would hit me, out of all the people at the event. He said, "Because you were not supposed to be there. That was the Lord giving you a sign that the place where you were was not for you." I didn't listen. I just thought it was a coincidence.

Keith couldn't stand that Kevin liked me, though. I wasn't taking Keith that seriously, so I would tell him about guys that I was dating. I would see these little tendencies of control that Keith would have, and I would see these signs of obsession with me. I would ignore it. Sometimes he would be telling me how much he liked me and wanted to be with me and would start crying. They weren't good signs. I would laugh it off and think it was cute, but I mean seriously, who's going to tell you that he likes you that much, when he barely knows you, and then just starts crying? That isn't a stable person. He also wasn't stable with his job, and he would play at different churches. He lived with his grandparents… It just wasn't a good situation. It didn't make me comfortable to be with him, yet I was comfortable enough to keep him around. It was hard to walk away because we had unbelievable chemistry. But I just knew it wasn't for me.

One particular day, Tia and I were meeting with Kevin and some other guy at this restaurant, and Keith kept calling me constantly on my cell phone, asking me where I was. I told him where I was, and that I was with Tia. Of course I didn't tell him that I was with Kevin, because I didn't want him to know.

I continued with dinner, and we all ate and had a great time. After dinner, Kevin walked me to my car, and I got in and drove home.

All of a sudden, when I was in the car, my phone started ringing out of control. It was Keith!

"Hello?" I said,

"I know where you are."

"Yeah, I know you know where I am, I told you where I was," I said, confused.

"No, I know. One of my friends saw you with another guy."

I was thinking to myself, *One of your friends saw me with another guy?*

We were in a White neighborhood… Kevin is African American and Tia is African American. I didn't really see that many other African Americans besides who we were with. So who was his friend that saw me?

"My barber saw you at this restaurant, and said you were with another guy," he continued.

"Your barber? Who is your barber?"

I almost started getting nervous. Did I have people knowing who I was, and not only that, they were telling on me?

"Leah, just tell me who you were with. Just tell me."

"I was with Kevin and Tia. What's the big deal?"

"You lied to me. You didn't tell me that you were with Kevin!"

"Because I know how you feel about Kevin, so why would I say that I was with him? It was nothing."

The tone of his voice was so odd. It was coming off too harsh even if I had been his girlfriend. Why was he coming off so possessive? It was kind of reminding me of James, and it didn't make me feel good.

I got off the phone and tried to go on about my business once I got back to my apartment. But all night long he kept calling me, badgering me about who I was with.

A few weeks later, he kept telling me that he had something to tell me. He wouldn't tell me on the phone, though; he insisted on telling me in person. Something just wasn't right.

One night after my Friday Night Alive service at my church, Keith wanted to take me to the beach. I was thinking he wanted to have a romantic night, confessing his love for me. *Here we go,* I thought to myself. Once again, I was about to be put in another awkward situation.

As we were walking on the beach, he began to tell me, "Leah, do you remember that night you went out with Tia and Kevin?"

"Yes. Why?"

"Remember how I told you that my barber saw you there and you kept wondering how he knew you?"

"Yes, where is this going?"

"It wasn't my barber that saw you."

"Well then, who saw me?"

"It was me," he confessed.

I could tell he could see the confusion on my face.

"When you told me the name of the restaurant you were at, I came to see who you were with."

"You? Excuse me? You lied to me and said that your barber saw me when it was you?"

"I was so embarrassed that I did that, but I didn't trust where you were, and I wanted to see for myself."

"You didn't trust where I was? Why?" I started thinking to myself, *This man is a stalker!*

"I saw him walk you to your car and everything. I couldn't stand to see it."

"Keith, you followed me?"

I was speechless. I didn't think that was funny, I didn't think it was sweet that he ended up telling me the truth. He was showing me that he was crazy. But I tried to keep a calm demeanor. "Well, I'm glad you told me… but that makes me feel like I can't really trust you," I said.

"How do you think I feel? I can't really trust you either."

Couldn't trust me? I was starting to understand why Dr. Tigner told me that this wasn't for me. I had never been with a stalker before. I had never been with someone who went out of his way to find where I was. We weren't even in a committed relationship.

We left each other that night. I told Dr. Tigner about everything the next day, and all he said was, "Leah, if you don't get out of this relationship, it's only going to get worse!"

Deep down, I knew he was right. Yet I still felt so many emotions. Have you ever had chemistry so deeply with someone beyond physical attraction? No, we didn't have sex, but even our affection was just beyond. I could not break out of it! I was trying to break away, but it was hard. To be honest, I still dated him because of how nicely he treated me. I had almost forgotten about the stalking situation.

positive three

At my job at the elementary school, I was having a little bit of trouble because enrollment was low. When you teach at a private school, and your enrollment is low, that means that your pay will get cut, you may get laid off, and the school may close. The school was going through so many changes, and they were beginning to let some teachers go. They kept me because I was well liked with the students and parents. I had a good relationship with the principal as well. He told me that he really wanted to keep me, but that I might have to start teaching two grades at a time so that we could save the school. I told him that I was willing to do whatever it took to keep my position and my job. I had to continue paying for my rent, my other bills, and school at Pepperdine.

One particular day during the summer, in June, I went to work, and he told me, "I don't know what we're going to do next year. I don't know if the school is going to be open. I'll let you know, but we want to keep you!"

I had a great rapport with the children, parents, and staff, so I felt very confident about my job.

June went by, July went by, and August went by before I got a phone call from the principal.

"We tried our best this summer to keep First Lutheran open, but we're going to have to close the school. We can't even give you your last check—we have no money. I'm so sorry!"

That shouldn't be a problem, I thought to myself. I thought I could get a job at another school quickly. I started looking online for job openings. What I failed to realize was that it was August. Every school that I called to see if they had an opening didn't, because schools take teacher applications in March, and by August the school is already all staffed and ready for the new school year in September.

So I was living from my last check from July. As a teacher, you have a choice, since we get paid once a month: you can get paid a lump sum for ten months, or you can cut your paycheck so that you can get a smaller paycheck but be paid all twelve months. I'd decided that I wanted my paycheck all twelve months, so that I could have money every month. But this month since I wasn't getting paid, I was literally down to my last dime.

One particular night, I went out with Keith to a Stevie Wonder homage concert. Before I go out, I always call my bank account to see how much money I have to play with. But this night I didn't check until I was already at the concert. It was almost like God told me to check my account. I called my bank, and the automated Bank of America message said: *You have 82 cents available.*

Not even a dollar... 82 cents! I was ready to leave.

When the concert ended, I told Keith that I couldn't stay around and that I had to go. My first thought was to go to my parents' house. When you're still a kid, and you don't have any money, the first thought you have is to go to your parents. Well, I was 26 years old, with 82 cents in my account, and my first thought was still to go to my parents.

I drove over to my parents' house, and it was around 10 p.m. My dad was on the couch watching TV, like usual, and my mom was in her room. I walked in, and my dad was surprised to see me.

"Hey, Leah! What are you doing here so late?"

"I just had to come see you," I sighed.

"What's wrong?" he asked.

"Dad, you know how I got laid off? And they couldn't pay me my last check?"

"Yeah?" he said, puzzled.

"I called my bank today, and they said I only have 82 cents left in my account."

"Yeah?" he said again.

"Could you guys help me until I find something?"

"I'm sorry. I can't help you."

"But Dad! I only have 82 cents. What do you mean you can't help me?"

"I am so sorry, Leah, I can't help you," he said calmly.

I knew that I was on my own for college. They'd paid for my undergrad tuition, my wedding, they even paid to get me on my feet after my divorce. I'll admit that I put my parents through a lot, but I was a daddy's girl. I knew my dad loved me... so I was shocked!

I was raised in the type of family that, if one parent said something, you couldn't go to the other parent and ask again. So I couldn't go in the other room and ask my mom. She was definitely not going to go against my dad.

"All right, well, I'll talk to you tomorrow."

He didn't even get off the couch, nor take his eyes off the TV.

I left the house, walked back to my car, and immediately started crying. I couldn't stop. I kept feeling like no matter how much I progressed, I was ending up at square one. The tears were absolutely uncontrollable and unstoppable. I started thinking about rent, gas money, food… How was I going to do it?

I started driving back to my apartment, still crying. Out of nowhere I heard the voice of the Lord tell me, *Everything that hits your hand… give me 10 percent.*

Everything that hits my hand?! I have 82 cents! How am I supposed to pay tithes off of 82 cents?! I don't even have an income to tithe off of!

I heard the voice of the Lord again: *Everything that hits your hand… give me 10 percent.*

You would think that would be a weird instruction at a time like this. But I had nothing else to say than *Okay!* What else was I going to say?

The next day was church. I was at the 8 a.m. service. After singing praise and worship and in the choir, I went to take my seat in the audience. I was sitting in the audience on the far left side of the church, in the second row. I was trying to stay calm, but I couldn't stop thinking about my financial status and the fact that I wasn't going to get help from my parents.

I happened to look up, and saw my pastor's wife, Varie's sister, Cassie, was staring at me.

Why does she keep looking at me?

The pastor preached, and the service was over. As I was about to leave, I saw Cassie starting to walk up to me. At this point, I was thinking of anything I could have done that might have made her mad.

"Leah, I don't know why, but the Lord told me to give you this."

She reached her hand out and put something in my palm. I looked down, opened my hand, and it was a hundred dollars.

"Really?" I said.

"Yes! I don't know why."

I hugged Cassie and thanked her so much. She didn't even know what that meant to me!

Suddenly, I heard the voice of the Lord again. Everything you touch, give me 10 percent.

I quickly got change for the hundred dollar bill and gave the Lord ten dollars.

From that point on, every chance that I'd get, I gave the Lord His tithe. Whether it was five dollars, or two dollars, or even change, I'd put it in the basket.

Throughout that time, people were just giving me money. My grandmother even offered to pay my rent until I got back on my feet again. I wasn't wasting any money. Even if I needed my hair done, I would do it myself, because I didn't have enough money to get my hair done.

Every morning, I would wake up and get on my computer to look for any job openings in Los Angeles. I would look on Craigslist. I would send my resume in for every position from secretary to assistant to property manager. I had no experience, but I was fierce about it. I was sending in my resume for any job that was available that I thought I could do and going on interviews weekly.

For every interview, I wore the same suit. One of the things James taught me was how to be professional. I also learned from other people, listening to how they got jobs. Appearance at job interviews is key. I learned that you have to wear a navy blue suit for people to take you seriously. I had a navy blue DKNY suit that I got from Loehman's. It was pinstriped and very girly. It had a blazer and a skirt with ruffles, but it was very classic. I have it to this day. I wore that same suit to every interview. Every single one. Most of the jobs that I was applying to were for temp agencies. Big corporations would go through temp agencies to filter out job applicants. I didn't really realize it until every interview I went to was called through a temp agency.

When my blue suit started to get a little dirty, I would switch it to a black pant suit. But both were very classic. I was getting call backs for a lot of interviews. But one particular day, I got a call from a staffing company called Star Staffing. They recruited people for jobs for casting agencies or entertainment lawyers and offices like that. One of the ladies called me and said, "I have a job opening for an African American lawyer. He's really successful, and he's looking for an assistant. Would you be interested in interviewing with him?"

"Absolutely!" I said.

I put on my navy blue suit, and I went to go meet him. His name was Don Mullen. He had an office called Mullen & Peters in Beverly Hills. It was on Wilshire, one block west of Neiman Marcus. I thought it was amazing that he was African American and so successful.

I went to go meet with him the day after I got the call from the agency. He immediately started asking me questions about my resume.

"Oh, you went to UC Berkeley."

"Yes, I did."

"You must be very smart. Tell me about your experience there," he said.

"It was one of the best experiences of my life. I learned so much. I figured out how smart I was because in order to be there, you literally have to be smart," I joked.

He laughed. "You graduated in three years?"

"Yes, I graduated in three years."

"What made you do something like that?"

"Well, I just wanted to prove to myself that I could do it."

Of course I wasn't going to tell him that I did it to marry a man who didn't even marry me in three years.

"That's pretty impressive to go to UC Berkeley and graduate in three years," he said.

"Thank you!"

"So your background is in education. I'm looking for an assistant to work my front desk. Are you familiar with computers?"

"Yes," I confirmed.

"Word and Excel?"

"Yes."

"Are you familiar with faxing documents?"

"Yes," I said, even though I hadn't done that much.

"Are you familiar with doing conference calls and connecting calls together outside of the office?"

"Oh, absolutely." I had never done that before.

"Do you know how to create files, and file documents, and scan documents to get them to my clients?"

"Yes!" I didn't know how to do any of that.

All I knew how to do was to make lesson plans, teach kids reading and basic math concepts, control a classroom, and execute a curriculum. That's what I knew how to do! I didn't know how to do anything he was asking me. Yet I still answered every question with *Yes!*

I learned that in an interview, you should never say that you can't do something, or you don't know how to do something. You just say yes and figure out how to do it on the job.

My interview was going well.

"You know what, I really like you!" he said.

"Great!" I said.

"But there's one more thing I have to tell you."

"Yes?" I asked.

"If you work for me, you can't wear those stuffy suits."

I laughed.

"This is an entertainment law firm. You can wear jeans and a blazer, or something like that. But you have to be a little more funky, a little more fun! Do you understand?"

"Yes! I understand."

Right away, I really liked him. He seemed very conservative and very serious, but he also seemed to have a little fun spontaneous disposition going on that I kind of liked. But I felt like if he hired me, I could learn so much from him. He seemed like a respectable guy.

I went home and immediately got a call from Star Staffing. The lady told me that he really liked me, and he wanted me to start. He even wanted me to start the next week.

"Perfect," she said. "He's going to start you at $10/hr. Paid weekly."

It wasn't much, but it was better than not having a job at all!

"Amazing!"

I started that next week. It was basically a trial. I would work for 4-6 weeks as a temp, and after that time was up, he would tell the staffing company if he wanted to keep me or not. I was paid through the staffing company. At the end of every week, I would have to pick up a check from the staffing company. And I was happy to do so.

I still paid tithes off the money that I was now making from my new job. I was so grateful. The Lord blessed me; I was back getting paid on a new job. A job that I would definitely have to get used to, and also a job where I didn't know how to do anything. But I was going to learn how to do everything.

I was working eight hours a day (10 a.m. - 7 p.m.). I was used to it because this was the same time that I got off at my preschool teaching job.

After the 4-6 weeks, he hired me permanently. I was part of the team. There were two other assistants that were really nice. A girl and a guy. I worked in the front desk, and the other two assistants worked in the back office. Of course they were more experienced than me, but they taught me everything. They taught me how to compose professional emails, what to say, how to file records, scan documents… They taught me how to do conference calls, although that was the hardest thing for me to do. They taught me how to connect calls to both lawyers in the office.

There were two lawyers in the office. There was the lawyer that I worked for and another lawyer, Robert. Robert was more of an agent, so he had a very agent-like attitude. Agents in LA can be very rude and loud and are always on the phone, yet you hear their entire conversation because they want you to know that they're in control. He would bring his dog and take it on walks throughout the day.

He made it very difficult for me to work there. He had high expectations, where I had to make coffee in the morning and be at the desk exactly at 10 a.m. to answer calls. If I was even five or ten minutes late, he would definitely bring it to my attention. If I didn't get a call right, he would yell at me and call me all kinds of names, and even curse at me. I'd heard that agents acted like that, but it was just very uncomfortable. Some days he'd be super nice, and we'd have great conversations, and other days, he was yelling at me and being rude. It was strange and kept me off guard.

I was working there, and really trying to get my bearings and do the best that I could do, especially with not knowing everything and learning how to do the job. I was like a fish out of water, but yet I was so thankful to have a job.

One particular day, I didn't connect a call correctly for Robert. It was a very important call. He went off. He said that I was always fucking stuff up and called me all kinds of names, and even told me that I wasn't good at my job. But he would always do it when Don was not around, which I thought was so interesting. Why would he be talking to me crazy, but only when he was the only man in charge? Obviously, he knew that he could do it at that time.

But this particular day, I was really fed up with the way he was talking to me. I was trying to be professional and accommodating, but I didn't say a word. I marched down the hallway to Don's office, opened up the door, and said, "Don, if you don't do something about this man, I will!"

I was really bold. I had never been like that; I respected Don to the fullest. I would never just barge in his office because I knew he was super busy. But I felt like I had to because I was so sick of that man! It almost reminded me of how James used to talk to me, and I wasn't going to stand for that anymore. I didn't care if this was my first job since my job search; this man was not going to talk to me like that! When Don saw my face, he knew I meant business. It made him really respect me. Needless to say, Robert never talked to me like that again.

It seemed as though that was the turning point in our relationship. Don would have me do different things for him on the side. For instance, he would host parties at his house, and he would have me work as his assistant on the weekends at the parties. I would get food and decorations and make sure the caterers were there on time.

He was in the midst of remodeling his entire house, and he asked me if I would house sit and manage the construction while he traveled. He really trusted me, and it made me feel so good. He even allowed me to drive his car, which was a Porsche Cayenne truck! I guess he saw my car was getting kind of old by then and joked that I needed to be a little safer. I was so grateful to be working for him and assisting him for whatever the occasion: his home, his events, work. I was learning so much and becoming very business-savvy and contract-savvy. I was extremely tech-savvy with emails and scanning documents. I really appreciated him.

One day, when I was at his house for a Christmas party, his girlfriend, Taylor, was there. Taylor was a beautiful lady, petite and very sassy. She was in real estate. While we were preparing for the party, we began talking, and she asked me if I'd ever thought about owning my own home. In my head, I was thinking, *Oh Lord no, I just got out of 82 cents in my account!* I was just starting to be able to pay my full rent again without the help of my grandmother. I was not thinking about buying any property. I was just barely making it and making sure I gave the Lord His tithe, 10 percent of anything I made.

"You should own your own home!" she said.

"One day! My family is really into real estate, where they have apartment buildings and duplexes that they own. I'm just not ready yet," I explained.

"You know what, let's just get you pre-qualified! We can see if you even qualify for a house, and then we'll go from there."

"Okay." I hesitated.

I couldn't stop thinking about the situation I'd just gotten out of, owning the house with James. I didn't want to own anything. I just wanted to build my credit, have my little cash flow, and just be done.

That Monday, when I went back to work, Taylor came to the office to get my social security number and my information. She ran my credit, and some way, somehow, I was pre-qualified. I couldn't believe it.

"When you're ready, let's start looking for houses," she told me.

A couple weeks later, I was at my brother's football game in Redlands. I was with my grandmother and my parents. My grandmother and I were sitting together on this grass area, and I just happened to tell her that one day I wanted to own my own piece of property.

"Baby, if you find a house that you like, I'll help you with the down payment."

"What?!"

"If you find a piece of property, I'll help you with the down payment," she said again.

My life was turning around instantly! I couldn't believe it.

So when I got back to work after the weekend, I called Taylor and told her that I was ready to start looking for houses. She would send me all kinds of properties. Just like my mom told me, I would drive by and see if I liked the area and its surroundings. Taylor told me the same thing. I told her I was interested in living in West LA, Westwood, Hollywood, or West Hollywood. I figured these places were best because it was in the middle of everything, and I could have access to all the freeways. I was maybe considering the Valley, but it would have had to be Studio City.

We would go see new properties often. I would really like them, especially the ones in Westwood. Westwood would have condominiums that almost reminded me of hotels, which I loved. But it seemed like all the places that I loved, I would put in bids for them, but it would be counter-offered, or I wouldn't get it. It was fine, because I wanted it to be right. I figured what was for me, I would have.

On days that I couldn't go look at properties because I was working for Don, Taylor would pick my grandmother up (in South Central) and take her to the properties. I wanted my grandmother to like the place before I even settled on it. That went on for a couple months.

During my time working for Don, I was still getting better and better business-wise. Although I was still itching to get back working with kids, I was still grateful for the job that I had.

Keith was still in the picture, and every Wednesday he'd pick me up and take me to lunch and bring me back to the office. One particular day, one of the lawyers in the office, Jacob, saw Keith. Jacob loved the Lord, and we had so much in common. But he looked almost ashamed of me when he saw Keith. I rushed to introduce them to make it less awkward:

"Keith, this is Jacob, Jacob, this is Keith!"

After I came back from lunch with Keith, he called me in his office and asked if he could talk to me for a second.

"Sure! What is it?" I asked.

"What are you doing?"

"What do you mean?"

"He just doesn't look like he's for you," he said.

This was the third person to tell me this.

"I know, I know. He's just a friend!" I replied.

"Come on, Leah. No, he's not."

Once again I found myself trying to defend Keith and only acknowledge him as my friend. I was doing the same thing over and over again, and I just don't know why I kept him around.

One weekend, Keith was out of town for a gig, which was good because he was getting paid. I don't remember who it was for, but it was some celebrity. He asked me to do some errands for him, pay a couple bills, but specifically to go to the credit union for him. So we were getting pretty serious, and close. It was getting too far out of my control, if that makes sense.

I went to the credit union for him and put the money in the bank as he requested. I went to the mailbox for him, and he asked me to bring some things to his grandparents' house, where he was living, and I did.

Both of his grandparents really liked me and embraced me with open arms. But this time it was only his grandfather who was home. He was an older preacher.

"Keith asked me to leave these things with you," I said as he opened the door.

"Thank you! Let me talk to you for a second, baby," he said with a slow, old speed.

"Okay," I said. I walked in the house.

"You know, the Lord is going to give you somebody just for you."

"Wow, thank you so much. I receive that," I said.

"The Lord is gonna bless you. And give you a man just for you!"

"Thank you!" I said again.

"But it's not Keith!" he said.

"Okay, thank you so much, sir. I'll see you later, thank you!" I walked out of the house.

Everybody was telling me this. Even his own grandfather was saying this wasn't for me. I needed to get myself together. I needed to stop; it had gotten too far. I was hearing the Lord loud and clear. But how was I going to get out of it?

My grandmother and Taylor were still looking for homes, and sometimes I'd be able to go on weekends. I would always try to sneak and look online at house listings while I was at work.

Taylor began to send me some properties in the Ladera area. I saw this condo in Ladera that I wanted. We chose to bid higher than it was even worth. They declined me.

I felt like I was striking out on every end.

One day, my grandmother, my mom, and I were driving around Ladera, and we passed this duplex. It looked older, but it was pretty big. My mom looked at it and said, "I think this is it!"

"What do you mean this is it?" I asked.

"I think… I think this is it," she said profoundly.

It looked like a huge house, but it had two units. On one side, it was a two-story house with a full kitchen, breakfast nook, dining room, living room, den, and three bedrooms. It was beautiful. It was spacious with hardwood floors. Next door was a two-bedroom unit with a large bathroom, kitchen, and living room. The price was right, and my mom just knew this was it.

"Well, wait a minute! I don't know if I want to live in Ladera. I said West LA!"

"This is it! You can live in one and rent out the other. This isn't rocket science, this is perfect for you! This is income property. It would be a perfect move for you and set you up for success. This is it!" my mom exclaimed.

My grandparents were really into that, and they'd done it for as long as I could remember. They were professionals at buying apartment complexes and duplexes and renting them out. They did this because that was their way of obtaining wealth and leaving something for their children and future generations. They saw purchasing income property as a way for their children to have income and always have a place to stay if times got hard. It was really admirable for my grandparents, who came from meager beginnings. They came from a generation that wanted their children to have something, and she definitely wanted me to have something of my own. Something that could give me equity and stability even at my young age of 26.

Owning my own duplex just seemed perfect. My grandmother adamantly agreed and said, "Yes! This is it!" in unison with my mother. I immediately called Taylor and told her to go ahead and run the numbers. She ran the numbers and called the owner, and he accepted the offer!

I went from 82 cents in my account, living in an apartment where I needed my grandmother's help, to getting ready to become a home-owner and a landlord. What a huge difference. It was a huge blessing. Talk about recovery... God was doing everything He'd promised He'd do. Remember when I prayed the prayer, "Lord, show me what my life would be like with and without James?" God told me that without him He would restore all that I had lost, and He was doing exactly what He said. I also learned that tithing works. By just obeying God when He said to give Him 10 percent of anything that hit my hand, He began to bless me beyond my wildest dreams.

I was back in school getting a master's degree in a few months. It was a complete transition, a complete turnaround from where I'd come from. I was scared and excited at the same time. The process happened really fast. The owner accepted my offer, and as prom-ised, my grandmother made the down payment. Then it was getting a first and second loan because I was young. That was the only way that I'd be able to afford the house. So I had a first mortgage and a second mortgage. I had to sign all these papers in front of a notary. Taylor had all kinds of people that met me at Don's office where I worked to sign papers. It was going so fast that I was getting scared. I would have to be paying $2,300 a month. That was the first mort-gage. The second mortgage was around $400. That may not sound like a lot to some people, but to me, it was a lot of money! However, I knew that from renting out the second side of my duplex, I would get the money for the mortgage. In addition, with my income from working, I would have enough to pay for everything. Everything seemed to be great, but I was just so scared. In fact, I was house-sitting for Don one weekend while he was traveling, and I had a panic attack.

I called my pastor and said, "Pastor Tigner, I am scared. Is this something I should do? It's a lot of money. Should I stop the process?"

"Are you crazy?" He chuckled. "The Lord is blessing you right now! He is opening up the windows of heaven and pouring you out a blessing! This is your blessing, just walk into it. Just walk in it, be happy and be grateful," he said calmly.

I was so thankful for that phone call.

I signed the papers, and it was time for me to move in. When I was preparing to move out, I had to tell my property manager at the apartment that I was leaving. I had made so many friends with my little Jewish ladies in my apartment complex. The property manager cried when I told her I was leaving.

"We're going to miss seeing you and your cute outfits walking out of your apartment. You are so clean, and so quiet, we're going to miss that! How are we going to find somebody like you?"

I was sad, too, because she had given me a chance. She didn't even check my credit. I knew it was a new chapter in my life, but it wasn't easy. I kept hearing Dr. Tigner telling me to just walk into my blessing.

Before I moved in, I wanted to make the house mine. I wanted to paint everything. I painted the inside a cream color. All the crown moldings were bright white. That was downstairs, in the living room. I already had my cream Ultrasuede couches and furniture that I had from the garage sale. In fact, I already had everything that would be in my living room. I had my piano that my grandmother bought me, and even a den that needed furnishing. I had three bedrooms upstairs. I wanted my room to be pale pink with white crown molding around the edges. I wanted the closet to be painted white. I had my cherrywood sleigh bed that I'd had since college. I just had to figure out what I was going to do with the other two bedrooms. I decided to make one of them my office with my computer and desk. I had no clue what I was going to do with the other bedroom and didn't have enough money for more furniture. I needed to give that one some thought.

Anyway, I was so excited about making the house mine. I couldn't wait to make it beautiful and girly, like I had with my apartment.

The outside was beige, with chocolate brown trim. I changed the trim to white for a cleaner and crisp look. My grandmother and I planted huge white rose bushes that surrounded the entire house. We decided to plant miniature palm trees in the garden, too. I even had beautiful brick walkways going into each doorway. There were three doorways, one for my tenant, one for my front door, and one that went straight into the kitchen. There were beautiful garage doors, one for me and one for my tenant. It was just gorgeous, and we were making it even more beautiful.

Everybody was so excited and proud of me for getting the house. I was taking my time to move in because the lease on my apartment wasn't completely up. Besides that, the house was still getting painted, and the floors were being refinished.

I was finally in my last few weeks of school, getting ready to graduate with my master's in education. I decided to have my housewarming the same day I graduated from Pepperdine. It was a graduation party/housewarming. Keith helped me bring some things back and forth into the house.

It became time for me to tell Don goodbye. I'd loved working for him, and I'd learned so much from him, but to tell you the truth, law was not my thing. I learned all about contracts and filing, how to do conference calls, databases, and even how to be more professional, but my heart was with teaching. One day while I was working at the front desk at Don's office, I got a call from one of my students' parents at one of my old schools.

"Ms. Walker, we have a position at this other school my kids go to, at Wilshire Private School. There's an opening for a third grade teacher. I would love for you to be my daughter's teacher. Could you please apply?"

I didn't tell Don because I didn't want to get my hopes up. So I called the school, and they said they wanted to interview me on a Saturday, which was strange, but it was a private school, and they make up their own rules.

That Saturday morning, I went dressed in my navy blue suit that I wore to all my other job interviews. He interviewed me, and I gave him my resume and told him about my prior teaching experiences. He loved that I was in school getting my master's in education. He was very impressed.

"How about I offer you the job right now?"

I couldn't even get the words out of my mouth.

"Yes. You can start in the fall. Would you like that?"

"Absolutely!" I said.

I was so happy, and I could barely believe it! It all felt so surreal. It was as if God was bringing to pass all the desires of my heart, even desires I hadn't communicated. He was putting them all at my feet, and all I had to do was walk in them. The only challenging thing now was it was time for me to tell Don that I'd gotten another job.

That Monday when I got to work, I called Don on the intercom and asked him if we could meet briefly. I went in the office and said, "I just want to give you a two-week notice."

"What do you mean?" he said desperately.

"I got a job... teaching."

"I knew it... I knew it. Well, it's a great way to start fresh. You'll be teaching again, you have a new home... Leah, I'm proud of you. You've been great here, but I can't hold you back."

I could tell he was sad, and I was really sad too. I called Taylor and told her the news, and she was sad as well. But they wanted the best for me, and that meant a lot to me. They both were responsible for changing my life. God had used Don to hire me, to take a chance on me, then to respect and trust me enough to give me the responsibility to house sit and manage his remodel, and that meant everything to me. Then for Taylor to be used of God to encourage me to step out on faith to become a homeowner, our connection and relationship was truly divine. God orchestrated me to lose my job at the school to work for Don in order to change the trajectory of my life. They were a true blessing, and I will never forget them for what they did for me.

I was closing so many doors in my life and opening so many beautiful and wonderful new doors. I knew it was time to close the door on Keith.

I knew it was bad once his grandfather told me to leave him alone and that God had someone just for me. It was amazing that his grandfather would tell me something like that. It was inevitable that I end this relationship. I just couldn't let him go, and I didn't know why. But finally, after moving into my home and preparing for my open house and moving into my new classroom, Dr. Tigner called me. It was as if he had enough and had to relay this message one more time loud and clear.

"Leah, I have to talk to you," he said.

"Yes?"

"You NEED to let Keith go! That's not your destiny, that's not your future! You're holding yourself back! You're making a mistake! He is not for you! He is not on your level! I hate to say it, but he is beneath you, a loser! I can't stand seeing you like this. End it today!"

I started crying.

"But how do I do it?" I asked.

"Just let him go! It's not even a how, not even a what, LET HIM GO! IT's OVER. Tell him it's over! This is enough! This is not your destiny. LET IT GO!"

And then he hung up. He was so angry, yet passionate. I guess he did not want me to go down the wrong road again and end up worse than when I was with James.

I knew it was the Lord talking through him, because I literally had to let him go. That night I called him, and said, "I'm so sorry, this has to end. We can't do this anymore. I have to move on with my life."

I said the famous line that everyone hates: "It's not you, it's me... You deserve someone that likes you and really loves you."

Well, he didn't get it. We went through a few weeks of back and forth dialogue.

A few weeks passed. I moved into my house and graduated from Pepperdine University with my master's in education. I was 27 years old, a new owner of a duplex with a tenant and was just starting a new job. I was having an open house and graduation party together. I invited everyone. I didn't want anyone to walk on my new hardwood floors, so I got these little painter shoes that people had to wear. I had a nice size backyard, and we had food that filled up the entire yard. I wanted catered Mexican food. Who doesn't like Mexican food? Tacos, enchiladas, both beef and chicken, rice and beans, and of course a salad.

Everyone loved the house. I was taking people on tours and showing them the bedrooms and bathrooms. Don had given me all the furniture from one of his bedrooms since he was refinishing his home. It was what I needed for that third bedroom that I did not have any money to furnish. He gave me a beautiful pristine white queen bed set with nightstands. Downstairs, in my den, I didn't have any couches yet, but I had an open space that people could walk around and mingle in. They understood that I had just moved in. There was new carpet and new floors, and everything looked absolutely gorgeous. Keith even came to congratulate me. He put together a playlist for the guests to hear. I was happy he did that for me, but I kept wondering why I was holding on to him and hearing Dr. Tigner's voice, "LET HIM GO!" constantly ringing in my ear.

It was just a great occasion. My grandmother was so happy and was greeting everyone. She was so happy for me, almost like it was her house. She was so proud of me, and I was just so happy that I had her. I told everyone how grateful I was for her and thanked her in front of everyone. I gave a nice speech before we cut the cake. The cake looked like a house, just like my house. I'd drawn a picture and taken it to Hansen's Bakery, and they made a house! It wasn't even like a sheet cake, it was a layered cake. It was so beautiful. The entire afternoon was just amazing.

Pastor Tigner and his wife Varie came to support me, and they kept giving me the eye for the entire party. Keith was looking really weird in the background. They kept pulling me to the side, of course, telling me to get rid of him. Varie told me God was showing me a sign by me getting my own house, and him still living with his grandparents.

A couple days after the party, I called Keith again and repeated that I didn't want to be in the relationship anymore. I begged for him not to call me or come over anymore.

Immediately, he came over to my house and started banging on my door. I called Dr. Tigner and told him that Keith was at the door and asked what I should do. Remember, I couldn't talk to my dad about any guys, because he was completely over it after James. Dr. Tigner was the only one I could really talk to about my guy problems.

He was ringing the doorbell and banging on the door so much that I was almost a little scared that he was going to break it down.

"Leah, do not go to the door. He will leave," he instructed.

"Are you sure?"

"Leah. He will leave."

After about an hour of ringing the doorbell and banging on the door, he finally left. It was finally over. Finally over. He didn't call me anymore, he didn't come over anymore. Of course I would still see him at church, but it was from a clear distance. I was done. Finally, I was done.

Although I was done with James, I was never done with some of the beautiful people I met while I lived in the Bay Area. Gigi and Papi were still very dear to me. I would talk to them weekly to catch up. Gigi would always keep me updated with everything that was going on at the church. Whether I wanted to know or not, she would fill me in on all of the gossip and the shenanigans of Chipmunk 2 and Dianne. It was a never-ending saga, and I was so glad I'd exited stage left! Gigi and Papi would both have their bouts with sickness, and every time they would, I would fly to Oakland, check on them, and fly right back to LA. That is how much I loved them. They were my family when I was away from my family. They fed me countless meals, listened, and consoled me through all of my James ordeals. The least I could do was be there for them like they had been for me.

One day while I was at work teaching, Gigi called me.

"Hi Gigi! How are you?" I asked

"Hi Leah, I am okay, but I wish I would have called you earlier to tell you," she said.

"Tell me what?"

"Papi passed," she said in a sad and somber tone.

"What?" I started crying uncontrollably.

"James did not want me to tell you, but I had to. I could not keep this from you. Papi loved you, and I know you loved him. He would have wanted you to know," Gigi explained.

"When is the funeral?" I asked.

"It's tomorrow. James did not want you to know because he didn't want you coming to the funeral."

"I don't care what James says! He can't stop me from coming to the funeral of a person that I love! I will see you tomorrow," I said firmly.

"That's what I want to hear. I'm so glad I called you. Papi would not have had it any other way. I will be looking to see you tomorrow. Love ya!"

"Love you too, Gigi." We hung up.

I was sad and furious at the same time. I was devastated that Papi had died, and I was furious that James did not want me to know. *He is a horrible person!* I thought to myself. *He is always trying to overpower me. Not this time!* I was going to show him who had their power back and who was not going to run or ruin my life any longer!

After I got myself together, I called my grandmother and told her that I needed her to fly with me to Oakland in the morning because Papi had died, and his funeral was that day. She agreed without hesitation. I quickly got two airline tickets from Southwest, asked my principal for the day off, and everything was set.

The next day we flew to Oakland and got there an hour before the funeral. We did not have any bags because we were going to fly right back home. As soon as we landed, we rented a car and headed toward the church. I was not nervous at all; I was more angry than anything. How could he tell Gigi not to tell me? How could he do this?

When we got to the church, we parked and walked in. This would be the first time I had been to the church since I'd left. All of the memories flooded my mind. All I could do was thank God that I had been delivered from that horrible place. Chills filled my body as I walked into the church and saw those famous steps I'd had to climb daily. My spirit cringed at the thought of all the misery I'd gone through at that church. But thank God, I was on the other side now. I could hold my head high because this episode was over, and I was better and stronger than ever.

We walked down the aisle and sat on the left-hand side of the church. The funeral had just begun. James was in the pulpit with some other ministers. When we were seated, I could see James glance over at us. He looked like he had seen a ghost. He kept glancing over at us in disbelief. I could tell by the look on his face that he was shocked that I was there. I did not care. My grandmother and I sat there with our heads held high, dressed to kill and not moved by his looks. We were there, and he could not do anything about it.

The next thing that happened was literally unbelievable. After James realized it was us, he reached down, grabbed his things, and left the pulpit. He went out of the side door and up the stairs to his office and never came back down.

He was the one who was supposed to deliver the eulogy, and he never came back! He didn't even tell the other ministers that he was not coming back. When it was time for the eulogy to be done, the other ministers looked around and had to decide who would do it. It was embarrassing and totally uncalled for. My presence made him forfeit his obligation to preach the eulogy? How inconsiderate and selfish.

I felt awful for Gigi. James was the one who called them his other parents. They had fed him, they were the ones who always picked him up from the airport, and they even did our laundry for us when we lived in the church. How could he do this to her? I know he was mad at me, but to leave the funeral and never come back—that was beyond disrespect. Then again, what else can you expect from someone like that?

After the eulogy, all of the guests walked around to view the body. As my grandmother and I walked around, I went over to hug and kiss Gigi. She looked so disgusted. Not only was she putting to rest the love of her life, she was so disappointed in James.

After the funeral, we headed back to the airport and flew to LA. That night after I returned home, I called Gigi to check on her. She was so glad that I had come despite James' wishes. She also talked about how mad she was at him and how he did not even call her to apologize. She admitted that she would never get over this. This was one of the saddest things I had ever witnessed. This was just another confirmation that I'd made the right decision to leave.

positive four

Terry had grown a little frustrated with me because at this point, years had gone by, and I still wasn't committed to him. I really felt like I shouldn't commit to him because he would be coming in and out of my life so much. I wouldn't hear from him for months, and then he'd pop up and call with his famous "Leah" voice-mail. That meant to call him. We'd catch up, and then I wouldn't hear from him again. Sometimes he'd send me a book that he wanted me to read or a program from where he was preaching. Sometimes it would even be a postcard or a picture. It was just so inconsistent I did not know if he really wanted to be with me. To me, it made no sense. When he would call, his voice would sound frustrated. I would be wondering why he was so frustrated if he hadn't called me for months. We hadn't seen each other in months, and if he'd come, it was for his revivals. We'd be together every day, and then I wouldn't hear from him when he got back home. I really compartmentalized our relationship into what it was: We were fond of each other, but it wasn't serious because I would not hear from him. I will be forever grateful for what he did for me. He'd shown me unconditional love at a time that I needed it most. He encouraged me, and he lifted me. In a perfect world we should have been together. We were perfect for each other. I even adored and had the utmost respect for his parents, but for some reason we couldn't get it together. It was like we were two planes that constantly passed one another, never making a clear connection or stabilizing what we were going to do with our relationship.

I loved him but was never settled on what we were. Were we together or not? We couldn't be because he was so inconsistent. One particular time, he came to Los Angeles to do a revival for a church, and he told me that he was going to be there for about four days. So I went every night of the revival, and afterward, we'd go out to eat and be affectionate and loving. We'd catch up and talk about current events and music. Then I'd take him back to his hotel, and I'd go home. I'd be excited about it, but I just didn't know what we were; I didn't know where we stood. On his last day of being in LA, he said that he wanted to have lunch. I agreed. My school was in Koreatown. So I could leave school and go to his hotel. He was staying at a hotel downtown. I only had about 45 minutes to an hour for lunch, so I literally let my kids out for lunch early so that I could get in my car, get downtown, have a bite to eat, and come right back. It was feasible; I could do it.

He told me what room of the hotel he was in, and I kept knocking on the door, but he wouldn't answer. I kept knocking. No answer. So I started wondering if he was okay. He had a history of being sick a lot. He'd be in and out of the hospital for different things.

Was he sick and unconscious?

I went downstairs to have the concierge call the room, and still there was no answer. I called his cell phone. Nothing! It was about thirty minutes of me knocking on the door and calling him, with no response. I didn't feel like I should call the police or anything. I just felt like maybe he possibly could have forgotten. I left, and on the drive back I was so deflated and disappointed.

Why wouldn't he tell me not to come or that he had other plans? Why wouldn't he call? Why would he make me leave my job? It wasn't even my idea to have lunch; it was his!

It was a lot for me to do that. I had a responsibility for the kids; I was a teacher. It's hard to leave and come back.

I didn't hear from him until I was back at work. He called me and said, "Oh, I was asleep."

"Okay. Let me call you back," I said.

That was just what our relationship was. It became frustrating for me, and so I just did my own thing. That's why I dated other people. I felt like I didn't understand what he wanted from me. Then I would hear from other people that we were a couple. I'd be wondering how they could even think that when I never heard from him. It was just really strange. Of course I would always honor and appreciate him for what he did for me, and how he encouraged me to know my value and know how beautiful I was. He really made me realize my self-worth, and I appreciated that so much. I admit that if it wasn't for him and his encouragement, I would never have left James. I would have never taken that step to go back to LA with nothing. I owed him that. And I thought that he was the one, but all of the in and outs, and no calls, and popups, I just couldn't wrap my head around it. I couldn't. I also don't think that he liked the fact that I volunteered to work at Dr. Tigner's conference. He said there was a certain stigma for ladies who did, that they just wanted a man. But he knew me; he couldn't say that. We had never slept together, he had never seen me naked, and I had never seen him naked. So how was I going to be that girl? That also caused me to feel like something was wrong. I knew that he was very conservative and very private. He didn't want anyone to know any of his business; he didn't like telling anyone about anything. I just didn't know how to act. One day, I was driving to the grocery store over by my house, and he called.

Oh! Haven't heard from him in about two months.

"LEAH!" he yelled.

"Yes?"

"This is your last chance."

"What?" I said, confused.

"WHAT ARE WE DOING?"

"I don't know what we're doing, Terry... What do you mean?"

"Leah, this is your last chance to be with me."

"My last chance?" I said, feeling disrespected.

"Yes, your last chance. Tell me now. Either you're going to be with me or you're not. This is your last chance."

What kind of relationship are you in when you don't hear from somebody for months? What relationship is that? I'm just not supposed to talk to anybody, and I'm just supposed to wait for him to call me or pop up?

"Well, I guess this is my last chance," I said calmly.

"Okay, Leah. All right," he said.

"All right."

He hung up. And I never heard from him again.

Now I had to deal with the condition of being alone again. Which is not fun. But at the same time, I had so much to be grateful for. I had my house, I was a landlord, I had a new job. I was still in the process of decorating my house and getting all kinds of pillows and nice décor. I was getting my life together. Finally. But I was still alone.

I also had to deal with the fact that Terry and I were over. Although I felt grateful and indebted to him for all that he had done for me, we were over. I heard that he was very angry about it, and he would voice his frustration to other people and his family. Because I had a relationship with his family, I desperately wanted to share my side of the story. I didn't want them to hate me. I highly respected them and would run into them often at church events and conferences. It hurt me that Terry hated me so much; I mean, he was vehemently mad, and there was nothing I could do. I knew the truth and held on to it. I would have to deal with his family's feelings internally because I decided to not have the conversation with them. Plus, by their actions and distance I realized he had definitely communicated his side of the story, so my side was null and void. This whole situation was hurtful, but another outcome just wasn't possible. We were over, and what he had meant to me would be written on the walls of my soul and as a chapter in my past.

I was dating a little. Which was fun, I guess. I reconnected with a lawyer that I'd grown up with at my old church who was a little bit older than me. He was single, and we'd go out to the movies and have dinner sometimes. We had great conversations, and he was very respectful.

Then I was also hired as Dr. Tigner's personal assistant. His last one had moved to Texas, and he needed someone to take care of his calendar, travel, organize his office, and type his sermons. He had a church secretary that dealt with all the matters of the church, but he still needed a personal assistant to deal with his personal matters. Because I had worked for Don and was good at what I did, he hired me to work for him.

So now I was working as a teacher, tutoring after school, and working for Dr. Tigner. Even though I was trying to date, my schedule was so full. I would even travel with Dr. Tigner and Varie for different engagements, which was really fun. Although sometimes with the pressure of having the sermons ready and making sure his travel was on point, it wouldn't be a leisure trip; it was a work trip. But I enjoyed it, and it was another source of income, so I appreciated it. Not only did I type his sermons, but I helped to write one of his books, *A Making of a Champion*. Working for him was a privilege, and I also felt it was my calling and purpose. It made sense. When I joined his church he'd told me that he had a job for me, and he did. He said he knew way before he hired me that I was going to be his personal assistant. He said that God had already told him, and now I was doing exactly what God had ordained.

Dr. Tigner has a conference every year called WHW Expository Preaching and Teaching Conference, and this particular year, he wanted to do something different. He and Varie wanted to have an LA night for the first night of the conference. The LA night would bring out all of the churches in the Los Angeles area and have a famous MC. Being the coordinator that I am, I suggested getting one of the local gospel radio station DJs to be the MC for the first night. Dr. Tigner and Varie loved that idea. I thought of one that would be perfect. His name was Andrew Roland, and he worked for KGFI. They had a broadcast on Sundays called Spread the Gospel, which played gospel music all day. The radio show was known all over the country.

I called the radio station to get Andrew Roland's number to see if he was available to MC the first night of the WHW Expository Preaching and Teaching Conference. They connected me to his voicemail, and I left a message. I ended up having to email them a flyer of the event and explain why we wanted him to be the MC. He ended up calling me back and told me that his fee was around

$350, but that he would be there. That would not only give us promotion on the radio, but it would also be good to put on the flyer. It was great marketing.

Dr. Tigner wanted me to introduce him as the MC for the night. This was fine with me because I loved speaking. I went on the KGFI radio station website, found his bio, typed up a beautiful introduction, and we were ready to go.

That day the conference started, and I was standing in front of the auditorium so that I could lead him onto the stage. I was wearing a black pants suit with a ruffled blouse. Almost like the one Beyonce had on in "Dreamgirls" during the scene when she's walking into the office building with the black pantsuit with the black hat and ruffled blouse. I was trying to imitate her outfit. I did my hair myself, my makeup was fresh, and I felt amazing.

It was really easy for me to do this, because assisting Don for so long had taught me so many personal skills. He came into the lobby of the LAX Hilton, and he asked for me.

They brought him to me, and I introduced myself. "Hi, Mr. Roland! I'm Leah Walker, nice to meet you."

All he could do was stare at me. And stare, and stare.

"Ms. Walker, you are very attractive."

"Wow, thank you, Mr. Roland. Here's your program for today. I'll be introducing you."

"Wonderful," he said as he stared deep into my eyes.

It was a bit uncomfortable. I knew he was a little older, and I was used to that, but it still was a little odd to feel.

I did my introduction in front of the crowd, which was amazing. He MC'd the evening and did a great job. The program was flawless, and the attendance was superb. The night went off flawlessly.

Right before the service was over, I was in the lobby of the hotel talking to some people. I had noticed that Mr. Roland had made his way off the stage and into the lobby where I was. He came over to me and proceeded to say that I was very attractive and asked if he could have my phone number so that we could stay in contact. He was very professional about it and made me wonder if he was trying to get me a position on a radio station, which would be awesome. But I of course knew what he wanted it for. I gave him my number.

All of a sudden, I got a text from Dr. Tigner asking me where I was. I texted back that I'd be right there. I told Mr. Roland that it was nice meeting him, gave him his check, and told him that I'd keep in touch. I headed back to the auditorium where Dr. Tigner and Varie were.

"Where have you been? You left early, and you know I needed you to be here!" Dr. Tigner said.

"Sorry, I was talking to Mr. Roland," I responded.

"Oh I know. I could see him staring at you all night!"

"You could?" I said. "He asked me for my number."

"I knew he was going to ask you for your number! I think he's a predator," he said.

"You are always saying something's wrong with these guys!" I said.

He was so overprotective of me.

"I don't know. I just think he's a predator."

"It's fine, don't worry about it," I pushed.

"Okay, I'm just trying to tell you."

"I know, but I'm good," I mocked in his voice.

I proceeded to help him for the rest of the night, and then I went home.

The next day, Mr. Roland called me and asked if I wanted to meet up for coffee or for dinner. I was getting back in the game and figured he was a pretty successful guy, so I agreed to meet him. We'd talk on the phone and go out often. Things seemed to be pretty great. Plus, he had a little bit of celebrity status because he had been on the radio station for a long time, and people knew him. I thought that was a plus. So basically, we started dating.

He said he was 40, but I felt like he was a little bit older than that. I was fine with it. He liked movies, going to dinner, and different showcases. Of course I would tell Dr. Tigner about our different dates, and he didn't really take an interest.

"I'm telling you, Leah. I don't get very good vibes from this one," he would say.

I continued dating, and we were still going out often. He seemed to be really into me, I thought. There was consistent calling and going out. He had his own place, car, his own everything, and I really liked that about him. He treated me very nicely and would always hold my hand. But in the back of my head, I had Dr. Tigner saying that he was a predator. So every time we were around each other, I had that voice in my head saying *predator, predator, predator.* It was kind of weird, and I laughed at myself for it. I tried to ignore it.

One day, I was at Dr. Tigner's house, and we were about to do some work and type the sermon for Sunday's service. Varie called him, and Dr. Tigner picked up the phone.

"Hey, V, how are you doing?"

"Good! I'm at the grocery store, picking up some food for us. Is there anything you need?"

"No, I'm not hungry right now," he responded.

"Well, guess what. Guess who I see in the grocery store?"

"Who?" he asked.

"I see Andrew Roland walking in the grocery store, pushing a basket with a woman! They look like they're in love or on a date or something!"

Dr. Tigner looked at me. "On a date?"

"You better tell Leah!"

Of course my whole body went into shock. The idea of somebody I was dating being involved with another woman brought back so many flashbacks and feelings from James. It didn't make me feel good, to say the least. So of course I didn't call him, and I waited for him to call me.

He finally called and asked if we could go out again. At this point I began feeling a little weird about it. I didn't really want to go out because I was feeling like he was the exact person Dr. Tigner said he'd be. But I would still go out to dinner with him, because we'd never decided on being exclusive.

One night, we went to this showcase in Hollywood, where he had to announce an artist, and afterwards, we went out onto the street and saw a Hustlers store.

"Let's go look and see what the store is all about," he suggested.

I already knew what the Hustlers store was all about.

We went in, and he was acting so fascinated with these sex toys. Of course when we first started dating, I told him that I wasn't having sex with anyone until I was married. I always made that clear so that I wouldn't give anyone the wrong impression.

So when he was looking at the sex toys, I was looking at him like *Did you forget?*

He could feel my discomfort. "Oh no, no, no, I'm not trying to have sex, but maybe I thought you would want to have a little fun."

What in the world? Who is this guy?

"Okay, let's leave and go get something to eat," he said.

We ended up going to a restaurant a couple of blocks down. Our relationship was a little weird after that, but I still tried to hold on and see what the end was going to be.

One day, he called me, and we were talking, and I told him that one of my best friends Tia was the rapper Shakeer's assistant. Shakeer was really hot in the hip-hop game, and he had several hit albums and star-studded relationships. He was known for his conscious rap songs and his activism. He was very attractive, and everybody knew who he was. I was talking about how she had just gotten the job being his assistant, and how they were always on the road. I was really just venting because I missed her.

"Do you think Shakeer would want to perform at our Christmas Toys for Kids Concert?" he asked me.

"I don't really know. I mean, I've never asked her for something like that before," I responded.

"Why don't you give her my number? Of course he'll get paid; it's what we do every year. We would love to have him perform, and we'll take care of him and all of his expenses. It would be awesome to have him on the lineup."

"Okay," I agreed.

I called Tia and told her about the gig for Shakeer. I gave her his number, and she gave Andrew his manager's number so that he could do the deal with him. They got all of the logistics together, and everything ended up working out. Shakeer was scheduled to do the gig.

I felt really empowered that I had really gotten a deal for someone. I had never done that before. So I was pretty proud of myself. I talked to Andrew, and he was thanking me so much.

"This is so great, everybody's going to be so thrilled that he's on the lineup!"

"Great!" I responded. "I can't wait to go to the concert!"

"Oh—you wanted to go?"

"Ummm, I just helped with this whole situation. Why wouldn't I want to go?"

"Oh, I'm going to have to see if we have enough tickets." He sounded scattered.

"You're the coordinator for the whole concert. How could you not have tickets?"

"I'll check and see if we have extra tickets, but it's probably not going to happen."

I was so disappointed. I called Tia and said, "Do you know what Andrew told me?"

"What?"

"Do you know that after we did all that, Andrew isn't even bringing me to the concert? He said he didn't know if he could get tickets."

"He didn't tell you that… did he?" she said, surprised.

"Exactly! Is that crazy or what?" I yelled.

"Hold on, let me call you right back."

A few minutes later, she called me back. "Leah!"

"Yeah?" I asked.

"It doesn't matter what he said. You're coming with us!"

"What?"

"Yes. With us. I'll give you all the details of where to meet us. You'll ride with us and be backstage with us. Don't worry about it. You'll be with Shakeer, the team, and me. Now let's see what he says," she said confidently.

"Thank you so much," I said.

I was excited.

The night for the Toys for Kids Concert arrived, Tia called and told me to meet them at The Four Seasons in Beverly Hills. She told me to park my car in valet so that I could ride with them. I tried to dress really cute. My hair was not done, so I resorted to wearing a slick bun making sure my edges were neat. My makeup was flawless, because I'd learned that if you wear your hair in a bun, your makeup has to be amazing. Eyebrows on point, eyeshadow, lip gloss, everything. I wore a gray sweater dress with the back out, paired with gray ankle-buckled pumps that were suede. I had a matching clutch to go with it. So I was conservative, yet a little sexy. I felt like I was concert ready. Plus, I wanted to make Andrew jealous. I wanted to look so good that he felt stupid for not inviting me to the concert.

I drove to The Four Seasons and parked in the valet, like Tia instructed. I took the elevator to the penthouse suite and rang the doorbell. To my surprise, Shakeer answered the door. He was on the phone as he opened it, and he looked as if I'd completely distracted him from his conversation.

"Boy, there's some really pretty attendants working at this hotel!" he said.

"Umm, I'm actually not a hotel attendant."

Tia yelled, and interrupted before I could introduce myself. "Shakeer, that's Leah! Let her in!"

I started to laugh to myself... *Do I look* THAT *conservative? Hotel attendant?*

"Oh, oh, oh, I'm so sorry!"

"No problem!"

God, was he fine... He was finer than he was on TV and music videos!

I walked into the room where Tia was. She was in the bedroom getting all his clothes and shoes together for the night's performance. We stayed in the room for a while. I guess he had a certain call time, so we didn't leave right away. Tia and I were laughing and catching up.

"You look cute!" Tia told me.

"Thank you! So do you!"

For her to say that I looked cute made me feel less like a hotel attendant.

I noticed that Shakeer kept walking back and forth to the room. I was very nervous, but I could tell he was trying to be very friendly and make me feel comfortable, which I appreciated. But at the same time, I kept telling Tia how absolutely fine her boss was. I still kept it very professional, though.

We finally left to go to the concert. We got into a black suv, and it took us straight to the venue. In the car, Shakeer had lots of questions for me. He wanted to know what I did, and even what kind of movies I liked. I later learned that he's a movie junkie. Because of Andrew, I had seen every latest movie that was out, so I had tons to contribute to the conversation. The conversation was cool, and he seemed very nice and laid back.

We got to the concert venue, and we walked backstage, where he had a green room just for him and his team. Tia had all his clothes and water ready. Shakeer was very detailed, but Tia had every single detail on deck. I admired how organized she was and how well she took care of him. I was taking mental notes on how to take care of Dr. Tigner better. Shakeer was getting ready to go on stage, but right before, he said, "Okay everybody, we gotta pray."

Oh wow. He prays before he goes on stage? That's great!

"Leah!" he said.

"Yes?"

"Tia told me you're a church girl. Why don't you pray for us before we go on stage?"

I looked at Tia so fast, and she looked away even faster. She always did that to me! Why couldn't I just be regular? Why did I have to be a church girl?! I gave her the forreal?! look.

"Okay, please bow your heads," I said. "Lord, I thank you for this day, and I thank you for this opportunity. I pray that you bless Shakeer and his band as they perform tonight. Allow them to be a blessing to the crowd that is here tonight and be blessed as a result. We give you the praise and the glory. In Jesus' name. Amen."

"Wow. Thank you so much," Shakeer said. "Wow."

I don't know what the Lord did through me with that prayer, but all I know is for the rest of the night, we were talking and laughing and joking. We were talking about church and even bagging on people backstage. He was just the coolest person ever!

As we were backstage and he was getting ready to go on stage, here came Andrew. He saw me, and his whole face was in shock.

"Leah?!"

"Hey!" I said confidently.

"How'd... how'd you get back here?"

"Oh, I came with Shakeer and Tia!"

"Oh.. oh... wow!" He looked at Shakeer in amazement. "Nice to meet you, man!"

He turned back to me. "You look good, Leah! Wow! Thanks for hooking all of this up! I'm so glad you got to come!"

I was looking at him like... *nigga what?* Andrew was so nervous and looked so deflated. He thought that he'd blocked me, but I came through like gangbusters. It was such a proud moment.

Shakeer and Tia started talking, and Tia said, "Yeah, that's that man that didn't let her come after Leah worked out the whole deal!"

"That's the nigga?" Shakeer said.

"Yep," I replied.

"Leah. You like old dudes?" Shakeer said.

"What?"

"That nigga looks like he's about 55."

"No, he's not. He's 40," I said.

"That nigga ain't 40."

"Yes he is! He's 40!"

"Leah! That nigga is OLD! You like old dudes! I see how you roll!"

For the rest of the night he kept bagging on me. I wasn't letting somebody get me with those digs; I had a comeback every single time. It was pretty funny.

Shakeer's performance was amazing. The crowd went crazy. After he performed he wanted to go get something to eat. We got back in the SUV, and it took us to a restaurant on Melrose, in Hollywood. We were still talking and laughing, and we were just having a great time together. All of us were. We got back to the hotel, and he asked if we wanted to come up and hang out for a bit. Tia and I looked at each other in agreement.

So we went back up to his hotel room. The conversation just kept flowing easily.

"Yeah, I was raised in church! You know that one song that goes... can't you see the clouds gathering!"

"Oh my gosh, you know that song?! I love that song! You better run to the arc before the rain starts!" I finished.

We were singing and dancing and laughing. It was so fun and easy. But I had to get up early for church the next morning, so I ended up having to break up the party.

"I have church in the morning, but I had so much fun. Thank you so much for having me, I really appreciate you guys for allowing me to tag along. It was nice meeting you!" I said.

"It was really nice meeting you, too!" he said.

We gave each other a hug before leaving the room. Tia was leaving too, so we walked down to the valet together.

"Tia. He is SO fine! Oh my gosh! How do you take it?!" I asked.

"Girl! I think he thinks you're fine too," she said.

"What do you mean?"

"He has never talked to anybody like that or hung out this long with anyone. Oh no. I think he thinks you're fine."

"Nah, no way. But anyway, thanks for having me. I really appreciate what you did for me. You're really my girl!"

I got in my car and left. I was thinking about Shakeer all night long. I had the time of my life. And he was sooo fine!

The next day I went to church, and Dr. Tigner wanted to know everything. I told him about how Andrew was looking crazy when I was backstage, and how he looked so stupid. I even told him about how much Shakeer and I hit it off.

"I knew it. I knew it!" he repeated.

"I didn't know it! I would never think he would talk to me," I said.

"Leah, why do you always do that to yourself? Why do you always think that you're not attractive and that people won't like you? Why do you think low of yourself?"

"It's just so weird!" I said.

"No! It's not weird. You have to start expecting things like that. I expect people to like you. You just have a low value of yourself because of how James treated you, but not everybody feels that way about you. People really like you, and you are likeable."

"I don't know. I just didn't think he would be somebody that would like me," I replied.

"Leah. Just keep going with the story," he urged.

"Well, when we were backstage, he asked me to pray! First I was frustrated with Tia for telling him that I was a church girl. Why does she always have to tell people that I'm a church girl? Why can't I just be a regular girl?"

"Because that's who you are. And that's what the Lord uses. Did you pray?" he asked.

"Of course I did. After I prayed, I don't know what happened, but we just clicked! We talked all night. He called Andrew an old man too!" I joked.

"I told you that man was old!"

One of the associate ministers at the church happened to be close by and overheard our conversation.

"Leah, do you know Andrew is 50?" he asked.

"No he's not. He's not 50," I said confidently.

"He's definitely 50 years old."

"He's definitely 40 years old," I said.

"No. He's 50! I know that for a fact. He knows one of my friends and they were talking about how old they were. He's 50!"

Sheesh. Shakeer was right!

Later on in the week, I was at the Gap in Century City, one of my favorite malls in Los Angeles. While I was looking for some good deals, Tia happened to call me.

"Hey! What's going on?" I asked.

"Girl! Guess what?" she said.

"What?"

"My boss cannot stop talking about you."

"Me??"

My whole body started getting butterflies.

"Yes. He cannot stop talking about you! He wants you to hang out with us more. He wants to know if you want to go eat!"

"Really?!"

"Yes, girl! In fact, he wants you to go with us to the 'Dreamgirls' screening."

"Wow! I would love to go!" I said. "Let me try to work out my schedule, and I will call you right back."

I had to call Dr. Tigner. I always wanted him to coach me. I had made so many bad decisions with guys and relationships, and I would always just want to double check with him. I told him what Tia said, and that he had invited me to the screening.

"GO!" he insisted.

I called Tia back, and she told me that the screening was on Thursday at 7 p.m., at ArcLight Theatre in Hollywood. I was so excited.

The next day Tia called and told me that Shakeer had a movie that he was filming. He was currently on set and wanted to know if I wanted to come hang out. I agreed. I had nothing else to do. Plus, I wanted to see him.

I put on some cute sweats and a cute hat and met him on the set. It was in Hollywood. When I got there, he seemed to be super excited to see me. I didn't want to bother him too much because he was working. I was just happy to be there.

Afterwards, he wanted to grab a bite to eat again. All of us went out, and we had an even better time than our previous outing. We were getting even more comfortable with each other, and still laughing together.

I got home late that night. Every time I went out with them, the night didn't end until about 1 or 2 a.m. I would have to get up by 6 so that I could be at work by 7:30. It didn't matter to me because I was having so much fun and really enjoying myself.

The night finally came for the "Dreamgirls" premiere at the ArcLight Theatre. It seemed like he was really glad that I came. We all sat next to each other in the theater and enjoyed the movie. During the movie, Tia leaned over to me and said, "I know he's going to ask us to get something to eat, but I have a date tonight. If you want to go with him, you should go, but I'm going on my date!"

"Okay," I whispered.

"If you don't feel comfortable going, then just say no. He'll understand."

If Shakeer asked me to go out to eat, I definitely wasn't saying no!

"Okay," I agreed.

"Dreamgirls" was AMAZING. As we were walking back to the parking lot, Shakeer asked us if we wanted to get something to eat.

"I'm going out tonight, so I can't," Tia said.

"Leah, how about you? You hungry?"

"Sure," I agreed.

"Okay, cool. I'll ride with you," he said.

I agreed, but I was feeling so insecure to have this celebrity in my green Ford Explorer. But if he said he wanted to ride with me, so be it. I just had to bite the bullet. I swallowed my pride.

"Okay, come on!" I said.

We went to this little diner on Melrose. We were just talking. He loved french fries. To be so fit, he sure did love his french fries and pizza. He was just so fun and normal. Our conversation always flowed so easily. Without a doubt, we had a connection. We always started our meals with prayer—he would either ask me to pray or he'd pray. We'd hold hands, too. This guy was just amazing to me.

"So I noticed you've been kind of shy to hang out," he said.

"Yeah..." I said with a sly smile.

Even though we'd only hung out a couple of times, I would kind of keep my distance and remain respectful. I heard that he had a girlfriend who was an actress and was pretty well known. So, even though I had a crush on him, I was still respectful. I just knew that was bad karma when you date someone who's already with someone else. Plus I went through that with James, and we all know how that turned out. Besides, who knew if he even wanted to date me? That was just something that was going on in my head.

"I just feel like you're trying not to hang out with me. What's up with that?" he said.

"Mmmm. Well, you do have a girlfriend."

"So? I didn't say anything about that. We're friends," he said.

"Yeah, we're friends," I replied.

"And I just want to let you know something... You going to be close to me," he asserted.

"What?" I asked.

"Yep. You are going to be close to me."

I don't know what it was, but there was something about his manhood and his assertiveness that did something to me. He always said what he wanted, yet still kept it respectful. He knew what he wanted and was determined to get it. That confidence and swag was so attractive.

After that night at the diner, Shakeer and I would talk on the phone often. He would ask me to pray for different things for him, like if he had an audition or was reading a script for a movie. He was also recording a new album at the time. He would always call me to see what I thought about certain things, and I really appreciated that because James really didn't include me or care much about what I thought. Shakeer, though, would ask for my advice. He sincerely wanted my input and sincerely wanted to know how to proceed. From clothes that he was wearing to being on the Oprah show, he wanted my opinion on how he did. He would talk about different movies with me because he loved movies. We would catch matinees and shows after I was done with church. Then we would discuss the movies over brunch. He'd even have me at the studio. Of course I was trying to be conservative at first, because he had a girlfriend, and I knew about it. But as time went on and I would bring up his girlfriend, he would brush it off. I began to not go out as much with him, because I just wanted to be respectful. I didn't want to kiss him or be affectionate because I just didn't want to send the wrong message. My desire was not to be "that girl" who would fool around with someone that was taken. It was so hard not to be affectionate with him because he was so loving and doting himself. I slipped a couple of times and vowed that I would not do it again. Those vows became nonexistent.

One weekend, I had to travel to Houston with Dr. Tigner and his wife. Dr. Tigner was thinking about starting a new church there, and he was scouting out vacant churches. He was originally from there and was considering doing a Friday/Saturday night service in Houston and keeping the Sundays at our church in Los Angeles. We were all staying together, and we happened to be driving back to where we were staying when my phone rang. It was Shakeer.

"Hey! What's going on?" I asked.

"Hey. Just want to talk to you about something," he said.

"Yeah?"

Because we had developed a friendship and a bond through advice, I was thinking he wanted my opinion on a business deal or a new song.

"I just wanted to let you know that we broke up," he said.

"You did?" I asked.

"Yeah. We broke up because I want to pursue this thing with you."

"Really?" I said in disbelief.

I was shocked because he was still this huge, well-known celebrity. He had been in the game for a long time, not just with his music, but his acting, too. All of his relationships were high-profile, with other high-profile people. I was just Leah. So it was hard to wrap my head around it.

"I just wanted to let you know that. I feel good about it, and I knew it was ending with me and her. I just want to do this with you, Leah."

"Okay," I said.

Everyone in the car was trying to ear-hustle. There were about seven people in the SUV, and although I was trying to keep it on the low, they all wanted to know what that phone call was about. Dr. Tigner was looking in the rearview mirror with those curious eyes. I knew I was going to tell him, but I didn't want to tell everyone in the car.

I got out of the car and told Dr. Tigner what had just happened.

"I want to tell you something," Dr. Tigner said. "Proceed with caution."

"What makes you say that?" I asked.

"I don't know. I just think you need to proceed with caution. He's a nice guy, he seems to really like you, and I like the way you guys pray together, but I want you to really proceed with caution. Keep your guard up."

"I understand," I said.

"He's a celebrity, and you're not having sex. You have to understand this. If you want to get into this game, you have to put your head in it, and not just your heart. He's going to expect certain things from you that you just can't give. He may get that from other people. And therefore, you need to proceed with caution. Don't put all your eggs in one basket."

"Okay."

I agreed, but it hurt my heart because I really liked Shakeer. Every time his name popped up on my phone, I got butterflies. Every time he opened up his condo door, and I saw his smile, my heart jumped. Every time I heard his songs on the radio, I couldn't believe I was actually talking to him. It would make me feel so special. To hear "proceed with caution" put a halt on my feelings, yet I trusted Dr. Tigner, and I knew he knew what he was saying. But it is so hard to proceed with caution when you really like somebody and have that special connection. Our chemistry was one in a million, and overwhelming. When he would hug and kiss me, I would just melt. But I would always have to stop because I couldn't have sex with him. I was honest about that. I wanted him to know I wasn't having sex until I was married. He said he was good with it. I was falling for him, and I couldn't help it.

No one that I had dated previously had ever thought of me as valuable like Shakeer did (in a sense of the spiritual world, or in my relationship with God). So for him to want to be a part of that meant a lot to me. I took it personally and spiritually, and I was grateful for it. I would keep a journal about all of our conversations, when we went out, and things he would ask me. Every night when I got home, I would write about what we did. Dr. Tigner told me to do that so I could track our progress and to keep myself grounded. My journals would be prayer entries, and sometimes I'd even ask the Lord for him to like me. I wanted him to love me, although he always stressed the fact that we didn't need to put a title on our relationship because I should know what I was to him. He always reminded me how beautiful I was. He would see me in different settings and say, "I don't think you know how beautiful you are, but I want to remind you. You are beautiful. It doesn't matter who you're around, or what setting you're in, or how many women are in the room. You are beautiful." I really appreciated that and probably needed it.

He wrote a children's book and wanted to film it with him reading to kids. Being a third grade teacher, I had kids. One day Tia called and asked, "Do you know a setting where we could film Shakeer reading to the kids?"

"You can come to my school! I can get approval from the principal."

So I went to the principal and got all the guidelines from the school and had Shakeer's team talk to him. We ended up getting clearance, and we were all set. He was able to come read to my students and get footage. I was so excited to have that happen. The students were so cute. They knew who he was, and it was so great that I got to share that moment with them. Even then, he found time to talk to me privately, without raising suspicion. That night, he had a screening for his first movie that he was in, and he asked if I could come to the after party. Of course I agreed. Everything that he was doing was just making it so hard to proceed with caution. I went to the premiere party, and he was surrounded with so many people and celebrities, yet he made time for me. He wanted to take a picture with me, too. I felt very welcomed and special. It really did something for my ego and my self-esteem to have someone like him interested in me. It gave me a sense of confidence.

He would know about the most private restaurants that would be booked for months in advance. Yet he'd always manage to get reservations for us. I loved it. He loved different kinds of fish. He tried to eat very healthy because he had a strict workout regimen. Growing up in Los Angeles, you would think I would know about all of these restaurants, but I didn't. They were so high-profile and exclusive.

One particular time, he took me to a restaurant in Hollywood, and he said, "I'm not mad that you were married before."

I was so confused that I put my fork down and just looked at him. "Excuse me?" I asked.

"I'm not mad that you were married before. Tia told me how you were so hurt, and all the things that happened, and to not hurt you since you've been through a lot."

Why would she tell him that I was married before? Why wouldn't she let me do that?

I realized that she told him because she literally saw me go through that terrible time, and she did not want me to get hurt. But him knowing it made me feel bad. I felt bad because in my past, when I would tell men that I had been married before and was divorced, it didn't end well. Nobody ever took it well. I just thought that I didn't want to share that with him because I didn't want him to look at me differently.

"I don't care about that. I don't care about that at all. I just care about you," he proceeded. "It doesn't matter. The past is what makes everybody who they are. I heard he was really crazy, and did you wrong, and you should grow from that."

I was looking at him like... *okay*... Yet it did make me feel good and special that he felt that way. I could tell that he was waiting on me to open up.

"Well, it's true. I was married before."

"You're over it?"

"Yeah, I'm over it. I'm good. I learned a lot," I confessed.

"That's good. Don't feel bad about that. We all have a past."

He started talking about his past relationships, and how he thought he was in love, and even how he had been engaged before. It opened up a new level of our communication and our confidence in each other. It made me appreciate him even more, because I was very insecure about that part of my life. How was I supposed to proceed with caution with someone like this?

It was even harder to proceed with caution when he wanted me to spend the night at his house. I would have to remind him that I couldn't do certain things with him in bed because I wasn't having sex until I got married. Spending the night with someone would make me really vulnerable. He would understand, but he would be very disappointed every time. I understood his frustration. He would ask over and over for me to spend the night with him, but I knew I could not do that if I wanted to keep my promise to God. It was so hard to refuse. Being with him would make me feel so good. I could kiss and cuddle him all night. I knew if we ever made love it would be electric, but I just could not do it. No matter how sexually attracted I was to him, I could not go against my promise to the Lord. I had to hold on to it, no matter how hard it was to keep.

After church, Shakeer would always ask me what my pastor preached about. Plus, he knew that I would work on the sermons. I would share what Dr. Tigner had preached, and he really valued and respected it. Even if we were out on a Saturday night, he would always want me to call Dr. Tigner and ask if I could catch a movie before heading back to help with the sermon.

One particular day, he said, "You know what? I want to go to church one day with you. You think that would be all right?"

"Okay…" I hesitated.

"Let's shoot for this Sunday," he said.

Inside, I was really excited, but I was trying not to be, because if he didn't show up, I would be disappointed. I also wanted everyone to treat him respectfully, and I didn't want anyone to flock around him and ask for pictures. So I was worried yet excited that he wanted to go.

Saturday night he called and confirmed the time and promised that he'd be there.

I sing in the choir on Sundays. So I told Dr. Tigner that he was coming. I was in the choir stand when the service started. I was in the alto section. We were singing praise and worship when all of a sudden, the doors opened. Varie was walking down the aisle, and guess who was behind her? Shakeer.

She walked him all the way down to the second row in the center section, and he had the biggest smile on his face when he saw me in the choir. He did a little wave, and I was so ecstatic that he'd really kept his word and came.

Dr. Tigner got up to welcome all the visitors, and he said, "Shakeer is here! This is Leah's friend." Everybody started cheering.

Keith was on the organ, and I could tell he was upset. My friends at church felt sorry for him. But my focus was on Shakeer. After I sang in the choir, I sat by Shakeer for the service. It was just so great, and it felt like it couldn't get any better. Proceeding with caution was just so hard.

After church, Shakeer was ranting and ranting about how good it had been. He loved the music and preaching, and especially liked how Dr. Tigner taught the word of God. He even wanted to come back the following week.

"Let's go get something to eat!" he suggested.

"Well, I can't leave church right away because I have to make sure Dr. Tigner has everything he needs."

"That's fine. Tonight we can order in, watch some movies, and chill. I just want to see you."

"Of course! Let me just get finished, and then I'll meet you at the house."

As we were walking to the parking lot, my dad was walking to his car as well. My dad saw that Shakeer had been in service the whole time and knew exactly who he was.

"Shakeer, this is my dad, Mr. Walker!" I said.

"Hey! How are you? It's so nice to meet you!" my dad said. He was overjoyed. Anybody other than James would be amazing, right? "Thanks for coming today. I hope you enjoyed it!" he continued.

"Thanks, sir! It's great to meet you!" Shakeer said.

It was just so cool, and the day was going so well. It couldn't get better. I said my goodbyes to Shakeer and gave him a hug, and he started looking at me intensely. It's like he saw another level of me that he liked, I guess. I was just falling hard and I couldn't get up. Not only was he so fine, but he was into God, and into what I was into. That made it even better for me.

I went back inside the church after he drove away, and everyone rushed up to me with questions about him. People were so amazed that I had gotten him to come to church. I was trying to tell everyone that it wasn't really that hard because he loves the Lord.

I went to Dr. Tigner's office, and he said, "You did good!"

"I did?"

"You did great! You got him to come to church, and he actually came. He enjoyed himself. You did GREAT!" he said.

"Do you think he likes me?" I asked.

"Leah, I'm not changing what I said. Proceed with caution."

"Okay, okay. It's just so hard, though," I said.

"I know. I know you like him a lot, but guard your heart."

"Okay."

I just went along with it. I finished up at church and changed into something cute and casual before heading to Shakeer's house. I wore a little bit of makeup, lip gloss, and I smelled amazing.

I went over to his house, and we watched movies and ordered dinner. We were joking around and also talking about church. Every time someone would call him, he wouldn't forget to mention that he'd gone to my church earlier and explained how good it was. Even Tia called him, and he told her.

We continued enjoying the rest of our night, and of course he asked if I could stay.

"Can you please stay with me tonight?"

"I can't. I can't do it," I said.

Everything in me wanted to stay. EVERYTHING! My mouth was saying no, but my body was screaming YES! I mean, what could be better than a whole night of lovemaking, sleeping, and waking up next to his beautiful face? I don't know why, but everything about him was so special to me. I still couldn't believe that he liked me.

I ended up getting out of it because I had to keep my vow to the Lord. I left, and he told me to call him when I got home. I got into my car and drove off, thinking about how lovely the night was. When I got home and called him, he couldn't stop raving to me about how much he'd enjoyed the time. I really did as well, but I was trying to keep my guard up like Dr. Tigner told me. I got off the phone and wrote in my journal before going to sleep.

For the next couple of weeks, we would go out and have a good time, but I started really questioning if he liked me. Sometimes when he would invite me to events, he would be so consumed with the event and other people. Of course there would be other women around, and I tried not to let it bother me, but I did begin to question it. Sometimes I wouldn't hear from him after video shoots or sets where they were filming. He would have other actresses and singers on set who were just gorgeous. I would feel a little insecure, and then he would sneak a smile at me that would make me forget everything.

Every time I would see him, I would bring something to give him. He loved those soft peppermints, so I would make sure to have some in my purse. Even if I was going to the studio, I would call and ask him if he wanted anything, and he would always say yes and request what he wanted. Most times, it would be Pinot Noir wine. I had no clue what that was because I don't drink, but I still would figure it out and bring it. Whatever I could do to show him that I liked him, I wanted to do it. I don't know why. I just wanted him to know how I felt. But it wasn't really being reciprocated. I couldn't lie; I knew that I was doing more for him than he was for me.

Anytime I would talk to Dr. Tigner about it, he would say, "Leah, I told you to guard your heart."

"I know, it's just so hard," I would constantly say.

"You just have to back up a little. If he asks to go to the movies, say you can't go sometimes."

So I would do that. I would purposely dodge different outings that Shakeer would invite me to. It really began to bother him.

"Come on, Lee! We can't go to the movies? I haven't seen you all week!" he would say.

"I'm sorry, I have to be up early for work," I replied.

"You know I always make sure you're back in time for work! Come on, it'll just be a couple hours!"

"I can't, I'm really sorry."

"Okay then, bye," he would say with a horrible attitude.

Even though I would decline the invitation, I always wanted to go. I would usually spend my night wishing I'd gone. So the next time he would invite me out, I'd be jumping to go. It became really weird. Was I falling into the James thing again, where I liked him so much that I was forgetting about myself and then falling into those depressions when I wouldn't hear from him? I could not feel that type of pain again. So I would go through these battles with myself in my mind about whether I should keep pushing forward or pull back. I didn't know what exactly to do, but I knew that I was confused. I wanted to be optimistic but was afraid to repeat history.

There was a specific video shoot that he had with two celebrity women that he didn't invite me to. I was wondering if he didn't want me on the set because he liked them. He never mentioned it, not one word about it. A lot of things happened like that, where I would really question how he felt about me. Even though I wanted to pull back so badly, I liked him so much that I wouldn't.

One day during the WHW Expository Teaching Conference, I was getting ready to go to the banquet, and he called. Of course I answered. He was out of town at the time.

"Hey, what's going on?" I said.

"Hey, Lee—there's something I need to tell you."

"Okay, what is it? Is there anything you need me to pray for?" I asked.

"There's an article coming out about me and another girl," he said.

"Okay..."

"I just want you to know it's not true, and you know how I feel about you."

"All right..." I said.

"We don't have to put any titles on our relationship, you know how I feel about you. You're beautiful, and you know that. You never have to question who you are to me," he said.

"No problem," I said hesitantly.

"Are you good?" he asked.

"Yeah I'm good. I have to go to this banquet, and then I'll call you later."

Is he preparing me for something that I don't want to know about? Does he realize that I like him so much that the article would break my heart? Who is the girl he was talking about?

I didn't look for the article at all. I didn't do any investigating like I would normally do. I'm a nosy person. I look up everything and hang on to people's every word. I remember every event, and even what people were wearing. I'm like a human tape recorder with a photographic memory, and I want to know every single detail about everything. But with this, I didn't even bother to look. I couldn't. I absolutely couldn't bear to find myself in that type of pain again.

That conversation did bother me and caused me to ponder it heavily. Of course I talked to Dr. Tigner about it, and I asked him what he thought.

"Leah, he probably is involved with someone. You're not having sex. You have to have this in your head. He probably is dating other people although he might really like you and see you as different. He sees you as a good luck charm, and he asks you for advice. He knows you have a relationship with the Lord, and he respects that about you, but you have to realize that he is definitely dating other people."

Of course, deep down inside, I knew that, but I didn't want to accept it. One day, he had a performance on a college campus that he wanted me to go to. I finished my work with Dr. Tigner early so

I was able to attend. I was driving over to his house when I got a call from Tia. I think she felt a kind of way about us dating but didn't really know how to express it. She would say little things to me, but she had seen me go through so much and had been with me when we saw James in bed with another woman, and had even helped me pack all my clothes to leave James. I knew that sometimes she could come off as harsh, but I felt like it was protective.

"Hey, Tia, what's up?" I asked.

"I just wanted to talk to you. I know you're coming today to the college campus. You're not telling me too much about what's going on with you and Shakeer, and to be honest it is bothering me. I mean, are you gonna have his baby?"

I started laughing hysterically. "You're so funny. No, I'm not having sex with him. You know that!"

"Yeah, but you're not saying anything, and we're close. What's going on?"

"I mean, I really like him, but I don't know what's going on. I've been trying to take it slow," I said.

"Leah, you need to take it slow. When he dates people, if he's done, he's done. I've seen a lot of things. I'm with him every single day. I know him very well. You need to be careful! You guys are very different. I don't see this really working out. Yeah, you're the kind of person that he has never dated before because of your values and your education and your connection with the Lord. It's definitely totally different than what he's used to, and I know he likes that. He thinks you're fun, and he tells me all the time how pretty you are. All that is good and everything, but I just don't see it working out. You have to know that I know him."

This was a lot for me to take in. This was the first time that I had liked someone this much since James. I was wondering why she was so hard on me about it. But at the same time, I had to keep reminding myself that she was being a friend and being protective. Also, this was her job, and this was what she had to do. I knew she had to play both sides, but I did feel some kind of way. *Why doesn't she like us together? What is it that she doesn't like? I'm a good person, and she knows that.* I knew that she knew I wouldn't do anything disrespectful or carry myself in a bad way. She knew what I'd gone through, so why would she do this? But I had to respect it and move forward. I didn't let that halt our day because she was one of my closest friends, and I knew she loved me.

So I went to his house, and we all went to the event together. I could see there were a lot of guys there, and a lot of them were checking me out. I think Shakeer could see that, and he wanted to make sure that they knew that I was with him.

He asked in front of a lot of people, "So you're coming to the house after the show?"

"Yeah, of course," I agreed.

He made sure that he was marking his territory, and I could definitely tell that. That did make me feel good, but I couldn't stop thinking about what Tia and Dr. Tigner had said. It was so hard for me to feel completely comfortable when I knew what they thought. But I still kept going. I still kept hoping and wishing and praying that we would work out.

His album came out, and it was really amazing. I felt a part of it because I was in the studio for a lot of its recording. He would ask me about different songs, play them for me, and ask my opinions about different verses. I felt connected to it. He even mentioned me in the special thanks portion of the album. He said, "Leah, you have a beautiful spirit." I was so happy he did that. It meant the world to me.

The night of his release party was quickly approaching. I had my hair freshly done and made sure that my outfit looked really pretty. I picked out a beautiful dress and strappy heels. Tia called me the night before and told me that she didn't have anyone to do her hair and was wondering if I could do it. Of course I agreed. I did her hair all the time and loved doing it because it was so long and gorgeous.

She came over, and while I was doing her hair, Shakeer called me.

"Lee—the release party is tomorrow. Let's go out and celebrate! Come to this restaurant, I want to be around people who I love and enjoy!" he said with excitement.

Of course my heart was jumping up and down, but in front of me was Tia with freshly washed hair that I had to do. "I wish I could. I can't! I'm doing Tia's hair right now," I said.

"Doing Tia's hair? Man, tell Tia that you'll be back. Come with me!"

"I can't. I just washed her hair."

"Man, this is a celebration! I want to celebrate with you! You were with me the whole time. This is epic!"

"I... can't," I said again.

Tia was looking at me like *Girl... you have to do my hair!*

"All right then. Well, I'll see you tomorrow at the party," he said bleakly.

"Yes, see you tomorrow," I said.

"Good. Our loyalty to each other comes first," Tia said.

"Yup, you're right," I agreed. Inside, I felt so bad because I really wanted to be with him, but I knew I had made a promise. I felt like I had to make it up to him, so I told myself that tomorrow at the wrap party, I would look my best and make sure to be with him.

The night of the party came. There were SO many people there that I loved from the big screen. All of our friends, and even people that Tia and I had known from high school were there. We were all hanging out and having a great time, but Shakeer was in his own section. There were lots of girls there, from movie stars to artists to tennis players—I mean, everybody was on the scene. People kept asking me why I wasn't with him, and I would keep telling them that this was his moment, and I wanted to let him shine.

I did see him talking to a bunch of girls, though, and I just felt awkward and out of place, but I was trying to enjoy myself. I didn't want to drink, but I was trying to talk and laugh and keep my spirits high. Tia was working really hard because it was a big night for her, too. I just kind of felt like I was forgotten. He didn't spend that much time with me, and he didn't come up to me at all. I ended up going over and congratulating him on his success. He saw me in the cut but didn't go out of his way to come see me.

You know what… it's time for me to go. I was so disappointed. I decided to go up to him and say my goodbyes.

"Hey, Lee!" he said.

"Hey! I'm going to get ready to leave," I said.

"You're leaving?"

"Yeah, I'm getting ready to leave. I just wanted to come up and tell you how proud I am of you, and I'm so happy for you. This is going to be so great, thank you so much for inviting me tonight."

"Okay, I'll call you when I get home," he said.

"All right."

And I walked out. By myself. My heart dropped. I thought this was the night that we'd celebrate, I thought that we'd be together, but there I was again, walking to my car by myself. I could hear the music playing from the party as I went. I felt alone. Again. I felt it was my fault, though. They'd warned me.

That night after the release party, I was really down on myself by the time I got home. I called Dr. Tigner and told him what happened. He suggested that I should have known that this was going to happen.

"You aren't too good at this proceeding with caution thing, are you?" he asked jokingly. "He is a man. He has a lot of girls. He is going to have sex! Since you aren't doing that, he's going to get it from somewhere else. You need to really get a grip on it and know that this is what's happening."

Shakeer not giving me any attention that night was showing me where I really stood. Yes, he said I should know what I was to him, and yes, he said that we didn't have to put a title on our relationship, but obviously if he wasn't putting a title on the relationship, I should have known that we weren't more than friends. I wasn't his girlfriend, and I should have known that. It was a hard pill to swallow, and I chose to resort to my journal. Although I wanted him to solidify the relationship, I understood it wasn't going to happen. I was getting ready to go to sleep when the phone rang. It was late; after 2 a.m. It was him.

"Hey, how are you?" I asked.

"Good. I just wanted to tell you how much I appreciate you coming out tonight. I wanted you to know that you really helped me with this project, and I didn't want you to think that I didn't appreciate you. I appreciate all the support and everything you did for me. I just really wanted you to come out with me last night before the party to celebrate, but I know you had to do Tia's hair. I was really disappointed in that, and maybe that's why I was acting like that tonight. But I just really wanted you to know how much I appreciate you for everything."

I felt like maybe I should just go with that and appreciate him calling me.

"No problem," I said.

"Well, I know you're in bed, so go ahead and go to sleep. I'll talk to you tomorrow."

"Okay," I said.

"Love." He always ended his phone calls with this. He never liked saying goodbye.

So I got off the phone and went to bed happier than I had been when I left the party. At least he'd called me. But I still had to understand why he did what he did. And although he called me, and although I felt better, I had to really understand that. I didn't want it to be like that. I genuinely wanted to be in a relationship with him. I wanted him to love me and put a title on us, but he wasn't going to give it to me. I guess I had to be satisfied with what he was giving me.

With the release of an album, there's several things that happen. He had to tour, do different venues and shows to promote the album. He would invite me to some of the events, and it would be great. But he wouldn't invite me to certain events.

He also had a movie deal in Prague. He called me so excited. "Lee, I got the role! The one that we prayed about, for that audition! Remember? Can you believe it?!" he gushed.

"I believe it! I'm so happy for you."

"I'm gonna be doing the movie in Prague. It's with a lot of A list celebrities. This is so amazing! I can't wait. Thank you so much for praying for me and believing in me! God is great!"

As we got off the phone, I was really excited for him. Of course, the next thing I was wondering was if he was going to invite me to go. Every day I was waiting on him to ask me to go with him. He was leaving in about a month. I just knew he was going to ask me to go with him. *I'm the one that prayed with him about this. He's going to ask me to come.* I was constantly reminding myself of this. Every day he was talking about the movie and getting into character. We went to see all of these movies that he felt would prepare him for his role. He was reading up and doing a lot of research on his character. He was a researcher and a very hard worker. His album was #1, and then he got this movie, so his career was really taking off. He was a movie star in the making. It was really exciting to witness.

I would constantly ask Dr. Tigner if he thought I would get invited to Prague. He would always just say he didn't know, and I think he was just trying to spare me the heartbreak.

Shakeer and I were still going out to dinner and the movies, and he still didn't ask me. Then it got to the time where he was supposed to go, and we talked the night before. He told me what time his plane was leaving, we prayed, and then he took off.

I didn't really hear from him.

I figured it was going to take about twelve hours for him to arrive and get settled. So I expected to hear from him the next day. Two days passed, and I didn't hear from him. Three days passed, and I still didn't hear from him. Four days…

Then I decided to just call and make sure that he made it. I honestly began to get a little worried. The ringing was different, so I knew that he had made it to another country. But he didn't pick up. The next day, he called and said, "Hey, I made it! We've been working, and it's so much fun. The whole crew hangs out, and they're so cool. They're treating me so well. It's such a blessing. You know, I was going to ask you to come out here, but I figured I shouldn't ask you because I really need to concentrate on my work, and some of my crew is here with me. They asked me if I was going to bring you to Prague with me. I really thought about it, but I figured it wasn't the best idea. But I miss you! I really do miss you, and I wish you were here. It's cool, though. We'll have other trips that we can go on!"

My heart dropped. It's like he knew that I was anticipating him asking me to go to Prague and he didn't.

"It's okay," I assured him. Typical Leah. Never wanted anyone to see me sweat. "This is your destiny, this is your blessing, and I want you to enjoy it! I want you to have fun. Don't worry about me, I'm good. I'm so proud of you! I'm praying for you every day."

"Yeah, man, pray for me. You gotta keep praying for me. But this is just crazy. God is so good," he said. "All right, well, it's late here. I'm gonna go so I can get some sleep, but I'll be calling you."

"Okay, cool! Bye!" I tried to use my happiest voice.

I was so sad. Even the crew was asking when he was going to bring me? So obviously people knew we were close... Why wouldn't he just bring me to hang out? I called my go-to, Dr. Tigner, and told him everything.

"Woah, woah, woah. Leah, can I ask you a question?"

"Yes?" I asked.

"Do you have a passport?"

"No, I lost it."

"So even if he did ask you, you still couldn't go. How can you be mad if you are not even prepared?" he inquired.

"You're right..." I realized.

"Trying to get a passport isn't overnight. You gotta apply for it, and it takes a minute to get it back. It would be different if you were prepared to go, but you weren't. You can't be mad at anybody but yourself. If he didn't invite you, there's a reason he didn't invite you, Leah. That's why I keep telling you to proceed with caution. Guard your heart! You're in this far more than he is, and you need to wake up! Now can you get a passport, so that when somebody asks you the next time, you can go?"

He was right. He always was. I started applying for a passport.

About a month and a half later, he got back from Prague. I was so happy that he was back. He did call me several times while he was out of town, which made me feel good. It made me feel like he was thinking about me. I got a passport and everything, and I was prepared, so that if he had any more movies in any more locations, I would be ready if he asked.

As soon as he got back from Prague, he ended up landing another movie. I mean, his career was just going through the roof. For this movie, the location was in the hood. He wanted me to drive him to the hood so that he could get a taste of what it felt like. I drove him near my grandmother's house because she lives in Watts. I showed him the Watts Towers and different things like that, and he really enjoyed it. Anytime he got a new character, he really got into it and wanted to study it to the best of his ability. He soaked in the environment, and even wore the attire when he didn't have to. He was all in, which was great. He was studying his lines and asking different questions. He was still asking me to pray for him. It seemed like every single thing that we prayed for, God answered, and it came to pass. It was really a fulfillment of what Dr. Tigner said: I was like a good luck charm to him. He would never not ask me what I thought, and he wouldn't make a deal before we prayed about it. He would always do exactly what I said. He was blowing up in front of my eyes.

It was the 4th of July. He told me that he just wanted to spend the day with me.

"We don't have to go to any parties or anything. Let's go to Malibu. We can drive up the coast and go to the beach."

I knew a private spot on the beach that we could go to, because everywhere we went, people would try to swarm him for pictures and autographs. While I would be behind him getting all of this attention, girls would always be in my ear telling me how lucky I was. So sometimes it was nice, but I could tell that sometimes he just didn't want to be bothered. I figured that's why he would go to those private restaurants and those in the cut type places.

I took him to Geoffrey's in Malibu and then to a private spot on the beach where we could walk by ourselves. We had a really great day. As we were driving, he was telling me about how he had an invitation to go to the Essence Festival.

"Wow, cool, I've never been to Essence."

"You've never been to Essence?" he asked.

"Nope!" I joked.

"You wanna go?"

"Yeah! Sure," I said.

"Really? You would come? I can make arrangements for you to go. It would be fun! Everybody's going out there, my whole crew is going. It would be great!"

"Okay, well, cool!" I agreed.

He called his travel assistant and gave her my name. He told me that she would be reaching out to me later to get more information for my ticket. I was so enamored. I didn't go to Prague, but I was going to Essence! We drove back to LA and ended up going to the movies when we got back. After the movies, we talked more about Essence, which was the following weekend.

"Are you going to stay in my hotel room?" he asked.

"You know I can't!"

"Okay, so I have to get you another hotel room?"

"Yes," I confirmed.

"Okay. You know I don't like that, but okay. That's fine. I'll do that for you because I want you to come."

That night when I got home, I called Dr. Tigner and told him that Shakeer had invited me to go to New Orleans for the Essence Festival.

Dr. Tigner thought that it was a great idea but had a couple of reservations.

"You know he's going to want to sleep with you," he commented.

"No, no, I took care of that. I told him that he had to get me my own room, and that I wasn't going to be able to stay with him," I confirmed.

"Okay, that's fine. But Leah, you have to know that when a man is taking you out of town, that is one of his expectations. He's paying for everything, getting you a room, paying for your flight... just know that this is one of the expectations. You have to stay strong on your convictions and your promise to the Lord."

"I will. I promise I will," I said.

Having this warning in my head on my way to New Orleans was good, because it kept me on my toes. I definitely wanted the Lord to bless me, and God is way more important than Shakeer, even though I liked him so much. I called my parents and let them know that I was going to New Orleans. My dad was excited and wanted me to enjoy myself. I told him that I would be leaving on Friday morning and coming back Sunday morning right before church. I never missed church. I wanted the Lord to know that He came first in my life, and any relationship was second. Shakeer and his team were staying until Monday, but I asked his travel assistant to make my arrangements to come back Sunday morning. I would leave right from the airport and go straight to service. My dad approved and just wanted me to be safe.

Shakeer called me and said that he heard everything was set.

"Okay, I made arrangements for you to stay with Tia. You know I want you to stay with me, though."

"Yes, I know."

"But I know your standards, and I know what you stand for. I'm just happy you're coming."

"Thank you so much! I'll see you Friday!"

Friday morning, we got to the airport. I was ecstatic. I'd planned every single outfit. I knew what the itinerary was: There were different shows, different appearances. He had the entire weekend booked. I wanted to look flawless for every event. I knew I was going to be super tired when I got home on Sunday. I bought him a card to thank him for inviting me and planned to give it to him Sunday morning before I went to the airport.

We got to the airport, and after we all compared tickets, I learned that Tia and I were sitting together. Shakeer was in first class. I thought that was kind of weird that we weren't all sitting together, but I thought that maybe he didn't want to make a difference between me and Tia. We arrived in New Orleans and got picked up in a black SUV that took us straight to the studio where he had practice. When I showed up, I could see the whole team was looking at each other in disbelief that I had come. It made me feel special because they were happy to see me at the same time.

I was with Tia a lot because he was really busy. Tia and I always had fun together. Yet I could feel her protective side coming out. She was still making comments about how Shakeer loses interest quickly, and so I was listening to her, while at the same time just so happy that I was even there. I wanted to enjoy it.

I found the most joy in the smallest things, like when we could eat together or hang out in Shakeer's hotel suite. I'd be joking and laughing with the whole crew. When we went to the different venues and shows, Shakeer couldn't really be all hugged up on me because he was so busy. I completely understood. He was definitely about his business, and I was definitely a fan of that.

The girls were going crazy over him at every single appearance. He was getting autographs, he was doing freestyle appearances, and then he had several different hosting gigs throughout Essence. He had his own concert that night as well. We were all backstage, and there were a lot of different people from LA that were backstage, too. He kept checking on me the entire time but wasn't really giving me that much attention. I was trying to just be good with the fact that he wanted me to come. That had to mean something. After the show, along with some girls that we knew from LA, we went back to his suite where he hosted an after party. He was drinking quite a bit of red wine. That was his favorite. He kept complimenting this one girl. It just made me feel a little odd. *I'm standing right here...* Tia would just look at me with those *I'm trying to tell you* eyes. I was listening, but I still just liked him so much. So he had a lot of drinks, and he was really enjoying his free time with his team. He would call me over sometimes to sit next to him, and I would sit next to him for a while, and he would be playing cards and drinking. The night started to get a little late, and I had to catch that early flight so I wouldn't miss worship service, so I told him that I was going to have to head back to my room so that I could pack and plan to leave early in the morning. He understood.

"Yeah, I know you have to wake up really early in the morning for church. I really appreciate you coming. I had fun with you!"

"No, thank you for even bringing me out here. I had a blast, you were great! I'm so proud of you!" I said.

"Man, thanks! Well, call me when you land in LA."

Tia walked back to the room with me, and she even helped me pack before she headed back to the suite.

"I'll have the team have the car ready for you in the morning to take you back to the airport."

"Thank you, I really appreciate that," I said.

I tried to go to sleep, but I started crying out of nowhere. As I lay down, I just couldn't help but notice that the trip was nothing like I had hoped it to be. I was happy that I'd gone, but in my head, I'd seen it going completely differently.

That morning, I got up really early. I only had a couple hours to sleep in order to catch the first flight out of New Orleans to get to LA on time. As I got up, I signed the card thanking him for the trip and for taking care of everything. But for some reason, I couldn't give it to him. I just put it in my suitcase and told myself that I would give it to him when he got back to LA. I texted Tia, and she met me downstairs in the lobby. She made sure that I got in the car, and we hugged before she sent me off. I wish I could have stayed with the team for a little while longer, but I knew my obligation.

I got back just in time for church. I ran straight to the choir stand and sang, and everyone had already heard that I had gone to Essence. They wanted to hear all about it, and I completely acted like I'd had the time of my life. I told them about the amazing culture and food that I had experienced.

But when I got into Dr. Tigner's office after service, of course he wanted the full details of the trip. I gave him a blow by blow. I told him about the flight, and how he was in first class. I told him about the different appearances, and how he didn't have that much time. I even told him about how he was giving a lot of attention to the girls in the suite, even though I was standing right there.

"Leah, I told you! You're not giving it up. You have to understand that he didn't make the vow that you made to the Lord, you did. You can't be upset about him wanting to have sex. That's your choice, and you have to just stand firm in that. The one that loves you will fall in line with that. But you can't expect everybody to respect this oath that you gave the Lord. This is exactly what I thought was going to happen."

"Then why do I feel so hurt?" I asked.

"Because you really like him. I know you do. But he doesn't like you like that, Leah. You have to know that. He's not ready to get married. He's career driven. He is in the moment. His career is blowing up. You have to understand that. He's not ready to settle down. You are. He's not. And you can't be mad at that. He treats you nicely, he doesn't disrespect you. He spent money to get you out there—that was nice. He clearly appreciates you and sees you as a spiritual advisor, someone who can help him along the way. And that's what it is."

So once again my heart sank because I didn't know how to stop liking him. I just wanted him to like me as much as I liked him. But I wasn't sure if it was going to happen.

It seemed as though Shakeer always knew when I was feeling kind of bad. Every time that I would feel bad or like I was unappreciated, he would call. Even though I was back in LA and he was still in New Orleans.

"Hey Lee, you good? How was your flight?" he inquired.

"Yes! Thanks again!" I said.

"I just wanted to call you and tell you thank you so much for coming! I really appreciated you coming."

"Thank you for bringing me out there!" I responded.

"Yeah, I just wanted to make sure that you knew that I really appreciate you, and I appreciate our relationship. I'll call you when I get back in LA tomorrow. Love."

I felt better that he called me, but still I was uneasy. I just knew that he didn't like me as much as I liked him. I trusted Dr. Tigner and his advice, so I knew he was telling the truth; I just didn't want to wholeheartedly believe it.

When Shakeer came back, things were back to normal for the most part. Not every day, but sometimes. He'd check in and see how I was doing and tell me about some projects that he was working on. Sometimes the whole conversation would be him talking to me about what projects he had and my opinions on them. Upcoming tours, potential movie roles, TV shows… He would think out loud with me. Sometimes he wouldn't even ask me how I was doing, it would just be about him and advice. And then after he got the advice, he would say that he would talk to me later. It became kind of like counseling sessions and prayer sessions. It didn't matter to me; I just wanted to hear from him.

He was getting ready to go on tour all over the world. He was going to be gone for a while, and I knew it. So when he left, I didn't hear from him for about two weeks. Every day I was looking for a phone call and didn't get one. Not one. Nothing. Tia was on tour with him as well, and I would text back and forth with her, but no word from Shakeer. I wouldn't ask her about him because I knew how she felt about it, and I did not want to jeopardize our friendship by asking her too much about him.

So two weeks went by without hearing a peep from Shakeer. Nothing. And he wasn't a texter, so he wasn't going to text me. I was really upset… How could he not call me for two weeks? I kind of got disgusted and wasn't even looking forward to his calls anymore.

One of my girlfriends, Sarah, asked if we could go out. We went to this cute little restaurant on Third Street called Toast Cafe. It had really great salads and sandwiches. It was in the West Hollywood area, near the Beverly Center. It was like my old stomping ground. We went there around 7 p.m., and the night was just beautiful. LA always has the best nighttime vibe, especially during the summer. We were eating our salads and laughing about different things going on. Just catching up. Then she brought up Shakeer's name. She was telling me about how well his music was doing, and how everywhere she went she was hearing his name. I didn't really want to talk about him, though. I tried to change the subject without raising any red flags and suggested that we not talk about guys for the rest of our dinner.

"Oh, I know why you don't want to talk about him. You heard about Stacy Walker, the tennis player, huh?"

"Stacy Walker?" I asked.

She dropped her fork and looked at me intensely. "You don't know about Stacy Walker?"

"What about Stacy Walker?" My heart started pounding.

"Oh shit," she said as she put her head down.

"What?!"

"You really don't know about her, do you?"

"Know about what? What are you talking about?"

"No one's told you?"

"No! No one's told me. What are you talking about?"

"I can't tell you, but all I can say is… when you go home, log on to bossip.com, and type in Shakeer with Stacy Walker."

"Okay." I squirmed.

After dinner, I must have driven home in less than ten minutes. I got upstairs, logged on to the website, and put in the key search that Sarah had told me. The first thing that came up was him and the tennis star walking out of a London hotel. Her stockings were ripped at the knees, and his lips were greasy and glossy. They looked like they'd just had sex. My heart sank to my feet. I immediately started shaking… The blogs said that they had been together, that she was on tour with him, and their dating was sparking a lot of noise. It was almost midnight when I found the pictures.

I didn't know anything else to do except call Dr. Tigner. I was hoping that Varie didn't get mad at me, but I had to talk to somebody.

"Dr. Tigner, I'm so sorry for calling so late. Are you up?"

"I'm up," he said.

I told him to go on bossip.com and type in the exact keyword search.

"What am I going to see? Stacy Walker, the tennis player and Shakeer?"

"Yes. The tennis star."

He logged on and saw the same picture. "It looks like they just—"

"I know," I said.

I began to tell him the story of what Sarah told me, and that I hadn't heard from him in two weeks. I started crying frantically, asking Dr. Tigner over and over, "How could he do this to me?"

"Leah. He's been trying to tell you. Can't you see? I told you, proceed with caution… You are not giving out, you are not having sex. You can't expect that people are following the same rules! This was bound to happen. He couldn't get it from you, so he had to get it from somewhere else. Remember, he is career driven, it's good for his career to be seen with somebody like her. You're just the good luck charm, you're not the only one. You have to understand this. Be a big girl, take this in, and know he didn't want you like that. Didn't you say that you saw Stacy Walker at the launch party for his album?"

"Yes... I did," I confessed.

"They've probably been dating!"

"But they weren't together," I noted.

"Of course not. He can't show who he's with. Especially if you were there, and whoever else was there. Wasn't she at the video shoot, too?"

"Yes... she was," I sighed. I was sobbing by this point.

"Leah, that's why I kept telling you everything. I didn't want to be harsh, nor to hurt your feelings, but I wanted to prepare you. That's why I kept saying to guard your heart... Now try to get some sleep. I know it's going to be hard. You're going to be okay... you can get through this."

"Okay, thank you so much," I said before hanging up the phone.

I cried myself to sleep.

In the morning, I woke up hoping that it had all been a bad dream. I was just completely beside myself. I was hurt and confused. I didn't know why Tia didn't tell me, but I understood that she had been trying to. I still wished that she had told me exactly what was going on... Later in the day, I ended up getting a text from her that said, *I know you're really hurt.*

I couldn't even get myself to respond... I was completely distraught. Devastated. It took me a really long time to get over it. Then he started calling me. He was calling my phone nonstop, but

I wasn't answering. I had nothing to say. I asked Dr. Tigner when it would be right for me to talk to him, and he told me to answer when I was ready. He understood me not wanting to talk in that moment and suggested that I give it a couple weeks.

So I held tight for two weeks. He was leaving me voicemails begging me to talk to him, and I could tell he knew why I wasn't answering the phone. He knew something was wrong, though. I knew he could feel it.

Finally after two weeks, he called me, and I answered.

"Hey, how you doin'?" he asked.

"I'm good." I really didn't have anything to say, so I was really short about it.

"Why haven't you returned any of my calls?"

"Shakeer. You know why I haven't called you back."

"I know, I know, I know. I was going to tell you—"

"Shakeer, we talk about everything. We prayed about everything. Every movie, every audition, every script, your ideas, your dreams… You couldn't tell me this?"

"I-I was gonna tell you," he stuttered.

"No."

"She's not my girlfriend, though, Lee! I want to date both of you!" he exclaimed.

"Shakeer, I don't share my man. I don't do that."

"I know… I know."

We had a little talk. He asked about Dr. Tigner and how he was, and how everyone at the church was. I knew he was trying to change the subject. He even asked me if I had seen any movies.

"All right, well, I'll talk to you soon," he said.

"Talk to you soon," I replied.

And we hung up. I didn't hear from him for months after that, but it was okay because I was way too hurt and devastated. The one time I had finally really liked someone after James and gave my heart to them and let my guard down, I got hurt. I couldn't handle it.

I couldn't show anybody how much that damaged me, because we'd never even put a title on our relationship, so I couldn't treat it like a breakup. I was basically treating it like I was just really dumb and stupid, and I should have proceeded with caution as Dr. Tigner told me. I should have known that he wasn't taking me as seriously as I was taking him. I should have known that I was just the good luck charm. I began to question myself and my decisions. But I knew that if I could get through a relationship with James, who was the ultimate player, then I could get past Shakeer. I should have known the signs. I learned so much about relationships once again. I learned that if someone isn't putting a title on your relationship, you are not together. All of the *You should know who you are to me* doesn't matter at all; it's complete manipulation. They do not want to claim you as theirs. They do not want to be in a relationship with you... You have to know that if they don't invite you somewhere, then they don't want you around, and there's a deeper reason behind that. I should have recognized all of these signs and red flags. James did the exact same thing—so why didn't I catch it?

Another thing that Dr. Tigner would constantly ask me was if Shakeer ever asked about my bills. I would always say, "No, why would he ask me about my bills?"

"Has he ever tried to give you any money?" he would ask.

"No. He's never tried to give me any money."

"Never? But he knows your position. He knows you're a teacher, and don't make that much money. You assist me, and you don't make that much money doing that either. You're not making a lot of money, and he knows that. He knows you work hard… He should want to help you with your bills and alleviate some of those burdens. Has he ever bought you a big gift?"

"Well, he took me to New Orleans, and he brought some flowers to my school."

"What color were the flowers?" he asked.

"Yellow," I said.

"Not romantic. Yellow means friendship. So no gifts at all?" he asked again.

"Well, for my birthday, I really liked this luggage that Tia had, and he bought me that piece."

"He… bought you a piece of luggage?" he asked sarcastically.

"Yeah! It was really expensive," I confirmed.

"It was really expensive? A piece of luggage? So he never gave you money, he never gave you an expensive gift, and when it was expensive, it was a piece of luggage? Leah, you can't see friendship written on that?"

"I guess you're right…"

"If it was romantic, the flowers would have been red. If he really wants to be your man, a man steps up and is your man. He should want to pay your bills, or at least help alleviate some stress. He should want to."

"Well, he would give me gas money whenever I drove, and—"

"Leah, stop talking. Just stop… Don't say that. That's the least he could do. And I bet that you're gonna say he paid for all your food, too?"

"Well, yeah he did, I didn't have to pay for any food when we were together."

"Leah. Once again, that's the least he could do. He wasn't trying to be your man! Your man would step up and do whatever is necessary to be your man. He would at least offer to pay your bills, pay your car note, do something for you! Something!"

This conversation didn't quite hit home until after I found out about Stacy and was trying to get myself together from that. When I had to shake myself back into reality, that's really when I realized how dumb I was, and not only how I wasn't paying attention to the signs, but how I wasn't applying the lessons that I'd learned from James. I guess it was never like I'd thought it was. It really hit home. Although I really liked him, I really needed to know that the person I settled down with needed to like me more than I liked them. Because this hurt way too much, and I couldn't feel like this anymore.

positive five

So the year went by, and throughout that year, I would still see Stacy and Shakeer together in different blogs and magazines. It just seemed like I could not get it together, I was just so hurt. His album was nominated for a Grammy, and he actually won. He was in all of these movies, and I saw every single one. His name was undeniably everywhere. And every time I would see it, I would be so sad.

Every time I was with Dr. Tigner getting ready to work, I would ask him different questions. He would have to counsel me and help me get my head back in the game. He would constantly tell me that there was somebody else out there who was going to love me and do everything right for me. It just took me a while to get over it completely. My heart was *broken*. Several of my friends didn't ever talk about it because they knew I was hurting, like Sarah and Tia. But one of my close friends, Natasha, who I'd gone to college with, came over for a Christmas party. I was doing anything that I could to help get my mind off of Shakeer. Since I had my house, Sarah and I wanted to have a Christmas party for all of our friends. We decided to make it an Italian theme and invite everyone from high school to college friends. We had drinks and music, and made it really fun.

Before the party started, Natasha wanted to come over to talk to me. I love Natasha so much; I met her my sophomore year at Berkeley. Her mom and my mom were both teachers at the same school, and they planned for us to meet. I was in my Mass Communications 10 class when I remembered my mom telling me to look out for a biracial girl with long, curly hair. I looked around the room and spotted this beautiful biracial girl with long, curly, black hair. She had a beautiful smile. I knew it was her.

I walked up to her and said, "Hi, my name is Leah, and my mom works at Brentwood Science Magnet—"

"Oh my God, my mom's been wanting me to meet you!" she exploded.

"My mom's been wanting me to meet you, too!" I said.

We just hit it off from that point on. Our apartments were around the corner from each other, and we would drive back and forth from Oakland to LA for holidays. We developed a really close-knit friendship. She was really soft-spoken, but always so positive.

When Natasha arrived before the party, we went upstairs to my room so that we could catch up privately. She lay on my bed.

"You know I've heard a lot of things from other people, and I just want to check in with you. How are you doing?"

"I appreciate that so much. My heart is hurting so much. I really liked him," I confessed.

"I know you did... I heard people talking about it and how it would not likely work out because you guys are so different, but I just wanted to see how you were doing and just check on you. I love you, and I'm here for you."

That conversation meant so much because no one was saying anything. Everyone was tiptoeing around me and not really talking about it. For her to just come to me and talk to me about it just made me appreciate her so much. I needed someone to understand how I felt. Natasha was in my first wedding, so she knew all about what I'd gone through with James. She'd seen everything. So she knew I was trying to get my heart and head back in the game and was now witnessing me getting my heart broken again. It meant a lot to me that she sat me down and told me that she could see my pain.

We went downstairs as people were finally arriving at my house for the party. Tia surprised us and came, and I was so happy to see her because she was supposed to be out of town with Shakeer. We had a great time, the party was a lot of fun, and everyone loved my house. I felt good about that, I really did. There were several guys that were there who wanted to be introduced to me, and it just made me feel like I could get back in the game. I felt good about that. It was that night that I told myself to snap out of it. After that, I finally allowed myself to start going out on dates and getting to know different people. People who were really interested in me and wanted to talk to me.

Even though I had my head back in the game, and I was trying to submerge myself in work and new people, I was so busy, yet so lonely. My dating life was very sporadic, and nothing serious. I didn't really like any of those guys; it was just something that I was doing to try to stay social. It just wasn't really working. I found myself still really lonely and sad. It seemed like Shakeer was doing so well and didn't really care about me. He was really open about his relationship with Stacy all over the world. It kind of brought me back to my depression and back to the place where I was after leaving James. It brought back really bad memories. I just didn't feel good about myself, and I couldn't shake my loneliness, as hard as I tried. There would be days where my phone wouldn't ring at all. Nobody would call me. It wasn't like things weren't going well. I wasn't broke; I was doing amazing financially. My house was beautiful. My first tenant was absolutely crazy, and she ended up leaving. She was a single mom with a few kids, and a very pretty girl, but she just couldn't get it together. She would talk to my grandmother any kind of way, and I couldn't handle that at all. My grandmother managed the property and would collect the rent and make sure everything was running smoothly. She'd even come over to my house every Thursday, do my laundry, and cook for me, too. It gave her something to look forward to. I looked forward to it as well. Can you imagine the excitement I would have coming home every Thursday to a clean house, a home-cooked meal, and my grandma? She was so proud of the home she'd helped me buy. She truly treated it like it was her own.

My grandmother told my tenant the day before that we were going to fix her heater, and we were supposed to give her a 24-hour notice, but we didn't. Our mistake. But the way she reacted was completely uncalled for. My grandmother went over to fix the heater, and the tenant started cursing her out.

"You didn't give me my 24-hour notice. Leave my damn house!"

My grandmother was 79 years old. How do you talk to somebody like that? I heard this from upstairs in my room. I just knew she wasn't talking to my grandmother like that. I ran down the stairs, not remembering that I had just mopped the kitchen floor, hit that bottom step, and slipped horribly. My feet slid out from under me, and I hit the back of my head on that last step. I could tell it was bleeding badly.

My grandmother rushed in from the side door after she heard my tumble. "Oh my gosh, what happened, baby?!" she said as she tried to run to me.

"Mama, call 911!"

"Huh?" My grandmother had a hearing problem but would never admit it.

"Mama, call 911."

"Huh baby?"

"CALL 911!" I yelled.

"Baby, I just don't understand what you're saying!"

"Just give me the phone!" I said. She understood that.

She gave me the phone, and I called 911. The paramedics and the fire department, who were really close by my house, came in less than five minutes. They got me off the floor and saw the gash in my head. I explained to them that I'd heard the tenant yelling at my grandmother, and I had slipped on my freshly mopped floors.

I looked up, and all the firefighters were these handsome young African American men. They were all muscular, and there were at least five of them. I started crying. *This is a shame! They are seeing me with this gash in my head, pajamas on, looking crazy! And they are fine!*

I went to the emergency room, they gave me pain medicine, and thank God it was just a gash. They sent me home, and I was happy about that, but I was still lonely.

All these things, good and bad, were happening, and you would think I wouldn't have the time, but I was lonely. Dr. Tigner and Varie invited me on a trip to Hawaii, and I had never been to Hawaii before. They paid for my ticket and said it was because I had been such a good worker for them. I had a phenomenal time. We went horseback riding, ATV riding, the shooting range, swimming—it was something that I needed so desperately, and I was so grateful.

I had such a great time and didn't have to pay for *anything*. They treated me royally. And even then, I would be in my hotel room crying to Dr. Tigner about Shakeer. It was so bad that Varie finally said, "Girl, you still talking about this?!"

So things were happening—good things. I was being blessed, but I was still lonely.

When we got back from Hawaii, I continued to submerge myself in my work. We went to Hawaii during the December holiday, which is the best time to go. The whole United States will be freezing while Hawaii is sunny and beautiful. I got back to LA and went straight back to work because the holiday season was over. I was trying to keep myself busy with different things like teaching and tutoring. I even started a little dance group after school, where the kids would pay me to teach them dance. I was doing really well but still couldn't shake the loneliness. It seemed like nobody was calling me. I didn't even get calls from my friends. Even those little dates that I didn't really care about, those guys didn't call me, either. Nobody was inviting me anywhere. I mean NOTHING! It was a dry season. It went on for months and months. I would even call myself to see if my phone worked because it would NOT ring! I would just work, do my tutoring, then go straight to Dr. Tigner's house. I did that over and over. I would even try to jump on Dr. Tigner and Varie's dates because they loved going out to movies and dinner. They would do things together all the time. I knew it was getting really bad when I invited myself on their movie date one night, and Dr. Tigner said, "No, me and Varie are going to the movies! **You** are doing something else!"

"Nobody invites me anywhere! Nobody even calls me, ever!" I said as I burst into tears. "I'm so lonely!" I howled. "I try not to show you, but I'm so depressed and sad all day! This is such a bad season! Can't I just get a date?!"

"What?" Dr. Tigner said.

"Am I not attractive, smart, or fun enough for a date? Can the Lord just get me a date?"

Dr. Tigner started laughing at the top of his lungs. I mean hysterically. This was not funny!

"I'm serious!" I said.

"No, I'm laughing because this is funny, and... I'm gonna pray for you."

So he prayed for me and asked the Lord to help me during this time. After he prayed, he said, "Leah, in 38 days, you're going to have a man."

I dried my eyes. "What?" I asked.

"I want you to fast for 38 days. Take a time out. No food in the day for a certain amount of hours, for 38 days. After the 38 days, you're going to have a man."

I got excited. "Thank you, Jesus! I receive that word in the name of Jesus!"

And so I began to fast. One day turned into 38 days.

No man.

No calls.

No nothing.

I began to get a little frustrated as the 38th day approached. During that time, I started working out. Every morning before I went to work, I would go to the gym at 5 o'clock, go back home, shower, and get to work by 7:30. During my time at the gym, I would run, I would work on my legs, and I even started making my own regimens. Two days out of the week, I would do upper body, and two days I would do lower body. I was also doing cardio every day, running 3-5 miles. I was getting into great shape and building muscle.

During one of my sessions at the gym, it was like the Lord began to talk to me. He began to show me the LadyLike class. He began to show me different things I could do with it, like giving college scholarships, having teas, etiquette classes, and selling merchandise. I even saw myself holding big sessions like health and fitness, girl talks on Friday nights… I just started thinking of all these things that I could do. I remember my girlfriend Sage at my church, who told me during my 38 days that I needed to make LadyLike a legal non-profit 501(c)(3).

"This is yours. This is your baby. You need to capitalize on this, Leah. I see this blowing up. This is needed. Every girl needs Lady-Like. You need to set up an office, set up a website, email, everything. This is yours."

Maybe this is something I need to do, I thought to myself. So on the 38th day, I went to Dr. Tigner and said, "Dr. Tigner, it's been 38 days and I don't have a man!"

"I know. But what did you get?" he asked.

"I think instead of a man, the Lord gave me a ministry," I replied.

"What do you mean?"

"I know I have the LadyLike class, but I think the Lord wants me to take it to another level."

"How so?" he asked.

"I think the Lord wants me to make this a legal non-profit 501(c)(3). My grandmother used to be a part of this team of African American administrators called ICA. From their own pockets, they would raise thousands of dollars and send African American teenagers with a certain GPA to college. They would support them all four years. These students went to Stanford, Harvard, Berkeley, USC, really prestigious schools, even Historically Black Colleges. I think I want to do that because they no longer exist. I think my grandmother would love it if I could continue the legacy."

In fact, she and my grandfather would give all the teenagers at our church who were going to college personal scholarships out of their own pockets. They would support them all four years. They believed in education and wanted to assist any African American financially to go to college.

"I think that's what LadyLike should do next. We should honor people in the community!" I continued.

"I think you've got something here!" Dr. Tigner said excitedly.

"Okay, so how do I get a 501(c)(3)?" I asked.

"You know, my WHW Expository Preaching and Teaching Conference is a 501(c)(3). This lady helped us put it together. Ask Varie to give you her number, and she will help you put the Ladylike Foundation 501(c)(3) together."

I called the lady, and she had me do this whole workbook on LadyLike. She had me put together an executive board, which included my mom, my grandmother, and me. I was the president and CEO, my mom was the VP, and my grandmother was the treasurer. I put together a list of other board members, which included my friends. She wanted me to do a mission statement, by-laws, and write out all the different activities and programs that the LadyLike Foundation would facilitate and the age range of the girls I wanted to target, which was 12-18. I also wanted to do some things with younger girls from 7-11. I called them the Little Ladies.

Then she told me I would need $800 to send to the city of Sacramento. That is how much it costs to have the application go through, and then you'll receive a 501(c)(3) number, which is an EIN number, which then is what you give to people who want to donate money to the organization, and it becomes tax deductible. If you want a non-profit organization in California, you have to send it to Sacramento, where they approve it, and that's when the 501(c)(3) status is given.

I had no clue where I was going to find that $800, so I just started to pray. I started saving from my paychecks and tutoring appointments until I managed to get $800. I sent in the packet, along with my $800 to the city of Sacramento, and about eight weeks later LadyLike Foundation became a non-profit 501(c)(3) organization. I had the paperwork and everything. In the end, the Lord did not give me a man—he gave me a ministry.

Having a nonprofit organization monopolized all of my time. I was no longer lonely; I was too busy. I was putting together events and trying to get T-shirts made. I had to get a logo. My friend Sage, the one that inspired me to start the nonprofit, helped me get it. She had worked in the nonprofit world for a long time, so she knew everything that I needed to do. She even had her brother design the logo for me. My next task was finding somebody to make a website for me, because I had no clue how to do that. Sage knew someone who could design it and helped me get everything together.

The next item on my list was to open a bank account for the organization. I had to take the papers that I'd gotten from Sacramento to the bank, showing them that my nonprofit organization was legit. They requested my EIN number, which I had just acquired. So on my lunch break, I went to Bank of America on Wilshire and set up a checking account for my business. I put my grandmother on it as well. All I had to open the account was $100. I was really excited about my new organization.

Next, I had to create my first event, kind of like an open house. This would be an informational event to invite some of the girls from my church and other teenage girls that I knew to talk about what the LadyLike Foundation was all about. I wanted them to know that it was a real organization, and I wanted it to be professional and be taken seriously. Although we already had real events, these were going to be professional events that would put them on a platform for success, educate, empower, and inspire them to be everything that God created them to be. I had all of these ideas!

Varie would always get T-shirts for the WHW conference, so I asked her where she got them made, and I got the factory's number. I had absolutely no clue that T-shirts were so expensive. It was going to be about $150, and I started to get worried because I only had $100 in the business account. So I definitely had to pay that out of pocket. I just wanted twenty T-shirts, from sizes XS-XXL. They were pink V-neck T-shirts with the white LadyLike logo. The logo had a picture of Audrey Hepburn from her famous movie, Breakfast at Tiffany's in between "Lady" and "Like." LadyLike means to be a classy woman who's well-rounded and has everything together. Not just knowing how to sit or dress appropriately, but a lady who knows how to do whatever it takes to get where she needs to go. She's educated, she's articulate, well-read, and knows what is going on in the world around her. Her makeup is gorgeously applied, her hair is neat and perfectly done in the style she chooses, and she can take care of business because she is financially literate and invests wisely. She's everything! She's every woman. I wanted to embrace the elegance, yet the sophistication and intelligence of a lady.

I sent the logo to the T-shirt lady, and she made the shirts for me. "I have these little pink thermals. Would you like to put the Lady-like logo on these for $10 apiece?"

If I already spent that much, I figured I might as well spend another $40. So I got 4 of those T-shirts and I gave one to Sage because she was so influential in helping me. I decided that on the opening day we would wear the thermals and give the T-shirts to the girls. Then I needed to figure out how I was going to send invitations. This was before electronic invitations were so popular. We were still doing paper invitations at the time. I went to Kinkos Copies and saw how much it would be for 100 invitations, which was *so* expensive. I called Sage looking for advice on how I was going to get them out.

"Leah, you need to find a little mom & pop copy place to do all your printing. You'll get to know each other, and you can work hand in hand with them instead of going to a commercial place like Kinkos Copies," she told me.

I just happened to be driving to work one day, and a couple blocks away from my school I saw a place called *Color & Copy La Brea*. It was a small print shop. I planned to go there on my recess break and see if they could design a little flyer for me. So on my break, I walked down to the copy place and saw that Koreans worked there. I figured it was a sign because I taught at a Korean school, and both the children and parents loved me. The business was run by a father and daughter. The daughter's name was Jenny.

"Hi! My name is Leah, and I'm looking to make some flyers for my upcoming event. It's a girl talk/open house for my foundation. I'm thinking about something really girly, and I'm looking for about 150 copies or so."

"Okay, what size do you want?" she asked.

I showed her the size I would be interested in.

"Do you want it in color or black and white?"

"In color, please. I would like for you to design it."

"Okay, no problem! Just give me your email. I'll send you a couple of proofs, and everything should be good. It will probably be around $60, is that okay?"

"Yes! That's fine! Do you have envelopes to match?"

"I'll find some envelopes to go with them," she confirmed.

By the time I got back to work, I had the proofs, and they were designed beautifully! The invites were decorated with pearl necklaces, lipsticks, dresses, and everything girly.

Oh, this is perfect!

She printed them out and got envelopes for me. I started collecting addresses from my church. I sent out the invitations to my opening, and I couldn't wait! I was so anxious and excited. The open house was in two weeks, and it was going to be at my house, of course.

Next, I had to figure out what I was going to feed them. Of course, when you have kids come out on a Friday night, you have to feed them something. My budget was very small; I was only making $35,000 a year as a teacher. I was making a couple hundred working with Dr. Tigner, but I still had my mortgage and other bills. So I planned to resort to making a pan of spaghetti, salad, cookies, and some punch. That would be about $50, and I could do that. I bought all the ingredients and prepped the food.

Then Sage brought up a good question: "How are we going to give away the T-shirts?"

She was right. Presentation is everything to me; I've always been all about presentation. I started looking around for white bags and figured I could put some LadyLike stickers on them. We could put the T-shirts inside and give them away as the girls left. Sage said that she had seen some white bags at Party City.

"I think they come in groups of ten," she pondered.

I had about 40 people RSVP, so I got 40 bags, and then I asked Jennifer from Color & Copy to make some stickers for me, and she did. We also had hats made. I had about 20 pink hats made with the LadyLike logo embroidered on them. Everything was getting to be a little expensive, but it was an open house, so I didn't want to ask anyone for money. I wanted to pay for everything. I ended up spending about $350 on all of this. I was going broke over the open house, but it was so worth it.

I got the bags, added the stickers, and put the T-shirts inside. I made the spaghetti and the salad and got the cookies and the punch. I set up my living room with pink candles everywhere. Everything in my living room was really girly anyway, so I didn't have to do anything extra. I was ready!

There were *so* many people that came out to my open house. The girls were sitting on the floor, on the couch, and even standing all around the walls. There was no place to walk in the living room because it was *that* big of an opening. Tia came, and even Sarah, and of course Sage came and helped. Sage had one of her friends, Pat, take pictures. There were just so many people, and I was so happy.

I started crying when I opened up with why I'd started Lady-Like and thanked all the girls that had already been with me for a number of years before I made it a nonprofit 501(c)(3). I wanted them to know that they could look forward to events monthly. I taught a lesson about self-esteem and confidence. Then we did the *question box* where girls could put anonymous questions in the box, and we would answer them. It was just amazing... The LadyLike Foundation was off to an amazing start.

After the open house for the ladies ages 12-18, I wanted to do something for the Little Ladies of LadyLike, ages 7-11. I wanted to create a princess party, where I would talk about Esther, the princess. In the Bible, Esther was a Jewish girl, and she was an orphan. She was brought into the kingdom so that the king could pick a wife. Out of all the girls, the king Xerxes chose and married her. But in order to be presented to the king, you had to go through all these beauty treatments. So one of the attendants of the kingdom helped Esther get ready to be queen. She took bathing rituals and other beauty routines, making sure everything was fit for a queen. I taught the little girls about Esther, and then did a spa party for them in my backyard. There were about ten little girls. My friend Charlotte who worked with me at my school was on the nail station, and she absolutely loved the idea of LadyLike. I had another friend who was doing glitter makeup for the girls, and then there was another station where they did vision boards. They could paste all the things they wanted to do and accomplish on a poster board. They were to rotate the stations in groups. They had a ball!

Of course on my limited budget I put together a meal that was inexpensive, so I decided to have what I had for the open house. It was cheap, and the kids loved it. As they walked in the door, I gave them all plastic tiaras so that they felt like princesses. I also invited some of my Korean students from Wilshire Private School. Their parents brought them to my house, and they stayed for a few hours. All the girls had a really good time at the Little Pretty Princess party. Things were looking great. I was now ready to plan my next monthly activity.

The next month I held a Mother-Daughter tea party at the Pasadena Tea Rose Garden. Pat, Sage's friend who took pictures at the open house, taught an etiquette lesson that was so fun and interactive. The girls loved it. They learned how to sit, how to eat, how to stir their tea when putting sugar and cream in it, how to properly drink tea, and even what conversation they should have at the table during tea time. They learned how to cut up their food, and not talk while they ate, and even how to properly place their napkin on their laps. I wanted them to know all the little tips about dining etiquette.

I figured out that I couldn't really do these events the way I wanted to do them without proper funding. Yes, it was my passion and ministry, but paying out of my pocket was becoming stressful. I thought it would be a great idea to have a fundraiser. I decided to have a luncheon: The Women of Excellence Scholarship Luncheon. I would honor mothers and daughters in the community who were excellent in the areas of community, in philanthropy, and in their various fields of occupation. We would sell tickets and also give college scholarships to college bound young ladies with a certain grade point average going to prestigious universities. I wanted to target African American girls and other minorities, giving them a chance and setting them on a path for success. It sounded like an amazing idea. Being the party planner that I am, I was already thinking about different venues. I wanted it to be at my favorite place, the Beverly Hills Hotel, where I'd had my wedding reception when I married James. Although the marriage carried horrible memories, the hotel I still held dear to my heart.

I scheduled an appointment, and I went. I only needed a smaller room for about 100 people, with a basic chicken lunch for the afternoon luncheon. I also needed a dance floor so that my praise team could dance. I planned to give awards while everyone ate lunch. Then I remembered my uncle played the piano, and he could be the entertainment. When I met with the hotel, they thought the idea was great. They were happy about it, and we planned to have the event in May. Everything was lining up perfectly—until I got the bill. For one hundred guests, that would be about $10,000.00. I would have to give a deposit to solidify the date for the luncheon. Of course, I didn't have a deposit, and like always, you know who I turned to.

I went to my grandmother and told her that I wanted to continue the legacy for ICA, and she thought it was an amazing idea. I told her I didn't have any money, but it didn't faze her.

"That's okay! I will pay the down payment, and whatever proceeds you make from this, that's what you can use to pay me back," she planned.

"Okay, perfect!" I said as I hugged her.

So we put the deposit down and signed all the papers. I brought her with me to do so. Now it was time to sell tickets. I just didn't know how much the tickets should be. I began to break it down. The meals were about $38 apiece, not including tax. Including tax and tips, it would have been $55. If I wanted to make any money, I had to make the price of the tickets more than $55. So I called Sage to see what she thought.

"Just make the tickets $100! Who's not going to pay $100?" she said.

"That sounds pretty good!" I agreed.

I went back to Jenny at Color & Copy, and she printed out the invitations and the envelopes that Sage had her friend design. I got about 150 invitations. I then started collecting addresses, including those from the ICA board so that they could come as well.

I wanted to honor Taylor, who was now the wife of Don, the entertainment lawyer I'd worked for, because she had been so instrumental in my life in helping me to become a homeowner. Her daughter had recently followed Taylor in her real estate footsteps, so I decided they would be the first mother & daughter duo that I would honor. Then of course, I had to honor my grandmother as a Woman of

Excellence. I also wanted to honor Varie for not only being the first lady of my church, but for embracing me and helping me in so many different areas. Finally, I planned to honor one of the teachers at my school, who was very influential in my life, as far as my teaching career went. She was a 6th grade teacher and happened to be an African American woman. She was also very powerful in the education world.

The invitations looked amazing, and we sent them out a month in advance. I thought that I was going to get an overwhelming response.

Nobody was buying tickets. No one.

I started to get nervous, because how was I going to pay for this event when no one was buying tickets? I went to my mailbox every single day, only to consistently find that there was not even one response. I kept going back and forth to my mailbox until I was two weeks away from the event.

I literally started praying.

Lord, if you don't want me to do this, I'll understand. Maybe I'm going too fast, too soon. If you don't want me to do this, let no one purchase a ticket. If you do want me to do this, at least let somebody purchase a ticket.

I went to my mailbox, and lo and behold, there was one RSVP envelope with $100 in it from my choir director at the church where I grew up. I was over the moon!

Okay, Lord! I've got my sign. I guess you want me to do this!

Every day, more and more tickets were coming in. My grandmother was also selling some tickets at her church. Don, my former employer, purchased a table, which was $1,000, for Taylor and her daughter and some of their friends. Things were looking great. We had about 100 people that were scheduled to be at the event. Everything was prepared, and I was ready!

I had pictures of the spa party in my backyard, as well as pictures from the opening. Sage's friend had amazing images from the open house and the tea party. We put the images on easels all around the entrance of the auditorium where the luncheon was going to be held. The assistant pastor of our church put together a video montage of all of our images to showcase to the guests. The entrance was beautiful; it had a nice space before you entered the dining hall. In that entrance was a baby grand piano that my uncle played as people walked in. They could listen to the piano, look at all the pictures, and enjoy the cocktail hour before they came into the luncheon.

My girls Tia, Sarah, Charlotte, and I were all on the hostess committee, as well as on the board. We made the program happen. Tia was the MC, making sure the program flowed. My praise dancers from church did a dance for everyone at the beginning of the luncheon. Sage had her husband contact a leader in the Korean community, to give the keynote address.

Then we had our awards, which we got from Crystal Factory. They were real crystal awards with their names engraved on them, so they looked great. Everything was professional, as I wanted it to be. My grandmother had her friends do the flowers. And everything just looked so beautiful and "LadyLike." Don told me that he was so proud of me, and Dr. Tigner was just beaming from ear to ear. My mom and dad were also proud; they couldn't believe I'd pulled this off. My dad could not stop raving about how amazing everything was.

All the honorees had the best speeches, and I felt so good about everything. It was just a sign of approval that the Lord wanted me to do this. I didn't make any money. I just barely met the bill, so I couldn't even pay my grandmother back. I couldn't give any college scholarships either; in fact, the only money I made was about $200, which I gave to one of the girls from my church that was going to Cal State Dominguez Hills.

I gave her the money and said, "I hope you can buy some books, and hopefully next year we'll do better!"

"Oh, no, Ms. Leah, this alone helps me so much! Thank you so much," she said.

The first Women of Excellence Luncheon was in the books. Next, it was time to think about more events so that I could make some money and really bless these girls.

The summer after the first luncheon, I continued to have girl talks and covered different topics pertaining to relationships. I planned a sewing class, where I talked about Dorcas in the Bible, who sewed for the homeless. My mom taught the Little Ladies how to sew, and how to make potholders with material that consumed heat so their hands wouldn't burn. Most of the events were at my house, but I began to rent little spaces so that I could have my events there instead. Everything was going pretty well. Yes, I was paying for a lot of things out of my own pocket, but I had faith. I found myself buying a lot of Subway platters, chips, punch, and cookies.

My next fantastic idea was that I wanted to have a conference. In the conference, I wanted to have different classes where the girls could pick what they wanted to do and what classes they wanted to participate in. I planned for it to be at a hotel. So I looked around for conference spaces that were affordable. I found a space at the Sheraton Hotel in Culver City. I met with the catering director and told her my idea. They had classrooms and a ballroom that was in the middle of the classrooms, which was perfect. I wanted classes like: *How to be LadyLike* (covering beauty, how to know you're valuable, and how to make wise decisions, which I based on the virtuous woman in Proverbs 31), *Relationships, Etiquette, Current Events, Fashion, Makeup, Debating,* etc. I had about ten different classes with my friends teaching them. Tia taught the *Relationships* class, and my mom did the whole summit with the kids ages 7-12, where they could do arts & crafts. I wanted the girls to be able to walk around and pick three classes that they found of interest. They'd spend 30 minutes in each class and then navigate to the next class of their choice. We had a group session in the morning to introduce all the classes and another group session where we would eat lunch together. There was a small fashion show during the lunch period, and after that, we would break out into the last session of the day.

I wrote all my ideas down and had Sage's friend Pat do the graphics. I wanted a brochure that kids and parents could fill out. It was $30 per girl for the whole day. I sent the brochure to different LAUSD schools, church friends, family friends, and even mustered up strength to ask Andrew if I could go on the radio to promote the Excellence Conference. He said yes, but I had to pay $350 to do that. I chose to also run an ad in the LA Focus, as well as other local newspapers. I really wasn't getting any registrants, even with all the marketing I was trying to do.

It's so funny when you think you have this great idea that everyone will buy into, and then everyone does not. I had to literally start making phone calls just to get people to believe in me. I would go on local radio stations in Inglewood that were internet based as well. I tried my best to get people to come without any success. I decided to start giving out free registrations because people weren't registering. It was very discouraging. You never realize how hard something is until you try to do it.

I had friends that were helping me put everything together, but they didn't see the vision that I saw in my head, so sometimes it would be hard for them to grasp it. They also didn't see any money, so they didn't see the benefit in it. I knew if I could just get through this one conference, I could have many more. It just wasn't working, and I knew I was going to have to bite the bullet and ask my grandmother if she could finance the event *again*, just so I could get it off the ground and make a name for myself.

One Sunday, I was assisting Dr. Tigner with an installation service for one of his sons in the ministry. There were a lot of pastors that I had known from working in the ministry with Dr. Tigner. There was a particular pastor who had just gotten installed in a very well-established church in the community, Pastor John Harrington. After the installation, John wanted to meet with Dr. Tigner to give him some tips about pastoring and to surround himself with distinguished pastors in Los Angeles. Dr. Tigner ended up referring him to me because I was his assistant and scheduled all of his appointments. Pastor Harrington came up to me, introduced himself, and I got his phone number so that I could schedule a meeting for them.

Later on that week, I called him, and we ended up talking on the phone for a while. We talked about different things after we found out we were around the same age and had the same views on current events, sports teams, and movies. He told me that he had heard about my foundation and about the conference coming up. I explained that I was having a difficult time getting people to come.

"Well, I can send ten of our teenage girls to your conference if that's okay with you," he said.

"Absolutely!" I agreed. "You would do that for me?"

"Of course! I've never personally met you before, but I've seen you around for years and always admired what you do for young girls. I'll send ten girls with a check from the church!"

I was amazed, because he barely knew me, yet he believed in me so much!

The day of the conference, we sold about 50 tickets altogether, but we had about 100 people there, from kids to parents to vendors. The vendors agreed to give a percentage of whatever they sold to the foundation. I even had one of my old college friends, who had become a very established professor, teach a class for the girls. And as promised, John sent ten girls from his church. That morning, one of the girls came up to me with an envelope and said, "Hi, we're from Pastor John Harrington's church. There's ten of us, here are our names, and here is the check. He told me to put this in your hands."

I thought to myself how great it was that Pastor Harrington had really followed through and kept his word. It just warmed my heart that someone who didn't even know me still supported me. It didn't stop there. Whatever event I had, he would send girls and financial support.

We started a friendship and would talk often. I believe that we were very fond of each other, but life got in the way. He was a new pastor getting acclimated to his new position, and with all of the things I was doing to create LadyLike, it just never worked. However, we still chose to support each other through everything.

The conference was a success. No, I didn't make any money, and on top of that, my grandmother had to pay all of the teachers. The night before the conference, my grandmother spent the night with me. I told her that I really wanted to pay the teachers, but I didn't have enough money.

"Baby, what do you want to pay everybody?" she asked.

"How about $250.00 each?" I asked.

"Perfect. Give me the names of all the teachers."

She started writing $250.00 checks for each and every one of the teachers. Once again, my grandmother came through for me like a champ. She believed in my dream and made it happen. I just love her so much... She didn't even ask me to pay her back. I couldn't have done it without her. LadyLike was off to an amazing start thanks to the Lord, my grandmother, and all of my friends who believed in me.

After a big event, if you're the spearhead and brains behind the event, it's such a high when the event is taking place. It's stressful, upsetting, and frustrating, but you're so happy when it's all over. It's very rewarding. It's like you go from a low to a high really, really quickly. When it's over, you go back to a low because you have nothing to look forward to. Especially if you aren't dating anyone, and I wasn't. God gave me a ministry, and not a man, so I put my *all* into LadyLike. When I wasn't doing LadyLike, I was teaching, and I put my all into that as well. If I wasn't teaching, I was putting my all into working with Dr. Tigner. I would have to alphabetize and organize all his sermons, which kept me mentally busy. So I was definitely busy, but still lonely. When you're lonely, you latch on to whoever gives you attention. At the time, Tia and Sarah and our whole crew would hang out with different guys. We had a male friend, Aaron, who worked at SAG (Screen Actors Guild) and had a really nice apartment in West Hollywood. His place overlooked the city of LA. He would invite everybody over to watch movies and eat. I could kind of tell that he was attracted to me, and so one night when everyone was over, I ended up staying after everyone left. We just talked and drank wine, even though I'm not a drinker.

He was very attractive and had a good job. He was also very articulate. He had a male roommate and seemed to be stable and mature. We started hanging out more, and he would come to my job sometimes to take me to lunch. It was cool, but I didn't see a future in it. Like I said, whoever gives you attention when you're lonely, you latch on to them.

Of course I told Dr. Tigner about Aaron and everything he had going for himself.

"That sounds really nice," he commented.

"Yeah. But he has a male roommate," I said.

"A male roommate?"

"Yeah."

"You sure he likes girls?" he asked.

"You're stereotyping, and that's not cool," I noted.

"No, I'm just saying. Men don't really have male roommates at your age. I understand college, I understand early twenties, but late twenties? I don't know about that, Leah."

"Don't be a hater, he's cool! And we have a lot of fun!" I added.

"Okay, we'll see how this works out," he said.

Well, of course, it did not grow or mature into anything. Aaron was just a friend to hang out with. But I was still so lonely. I missed Shakeer so much. I would engage with anybody that could get my mind off him. I mean, I even dated a waiter from Grand Luxe who was really cute and an aspiring actor. I was just needy for companionship.

With Pastor Harrington, even though we were very fond of each other and had great, stimulating conversation, it just seemed like bad timing. I figured that something had to be happening. God had to be getting me ready for something—I just didn't know what.

One day at work, I was on my lunch break surfing the internet to pass time. All of a sudden, I heard God speak something into my spirit.

"Your life is about to change drastically."

It came out of nowhere. It was such a shocking word that I wrote it on a Post-It and stuck it to a bulletin board right by my desk.

"Your life is about to change drastically."

positive six

riday nights were always spent brainstorming and out-lining sermons. On Saturday, we would put the sermon together for Sunday. One Friday night, I was working on the outline with Dr. Tigner in his office when all of a sudden I got a call from one of my friends from church, Melissa. She never called me, so it was very random.

"Hey, Melissa! How are you?"

"Great! A bunch of my friends are going out tonight. I was thinking about you, and we want you to come! Meet us! We're going to be in Studio City."

"Oh, no thank you, it's okay. Why don't we go out another time?" I asked.

Dr. Tigner was sitting on the other side of the desk listening to my conversation. He was mouthing, *No, go!*

"Aww come on! We're just going to this lounge place, you should come!" she urged.

Dr. Tigner kept signaling for me to go.

"Well, where is it again?" I asked.

"It's at The Firefly in Studio City. Come! When you get there say you are with Dana Pump."

"Hmm, no, it's okay."

"Leah, come! We're just going to hang out. It'll be great, you'll enjoy it!"

"Tell her you're going," Dr. Tigner demanded.

"Okay, fine. What time?" I asked.

"We're meeting at about 8. But we'll be there for a long time. Just be there!"

"Okay," I agreed.

I hung up the phone. With overjoyed excitement, Dr. Tigner said, "Isn't that great? You have something to do! You never have anything to do; you don't have a life! You need a life besides all of this other stuff that you're doing, Leah. A *social* life. This is good for you!"

The truth is, I hated clubs, lounges, and bars. It was totally out of my comfort zone. I was a teacher. Since I didn't have a social life, I was completely focused on teaching and LadyLike. If I didn't have my hair done, it was in a straight, neat, low bun. Like a teacher. I wore cardigans and scarves and loafers when my feet would get tired from the heels. I was a real educator and a foundation president. I had no pizzazz; I was completely engulfed in what I did.

"Go home, wear something cute, and have a good time!" Dr. Tigner said.

I went home, showered, and got ready. I decided to go with a simple LA girl outfit. Jeans, black boots, a white tee, and a black leather jacket. I had a little handbag, put my hair in a bun, and made sure my makeup was good. I put on my hoop earrings and lip gloss, and I was ready to go.

I drove to Studio City and found The Firefly. Just like I thought, there was an extremely long line outside. I parked in valet and got even more irritated by the line. But as I was walking up, I remembered that Melissa told me to tell the person at the door that I was with someone named Dana Pump—which I thought was a really weird name, by the way. I looked at the line, looked at the bouncer, and instantly just wanted to go home. I figured I would call her and tell her that I'd decided not to come. As I turned around to walk back to the valet stand, the bouncer yelled out to me, "Excuse me, are you looking for somebody?"

I started walking back.

"Yeah... umm.... Dana Pump?"

"Ohhhh, yes! Come this way!"

So I bypassed the long line and went right in the door, still following the bouncer. I was thinking to myself... *Whoever this Dana Pump is, he must have some juice because I don't know anyone that could have gotten me past that line!*

The Firefly was a really dark lounge. It was dimly lit and had an exclusive aura about it. The bouncer walked me to a long table of celebrities and athletes.

"Oh, no, no, no, this is not my table," I told him. "You must have it confused."

At the end of the table, Melissa started calling my name. "Hey, Leah! This is our table, come over here!"

I was so confused.

"Come sit down here with us!" she said.

I went to her side of the table and sat down. I was star-struck; I had never seen that many movie stars and athletes at one table. Melissa was sitting in the middle, and on the other side of her was this Caucasian red-headed guy with freckles.

"This is my friend Dana. Dana, this is my friend Leah!" she said.

"Hi, Leah, how are you?" Dana asked.

"I'm good!" I replied.

"So what do you do?" he asked.

"I'm a teacher."

"What grade?" he asked.

"Third."

"Cool! What college did you go to?"

"I went to Cal Berkeley," I answered.

"Oh, you must be smart!"

I kind of laughed it off.

Melissa began telling me to order whatever I wanted.

"Who's paying for this?" I whispered in her ear.

Remember, I'm a teacher, so I was worried about my pocketbook and my foundation. I didn't have any money to waste. They were eating clams and lobster, and wine was just being poured everywhere you looked.

"Girl, don't worry about it! Just eat!" she said.

"Okay…" I hesitated.

I started ordering and eating different things off the menu. I don't drink, so I wasn't drinking wine, but I had a ginger ale, and I was having a good time. I was very star-struck, so I was very entertained by everyone at the table. Suddenly I saw that it had become really late, and it was time for me to go.

"Thank you so much for inviting me, but I have to be at church in the morning," I told Melissa.

"You have church?" Dana interrupted.

"Yeah, I have to be there at 8 a.m. tomorrow," I said.

"Hmm." He had this confused look on his face.

"But honestly, thank you so much. This was such a nice gathering! I really had a great time."

I said my goodbyes, thanked Melissa again, and walked out. I got in my car and drove home.

Two weeks later, Melissa called and said that they were going out again and wanted me to come.

"Melissa, who is going to be there? Because you can't lead me on like you did last time. You didn't tell me all those celebrities were going to be there! Who's going to be there so I know what to wear?" I said.

"Girl, you always look great, don't worry about it! Just put on something cute and meet us at The Green Door in Hollywood. It's this club."

This time I was excited because all those entertainers and athletes had been there the last time. I found something cute and told Dr. Tigner that I was going to go out again. I stopped at the Fox Hills Mall and got a cute little top from a boutique. I had black pants that I could wear from home. I paired it with some heels, and I was good to go. And this time, my hair was done.

I got to the Green Door, and this time it wasn't as dingy and dark as The Firefly; it was a little more open and well lit. But I started looking around, and I didn't see any athletes or entertainers. I just saw Melissa, some of her friends, and Dana.

I sat down on this little couch, and Dana sat right across from me.

"I know all about you," he said.

"What?" I asked, confused.

"Yes, I have googled you," he said seriously. "I know all about you. You're very religious, but I don't mind that. I am Jewish, but you being Christian does not bother me at all."

I had the most puzzled look on my face.

"I know that you have a foundation called LadyLike Foundation—that's really admirable. It's great that you spend your time doing charity work. I do charity work as well. I have a cancer foundation, so we're a good match with that," he continued. "I know you used to date the rapper Shakeer, but I'm not intimidated by that at all. McDonald's doesn't worry about Burger King. I'm a good person, and I think this will be really great."

I was looking at Melissa like *What in the world is going on?* Dana got up to get drinks from the bar.

Melissa looked at me and said, "Oh my God, Leah, he really likes you!"

"What? He doesn't even know me."

"Leah. He is super successful. Yes, he is Jewish, but it is okay. He has partnerships with Adidas, he has AAU basketball teams and camps, he is extremely connected, and he even has a cancer foundation. He is beyond SUCCESSFUL!"

I looked at him while he was at the bar. He had on flooding jeans, this corduroy sport coat, his hair was really red, and it was a mess with no gel on it, he was a little overweight, and had on these Ferragamo shoes with thick soles that made his toes turn up.

I turned back to Melissa. "Absolutely not."

"No, Leah, you have got to give him a chance! He's a great catch! He could be perfect to help you with LadyLike and show you how to do things! He really likes you. I'm telling you, Leah. This is a great opportunity."

I looked at him again, standing at the bar. "Absolutely not. I don't care what he does or what he has, no!"

As I was shaking my head, Dana walked back over, took my phone out of my hand, and called his own phone so that he would have my number. He was all over me the entire night. Hugging me, trying to hold my hand, rubbing on my back... I mean, he just gave me the creeps! I never met someone who was so affectionate that fast. It was a bit uncomfortable.

That night as I drove home, Dana called me. Which was weird, because I've never met a guy that called me the same day that he got my number. They usually wait a day or so and play it cool.

"Hello?"

"Hey, this is Dana."

"Hi."

"It was really nice hanging out with you tonight. I think you're beautiful, and I just really want to get to know you. I'm a good person, and all I want to do is get married and have some kids." *What the hell? Who says this in the first conversation? He's striking out on every level.* "I'm ready now. I'm 41 years old, and it's just time for me to settle down. I'm also an identical twin. My brother and I take my mom out to dinner every week. I'm a real family person," he continued.

I was just looking at the phone like.... *When is he going to hang up?*

"Okay, so I'll call you in the morning," he ended.

Call me in the morning? He is just moving way too fast.

"Okay, bye," I said.

The next morning, he called. In fact, he started calling me every single day. He'd ask me all kinds of questions. He wanted to know where my job was, my shoe size, what gym did I go to... He knew that I came from a really close family, and even that I had been married before. He'd tell me over and over again how it didn't bother him at all. He was just so much! I guess Melissa had given him the rundown because she had known me for years. She knew about LadyLike, she knew that I was Dr. Tigner's assistant and that I taught the praise dancers at the church and the youth Bible study because her kids had gone through my classes. She gave Dana great pointers about me, but it just felt like too much.

But I gave it a chance. For the next month, I dated him. Dana is a businessman, and a very shrewd and persistent one. When he was 16 years old, he started AAU basketball teams called Double Pump. He had most of the elite African American players play for him. He had exhibition teams and a search firm. He was so successful that his first check was for $250,000.00 from LA Gear. They branched off, and Adidas took them under their wing and began sponsoring all their tournaments and teams. Their partnership with Adidas caused their influence to reach all colleges over the country. Dana's dad passed away of cancer. Because he was treated at Northridge Hospital, in honor of his legacy, Dana and his twin brother David created a cancer foundation which has given millions of dollars to the hospital for cancer research. The foundation also enables those in the community who can't afford it to have access to medical treatment and screenings.

I liked that he was a businessman, but being a businessman, he was very rude and very direct with his instructions for me. He'd say things like, "Meet me at the restaurant at 7 p.m., don't be late. The attire is upscale." It was too much like James for me with all the directions. So I would purposely be late and not listen to anything he had to say. But no matter what I did, he would keep calling me and inviting me to different places. "You're late," was something I heard from him constantly. He was just so rude, and I didn't know if I liked this guy.

One day while I was teaching, this big box came to my classroom. I opened up the box, and there were two pairs of the most expensive running shoes Adidas made at the time. There were jogging outfits, leggings, T-shirts, jackets, and all kinds of things from Adidas. Even a workout bag. I was so thankful that he'd sent it to me, but I couldn't call him because I was still teaching. Yet he called me in the middle of my lesson.

"Leah, did you get your package?" he asked.

"Yes."

"Do you like it?"

"Yes."

"Well, were you going to call and say thank you?"

"Yes. Thank you."

"Okay, I'll call you back later."

I just kept thinking how weird he was. He would send me flowers upon flowers, but I would be teaching and couldn't call to thank him.

"Do you like your flowers?"

"Yes."

"Were you going to say thank you?"

"Thank you."

He wouldn't even give me a chance to say thank you because of how aggressive he was.

There was one instance where I had gotten really sick. Being a teacher, you get sick a lot. The kids always want to touch you and hug you. When I get sick, I always lose my voice. He called me, and I didn't have a voice to speak to him.

"Are you sick?" he asked.

"Yes," I whimpered.

"Do you need me to get you anything?"

"No, I'm fine."

In about an hour, there was a man that came to my school, and he had a delivery for me.

"Hi, this is from Dana Pump. He said you were sick and sent you some soup," he said as he handed it to me.

I was so confused again, but I took the soup and enjoyed it. I thought it was sweet. No one had ever done that for me before.

He was doing all of the right things, but I just didn't like him. I just did not like him. I tried and tried to like him, I tried to go out with him, I tried to converse with him, but I just didn't see it going anywhere. Plus, he was Jewish, and that was a waste of time for me. I'm really, really, really Christian. I go to church *every* Sunday, and *every* Tuesday for Bible study. I am a pastor's assistant, for God's sake! I'm about as Christian as they come; I believe in Jesus. I believe that He rose from the grave in three days. I believe He's coming back again. I believe my sins are forgiven, and I believe in the blood of Jesus. I believe the Bible is the word of God—the indisputable and incorruptible word of God. I can't be with someone who doesn't believe that, I just can't. I believe that Jews have a special place in the heart of God because they are His chosen people. I believe that they will always be blessed, always be protected, and I believe that they will always have a special place in heaven because God promised Abraham that. I believe there wouldn't be any Christianity if there wasn't any Judaism. Christianity is a fulfillment of Judaism. I get that. But yet, Dana and I were so different. I was Black, he was White. He was Jewish, I was Christian. Totally different backgrounds. It seemed like a waste of time, and I just didn't like him.

I called my friend Melissa to get some things off my chest.

"Melissa, thank you so much for introducing me to Dana. He's a wonderful person, I just don't want to lead him on. So could you tell him to stop calling me?"

"Are you sure?" she asked.

"I'm sure! He's a really nice person, he's very sweet. He's kind of rude with his directions, and how he wants me to be and look, and different things like that. I don't really like that. But I know it's because he's a businessman. I get that. However, I just don't think it's going to work."

"Okay," she said. She didn't even try to convince me. "I'll call him. I'll let him know," she said peacefully.

"Okay! Thank you so much. I'll talk to you later."

Well, she did tell him not to call me, and that it wasn't going to work out. He did stop calling me for about a month.

It was so crazy because right after I told her that, it seemed like I did something wrong. I had this pain in my chest, and it just seemed like something was not right—as if I had let someone down. I kept trying to figure out what it was, and I knew it wasn't the Lord. I knew Dana wasn't the person the Lord wanted for me, so I knew I hadn't hurt Him in this. I couldn't decipher the feeling. I felt it silently for weeks, but I didn't tell anyone about it. This went on for about a month.

One Friday, I found myself right back in the same position I had been in the same night Melissa called to invite me to The Firefly. I was sitting on the other side of Dr. Tigner's desk drafting the outline of the sermon as he dictated. All of a sudden, Dr. Tigner said, "Leah, you never told me about what happened to Dana."

"What do you mean what happened to Dana? Nothing," I replied.

"No, no, no. Tell me what happened. You haven't talked about him in a while. I know you were giving him a chance. I know you didn't like him that much, but what happened? You didn't tell me anything."

"Oh, I told Melissa to tell him to stop calling me," I answered.

"What?"

"I told Melissa to tell him to stop calling me... It wasn't going to work. We're just too different. He's not my type."

"Not your type?" he asked as he leaned back in his chair.

"He's not my type!"

I started getting frustrated at this point because I couldn't figure out why he was pushing me on this issue. He knew Dana was Jewish.

"He's not your type?" he asked again.

"He's just not my type! He's not my type."

"Is it because he's White?"

"No. It's not because he's White."

I went to White schools my whole life. My first crush was White when I was in sixth grade. He didn't like me back, so I don't know if it counts. I'm very used to being around White people, and I have no problem with them at all. I had never dated a White guy, but I had never been approached by one either. I'd never even received a compliment from a White guy or anything. This would be my first experience, but it wasn't why I didn't like him.

"Well, let's talk about your type," he said.

"Okay," I agreed.

"Your ex-husband was your type. He was a womanizer, and a cheater, and a player. He used you, he wouldn't own up to you. He didn't even tell anyone that he was married to you. He emotionally abused you—he deflated you of your self-esteem and made you insecure. But that's your type, right?"

I was silent.

"Then you get divorced, you come back, and you start dating a musician that has two kids, a baby mama, and lives with his grandparents. But that's your type? Next, you start dating a rapper, and you thought you were in a monogamous relationship where you knew who you were to him, only to find out that he was dating a tennis player. But that's your type. Then you got desperate and started dating a guy that has another guy as his roommate in his 30s. Hmm. But that's your type."

"Woah, woah, woah—"

"Woah, woah, woah, what, Leah?"

What he was saying was hitting me in my heart. All of it was true. All of it!

"Why don't you try God's type?" he continued.

"God's type? He's Jewish!"

"Leah. Let me just say this to you. You want God to bless you within your small little box that you can see, while God is trying to bless you *outside* of the box. He's trying to bless you BIG. I think this is one of the biggest blessings that you'll ever receive. So this is what you need to do… We're not working today. Close the computer, go home, and tell the Lord that you're sorry because whenever the Lord sends you something, and you reject it, that's sin. Go apologize to the Lord, ask for forgiveness, and call Dana."

What he was saying hit me like a ton of bricks. I knew it was the Lord because it brought back that exact feeling I had been feeling for all those weeks; I just wasn't honest with myself. I knew it was something that I was supposed to do, but I didn't like him, so why was I supposed to do this? But okay. I wasn't going to question him. I was going to obey the Lord. I did not obey the Lord with James, I did not obey the Lord with all of those other guys… *Let me just obey the Lord…*

I closed the computer, gave Dr. Tigner a hug, went home, and prayed.

Lord, I'm sorry. If You give me one more chance with Dana, I promise I won't let You down.

After I prayed, I called Dana. He picked up.

"Hello?"

"Hi, Dana!"

"Who is this?" he asked sternly.

"This is Leah."

"Leah who?"

"Leah. Melissa's friend."

"Mmm. Let me call you back." And he hung up the phone.

I looked up to the sky and said: *This is why I don't like this guy, Lord! I don't like him!*

As I was telling the Lord this, Dana texted me.

Why are you calling me now?

Because I didn't give us a fair chance, I admitted.

Immediately, he called me. We rekindled immediately. It was as if nothing ever stopped. It went straight back to old times, like the month we were dating. Then he said, "Hey, I'm in Arizona for the NBA All Star Game. Would you like to come up here with me?"

I had never been to an NBA All Star Game. I had watched it every year since I was a kid. I love it. It's my absolute favorite sporting event to watch. I love the slam dunk contest, the three point contest, special skills contest, and the celebrity game. I love every part of NBA All Star Weekend, honestly.

"Let me call you right back!" I said.

You know who I called. Dr. Tigner.

"Dr. Tigner, guess what?!" I exclaimed.

"What?!" He was as excited as me.

"I did what you said. I called Dana, and he asked me to go to the NBA All Star Game!"

"You should go! Just make sure you tell him that you're not sleeping with him and that you need your own hotel room," he said.

"Okay, perfect," I agreed.

So I called Dana right back and told him that I could go. He was so excited. He was talking so fast that he couldn't even get everything out of his mouth. You could tell he has ADD and has just never been diagnosed. He's just hyper, aggressive, and direct.

"Okay, I'll have my assistant call you to get all of your flight information. You'll fly up tomorrow."

"Great!" I agreed. "I don't know if I can go to the All Star Game because I know that's on Sunday, and I have church Sunday morning."

"No problem. I'll have you back before church."

His assistant called me about thirty minutes later and got all of my information for the flight. It was on! I had gotten a confirmation number as soon as Dana called back.

"Did you get your confirmation number?" he asked.

"Yes."

"Okay, good. You're all squared away to come up tomorrow?"

"Yes."

"Perfect. I have one question to ask you," he said.

"Yes?"

"Do you wear scarves when you go to bed?"

"Umm. Absolutely. I'm Black. I wear scarves. But what does that mean to you, because I won't be sleeping with you. You need to get me my own room. Did you think that I was coming up there to sleep with you?"

"Well, I don't think this is going to work out," he huffed.

"Me either."

And I hung up.

I called Dr. Tigner and told him what had happened.

"Just wait a few minutes. He's gonna call you right back. What you said just turned him on."

"Really?" I asked.

"Yes, you told him no! This is good, you're doing good. Keep it up! If you can't get your own room, then you can't go."

He was right. Dana called me back within minutes.

"You're right. I'll get you your own room."

"You know what? How about this..." I proposed. "How about I don't come to the NBA All Star Game, and we have a real date when you get back? How about that?"

"That sounds great. You know, I really respect you for your decision. There's a lot of hoes that come up to NBA All Star Weekend, and I was really testing you. You seem like a really good girl to say that to me. That just makes me respect you more. I'll be home on Sunday, and we can go out to dinner that night."

"Okay, that sounds great," I agreed.

When we hung up, I called Dr. Tigner back to update him.

"Good job! You did it! Good, now stay like this. I'm going to coach you through this whole thing, Leah. This is a blessing, and we're going do this the correct way. You just have to listen to me."

"Of course. I'm listening to you until the end! I'm listening to all your directions. You never lead me wrong," I promised.

That whole weekend, Dana couldn't stop calling me. I mean, we talked all weekend—about everything.

"Oh my gosh, Leah, I'm so glad you didn't come up here this weekend. There's so many hoes out here, it's ridiculous! Hoe, hoe, hoe, hoe, hoe!" he joked.

This man is crazy! He's White but he has a lot of swag!

It was enjoyable. I did not like him, yet... I was enjoying the attention once again. I was trying to get myself into liking him.

Sunday came quickly. It was February 14th, 2009. Our first real date, Valentine's Day, and his mother's birthday all fell on the same day. So our first date was at his mother's birthday dinner.

The birthday dinner was at Sisley, an Italian restaurant in Sherman Oaks. I got there a little bit late, and he was there with his mother, brother, and his wife. They had already started eating. He told his mom that a nice Jewish girl was coming to meet them for dinner. My name is Leah, and that's a Hebrew name, so of course his Jewish matriarch mother was very excited that a Jewish girl was coming to dinner.

When I walked into the private room, everybody looked surprised, but not too surprised. For one, I wasn't Jewish... I was Black. Later I found out that Dana had always dated Black girls. That was just his type. He did not like dating White Jewish girls, or White Caucasian girls. Actually, not any other culture except Black. He just loved Black women.

We had a good dinner. They asked me questions about being a teacher and my family. I talked about my parents and my grandmother. They seemed like a very nice family. I learned that a lot of NBA players had gone through Dana and his brother's programs, AAU Basketball & Grassroots Basketball. Players like James Harden and Paul George—Dana was even one of the first people to pick Kobe Bryant up when he first got to Los Angeles with his parents. Colleges would call them to choose their coaches for them, too. They also had a great relationship with Pac-12 teams, and a great relationship with the UCLA basketball coaching staff. They were very entrenched in sports, but specifically the business behind it. I found it very interesting because I had never really dated anybody in sports.

After dinner, Dana asked if I would like to go to the movies, which was right next door at the Sherman Oaks Galleria. We walked there and talked more about his business affairs.

Dana is the type of person that, if he can't get into the movie right away, he doesn't want to watch it anymore. I don't even remember which movie it was, but we stayed for about 30 minutes before he turned to me and said, "Okay, you ready to go?"

I could tell he wasn't really into movies. But it was fine because it was getting late, and I had to get up and be at work in the morning. Monday mornings are the worst when you're a teacher.

He walked me to the car and told me that he would call me later in the night. And he did. When we talked that night, he told me that he would call me in the morning. And he did. Right after my grandmother would call me to wake me up, Dana would be calling me. He would call me all during the day and always wanted to meet for dinner. It was full court press with him.

I was trying to wrap my head around all of it and remain obedient because Dr. Tigner said that Dana would be one of the biggest blessings I would ever receive. I was trying to be open-minded. But I just did not want to kiss him. I didn't even want to hold his hand. He would really try to force himself, but I just kept telling him that we were taking it slowly. Like I said—full court press with him, and he didn't take no for an answer very well. He was still sending all kinds of things to my job. Flowers, Adidas gear, food… everything!

Our second date was at one of his friends' son's Bar Mitzvah. I work on Saturdays, and usually all of his events were in the Valley. I would not compromise my work to do anything that he wanted me to do, because he was very rude and brash about what *he* wanted me to do. Dr. Tigner sternly advised me to not let him take over my life because I still had things I needed to do. I had to tell Dana,

"When I'm finished with the sermon, then I'll be there. I won't be there before. If I'm late, I'm just late."

I had to be very confident in what I said, and I couldn't be moved, shaken, or show any weakness. He is the type of person that if you show any weakness, he'll walk all over you.

So I was late to the Bar Mitzvah. I arrived during the ceremony session. As we walked in, his friend's son was speaking to everyone in Hebrew and doing all of the ceremonial details that you have to do at a Bar Mitzvah. I was seated right by Dana's mother. She was reading the program and leaned over to me.

"Look. The program says one God. You know we both serve the same God."

"Absolutely!" I confirmed.

She was trying to make it clear that they were Jewish, and I was Christian. I believed in Jesus, but I wasn't going to make it a big deal because I didn't want them to think I was coming in preaching. However, I was definitely staying Christian. I was not converting.

We all had a great time that night. We took a picture together, and even a family picture. I was brand new to all of them, and we were already taking family pictures. It was moving pretty fast, but we had a great time.

That Monday, I was at work when Dana called me.

"Well, I guess you're my girlfriend!" he said. "Because I have your picture right by my bed. And I'm putting it on Facebook that I'm not single anymore. I have a girlfriend."

I didn't even agree to this, and this guy was already calling me his girlfriend! I hadn't even kissed him yet. This was crazy.

Well, we kept dating. His calls and efforts remained consistent. When he said he was going to do something, he would do it. Every morning and every night he would call me. He wanted to meet for lunch even if I only had 30 minutes to eat. Full court press and I still hadn't kissed him.

Three months with Dana flew by. Dr. Tigner told me to not accept a dime from him. We knew he was very successful and financially affluent, and Dr. Tigner informed me that if he wasn't getting his way, he would try to buy me.

"Do not take any money from him. You're not a ghetto girl from the hood. If you do, he will use that against you. You have to be strong. You are not cheap. You're strong, you're valuable… you have your own house, your own job, your own things. You are okay, don't let him buy his way in."

I agreed.

But one day, Dana called me and said, "After you work for Dr. Tigner, I have a shopping spree for you at the Adidas store in Santa Monica. Would you like to go?"

I asked Dr. Tigner what he thought. He thought it was a good idea because Dana had a partnership with Adidas.

"It's not his money, it's a gift card. So yes, definitely. You work out every day and could use workout clothes. I say you go get some," he advised.

So I let Dana take me to the Adidas store. We got everything from sweat suits to running shoes to jackets to workout bags, hats, socks, everything. I asked him if I could get Dr. Tigner some golf shoes because he was golfing at the time, and Dana let me. When we left the store, we had all of these huge bags in our hands. He walked me to the valet and put the bags in my car.

"Leah. So I have to take you to the Adidas store for a shopping spree in order for me to get a kiss?"

I knew I had to kiss him. It would be wrong if I didn't.

"Okay," I sighed.

"So can I kiss you?"

"Yes."

I gave him a kiss. It wasn't that bad... It was actually pretty good. So from that point on, whenever we saw each other I would have to give him a little kiss because I wasn't giving him any affection. I just didn't feel that way about him yet. I was still trying to wrap my head around liking him. Have you ever had that "yuck" feeling when a guy is so into you, and you're just not that into him? Those kinds of guys always want to be all over you, and you don't want to be anywhere near them. Have you ever had that? That's what I had. It was weird.

I guess he could tell that all the gifts weren't really moving me. So it seemed like he started going another route—using LadyLike as an anchor.

"Leah, I have some tickets to the UCLA women's basketball game on Sunday after church. Would you like to bring some of your girls?" he suggested.

"Yeah! That would be great!" I agreed.

I brought about five girls to the game. I also brought Varie with me, and her daughter, Denise. We watched the game, and Dana was trying to sit next to me and hold my hand. I would just move away. He even tried to walk closely next to me as we went down the street to get something to eat, but I would casually move to the other side. Varie could feel the vibe.

"Leah, you can't do this. He's a nice man, and he really likes you! You have to give him a little bit of attention or at least a little bit of affection."

Ugh. I was trying to be obedient to God, but it was just so hard. I didn't really like him that much!

It was really a learning process, of really getting to like him and getting to know him. It wasn't until a certain point that I really started liking him.

One thing I really liked about Dana was that he was very family oriented. He had dinners on Sunday with his mom. Every Sunday. Then he was very interested in meeting my family, although I was kind of scared to introduce my family to him. Even though it was hard, I knew I needed to introduce him to my parents and to Dr. Tigner. Besides, he would ask me, "So when am I going to meet your parents?" almost daily. I told him that he was going to meet my grandmother first.

"Great! When can I meet her?" he said with excitement.

One day while I was having a garage sale for the LadyLike Foundation at my house, I invited Dana to come. My grandmother was the one collecting all the money and giving change.

My grandmother walked every morning and had swept the street for years. She would wear a hoodie, a beanie, gloves, scarves... I mean, it almost looked like she lived on the street. But she just didn't want anyone to bother her. So she had on that same outfit at my garage sale, because she had just come from walking.

My house was on the corner, so we got a lot of traffic. A lot of people were buying things at the garage sale, and we were very occupied. Dana drove up in his white S-class Mercedes. My grandmother was looking like *Who is this?*

He got out of the car and immediately asked me where my grandmother was. I pointed to where she was sitting down collecting money in her horrible outfit.

"That's your grandmother?" he whispered to me.

"Yes, she's the love of my life. She helped me buy this house. She's amazing!"

"Wow... okay. But... she looks like she's homeless," he commented.

"I know. That's just how she looks when she walks and sweeps the street. But she's not. Okay?"

I thought it was pretty funny.

He went up to my grandmother to introduce himself. I followed behind him.

"Hey, Grandma. I'm Dana, Leah's friend."

"Okay," she said.

"Well, how much do you think you need to make this garage sale successful?" he asked.

"Hmm. About $300."

"That's no problem," he said.

He reached in his pocket and gave her $300 in cash. She looked down at her hands, and her eyes widened before she turned to look at me.

"Who is this, Leah?" she asked.

"This is my friend, Dana."

"Oh, I like Dana!"

She was sold after that. From that point on, they had a great relationship. Dana would call and talk to her, and he had me bring him to Watts, where she lives, so he could see her house. So that was a wrap! My grandmother really, really, really liked him.

"Love sees no color, baby," she told me. "Love sees no color."

I was still trying to like him at this point. Next it was my dad and my mom. And I couldn't forget about Dr. Tigner and Varie, who had already met him at the UCLA women's game.

One day when I was with Dana, he looked at me and said, "Leah, I'm going to invite your mom, your dad, Dr. Tigner, and his wife to the Pac-12 tournament at The Staples Center. We'll all sit together, and I'll get to know them."

I was very nervous.

"Let me just say this, my dad is crazy," I warned.

"It's okay, I've seen crazy."

"Nope. My dad is *crazy*. He's loud, he's spirited, he has to have control... You don't know him!"

"I don't care. I want to meet him," he said.

So we brought everyone to the Pac-12 tournament as Dana promised. We were sitting on the floor and had great seats. Dr. Tigner was sitting next to my dad. I was sitting next to Dana, and my mom and Varie were sitting next to each other.

Pastor Tigner decided it was time to break the news to my dad. "Charles, you do know that's Leah's boyfriend, right?"

My dad looked at Dana and laughed. "No it's not. That's Leah's friend!" he said with confidence.

"No, Charles. That's her boyfriend."

"T"—that's what he called Dr. Tigner—"that's not her boyfriend. That's her *friend*."

"Charles, I know you don't want to think that, but that's her boyfriend. That red-headed guy that she's sitting with is her boyfriend."

"What?"

My dad was just blown away. But being that Dana was a sports guy and had the best tickets to all the hottest sporting events and knew all the athletes, of course my dad was game because he was a sports guy as well. Even though they were leery at first, Dana won them over because he wanted them around. If he was having a family dinner, he wanted my parents there too. He wanted to be a happy family, which I liked, and it was very endearing to me. However, it was moving so fast.

It was a little scary how fast he was moving; however, for everything, I was constantly checking in with Dr. Tigner to see if I was doing it right and making the right decisions.

My interactions with Dana were completely different than with James and Shakeer. With them, I would be waiting for them to call me and wondering when they would call. With Dana, he was calling too much. I was hoping and praying that Shakeer would like me, but with Dana, I didn't have to do anything. He just liked me for me. He was always complimenting me and always wanted to know what I was doing. He called five or six times a day. Not to mention he would call me as *soon* as he woke up.

One particular day, when Dana and I were on the phone, he asked me, "So what do you do every morning when you wake up?"

"When I wake up, I always pray," I answered.

"You do?" he asked.

"Yes."

"I'd like to pray with you," he said.

He's Jewish... why would he want to pray with me?

"Okay..." I responded.

"So what do you pray about?" he asked.

I sighed. "Okay, repeat after me... Our Father..."

"Our Father..."

"Who art in heaven..."

"Who art in heaven..."

"Hallowed be thy name."

"Hallowed be thy name."

"Thy kingdom come..."

"Thy kingdom come..."

"Thy will be done..."

"Thy will be done..."

"On earth..."

"On earth..."

"As it is in heaven."

"As it is in heaven."

"Give us this day..."

"Give us this day..."

"Our daily bread..."

"Our daily bread..."

"And forgive us our debts..."

"And forgive us our debts..."

"As we forgive our debtors..."

"As we forgive our debtors..."

"And lead us not..."

"And lead us not..."

"Into temptation..."

"Into temptation..."

"But deliver us from evil, for Thine is the kingdom..."

"But deliver us from evil, for Thine is the kingdom..."

"And the power, and the glory..."

"And the power, and the glory..."

"Forever."

"Forever."

"Amen."

"Amen."

"Oh, okay! Let's do that every morning," he suggested.

I was looking at the phone like... *What is even going on?* So every morning, he would call me when he woke up, and we would pray.

It would start with the Lord's prayer, and then when it breaks off into, "Give us this day our daily bread," we would each break off and pray for something that we wanted the Lord to do for us that day. Mind you, he wasn't saved. He had not given his life to the Lord. His mother was very adamant about how Jewish he was. So I really didn't push the envelope when it came to religion. I was a little worried about it because I didn't know how it was going to pan out.

I would go to church, but Dana wouldn't. He would call me in the morning before church and after church. One Sunday morning as I was getting dressed for service, he said, "I want to come to church!"

"You do?"

"Yeah, I want to come to church! You've never invited me to church."

"I know. I didn't think that you would want to come," I admitted.

"I want to come."

Of course I talked to Dr. Tigner about it.

"Are you crazy? Invite him to church!" he said.

"But what are people going to say?"

"Who cares what people are going to say? Invite him to church."

I was worried about how different we were, but I said forget it. I invited him. I told him where the church was and that it started at 9 a.m. He came, on time, and sat with me.

"Man, this is really in the hood! I've never been this far in the hood. I've been to USC, but never this far east," he said.

I laughed so hard.

"I've never even seen this type of hood before!" he continued. "This is pretty amazing! The people are so spirited and so happy! And Dr. Tigner is good! It's just singing and preaching and then you're done!"

It's safe to say he loved it. He started coming every week. It was like our thing to do. He would come to church, then after, I would go home, change clothes, and go to his house. He lived all the way in the Valley, going toward Six Flags. I remember one of the first times he invited me over to his house, I wasn't too sure if I should go. I asked Dr. Tigner, and he agreed that I should go.

"Go! See where he lives. I bet you he lives better than all of those boyfriends you've ever had."

It was a Friday night when I went to his house. He wanted me to meet him at his house and then we planned to go out to dinner. It took me about an hour to get there. Friday night traffic in LA is horrific, especially when you are going toward the Valley.

As I got off the 118 freeway, I had to drive up this long hill. I started to think I was lost. I kept following the directions that he gave me. I ended up at this gated community with these beautiful, huge gates and a call guard. As I approached the gate, I had to say, "Dana Pump," and he called him to confirm I was his guest. The guard then took my driver's license and gave me a pass, and I could then drive into the community. It was beautiful. These houses were absolutely stunning. Dr. Tigner was already correct.

I parked outside his house. I wasn't able to see the front door from the street. You have to walk through this outside hallway made of vines, which led to a courtyard, and then there was the front door. I rang the doorbell, and Dana answered in some basketball shorts, a T-shirt, and Adidas slides.

"Hey! You found it all right?" he asked.

"Yeah."

"You always look so conservative," he noted.

"Well, I'm a teacher, and I just got off work," I said.

I had on a cardigan, heels, and my hair was back in a bun. He walked me into the house and immediately gave me a tour. The house was beautiful. High ceilings. Everything was new and modern. Shuttered windows, beautiful kitchen, huge living room and dining room. Travertine tile floors. Huge bedrooms, beautiful bathrooms, beautiful office... I mean, just beautiful. Dr. Tigner was right. It was the most beautiful house I'd been to that belonged to a person I was dating. Better than Shakeer's, better than James'... just better. And it was just him. He was 41 years old, no kids, had never been married.

He had built this sports empire with his brother, and he was very proud of it. That was clear. He had pictures all over his house; he loved pictures. There were pictures with him and Michael Jordan, Magic Johnson, and Denzel Washington and his wife, Pauletta. There were different pictures of him at all his different foundation events with sports legends like Coach K from Duke, Isiah Thomas, Jerry West, James Harden, Gilbert Arenas, and the famous coach from the UNLV Runnin' Rebels, Jerry Tarkanian. I was just blown away from the pictures. Just looking at where he had been told me how successful he was. I was learning so much about him just by coming to his house. What really brought everything together was in his den, he had this huge painting of Jackie Robinson. *Okay. He loves Black people.* Every picture in his house had at least one Black person in it. From his college years to his young adult years to his AAU basketball team. I was simply amazed.

"Leah, do you like Mexican food?" he asked as I was looking at the pictures.

"Yes!"

"Okay, let's go to this Mexican place by my house. I'll drive."

So we jumped in his S550 Mercedes. Everything was showing me how authentic and successfully secure he was, but he was always so cool and casual about it. Very laid back. We got to the Mexican restaurant and sat down. I was the only Black person in the whole restaurant. We went to Los Toros in Chatsworth. Everyone was looking at me. I couldn't help but wonder if that was going to be our new norm for the next few months.

We sat in a nice booth and ordered fajitas. He got a tortilla, put it on the table, and started filling it up with meat and the sides. Not on a plate, but on the table.

"Boy! That table is filthy!" I said in disgust.

He did not care. He was just like that! He was stuffing his mouth and just talking so fast. *This is going to be an experience!* He was 100 percent him and 100 percent authentic.

He drove me back to the house and told me he'd had a great night. I knew I was not going to kiss him, but I gave him a hug, told him thank you, and drove back home. I called Dr. Tigner on my way back.

"The nicest house you've ever been to, huh?" he asked.

"Yes! How'd you know?!"

"I told you! Girl, you're about to be blessed!"

I couldn't see that far ahead, but I knew he wasn't just talking. I saw how nicely he lived. I told him about all the pictures I saw, and I also told him about that tortilla on that dang table! I mean, I just really found that gross.

Our dating was cool and very interesting. I was also getting to know his mother. Dana had no problem with me going to dinner to meet his mother, and my parents would join us often. Everything was just moving entirely too fast. He was still coming to church every Sunday, and we were praying every morning... This relationship was moving!

Even though we were dating and getting closer, and a little bit more affectionate, I still was hesitant to like him. I don't know why I was so hesitant. He was doing the right things and being the ultimate gentleman. What was it going to take for me to be into him?

One evening he invited me to get some drinks after work. He had a lot of consulting meetings at this hotel and suggested that I meet him after his meetings for a bite to eat and some drinks. Even though I don't drink, and neither does he, he would just say that because I guess it was cool to say. I agreed and met him.

"Leah, I know you're getting ready for your foundation event, and I know you're working hard and using a lot of your own money, so I want to help you. Here's a check for $1,000."

I looked at the check, and then looked at him. I remembered what Dr. Tigner told me—not to take any money. I gave the check back to him and said, "You know what? I don't want your money. I want you to teach me what you do. You have a successful foundation, you network, you fundraise... I want you to teach me how to do that."

"Really? You would want to learn that?" He looked at me with wild eyes.

"I want to learn," I confirmed.

"All right. I'm going to teach you how to do this successfully. Now are you a good student?" he asked.

"I'm an excellent student."

"Okay. Well, be ready because I'm going to teach you."

After that dinner, he started setting up all of these meetings for me. Dinner parties with all of these corporate people from banks, funds, and even with Nestlé. He would tell me to tell my story to them about why I have a passion for girls and why I started the LadyLike Foundation. He taught me how to communicate what I wanted to do with the funds and my goals for the foundation, how I wanted to educate, inspire, and empower young ladies to reach their highest potential and become everything that they were created to be. I told them about the workshops, the education, the scholarships, the experiences. My desire was to put these young ladies living in underprivileged communities on the path to success. I would tell the story, and people would be impressed. They would say they definitely wanted to learn more and would go to my website for more information. But when I had my meeting with Nestlé, he was very, very thrilled and excited about it.

"Okay, well, I'll look into it," he promised.

Dana saw that he was very interested. His name was Carter Bains. The next day, Dana told me to send Mr. Bains an edible arrangement with a note saying it was great to meet him, and that I looked forward to doing business with him. I did exactly what Dana said.

A few weeks later, I got an email from Mr. Bains saying that he would be a $5,000 sponsor for my scholarship luncheon. That was huge. It was my first corporate sponsorship. That basically took care of my entire luncheon at the time. I was off to a great start!

That's what made me really start liking Dana. He took me by the hand and showed me how to do fundraising the right way. He actually saw my dream and taught me how to make it a reality. That was so attractive to me. More than anything Dana had done for me, what he did for my foundation—which was my passion—endeared me to him. After we got the corporate sponsor, he asked me who I wanted to honor with the Women of Excellence awards that year.

"I have no idea," I answered.

"One of my good friends is the ladies' basketball coach at UCLA. You should honor her. Another one of my good friends is a reporter for Fox Sports. She should be your host. Plus, you'll have Carter Bains with Nestlé as one of your sponsors," he mapped out.

"I want to honor Verna B. Dauterive. She gave $50 million to USC, and she's my grandmother's best friend."

"What?! Get her!"

I knew I also needed to honor my mom because I'd honored my grandmother at the last luncheon. You know you can't honor your grandmother and not honor your mom!

"Perfect. You have your honorees. Now you need to get the place. I have a friend that works at The Ritz Carlton in Marina Del Rey. We'll get a great rate for you, and we'll have your venue," he said.

Dana met with his friend and had me call him. We confirmed all the logistics and signed the contract. He helped me with everything, and he was excited about it. He wanted to make this happen for me. He wanted my dream to come true.

"Okay, what about the scholarships?" he asked.

"We sent out scholarship applications to all of the high schools in LA."

"Make sure you pick good ones," he advised.

And we did. We picked a girl that was homeless and was going to Harvard. She attended Jordan High School. Then we had some other girls that were going to UCLA and UC Berkeley. Everything was just moving.

"In order to make the event a total success you have to make some money, so we're going to get you some silent auction items."

He collected paintings and memorabilia that were all donated, so that if anyone bought them, it was a straight donation to the foundation.

Varie thought about getting all the girls that were going to participate in the luncheon the same dress. She went downtown and got matching pink dresses. The girls looked so cute. They were by the doors greeting the people, they walked around asking the people how they were doing, and I taught them to say, "Welcome to the LadyLike Foundation. We're so happy that you came, please enjoy yourself." They did their speeches, they did the welcome, and presented what they learned in the LadyLike Foundation. Dana literally was the one to help me do everything.

I began to not be impressed by Dana but inspired by him. To be honest, I began to really like him. His drive and tenacity were infectious. In fact, it made me take another look at him, and I found myself truly attracted to him. He singlehandedly took my foundation to a whole different level, and he was proud about it. He took my dream and made it a reality. He listened to my thoughts and made them happen. No one I dated had ever done this for me, as far as when it came to my dreams. I was so blown away by him. When I did my speech at the luncheon and thanked everyone, I decided to confirm what I was feeling within. "I'd like to thank my boyfriend, Dana Pump."

Everybody was so shocked that I said that. I was also still trying to get my dad used to the idea. By my announcement, I think my dad got it. It was real.

My first luncheon only had about 100 attendees, and it was a struggle. The second luncheon had over 300 people, thanks to Dana Pump. It was packed, with standing room only. I had said I wanted 250, but with his invites and his network, I surpassed my goal. It was a huge success, and I had money even after I paid for the venue and scholarships so that I could do activities with the girls.

That summer, Dana had a really great idea to take the girls to the Montage in Beverly Hills for high tea. We rented a van and took them on a tour, and they saw different places that they had never seen before: Neiman Marcus, Saks Fifth Avenue, and different boutiques on Rodeo Drive. I wanted to expose them to these places and give them something to look forward to. Some of these girls had never been out of their neighborhoods or a three-mile radius from their homes. Exposing them to places they would not frequent was important to me.

We went to the Beverly Hills park, which is in the center of Beverly Hills. We took pictures there, and then took them to the Montage, where they toured the hotel, saw the spa and the pool, and then we had high tea in the restaurant. They wore hats and gloves and beautiful little dresses. It was so much fun! And it was all Dana's idea. He always had the cutest ideas for the girls. He was constantly getting us tickets to different sporting events and women's basketball games. He was really supportive.

I remember for some of the Friday night girl talks with the teenage girls, Dana would say, "Let me just take that burden off of you and bring all the food for them!"

He came with desserts, drinks, and sandwiches, and the girls loved it. He was always doing things that truly blessed me. I was starting to really feel the relationship and be good with it. I was falling in love with him and started seeing that he was the one for me. We were affectionate, we were holding hands, we were going to church every Sunday. After church, it was our day. We were still going to dinner with his mom every Sunday, and she would pick the restaurant every week, of course. But it was fine. As long as I was going after my church responsibilities, Dr. Tigner was fine with it, too. But driving out to Dana's house all the time Dr. Tigner was not fine with.

"You're not going to be doing that. You're driving your car every time, and that's a good 50-60 miles one way. That's thirsty and needy. Yeah, he has a nice house and all that, but no. He's going to have to come to *your* house or come pick you up. You also should let him know you're not sleeping with him."

When Dr. Tigner told me this, it reminded me of the lesson I taught to the girls about the Song of Solomon. How Solomon leaped over hills and valleys to get to his beloved on the outskirts of Israel. He did not wait for her to come to see him, he went to see her. No matter how far she was, it did not matter; he was going to get her and bring her to the palace. What Dr. Tigner said was right, and if Dana loved me, he would do what it took to bring me to where he was.

So now I had two things to talk to Dana about. He asked me to meet him in LA for dinner at this restaurant called Kate Mantilini. I was so late. I had gotten my hair done, and this particular hair-dresser was very meticulous because she was into natural styling. Dana waited for over an hour for me to get there. He would always send me these texts saying "ETA?" which means, "Estimated time of arrival," when I was running late, which I couldn't stand. He was always on time; in fact, he would get to places 20 minutes early. I felt really bad this time, because at this point I actually did really like him.

When I got there, I could see in his face that he was frustrated. But he waited, and he stayed. I knew I had to talk to him about my past marriage with James and the reason I wouldn't be sleeping with anyone until I was married again. In the past, I was always afraid to have this conversation, but this time I wasn't afraid at all.

"I'm so sorry I'm late, I had to get my hair done," I said.

"Oh, it's okay. You look exquisite."

"Woah, that's a big word!" I joked. "Thank you so much."

We ordered our food and began engaging with each other.

"There's a couple things I want to talk to you about," I said.

"Go ahead."

"I know Melissa told you that I was married before. It was a horrific situation. He was terrible to me, he disowned me, and it really hurt my self-esteem. So as a result, I made a vow to the Lord to not have sex with anyone until I get married again."

He made a funny face. "Oh, that's all you wanted to talk to me about? No problem. Sex isn't everything. You have to get to know the person and make sure you like them. You have to know you like to be around the person, you have to know what that person is all about. By the way, I love what you're all about. You work out, you're smart, you have a real family, a real dad and mom, and a real grandmother that I love. You take care of your family, you make sure that they're good. You work for the Lord, you go to church every Sunday, you don't just say you go to church. You *really* go to church. And you don't just say you work out, you really work out every morning. I know you're at the gym before work. I can see you're dedicated and driven. You keep your word, you have great character, great values… That's what I love. So no, sex isn't everything."

This guy was beginning to be a winner.

I began to really know him for him. I began to see how driven and committed he was to his affairs. He was so passionate about it and would raise a large amount of money and give it away to Northridge Hospital. The Carole Pump Women's Center (named after his mom) treated women that had cancer. There was another wing at the hospital named The Harold & Carole Pump Oncology Center that was named after his mom and dad. His foundation event raised money just for the hospital and the treatment of cancer patients. At their event they honored world renowned athletes and entertainers. This particular year, they were honoring Magic Johnson and Bill Russell. He was working hard every day for this event, raising money, meeting with corporations, telling the story of his father passing away from cancer, which motivated him to create the foundation. He talked about things he was able to do for the community, like screenings and health fairs for the San Fernando valley that had free mammograms and prostate exams, with free transportation to anyone who didn't have their own. All of these things were making me really love the person he was, and I loved his family, too. His mother was the matriarch, and I could tell that she loved Dana so much. I recognized that her world was her twin boys because everything revolved around them. Dana was the driving force in the twin towers. David, his twin, is the laid back one, whereas Dana is the aggressive one.

Every time I was with his mother, Carole, she would always give me tips on how to handle Dana, because he was definitely a lot to handle. You had to do a lot to keep his interest, although I didn't do anything, which I think made him even more interested. He was a driven guy, so I had to keep the challenge up. I did that. I barely called him, and he always called me. I rarely initiated anything; he always initiated.

His mother would tell me things like, "Don't ever let him get away with anything! If you ever let him get away with anything, he'll get away with everything."

Note to self.

"When you say no, mean it! Because he doesn't take no for an answer."

"Leah, he's aggressive, even when he was a baby. When I had anything for them, Dana was the first one to grab, and David would come second."

I would see these little traits that Carole warned me about. If he was being too aggressive, I was never afraid to say no and stand my ground. I was never afraid to be myself. If he acted a little rude, I would call him on it, and just not answer my phone. I wouldn't be pressed and wouldn't be moved. I was really finding my voice in this relationship. I was strong, confident, and not worried whether he would not like me or not. I was really seeing how someone can like you when you're yourself. I didn't have to do anything out of the ordinary. He didn't want me to dress a certain way, he didn't want me to wear a lot of makeup. I was myself at church, myself in my foundation, myself at school, and he loved all of it. He couldn't get enough of it. The more I pulled back, the more he pressed forward. If I wasn't talking to him, he would bulldoze his way to my house. He started driving down to my house, and if there were nights I told him I wasn't coming to his house, he would send a car service to come pick me up, bring me to him, and then take me back to my house. This was almost every week, sometimes two or three times a week.

Whatever was necessary, he did it. He made it happen. In addition, I was still not taking any money from him, which drove him crazy. Not one cent. He could pay for dinner, he could pay for the movies or wherever we went, but I would not take money. At all.

Next, he wanted to buy me a car. He hated my Ford Explorer, and I mean hated it. I did too, because at that point I had been driving it for about ten years. Every time he would see it, he would say, "Can I *please* buy you a car?"

Of course I wanted him to buy me a car, but I said no. Dr. Tigner told me to not take a dime, and I listened. Every time he was out of town, he would leave his Mercedes with me, and I would drive it, but I would not let him buy me a car. Whatever was necessary, he was willing to do in order to make me love him. Isn't that crazy? Not make him love me, but make me love him!

The only thing that was hard was getting him to give his life to the Lord. We would talk about it all the time, but he kept saying that he was Jewish. I knew it was his mother's influence, and I would have to explain to him that being Christian is just the evolution of a Jew. It's the end result. There's no Christianity without Judaism. It's the same faith, except with Jesus. Jesus completes the Jewish faith. He would say it's not necessary, but I was certain in letting him know that if he wanted a future with me, it was definitely necessary.

Summer came fast, and I loved that I was out of school so that I could have more free time to go out during the week with Dana. It was a lot of fun, and we were spending almost every day together just getting to know each other more. He kept saying that he wanted to marry me. I would hear through the grapevine that he was going to propose, and I just felt like it was way too fast. David's wife, Eunice, would talk about how he was ready to propose and that he was looking at rings. We had only started dating in February, and it was only July! No, no, no, no, no! I knew that he hadn't given his life to the Lord, and that was very important to me. I could not be married to somebody who did not share my faith, or at least believe in what I believed in. God had brought me through so much. I just couldn't do it. I know couples who do have different faiths, and that's completely fine to me. I definitely didn't want to take away his Jewishness and his upbringing, and all of his high holidays. I would never want to take that away from him. I felt like that's what made him who he was, even though he wasn't orthodox at all.

I wanted to minister to him in a way that he could understand. He was still coming to church every Sunday. When my pastor opens up the doors of the church, he always says, "If you are saved, and you know it, raise your hand," as we bow our heads and close our eyes. I would raise Dana's hand with my hand.

"Why are you raising my hand?" he whispered.

"Because one day, you're going to be saved."

He kind of laughed it off. But I kept doing that week after week. In addition, on our tithe envelopes, there is a prayer request box where you can fill out what you want the pastor to pray for. On the back of the card, I would put "Dana's salvation" every single week. Although he was reluctant and didn't think it was important, I was still praying and having the Lord work on his spirit.

My 30th birthday was coming up, and I wanted to do something special. But then again, I didn't. Dana and I were talking about what I should do, and I said, "Why don't we just have a barbecue at your house? Your house is beautiful, and you have a pool."

"Perfect!" he said.

And so Varie was going to cook all the barbecue, and some friends from my church were going to help her with the sides and other items for the party. Dana was going to get the DJ. And I wanted it to be an all-white party.

I wanted to try a full weave. So I had Melissa, who had started doing my hair, do a full weave. I wanted to have a new look for my 30th birthday.

Everybody came to Dana's house, and it was really great. My mom, my dad, my brother, my uncle, my grandmother, my godmother, Renee, and even friends from my church came. Everybody was so impressed with Dana's house and how it was in a gated community. They also loved the pool. It was beautiful. It was simply a wonderful day. The food was delicious. Varie outdid herself with the food. I mean, it was just great. Varie and Pastor Tigner provided all the barbeque. My dad and mom bought the cake from Hansen's, of course. I have had a Hansen's cake since my first birthday. Varie and my friends from church brought all plates, eating utensils, drinks, and finger food. They brought everything to Dana's house. All Dana had to do was get the DJ.

The party was outstanding, and everyone had a great time. It was on Monday, Memorial Day. My birthday was on Tuesday, May 26, but I figured Memorial Day would be a great day to have the barbecue, so I moved the celebration to Monday because everyone would be off work and able to really enjoy themselves. The music and entertainment was great, and to top it off Dana had Brian McKnight come and sing "Happy Birthday" to me. Brian McKnight's girlfriend was a friend of Dana's, and she got Brian to come and sing.

The day was absolutely perfect, to say the least. My hair was perfect. My outfit was perfect. The birthday party was perfect. The food was delicious. The cake was the best ever, and everybody wore white. Brian McKnight singing me "Happy Birthday"... can you imagine?! I had the best 30th birthday party ever.

The next day, Tuesday, I had to go to work, of course, but Tuesday was my actual birthday. May 26th. So during my break, I called Dana and said, "Since I had such a great birthday party yesterday, how about we just go with the family to Cheesecake Factory tonight to celebrate my real birthday and call it a day?"

I'm a birthday girl, and birthdays mean everything to me. My parents from since I can remember always made my birthday special. They said it was the day that you can do whatever you want; eat what you want, wear what you want, and go wherever you want.

My birthday party was the day before, but my birthday wasn't... So I wanted to celebrate on the day, too.

"Cheesecake Factory? I mean, you already had a big birthday party yesterday. Don't break the bank," Dana said in a matter-of-fact tone.

Don't break the bank? It's the Cheesecake Factory...

"Didn't you do enough yesterday?" he continued.

I knew Dana doesn't like to spend money, but he didn't spend any money. I mean, he did not go out of his way at all. He got the DJ and Brian McKnight, who lives in the Valley really close to him. He did not do anything extra special and didn't give me any extra special gifts, so I didn't understand. What was he saying? What? *Don't break the bank?* That just kept ringing in my head. It was almost insulting. He didn't do anything! Did he think that he'd done something big?

I started to take his comment very personally. Was I this little Black girl that he was trying to buy and now he was telling me that was enough? So I got off the phone and I called Dr. Tigner, of course.

"You know... I asked Dana if we could all go to the Cheesecake Factory tonight for my birthday, and he said don't break the bank."

"What did he say?"

"He said don't break the bank," I repeated.

"Don't answer your phone."

"What?" I asked.

"Don't answer your phone. That is insulting. You are not supposed to be happy over the little things like you're a little Black girl from the hood. What does that mean? Break the bank? He didn't pay for anything, Leah. He didn't do anything. Just because we had a birthday party at his house? Varie and I brought almost everything. We brought the food. We brought the supplies. We brought the plates.

Your parents brought the cake. What did he do? No, no, no, no, no, no, no. We've got to teach him a lesson. Don't answer your phone."

"But it's my birthday."

"I don't care. Don't answer your phone. Call me when you get off work."

"Okay," I agreed.

I was so upset... my feelings were hurt. I couldn't believe it. We were on such a great run. *How could he ruin my birthday? How could he say I was breaking the bank? I didn't do anything. Is he that cheap? Am I not worth it?* All these things were running through my head. So I didn't answer my phone, and Dana was calling me nonstop. I was not answering. He was texting me, he was calling me, he was spoofing me. He was calling me from different numbers. But I did not answer my phone.

So it was Tuesday, and although I didn't plan to go to Bible study, what else was I going to do? I had to go to Bible study because Tuesday nights were Bible study nights. I decided to go to church, and I was really depressed. Dr. Tigner saw my face.

"I don't know why you're so sad."

"I am disappointed in him," I confessed.

"Yeah, but, you know, you've got to teach him a lesson because he's going to keep doing this, and this is not okay. He can't act like he's the savior or Captain Save a Hoe when he hasn't done nothing. Oh, no, no, no, no. We have to teach him a lesson."

During Bible study, my phone rang, and to my surprise, it was Shakeer. He left a voicemail on my phone.

"Hey Lee! Happy born day! It's Shakeer. I wanted to know if you were doing anything today, and if you weren't doing anything, I'd love to take you out. All right, give me a call back. Love."

So I told Dr Tigner. "Shakeer called me."

"He did?"

"He called me to wish me a happy birthday and wanted to know if I was doing anything tonight, and if not, he wants to take me out."

"Call him," he said.

"What about Dana?" I asked.

"Dana messed up! Dana needs to be taught a lesson. Call Shakeer and go out with him."

"Are you sure?"

"Go out with him."

"Okay."

You know he's my coach. He knows what he's talking about. I called Shakeer.

"Heyyyy, Lee! Happy born day! How are you? I miss you. Are you doing okay?" he asked.

"Yeah, I'm doing good!"

"Well, do you have any plans for tonight?"

"No, no, I don't have any plans."

"I'd love to take you to this great Italian restaurant. It's really hard to get into, but I'd love to take you out if you let me."

"Okay. Yeah, that sounds good."

"Cool. Well, meet me at about 8:00 in West Hollywood at this address."

"Cool!" I agreed.

I was so excited. I hadn't seen him in months. He just happened to call me. *Lord, You're so good. On one hand, I was disappointed, but on the other hand, Shakeer called me. This is amazing!*

So I met him at the restaurant, and God, he looked so good. Oh, my God. That face, that smile... it just brought back all the old memories. But I had to remember that I was in a relationship. Of course, he didn't have to know that. We had dinner, and it was back like old times. This time, he prayed for me.

"Lord, thank you for allowing Leah to be born on this day. She is a beautiful light to this world. She has a beautiful spirit. Bless her today. Thank you so much for this dinner. Bless this food. In Jesus' name, Amen."

God, why did he always get me? He just got me every time. During dinner we were talking and laughing, and we started talking about his type.

"You like big girls, don't you?" I joked. The tennis star was very thick.

"No, I don't!" he said.

"Yes, you do."

And he was just laughing. We had a great, great dinner. I mean, the Lord really came through. After dinner, he walked me to the car and gave me a big hug.

"Man, this was so nice," he said.

"Yeah, it was. It was so nice to see you."

"All right, well, take care," he said.

"Thank you so much for tonight. You really made my day," I told him.

"My pleasure. My pleasure. Take care and I'll see you soon."

Dana continued to call me all through the dinner, but I didn't answer. I just kept the phone in my purse. When I went home, I called Dr. Tigner, and I said, "Well, when do I pick up the phone?"

"Don't pick up the phone for a week. He has to learn a lesson. He will never say that to you again."

"All right," I agreed.

And I did it. I didn't pick my phone up for a week. Of course, after a couple of days, Dana was showing up at my job with flowers and everything. I'd tell Dr. Tigner, and he would just say, "It doesn't matter if he got flowers. Don't pick up that phone for a week."

"Okay," I sighed.

So when a week was up, Dr. Tigner said, "Now call him and say you don't want to talk on the phone. You want to see him in person and to meet you somewhere **you** want to meet."

"Got it," I said.

I called Dana. Of course he was ready to talk that day.

"Wherever you want me to meet you, I'll meet you," he said.

"Okay, meet me at Katana at 7:30."

He agreed. So I met him at Katana, and I was serious. I didn't give him a hug. I didn't give him a kiss. I didn't give him anything.

"Why didn't you pick up your phone? Why weren't you answering?"

"Dana. Don't you ever in your life tell me that I'm breaking the bank. You didn't pay for shit. You didn't buy one stitch of food. You didn't buy any utensils. You didn't do anything. My family and my friends did that for me. All you did was get the DJ and get Brian McKnight to sing for free. Don't ever say that I'm breaking the bank, do you understand? If you ever say that again, I promise you it's over."

"Leah, I promise you, I love you. I'll never do that again. I'll never, ever, ever do that again. Please don't ever not answer your phone."

From that point on, Dana was on his absolute best behavior with me. We were back to old times, and I could tell that he knew that he'd really messed up, and he didn't want to lose me. I found out that he had found a ring for me and that it was beautiful. I even heard that his mom helped him pick it out. He was trying to plot all of these ways to propose to me, but he had to talk to my dad, and he had to talk to my pastor. So he made arrangements to talk to my dad. And of course my dad was thrilled because by now, he loved him. He loved all the celebrities that Dana knew, and he loved all the games and events that Dana invited him to. My dad also loved all the basketball tournaments, and honestly all the things that Dana represented. My mom was going along with my dad. So they were happy. My grandmother loved Dana so much. She would threaten me that if I didn't marry him, that she was going to move to Texas. And I would say, "Well, Mama, you're probably going to have to move to Texas, even though I love you so much. But I'm not marrying him until he gives his life to the Lord."

And I stood firm on that. Dr. Tigner kept me firm on it as well. But Dana was still very reluctant.

Dana went to visit Dr. Tigner one day because I was very adamant that if he wanted to marry me, he had to talk to Dr. Tigner. My dad wasn't really strict about the Christian thing, even though he was a staunch Christian. He didn't really make it a priority that Dana gave his life to the Lord. I think my parents saw me getting older, and they wanted me to get married. However, Dr. Tigner wanted me to make it a priority because David, Dana's twin, was married also to a Christian, but she never made it a priority. As a result, David never made it a priority to come to church with her. He would attend church with his wife on special events like Easter and Christmas, but he wouldn't come regularly. It really bothered her, and she would tell me about it. I wanted to make sure that this was done before I said that I would marry him, before we said I do, so that there would be no problems afterwards.

Dr. Tigner talked to Dana about the importance of giving his life to the Lord. Dana just kept saying that he was Jewish. Dr. Tigner told him, "You're really nothing because you don't even know why you're Jewish."

"Well, I was raised by Jews," Dana said.

"Okay. We'll say that you were raised Jewish, but you don't really know why you're Jewish. You didn't go to Hebrew school, you were Bar Mitzvah'd, but you were tutored for your Bar Mitzvah. You really don't know. So you're basically nothing. You're just culturally Jewish."

"Well, well, yeah, but my mom... she's very serious about me not changing my religion."

"It's not changing your religion. It's just accepting Jesus to be your savior. It's not changing who you are. It's just accepting the fullness of what Judaism is. It's accepting Jesus as your savior. Jesus came to save God's people, God's chosen people, which are the Jews. So not changing who you are, but accepting this lifestyle that enhances who you are, basically," Dr. Tigner noted.

"Well, my mom doesn't think it's necessary, so I don't think it's necessary."

"Well, you have a choice. You're either going to sleep with your mom or you're going to sleep with Leah."

"What?"

"You're going to either sleep with your mother... because if you're trying to make your mother happy in this, then you need to sleep with your mother. But if you're trying to marry Leah, and if you love Leah, then you need to accept the Lord."

That was put very, very plainly. Dana got it really quickly. But still, it took him some time to really see the importance of coming to Christ. In fact, he just put it on the back burner and would say, "You know, I'll do it one day, but I don't have to do it now."

I would hear about all of these little plans that he was going to propose to me. In fact, one of his mentors, Gino Roberts, called me one day. Gino Roberts worked for Nike Global. So I knew he had a lot of influence and knew a lot of things about fundraising and business. He was a business mastermind.

"Hey, Leah. There's a big summit in Santa Barbara that I want you to go to. Apple is going to be there, as well as other huge companies."

"Oh, yes! I'd love to be there."

I called Dana and told him I wanted to go to the summit. I felt like it could make LadyLike big and connect me with the people I needed to meet. Dana had gotten me on this networking kick, so I felt like I needed to be where all these people were.

A few hours later, I got a call from Dr. Tigner. "That Santa Barbara trip is a hoax. It's just a setup for him to ask you to marry him."

"Really?" I asked.

"Yes. And Leah, he has not done what we have asked him to do. He has not given his life to the Lord. So you cannot put yourself in a position where he asks you to marry him when he has not done his part. You're not the little Black girl that's hungry for a ring. No. We need him to do his part."

"You're right."

I called Dana. "I can't go to the conference in Santa Barbara. I have a couple things I need to do." I just made up some stuff. So Dana's plans were done. I knew he had the ring, but I wanted to make sure that this was right. I did not want to make the same mistakes as I'd made with James and other relationships that were not right. I wanted to make sure that God was pleased with my relationship with Dana. In my heart I felt he was the one for me, my perfect match. I just wanted to be sure, and him giving his life to the Lord would be the ultimate sign from God that this was the one for me. Even though he was so much fun, and he exposed me to so many events, sporting events and charity events, taught me how to network, taught me how to fundraise, taught me how to be successful, taught me how to be business savvy, I still did not want to give up on what was important to me, which was the Lord.

Dana's charity event was coming up, and it was his ninth year. It was at the Beverly Hilton Hotel. He had already given away millions of dollars to Northridge Hospital, and he wanted to give away even more. This year he was honoring Bill Russell and Magic Johnson, and the place was filled with over eight hundred people. He raised hundreds of thousands of dollars that he was going to give to Northridge Hospital, and I was his date. This was the first time I would be able to watch him in action, and it was really amazing to see. Everything he taught me I saw him do. He truly practiced what he preached. Every athlete, every Hall of Famer from every sport—baseball, basketball, and football—was there. He even had NBA rookies there. Celebrities such as Denzel Washington, Cedric the Entertainer, and even Snoop Dogg were all in attendance. It was like athletes versus entertainers all in one room. The ongoing funny theme of the night was that the athletes were star struck when they saw the movie stars, and the movie stars were star struck when they saw the athletes.

I was so impressed. Although I'd never been to his event, I got to see everything and watch the whole process of him raising money. I just had to tell him, "Dana, you and your brother are blessed." I had never seen someone have the gift of fundraising where he just could make a call and people gave thousands of dollars. A hundred thousand dollars here, ten thousand there, twenty-five thousand at a different table. I had never seen it on this level. He was really a genius when it came to fundraising. He was so passionate about it because he wanted to raise money to fight cancer. It was the most amazing thing. Taking a tragedy and turning it into a passion-driven foundation was simply admirable. I went to the gala, and I invited Dr. Tigner and Varie. My mom, dad, my grandmother and another pastor and his wife went with us. We were all dressed in after five attire.

Pastor Tigner was advising me on how I should dress that night. "Leah, you've got to look really good because this is your boyfriend's event. You have to look the best."

I went to Loehman's and got this little black dress and thought I was really going to look nice and classy. It was not too much and not too fancy; it was perfect to me. When it came time for the event, Dr. Tigner and Varie looked at my dress, and Varie said, "Well, I didn't think you'd wear that. You need to be the star!"

And so that always stuck in my mind. I was like, *Okay, next year I'll do better.*

We all truly enjoyed ourselves. The event was a complete success. The honorees for the night, Magic Johnson and Bill Russell, made speeches that were moving and heartfelt. I really was proud of Dana.

He called me as soon as I got home and thanked me for coming. He then went on to ask me for a blow-by-blow of what I thought of the event, since it was the first one that I'd attended.

"I'm so impressed with you. And I'm so proud of you," I told him.

After every event, his family's tradition is to go on a vacation. This year they were going to Cabo. Before the fundraiser, he asked me if I would go with him.

"Well, you know, I'm not going to be able to sleep with you," I said.

"That's fine. I respect that. The rooms are big. It's a loft. I wouldn't expect that from you, but I still really want you to come. All my friends are going, David's going, and his wife is going. I would love for you to go with me."

So of course, I asked Dr. Tigner what he thought. Dr. Tigner said yes, but to make sure I wasn't going to sleep with him. I told him I wasn't.

"If he respects your decision, then you should go," he said.

I told Dana I could go and made all of the flight arrangements. I didn't want to miss church. They were all leaving right after the event that Saturday, and I would leave right after church on Sunday. He knew how important church was to me. I always wanted to make sure that God knew that He was first. I felt that if God knew He was first then He would bless me. So after church, I flew to Cabo for our first vacation together.

We went to Cabo, and we stayed at One & Only Palmilla, which is a beautiful, beautiful resort. It had lofts and gorgeous bungalows that everyone stayed in. Our bungalow was two stories. The bedroom was on top, the living room was on the bottom, and it was right on the beach. I had never seen anything this beautiful. Yes, I know what you are thinking—of course I had my passport! After Dr. Tigner told me to get my passport, I had it. So I was ready for this trip when he asked me.

My luggage consisted of beautiful bathing suits and these beautiful dresses. I was ready for this trip and was so excited. I felt no pressure to sleep with Dana because we had been in several situations before where I would be in his house or we'd taken a nap, and he'd never pressured me. So I felt really confident that I was going to be good on this trip.

As soon as I arrived at Cabo, Dana was so excited. He was introducing me to everyone, and I was so happy to meet them.

"This is my girlfriend. This is my girlfriend! This is the girl that I've been talking to you about. This is the girl from the picture! This is the girl!"

I mean, he was so excited and telling everybody that I was his girlfriend, which was different from James. Can you imagine? I wanted him to say who I was, and he never did. Dana had no problem telling people who I was. He was proud to claim me and tell the world who I was to him. This made me feel safe and secure. It really meant a lot, especially because of all I'd gone through. It was validating and made me feel valuable—something that I had longed to feel. Yes, value should come from within, and I did value who I was and all that I had become. But to have someone put value on you like King Solomon and put a banner over your head telling the world who you are to him is truly something that causes you to know that this person values and loves you.

All the couples were nice and really fun to be around. It was wonderful meeting new people and being with loving couples.

As soon as I got into our bungalow, I had this cramping feeling in my stomach. I always have terrible, terrible cramps, but only when I am on my period or my period is coming. In my mind I said, *I know I'm not on my period. No, I'm not on my period.* It's like God had this sense of humor. I was in this beautiful place on the beach, in this beautiful bungalow, and I started my period? Yeah, right.

I went to the bathroom. And guess what? I'd started my period. I was like, *Oh God definitely doesn't want me to have sex on this trip.* Dana asked me what was wrong.

"Umm, I started my period."

"Oh, you did? Okay. All right. Let me make a call."

He called down to the concierge and said, "Hello? Hola, hola. My girlfriend started her period. Do you have any pads?"

Wow, he is a winner.

He didn't care. Any other man would have gone crazy to know that their girlfriend was on their period, because this was definitely a setup for sex. And there was none happening here on this trip.

He got the pads for me. They came right away to the room. He brought them to the bathroom for me.

"Here you go. Is this the kind you need?"

He is really something special, I thought.

Even though I was on my period, I still had fun. I still swam, I still wore my cute dresses. Intimacy was out, of course. Kissing and stuff was in, but everything else was out. I felt so good. I got to know all of his close friends, and we bonded. We would eat all of our meals together, which enabled us to talk and really get to know each other. We even went into the city. We just had a wonderful four days.

During the trip, Dr. Tigner had gotten salmonella and was very sick, and I couldn't reach him. I was so scared because he means so much to me. He wasn't answering his phone, and like always I was trying to give him a blow-by-blow, but I couldn't reach him. This was just not like him. There's never been a time when I couldn't reach him. So I finally reached his daughter, Bella, and Bella told me that he was in the hospital. Immediately, I wanted to come home. But everyone, including Varie and my family, was like, *No, this is the first time you're on a real trip with a guy that really likes you. We want you to enjoy it. And Dr. Tigner is fine. He was really sick, but he's getting better.*

I felt better hearing that, but I would get teary at the thought of ever losing him. After a few days, I finally talked to Dr. Tigner, even though he sounded so weak on the phone. After talking to him, I was able to enjoy the rest of my trip. But as soon as I got back, I went straight to Cedars-Sinai to see him. He was doing much, much better and was going to be released in a day or so. I was so happy.

At the hospital, of course, he asked me everything, and I told him everything. I told him I'd kept my vow and not had sex. But I told him I'd started my cycle, and he laughed so hard.

"That is crazy!" he said.

"I know, right? The Lord really, really, really didn't want me to have sex."

"Well, did he ask you to marry him?"

"No! I found out he was trying to ask me to marry him right before the trip. Eunice, David's wife, told me. But I told her to tell David to tell him no, I was not ready."

This was so crazy, right? Full circle with James. I couldn't wait for him to ask me to marry him. For Dana, I had to get him to stop asking me to marry him. At every chance he got, he was trying to ask me to marry him. I just wasn't ready! He had not given his life to the Lord.

It was a 180 degree difference. From one guy that you love so much, and you can't wait to be with, only to find out he doesn't want to be with you to finding a man who your pastor tells you is going to be one of your biggest blessings, and you've got to make him slow down on marrying you. Go figure.

Things were going great. Dana and I were falling in love. But I still kept my guard up because he had not given his life to the Lord. I started telling myself over and over: *Leah, if this doesn't work out, you're going to be fine. You're going to be great. You have a great job, a beautiful home, your students love you… if this relationship doesn't work out, you're going to be fine!*

I kept that attitude. It made me more confident. It made me be who I was, and I wasn't afraid of Dana. If we got in an argument, I would yell, scream, curse, fight, leave, hang the phone up, I mean it didn't matter. I could be 100 percent myself: my cocky self, my OCD self, my silly self, my professional self, and even my academic self. It didn't matter. He did not care; he just wanted to be with me, and I knew he loved me. He would call my parents and check in on them, then call my grandmother and talk to her for hours about how I wouldn't marry him. She would always reassure him that she would get me to marry him.

Dr. Tigner had several engagements out of state in August. My mom's birthday is in August as well. With Dr. Tigner being out of town, we didn't talk as much because he was very busy preaching, teaching and dealing with all of his preaching assignments. When we did get a chance to talk, he would be adamant and direct with me staying on course. He did not want me to let my guard down and tell Dana that I would marry him without him keeping his end of the bargain and giving his life to the Lord. Dr. Tigner would say over and over, "Don't get to the finish line and drop the baton. You have gotten this far, don't throw it all away." He was absolutely right, and his words kept me on my guard.

On my mom's birthday, she wanted to make my grandmother happy, so she wanted all of us to go to Hometown Buffet in Hawthorne. Since Dana was very comfortable with my family, and I was very comfortable with his family, I brought Dana with me to my mom's birthday dinner.

We had a good time at Hometown Buffet, laughing and having a good time. My dad was taking pictures of everyone and was the life of the party. Dana and my dad are a lot alike, and their birthdays are nine days apart: both Aquarius men. They both know it all, and both of them were very loud. Every dinner with them was a guaranteed good time. Dana was scheduled to go out of town the next morning.

"Do you want to keep my car? Why don't you take me home? I have to go to an event at Smokey Robinson's house. We can go to Smokey's event and then you can drop me off and drive home," he told me.

"Okay, no problem."

We went to Smokey Robinson's event, and then to his house after.

"Come inside before you take the car back to LA. Let's fight."

One of our favorite "couple things" to do was wrestle each other. We pretended like we were WWE fighters. I don't know why we found that fun, but we did. We would try to see who could push the other off the bed first. I know it sounds crazy, but it was really fun. I would win because I'm stronger; I work out. Even though he's big, I still would win.

So we had our tumbling match, and all of a sudden he said, "Leah, would you *please* marry me? Please. Marry me, Leah, please."

He had never done that before. He started crying, and he brought out this little basketball. He opened it up, and inside there was a ring. It was huge. It was a yellow canary cushion-cut diamond in the center with three levels of diamonds under it. It looked like a tri-layered cake. It was yellow gold and white gold. In my heart, I always wanted a mixed metal ring, because I always loved yellow gold, but yellow gold rings were not in style anymore. *How did he know?* I had never told that to anyone.

"Leah, I've never met anyone like you before in my life. I love you. I knew when I met you that you were the one for me. Your drive, your values, your upbringing... I'm a better person because of you. Can you *please* marry me?" His eyes were full of tears and passion.

I just felt so confused. I remembered what Dr. Tigner said, but he was crying, and I loved him too. I felt the exact same way about him. He made me better, he encouraged me, he was the one, my partner for life. What was I to say? He was proposing. No, he still had not done what he said he was going to do. I was caught off guard...

"Okay," I said.

He started crying even more. I didn't cry at all. I had no clue what I'd just done. He put the ring on me and called his mom.

"She said yes!"

Next, he called his brother, David.

"She said yes!!!"

He looked up from his phone. "You aren't going to call your parents?" he asked.

"No. I'll wait."

"I'm so happy, I'm so happy!" he exclaimed.

He walked me to the door, I got in his car, and I drove to LA. I wanted to call Dr. Tigner so badly, but I felt like I had failed. I hadn't made him do what he said he was going to do. I was driving down the 405, feeling so confused. I didn't feel happy; I felt like I had disappointed the Lord. The same disappointment I felt for not giving Dana a chance was the same disappointment I felt in my spirit on that freeway driving back to LA.

My girlfriend Emily was in town with her family. I called her and told her that I needed to come over. She knew that something was wrong, but I didn't want to talk about it until I got there. She lived in Arizona with her husband, who was an ex-NFL player. She'd just had a new baby boy. I'm the godmother to her first child. She was always easy to talk to and understanding. She was the first person I talked to about James, and now I needed to talk to her about what had just happened.

I got over to her mother's house, where she was staying, and she was holding and nursing her brand-new baby.

"So what happened?" she asked.

"This."

I put my left hand out.

"Oh my gosh, Leah!! He asked you to marry him?"

"Yes."

"Aren't you happy?" she asked.

"No."

"Why?"

"Because he didn't do what he said."

"Leah, are you crazy?"

"I know I sound crazy, but I just know he's supposed to do what he said he'd do. I just don't feel right. I feel like I failed," I admitted.

"No, Leah. You didn't fail. He loves you!"

"I understand that. I just feel really bad."

We just talked and talked about everything. She always made me feel better about my situations, and always made me feel confident about everything. She just made me feel good. While I was holding her baby, I said, "Should I marry Mr. Dana?"

He nodded his head. He was a newborn baby! It was the weirdest thing. Emily and I laughed so hard.

I went home and put the ring on my nightstand. I tried to go to sleep, but I couldn't. To be honest, I was scared to have to talk to Dr. Tigner the next day.

The next morning on my way to the gym, I called Dr. Tigner.

"Hey, Leah. I didn't hear from you last night."

"Yeah... I know. I have to tell you something," I said.

"What?"

"Dana proposed to me last night..."

"I KNEW IT! I knew the devil was going to do this to you."

"What?" I asked.

"Put you in a position where you had to say yes when it was not time for you to say yes, because he did not give his life to the Lord. I knew it, I knew it!"

Varie was in the background saying, "Why did you rush? What's the hurry?"

"I don't know… I don't know…" I confessed.

"Leah, you made a big mistake," Dr. Tigner said.

"I know! But how do I fix it?" I asked.

"I don't know. I don't know how you're going to fix it. Where's Dana now?" he asked.

"In New York," I answered.

"What is he doing in New York?"

"Business."

"Did he ask you to go with him?"

"Yes."

"And you said no? You can't say no, you're his fiancée. Call and tell him you're going to meet him in New York," he advised.

"But I don't want to go!"

"You made the decision to be his fiancée, so you need to go. That's what fiancées do."

He hung up the phone. I called Dana and told him that I would go to New York with him.

"You'll really come with me? Great! I'll get a ticket for you. I can't wait to see you!"

I was so nervous when I got to the airport the next day. Varie's sister, Cassie, took me to the airport. I was so discombobulated that I missed my flight and had to wait an extra three hours to catch the next flight out.

When I finally got to Dana, I was happy that I was with him. Yet I still had this sick feeling in my stomach. We spent time in New

York before I flew back home on Sunday. I called Dr. Tigner as soon as I landed.

"Hi," I said shyly.

"You know you made a terrible mistake?"

"I know."

"You know you're going to be miserable, right?"

"What?" I asked.

"If you don't get this straight before you get married... if he doesn't give his life to the Lord, and you don't hold him accountable for what he said he was going to do, he will never do what he says he's going to do, and *you* will be miserable. Mark my words. You need to give back the ring and tell him that you will not put it back on until he gives his life to the Lord. You mean business, Leah. Just like he forced you to do this, you force him to do that. You guys need to be on one accord, and he needs to see that it's very important to you. If you don't do this, you'll be miserable. I have been telling you not to drop the baton before you cross the finish line. At this point you have dropped it. Give. The. Ring. Back."

Now it was time to give the ring back because I knew what Dr. Tigner said was true. I had Dana come over to my house, and I gave him the ring back.

"Dana. I cannot wear this ring until you do what you said you were going to do."

"I'm not ready!" he exclaimed.

"Well, then I'm not ready to be your wife. And I will not wear this until you do what you said you were going to do."

Months went by. We were still dating and hanging out, but every time he would ask me to wear the ring, I wouldn't. He kept the ring in his house, by his bed, and he would always try to slip it on my hand while I was sleeping. I'd move my hand away every time.

He told his mother that I just wasn't wearing the ring because it was too big, but he knew the truth. I was not putting that ring back on my finger until he gave his life to the Lord.

A few months later, we ended up going on a trip to San Diego for a Stop Cancer event. He looked at me and said, "Leah, why won't you wear the ring?"

"You did not do what you said!"

"So what do I need to do?" he asked.

"You need the Lord in your life, and you know you do! We pray every day and everything, but *you* need the Lord in your life!"

"You are so right. Show me. How do I have the Lord in my life?"

"We have to pray the prayer of salvation," I answered.

"Okay. How do I do that?"

"Repeat after me," I said. "Lord…"

"Lord…"

"I repent of my sins."

"I repent of my sins."

"Come into my heart."

"Come into my heart."

"I accept you as my Lord and savior."

"I accept you as my Lord and savior."

"I believe you died on the cross for my sins."

"I believe you died on the cross for my sins."

"Make me a new creature."

"Make me a new creature."

"In Jesus' name, Amen."

"In Jesus' name, Amen."

Right after we prayed the prayer of salvation, he looked at me and said, "Now will you wear the ring?"

"Yes."

I started wearing the ring. But then I felt like I should wear the ring, but not set a date. I was unsure if he was really honest about his decision about the Lord. Dr. Tigner agreed with that as well.

"We've got to see if this is just for you to get the ring on, or if this is for real."

"You're right."

So I wore the ring, but I did not set a date.

December was approaching. Our first Christmas together. Dana *loved* Christmas. We got a tree, we furnished it, he went out of his way buying all types of gifts: a Luis Vuitton purse, a laptop, and a lot of small gifts he heard me say that I wanted. It was his first real Christmas that he'd had in his life, because he's Jewish.

"Wow, I love this Christmas thing! I've been missing out on this all this time?! Christmas is amazing!" he told me.

He bought a snowman and a bunch of little Santa Clauses and furnished his house from top to bottom in festive decorations. We had our first Christmas party together and invited all of our friends and family. We had a great time. A lot of people at the party were asking if I had set a date, and I made it clear that I had not decided on one yet.

Not too soon after, Tia had a birthday party, and I was going to bring Dana. This would be the first time that I would bring Dana around Tia and my other friends. Dana had invited the UCLA's girl's coaching staff to come with us to Tia's party at the SLS Hotel.

We all met for dinner, and then we went to the party. Tia's parties are usually the best parties of the end of the year. It's like a reunion for everybody from Los Angeles. You would always see somebody you do want to see and somebody you don't want to see. Everyone's in town for the holidays, and everyone would always look forward to it.

I was bringing Dana as my fiancé, and we were coming with a group of about ten people. One of my friends Sarah rushed up to me and said, "Leah! I've never seen these people! You have a whole new group of friends!"

"Oh, these are some people that I met through Dana," I replied.

I introduced Dana as my fiancé to Sarah and different friends. We got our own corner of lounge seats, and we were just having a really good time. The party was great. I saw a lot of people from high school, college, and the DJ was great.

Dana being Dana, when he's ready to leave, he is READY. I was ready to go too. I had already seen all the people I wanted to see. I saw Tia, gave her her gift, and I was ready.

Right before we were about to leave, I had to use the restroom. It was really crowded, and you really had to fight to navigate through people to get to it. Dana had to go too, so we were fighting through the crowd together. We both handled our business, and we began to walk out the only way you could exit the party.

As we were walking out, I saw this whole crowd of people. I looked closely, and it was Shakeer in the middle of people crowding him. Everyone was trying to get close to him.

Oh Lord...

Dana knew that I used to date him, so I was trying to bypass this crowd in a way that I didn't run into him. I just didn't want to have that moment; I just wanted to leave. I started walking and passed the crowd, when all of a sudden, bursting out of the crowd was Shakeer yelling, "Lee! Lee! Oh my gosh, hey! I haven't seen you in so long!"

He hugged me so tightly, for so long. You know those uncomfortable type hugs where you're trying to get out of it but can't? Dana was standing right there. I broke out of the hug and said, "Hey, it's so nice to see you too! Um, this is my fiancé, Dana."

Shakeer looked at Dana, and it was like he had seen a ghost. It was like time had stopped for that moment, it seemed like it was forever. He snapped out of it.

"Oh man, it's great to meet you!"

Dana was so excited to meet him. "Good to meet you too!"

Shakeer turned back to me and was like, "Wow, Lee!"

"Yeahhh," I said. "So good seeing you. All right, well, I'll see you soon."

"See you soon..." he said.

Dana and I walked away hand in hand.

I could not have written that any better. God really has a sense of humor! That was just classic.

The next day, Tia called me. "Girlllll, you know Shakeer told me that he met Dana!" she laughed.

"Really?"

"Yes, and I had to tell him that yes Dana is really your fiancé and he adores you. I told him you guys were so happy. Then he was like, 'Yeah, Leah's a really good girl, she deserves to be happy.'"

And so that was that for Shakeer.

positive seven

$\mathcal{J}$anuary went by... still no date... February... still no date.
Even March.

We found ourselves in his bed doing that wrestling match again.
He stopped fighting and looked at me.

"Leah, I can't take this anymore! What do I have to do to set a
date? We've gotta get married. I'm tired of this, I love you so much!"

"You need to give your life to the Lord."

"I did give my life to the Lord!"

"Nope! You need to walk down the aisle of the church and give
your life to the Lord."

"I'll do that tomorrow at 9 a.m. service. I promise you I'll do it."

That was a Saturday night. The next morning, I was in the choir
stand. Dana was there, suited, dressed to a T, and on time at 9 a.m.
After I finished singing, I came down to sit beside him.

As soon as Pastor Tigner finished preaching and opened up the
doors of the church, Dana looked at me and said, "You ready?"

"Ready!" I said.

Game time. He walked down the aisle and gave his life to the Lord. I will never, ever, ever forget that day. He finally did it! He did what he said he was going to do. I felt better about marrying him because he saw what was important to me, and he did it. I was so happy and in love.

His mother gave him a really hard time about it. She said it was completely unnecessary, and he shouldn't have done it. He went against his own mother to prove his love for me. He knew that the Lord had been working with him all this time because he said to me that it was a couple years ago when he was in his bed alone, and he was so tired of being single. He told me he said his first prayer: *God, please send me somebody.*

And it was me. He knew the Lord was real. Of course right after he gave his life to the Lord, he said, "So we're setting a date?"

"I guess we have to, right?" I joked. "Why don't we get married the weekend of your event in August? You'll have everybody in town. You'll have your event, and we can get married that Sunday."

"You're right! That's a great idea, because all my friends will be here! No one has to fly twice. They will already be here."

After church, we had family dinner with his mom. We told his mom that we'd set a date—August 15th. She was excited—in fact, everyone was. Now the wedding planning had to begin.

I told Dr. Tigner that we'd set a date, and he was so happy for me.

"Absolutely! That's exactly what I wanted you to do after he gave his life to the Lord."

In fact, he had been saying that if Dana did give his life to the Lord, I should know to immediately set a date because he had done everything that I had asked him to do. It took time; it wasn't abrupt. He had to think about how important it was for him to have me in his life and how important it was that he knew my faith is so strong that I'd hold out that long and not get married to him. Although he proposed in August, he didn't fully give his life to the Lord until April. So it was time. It was a long time that I had held out, and we still hadn't slept together. Just imagine all that he was going through as a man and seeing how firm I was standing. I didn't give in to a beautiful ring that was over 5 karats, nor did I give in to his success and lifestyle. I held strong to my faith and principles, and to who I was.

Now that it was time for planning, I began getting excited. My parents were so involved in the first wedding and paid for the whole thing. This time, they couldn't pay for the entire wedding. My grand-mother was in a totally different economic situation: she had given me the money for the house, was dealing with her own properties, and had also given an abundance to LadyLike. She wasn't in the position to just dish out money like she had been before.

Dana and I made an agreement that we'd split the cost of the wedding between both of our families. So all of the decisions were joint. I was excited about that, but I was also nervous because it was my second wedding.

Do you remember that episode on Sex and the City where Char-lotte is getting married to the Jewish lawyer Harry, and it's her second wedding? She isn't too excited about it, because she feels bad and worries how it will look to people that she was married before, although it is Harry's first wedding. Carrie and her friends try to convince her that Harry loves her and encourage her to be excited about it. That's exactly how I felt. Like Charlotte. It was my second chance at a marriage. But it was Dana's first wedding, so he was SUPER excited. He wanted our invitations to be in the style of sporting event tickets because he's a sports guy. He wanted to tell the world that he was engaged, so he changed his Facebook status to "engaged," although he'd done that back in August. Up until that point, I never changed mine until he gave his life to the Lord in April. So there was a frenzy on Facebook about me getting married. I didn't even say anything; I just changed my status, and it seemed like that just opened up the floodgates of people congratulating me.

The first thing Dana wanted to do was to send out a save the date card to everyone we were going to invite. Everything was moving so fast, but we only had four months to plan. Dana knew a lot of people, so this was going to be a big wedding. He wanted it to be a big wedding. We definitely had to get a wedding planner because although he wanted to be so involved, he still had to plan his foundation event, and this was his 10th year.

For his 10th annual event, he was going to be honoring Muhammad Ali, Denzel Washington, and Hank Aaron. So it was a huge year for him. Then I also had my foundation luncheon that was coming up in May. I decided to honor Dana's mother, Carole Pump, Kim Howland, who was the UCLA basketball coach's wife, and my godmother, Mack McKinney, who had built a successful business working with special needs children and adults. I was moving the luncheon from the Ritz Carlton hotel to the Luxe hotel. So we had a lot of planning on our plates for four months. Two foundation events and a wedding. Plus, I was still working at the Wilshire Private School. Things were getting a little crazy there because the enrollment had dropped, but the Korean consulate financed the school. The school wasn't closing, but they had to do some lay-offs to keep the finances feasible.

I was one of the only Black teachers there, and the principal at the time was this Caucasian man. For some reason, he didn't like me and wanted to get rid of me. He would say that I wasn't teaching curriculum, he would pop up in my classroom and say I was always on the computer or the phone, and even if I was two minutes late, he would dock me. It was just ridiculous. So when they were doing lay-offs, I just knew I was going to be the first one to be laid off.

The parents and kids loved me, and I was super successful at being their teacher. All of my students had excellent grades, and their standardized test scores were above par. I was going above and beyond with teaching, and my students were excelling at rapid rates, but the principal just hated me. Maybe it was because the kids and the parents loved me so much, and he couldn't understand why they did. However, I literally had too many other things going on to worry about why he didn't like me.

News was quickly spreading around that teachers were going to be laid off and that salaries were being cut. I didn't want to stop working because I did not want it to be like when I was married to James: nothing to do, and under my husband's control. I did not want that. I didn't want to be vulnerable. I wanted to have something to do every single day. Even though Dana was successful, and I didn't have to work if I didn't want to, I wanted to keep doing what I loved. As a result, I was really worried about losing my job. Really worried. But I just kept praying and talking to Dr. Tigner about it. He kept assuring me, "Leah, you're not going to lose your job. Just keep praying. The Lord is with you."

Every day, it just seemed like something was up. Then, by the end of the week, they fired the principal. I called Dr. Tigner and told him.

"I know. I told you that you weren't going to lose your job. In fact, I believe you're going to be the principal."

"Yeah, right!" I laughed.

Every day, I was on pins and needles about losing my job. I was hearing these private conversations, paranoid that they were about me. Especially since the principal had said so many bad things about me. I just knew that my time was up.

One day while I was teaching, the board president came to my classroom and said, "Ms. Walker, we would like to see you after school today."

"Okay," I sighed.

I knew that was it.

"Great. As soon as you dismiss your kids for the day, we'd like to see you in the office."

I finished teaching, dismissed my kids, and walked to the office. I was so nervous. I snuck a quick call in and asked Dr. Tigner to pray for me.

"Leah, you are not going to lose your job. They're going to give you the principal position," he said calmly.

He prayed over me, and then I walked into the office. When I walked in, the board president said, "Ms. Walker, the faculty really likes you. The students like you, and we've noticed that your students do really well academically. Their test scores are extremely high, and the parents can't stop raving about how good of a teacher you are. We really want to keep you on the staff of this school. We've realized that you're the only teacher on this staff who has a master's degree in education."

"Yes, I do," I agreed.

"Since you have the highest degree, we want to make you the principal of the school. Is that okay?"

"Yes!" I was speechless but had to force a word out.

"Great. We're going to offer you a raise in your salary, and in addition, you're going to have to continue teaching third grade for the rest of this school year because right now, we don't want to find another teacher. Then next year, you'll be principal without having a third grade class. Is this okay?" she asked.

"Absolutely. I can do that."

I didn't have that many students anyway. It was a small class, so I could definitely balance administration and curriculum.

I walked out of the office and immediately started praising the Lord. I was thinking about the 82 cents that I'd had a couple years ago, when the Lord blessed me with a house, then the Lord blessed me to come back to teaching. The Lord then blessed me with Lady-Like, and then out of the blue the Lord blessed me with Dana. Now the Lord was blessing me to be the principal? At 30 years old? This was unheard of! I had to call Dr. Tigner and tell him the news.

"Yes! I told you! The enemy was trying to get rid of you, but God was trying to promote you!"

"Amen!" I said with tears in my eyes.

I just thought about how tithing really works, and putting God first, even in my relationship. It works! Putting God first propelled me to higher levels that I couldn't even dream of. Not only was I planning a wedding, I was now going to plan an entire school year. I was the principal of Wilshire Private School.

In the midst of wedding planning and now being acclimated into being principal, Dana was still stressing about getting me a car. He still hated that Ford Explorer! But since Dr. Tigner told me to not take any money from him, I still hadn't accepted a car. I was paying my own bills and doing my own thing. Because we'd set a date, Dr. Tigner asked if he was still talking about getting me a car.

"Yes."

"Get your car," he said.

So I talked to Dana about getting a new one, and he was all for it. He was so glad.

"Let's go get a car!" he said. "Not only that, here are my credit cards. I called the credit card company and put your name on them so you can use them as you wish. Now that you're my fiancée, I want you to be taken care of. I don't want you to struggle."

Isn't it amazing how when a man loves you, he doesn't want you to struggle? He doesn't want you to have to fight to pay your bills? I was really learning the traits of what a man will do when he really loves you. He'll give his life to the Lord, he'll tell the world he's marrying you and even partner with you in his success. It was literally a dream come true, and I had never experienced anything like it before.

Dr. Tigner was really proud of me. He said that I'd recovered from dropping the baton before the finish line to picking it back up, and now I was crossing the finish line gracefully. That made me feel like I'd done this relationship right, and it really put things in perspective for me. I'd held Dana accountable for what he said he was going to do. Now not only did he respect me, but he was really trying to take care of me.

Not even two weeks later, we were driving to the Mercedes Benz dealer of Valencia, getting me a car. He put a down payment on a lease for a white 350E Mercedes sedan. I had already picked what I wanted, and that car was perfect. I wanted a white car with a beige interior because I thought it was so classy. He bought it for me, and we drove it off the lot. We drove back to his house in my new car, and I dropped him off and drove home in my new Benz. I was so happy! God was just blessing me left and right. Like God had warned me, my life had drastically changed.

We solicited different hotel catering managers for recommendations for a great wedding planner. Catering managers and wedding planners work hand in hand with venues. It's the wedding planner that works with the catering manager for all the logistics, permits, and details.

At the time, Dana had previously had his event at the Century Plaza Hotel and at the Beverly Hilton Hotel and had great relationships with the catering directors. They highly recommended this lady that owned Guilded Events, and she was Jewish. That was important to Dana's mom and Dana because we wanted to have a dual ceremony with a cantor and my pastor.

We met with the owner of Guilded Events, and she had done dual ceremonies before. She had so many beautiful ideas, and she seemed like a great fit. Dana told her his idea to walk down the aisle to the Final Four song, *One Shining Moment*. He was going to have a lot of basketball coaches in his wedding and wanted them to wear Adidas shell toe sneakers. He was going to get his tailor to do all the suits for the groomsmen. He had already picked out the men, too. He was EXCITED! By the time he picked his groomsmen, it was about 14 of them. There were coaches, athletic directors, David, childhood friends... just too much! So I had to pick out 14 bridesmaids. I literally did not even have 14 friends that I could think of. I knew I could figure it out, but life had just changed so much, and the people I used to be close to I wasn't really close to anymore.

My mom told me that I should have some of my childhood best friends that hadn't been in my first wedding. I chose my friend Ryan who I'd grown up in church with and Tina who went to Berkeley with me, who had met James that first day at the church. Then I wanted to put Tia in it, of course, Emily, Natasha, my friend Sophie from Oakland, Charlotte, who I'd worked with, and of course Melissa, because she'd introduced me to Dana. Dana wanted the women's basketball coach from UCLA, and I agreed. My friend Sage who encouraged me to make LadyLike a nonprofit 501(c)(3) organization, Varie, a few of my other friends I had met along the years, David's wife Eunice, and their daughter Laurie. After a while, I had 14 women for my bridesmaids.

Now it was time to find a dress for me and the bridesmaids. I wanted my grandmother to be my maid of honor, because she was literally my maid of honor in every way. She'd financed my dreams and my house and had gotten me out of my depression. When I asked her, she loved the idea and agreed without hesitation.

We were all set getting this wedding together. I didn't know anything about a "save the date" card. Getting married to someone in another culture, you start seeing things that you've never seen before. I was being exposed to so many traditions and details that were very important. I didn't do any of that for my wedding with James, so this was new territory. Everything was organized, professional, and laid out for us. We used a random picture that we took while we were in Santa Barbara for Michael Jordan's basketball camp for kids. It ended up being so cute, and we thought it would be perfect to use for our save the date. We sent it out, and to my not-so-surprise, it caused a huge buzz. Leah was marrying a White Jewish guy? This was crazy!

He and David are known as The Pump Brothers, and they are really popular and influential in the basketball world. I hadn't really realized how known they were. Everyone was calling me saying, "You're marrying a Pump brother? Do you know who they are? They're like the most powerful guys in sports! There are articles written on them, and the NCAA even made rules to stop them because they're so powerful! Do you know who you're marrying?" I got those questions ALL the time. I really had no clue I was marrying someone of this stature. I just knew him as Dana.

I did a lot of planning by myself, because like I said, my parents were not in the position. I just didn't want to bombard them with costs. I felt so bad about the first wedding, because I only stayed married to James for eight months, and they spent over $100,000. I didn't want to do that to them this time, so I was really trying to be cost effective.

I made appointments with different wedding dress places in Beverly Hills and would go look at dresses by myself. I went to Winnie Couture on Wilshire, and I didn't really find any dresses there, but there was this beautiful dress place called Pinache on Wilshire, which was right next door to my old office when I worked with Don. They have the most gorgeous dresses in the window. I made an appointment and went to try on dresses. All of the dress attendants were looking at me confused because I was alone. Every other bride was there with their mothers, and grandmothers, and bridesmaids. I shed a few tears in the dressing room, but I told myself I was growing up, and I could do this. My grandmother and my mother didn't even really have an interest in looking for another dress again. They just wanted me to get married, have some kids, and go on with my life.

So I tried on several dresses, and what I learned is that when you're wedding shopping, you have a dress in your mind that you want to wear, but wedding attendants always know what looks best on you. They see different body types often, and know what dress fits different shapes. It's best to let them choose the dress, because every dress I chose didn't look that good. When I let them choose for me, they were outstanding. In fact, they picked this beautiful dress that was on the mannequin. It was a tight, straight dress that had a rosette train and different dimensions. On one side of the sweetheart neckline, it had rosettes that matched the train, and on the other side it was straight. It was really different and really beautiful. It had a corset-laced back, which created a beautiful silhouette. I had been working out and losing a lot of weight, and I was so happy that I was able to fit into a dress like this. It was very form-fitting, yet very attractive and flattering.

I stepped on the round platform, and they fluffed out the dress so I could see what it really looked like. *It was absolutely gorgeous.*

"How much is this?" I asked.

"$5,200."

"Nope! Let me take this dress off and find something cheaper!" I joked.

"But this is your dress!"

"No, I'll get something cheaper!" I said.

I didn't want to spend that much money. They insisted on taking a picture of me in it, and I left the store. I was a little sad because I knew that was *the* dress, but I just couldn't afford it, nor did I want to ask my mom and grandmother to pay for it.

I drove to Dr. Tigner's office after that. I was still working for him. I was getting ready to type the sermon when he asked me, "Leah, what's wrong?"

"I think I found a dress, but it's just too expensive. I don't need to put that much effort into this. I just need to get a dress and call it a day," I sighed.

"Why?"

"This is my second wedding, and–"

"Leah. Let me see the dress."

He called Varie to come into the office so she could see the dress I'd found. I showed them the picture, and they both said, "That is it!"

"Really? It's $5,200."

"Leah, that's the dress. Get that dress," they confirmed.

"But how am I going to afford it? My grandmother's not going to pay for this."

"Call Dana and see if he'd go half with your grandmother," Dr. Tigner suggested.

So I did. I called Dana right in front of them.

"Hey, Dana. I think I found my dress, but I don't want to make my grandmother pay for too much."

"How much is the dress?" he asked.

"$5,200," I answered.

"$5,200? Sheesh… umm, okay… We can go half," he said.

"Really?!"

"Yeah. Call your grandmother and see if it's okay. Let's go get the dress. I'll give you a check tonight."

I called my grandmother and told her I thought I found the dress.

"You found the dress, baby? How much is it?" she asked.

"$5,200."

"Oh no, we're not getting that!"

"Well, Dana said that he'd go half with you!" I said with crossed fingers.

"He will?"

"Yes. Would that be okay for you?"

"Okay," she agreed.

"Can you go with me tomorrow to get it?"

"Absolutely!" she said.

The next morning, my grandmother drove to my house, and then I drove to the wedding dress store in my new, beautiful white Mercedes. My grandmother was so ecstatic.

"Never in my life did I think that I would be riding in a Mercedes," she said.

My grandmother could afford a Mercedes if she wanted to. They just weren't really into buying new cars. She drove a Lincoln Continental for over twenty years and a 1988 Ford Ranger truck that she absolutely adored. I know that she respected me for sticking to my guns and not marrying Dana until he gave his life to the Lord. She had threatened me several times that if I didn't marry Dana, she was going to move to Texas. She would give me all these different scenarios about how it takes time to get a man to commit. That was good and all, but I wasn't doing it.

I knew she was so proud of me and my new car. She was also so proud that I was principal, because she had been principal as well when she was working. I was doing everything that she had wanted me to do and had invested in me to do.

When I tried on the dress for her, she loved it.

"That's it. That's the dress."

She wrote a check for her half, and I had Dana's check, and I got the dress. So now it was time to find the bridesmaids' dresses. We planned on having champagne dresses and light heather gray suits. Champagne and gray were the colors. It was a beautiful combination.

The groomsmen were to have crisp white dress shirts, champagne ties, champagne pocket squares, and all white shell toe sneakers to go with their heather gray suits.

They happened to have a champagne bridesmaid dress in the same store as the wedding dress I had purchased. I called all the bridesmaids and told them where the dresses were to pick them up. They needed to be fitted and altered right away, because we only had a few months until the wedding. All of them were so happy, and they all did it. They were also excited to be a part of the wedding. I felt blessed that the ones that were in the first wedding said yes to be in my second wedding. It was like a total re-do, and I felt so blessed about that.

Dana's mother was really into the planning of the wedding, more than my family. I think that is what she loved to do, and I know that she helped plan David and his wife plan their wedding as well. From the invitations to the colors, she wanted to be involved in everything. She would set up all of our registrations, but specifically at Neiman Marcus for all of my pots and pans, silverware, and dining room items. She also had me register at Macy's, because she said that Macy's hotel collection sheets and towels were the best quality, and her son only sleeps on thousand thread sheets. I didn't even know what thousand thread sheets were! I was so used to getting my bedding from Ross, Target, or Marshalls. I didn't know any of those details, so I was happy that she was teaching me. Next, we registered at Bed Bath & Beyond so that our guests had various stores to choose from for their gifts.

About a month into wedding planning, Dana and I had our engagement photo shoot where we took photos at Venice Beach. The photographer was very eccentric, so she wanted some elegant photos by the water, and even photos by the graffiti wall, as well as with us on the swings. We picked the swing picture for our wedding invitation because we wanted it to reflect who we were: an always laughing, fun couple. We created invitations that were sporting event tickets with disclosures, just like a real ticket with a barcode on the bottom.

We sent out our invitations with our registry to over 400 guests. The gifts just started rolling in. People were buying everything I wanted on my registry!

One day I got a call from a Neiman Marcus salesperson saying, "Hello, Ms. Leah. Everything is bought on your registry! Is there anything else you want? Can you go back online and pick out some things? People want to buy things, but there's nothing else to buy."

It was crazy! They bought absolutely everything on our wedding list!

It was still more than a month away from our wedding day. So things were really moving. The house was getting remodeled as well. We hired a decorator for the house. The wife of one of Dana's friends was putting everything together: taking out old furniture and putting in new furniture. New bedding and decorative pieces in the house. Since I was going to move in, we needed to make it more feminine since it had been a bachelor pad for so long.

Before I knew it, May arrived, and it was time for my event. It was a success. I barely remember it because there were so many different things going on. Having an event and raising money wasn't even hard; it was actually the easiest thing; the wedding was more stressful. Dana's event was even more stressful because it was his tenth year.

I was still working for Dr. Tigner, but thank God it was the summer, so I wasn't working at the school. I did coordinate summer school and had classes for all of the grades, as well as extra-curricular classes. I was professional and organized on my education responsibilities, so I could really focus on being a new wife.

Dana and I had to attend several events together. I was getting my wardrobe together because he went to so many events, so I was constantly having to wear after five and professional attire. Because of James, I knew how to dress, I knew how to be appropriate and do my own hair/makeup. But I had a whole new look. I had a whole new vibe. I was wearing gowns and cocktail dresses every weekend. The events never stopped. We went to different charity events, sporting events, and sporting parties. It was never-ending. Every weekend after working for Dr. Tigner, I was headed to an event.

It was really preparing me because my life had changed drastically. I was meeting new people, I was getting entrenched in this new lifestyle of entertainers and celebrities and different charities all at the same time. I was getting involved in Dana's sporting tournaments in Orange County, where hundreds of teens from all over the world would register their AAU basketball teams to play. He was so successful with it. Coaches from Duke, Stanford, Kentucky, USC, Berkeley, and all kinds of great schools would be there. His Pump & Run teams were elite and excellent. Sometimes we'd have to go to Las Vegas for the tournaments and come right back to finish planning. So all of this was happening while I was planning a wedding! It was crazy, but it was fun. I loved my new life.

My bridal shower was being planned as well. Dana's mom wanted to plan it. So she, my mother, my grandmother, and all my bridesmaids were involved in the planning. It was to be on a Saturday in July, a month before the wedding.

My mom bought little wedding doll silhouettes from Ross, put flowers and ribbons on each of them, and put them in the middle of the tables. We had a three-course meal, and they got a 12-layer chocolate cake from a restaurant. Everyone was invited. We invited friends that I'd grown up with, my bridesmaids of course, and some of Dana's friends from the hospital and his foundation. I learned that you can't invite people to the bridal shower who weren't invited to the wedding, which caused a lot of ruckus since I didn't invite that many people. I only had 50 guests, and Dana had 350. It was just a handful of my friends and different people that I grew up with. I just wanted the people that meant a lot to me to be there. For Dana it was more about friends, business colleagues, wives of friends, coaches, etc. Which was fine for me; I wanted him to enjoy this moment.

The day of the bridal shower arrived, and it was absolutely gorgeous. Everything turned out beautifully, just as my mother-in-law envisioned it. I was really showered with love, and so many gifts. My mom made a game of words of wisdom so wives would get up and share their words of wisdom as well as recipes because I loved to cook.

Next, it was time for me to speak and say thank you to all of my guests. As I was speaking, I began to feel overwhelmed at how the Lord had truly done what He said He was going to do. Not only was I relieved with James and all the stress and heartache that came with that, but He had restored my life completely. He gave me back everything that I lost plus more.

So, in that, I said to the guests of the bridal shower, "A lot of you don't know my past, and a lot of you don't know where I come from, but I just want to tell everyone that God is so good. He can restore your life, and make your dreams come true. I'm just so grateful that I have a second chance at this, and that I'm around people that love me." My words were faint as I was fighting back tears.

People started cheering and clapping on their feet. Especially those who had known what I had gone through and knew that my life had truly, drastically changed.

My grandmother stood and asked if she could share a few words. She talked about how beautiful it was to see a multi-raced bridal shower with African Americans, Caucasians, Chinese, Korean, and Latina people all celebrating together. It brought tears to everybody's eyes. My grandmother said that she never thought that she would see something as beautiful as that, and how this marriage was bridging so many gaps and making so many people happy. We were on the road to a beautiful, beautiful wedding.

Everything was just so different than when I was getting married to James. Dana wanted to come so badly, he kept texting me saying, "Can I come now!?" Because usually, the groom comes at the end of the bridal shower, and everyone cheers the couple on. I told him the exact time to come. But guess who came before him? My dad! Boy! He came in, and everyone was expecting Dana.

"Hey, everybody!" my dad shouted.

He was just so thrilled about this. He, too, was enjoying every moment of this planning and being involved for the wedding. He just had to show up for this bridal shower. He called me the morning of the bridal shower and asked me, "Aren't you excited!?"

I was looking at the phone like... *What a change!* Another thing my dad was excited for was that he had never in his life had a tailored suit. élevée was tailoring all the groomsmen's suits, as well as my brother's, my uncle's, and my dad's. My uncle and I were planning a surprise for the wedding, so I wanted him to be dressed like the rest of the men.

All of the men who were participating in the wedding got to get measured and tailored for their suits. Neither my dad, brother, nor uncle, actually, had ever gotten a tailored suit. My dad was just overwhelmed and overjoyed about this experience. It was something that he had never experienced, and his soon-to-be son-in-law was just a dream! Sports, athletes, tailored suits, sporting events... what father-in-law wouldn't love this? It was so funny and so cute. Our relationship had revived; we were no longer mad at each other. My dad was just so proud of me, and I appreciated my parents and my grandmother so much for sticking by my side and rejoicing in my happiness. They loved who I had become. I'd reinvented myself with the help of the Lord and Dr. Tigner. My life was better, and my family couldn't help but celebrate.

Dana came at the exact time I asked, and not a second later. Everybody was cheering and overjoyed. He came and hugged and kissed me in front of everybody, and it was just a complete difference. Complete difference. We were so happy and excited to be husband and wife.

Everything was moving at a great pace. However, although he had given his life to the Lord, he had not been baptized. In my belief, you can be saved and not baptized, but baptism is a symbol of your new life of being saved. You're going down in the water and getting rid of your old life and resurrecting out of the water with your new life. It's a symbol to the world that your life has changed, which is important.

It was so hard to get Dana to walk down that aisle, and it was so hard to have him commit to giving his life to the Lord, that I didn't know if baptism was necessary. I figured it wasn't going to be necessary unless Dr. Tigner said it was. So I was going along with everything. Dana had these tournaments at Cal State Dominguez Hills, and after church, I was to meet him at his tournament.

It had been on my mind heavily for him to become baptized, and I knew the Lord wanted me to do it, but I just needed confirmation.

After church, I went to Dr. Tigner's office to see if he needed anything, and he was counseling someone. Perfect. I was just going to go in, wave goodbye, get my coat, and leave. So as I get my coat, he looked at me, took a break from his counseling session, and said, "Leah, Dana needs to be baptized."

Oh my gosh! How did he always know these things?! It was like telepathy. It was crazy!

I knew this was going to be another burden that I was going to have to do.

I drove to Carson for the tournament, and I was so anxious. I didn't know how I was going to tell Dana. I just knew the Lord wanted me to do it.

I arrived at the tournament, got out of my car, and Dana was waiting for me at the door. There were lots of coaches around, he was introducing me to everyone, and I pulled him to the side to talk to him about something. He was looking at me like, *Oh Lord, what now?*

"You've got to get baptized…"

"OH, NO, LEAH!!! COME ONNN!!! I'VE DONE EVERYTHING! WHY DO I HAVE TO DO THAT?!"

"You have to get baptized. You have to show the world that your life is changed."

"Man!! It's so unnecessary! Why!?"

"Because this is a visual! It's a visual example of what you've done."

"This is too much!" he said.

I could see the disgust on his face. I couldn't help but chuckle. I felt his pain, because he had done a lot already. I just kept talking to him about it every day and praying that the Lord would intervene.

A couple weeks later, it was my birthday. I was turning 31. I woke up to some disturbing news. On the front page of Yahoo, there was an article titled: "College Basketball Tickets Scandal," with Dana & David Pump and a couple others listed. It was really bad. It said that he was involved in this whole plot to get rich off of tickets during the college basketball tournaments. Somebody was really trying to sabotage all that Dana and David had been working on, and even their cancer foundation at Northridge Hospital.

He called me in a panic.

"Leah, I'm going to have to get a lawyer, this is really bad. David and I didn't do anything! This author of the article has always been trying to get us. This is just bad!"

It took a huge toll on Dana. He stopped eating and was completely depressed. He couldn't sleep. Even Dr. Tigner saw the article on the internet and called me to see what was going on. I had no idea; all I knew was that he didn't do it.

Dr. Tigner had to counsel Dana through it. It could have ruined his whole career and all that he had worked so hard for. Dana had to get a lawyer and fly back and forth to him. He had to complete all types of testimonies and make different statements. I was praying so hard during the whole thing.

One day, while I was at work teaching, Dana called me.

"Hey babe, I'm in class," I said.

"I know, but I really need to talk to you."

I stepped out of the room.

"Leah, if the Lord gets me out of this, I promise I'll get baptized."

I couldn't believe it!

Lo and behold, a few weeks later, all the charges against him were dropped, and the man who accused Dana and David got put in jail. Everything was erased; however, Dana had to work double time to clear his name from this terrible scandal. Things were starting to go on as normal.

Well, now I was keeping him to his word.

"Okay, everything is dropped, everything's normal. You have to get baptized like you promised!"

"Yeah, but my bachelor party is this weekend!"

Damn! I had already called the church clerk, the church secretary, and the person over the baptism to put his name in for the baptismal pool. You have to reserve it, so they know to heat up the pool. I had completely forgotten about his bachelor party.

"Okay, that's fine, we'll reschedule it for another time before we get married," I said.

So he went on his bachelor trip to Vegas, and they were all staying at the Aria. He had all of his friends there. You can imagine what I was going through that weekend!

Dana being Dana, he was calling me every second talking about the whole trip. I mean, he would keep me updated if they went from the pool to a restaurant. That night the guys were all going out to eat at Mastros in the Aria.

He called me from the table to check in with me before they enjoyed their steak dinners. About 30 minutes later, he called me again.

"Leah... one of my friends, Sam, he's—"

"He's what?" I said.

"He's choking on some bread. He went to the bathroom, and he hasn't come out yet."

"Well, go check on him!"

"I think he's allergic to gluten."

"Well, if he's allergic to gluten, why is he eating bread?"

"I don't know. I'll call you back."

Ten minutes later, he called back.

"Leah. I think Sam died in the bathroom."

"What?"

"Everybody's coming up here now. The police and paramedics are on their way. He was just choking, and excused himself from the table, and I think he died!"

"No, he didn't die," I said.

Immediately I started to pray.

Another thirty minutes passed before he called me back.

"Sam died."

"What?"

"He died, Leah. He's dead."

"Oh my gosh!" I exclaimed.

"We've gotta call his wife... Let me call you back."

It was just terrible... His bachelor party was ruined. They had to get the body out of the restaurant and file a report.

"Leah, what should I do?" he asked.

"What should you do?"

"Yeah, David wants me to stay and let the party continue."

"Baby, I think the party is over. Your friend died."

"You're right. I'll fly out first thing in the morning. Find me a flight."

So I went online and found a flight for him and called back to give him his confirmation number.

"Are you sure I shouldn't stay?"

"Babe, the party is over."

Dana's friend's death was so sudden, so tragic and awful. Everyone was shocked. It definitely ruined the mood of the bachelor party and had all of the men thinking of their mortality. Dana even mentioned that upon returning he wanted to keep his date to be baptized that Sunday. So he arrived back in Los Angeles Saturday evening. I called the church clerk and the person over baptism, and I said, "Put that water in the pool! He's getting baptized."

They did so.

I got Dana from the airport, took him home, and Sunday morning, I drove him to church.

"You're getting baptized today," I told him.

"What?"

"Yeah, remember you're getting baptized today," I said.

He replied, "Yes, I think God is trying to tell me something. I think it is something I really need to do."

I had already gotten his shorts and his shirt for the baptismal pool. I called the clerk again to make sure the pool was heated.

We got to church just in time for worship service, and after church he got baptized. What he did when he got out of the water was epic. He started waving to people like he was Miss America. It was the craziest baptism I had ever seen. It was hilarious! People were just clapping for him, and he kept waving and waving.

So now he'd given his life to the Lord, he'd gotten baptized, and even though it was a sad situation that caused him to be baptized, he still did it, and we were on the road to getting married.

We had about four weeks until the wedding. The house was coming together, the bridesmaids' dresses were all ordered, and the suits were being made. Our wedding planner was amazing, but Dana ended up not liking her because she was so expensive. I didn't even care. We had to have somebody to put this all together; we just couldn't do it on our own.

What we didn't know was that our wedding planner was getting married around the same time that we were. Plus she was pregnant. Just imagine the hormones that she had. Things were falling through the cracks; therefore, I had to really stay on her about everything. I don't remember who slipped and told me that she was getting married, but I had to confront her about it.

"Are you getting married? Are you pregnant? Please just talk to me about it."

"Yes, but we're doing this really fast. It's not going to interfere with your wedding."

I just didn't want to overwhelm her. Our guestlist was over the roof, along with 14 bridesmaids and groomsmen. I had three ring bearers, four flower girls, two flower dancers... it was a lot! She assured me that she had it under control, but to make sure, we had Dana's event planner, Linda, work hand in hand with the guest list. We needed to make sure that was tight because all of these high-profile guests were coming, and we needed to know we had their RSVPs and everything they would need. We wanted it to be organized and professional. The venue was at Sherwood Country Club. It was such an exclusive country club that you had to have permission from a member in order to have your wedding there. Dana's friend was a member and got us in. Having a wedding at a country club was more reasonable than having it at a hotel because you didn't have as many costs. It wasn't as expensive as a hotel would have been.

We were having the wedding in two locations of the country club. We were having the ceremony by the big iconic tree of the country club, which was in a grassy area. Then we were going to have the reception draped where the tennis courts were. We were bringing in a white dance floor, with a gobo light that had our initials lit on the floor. Dana wanted Brian McKnight and Jeffrey Osborne to sing, and so did I. We were bringing in chiavari chairs, rectangular tables, and circular tables to make it look family style. We had beautiful, huge centerpieces that would have beige roses, champagne roses, hydrangeas... It was gorgeous! I wanted an abundance of flowers. So as you can tell, the wedding planner getting married and being pregnant was throwing a monkey wrench into my plans. All of these pieces needed to be together; it could not be disorganized. I definitely couldn't do it all like I had for my first wedding. The coordinator was essential.

Dana's mother had a dream of me coming into the ceremony in a white horse and carriage. She loved the dream so much that she had gotten that for me and told me not to tell anyone so that it could be a surprise to all of our guests.

The cantor wanted us to meet with him to talk about the ceremony. So one evening, Dana and I went to meet with him. As soon as he opened the door, he said to Dana, "You and your brother owe me UCLA Basketball tickets."

Now Dana was already pissed off because he didn't like when people made it seem like they were trying to use him to get something. He hated that. Everything in the cantor's house was UCLA, so we could see he was a UCLA fan.

"So when are you going to give me those tickets? Your mom said that we also had tickets to go to your foundation event."

Dana was immediately turned off, so I was trying to reconcile everything and shift the conversation.

"Let us know about the ceremony. What are you going to be doing? We would like all the ceremonial pieces of a Jewish wedding. We're having the hupa [which is the tent that you stand under, which is like being under God], as well as the tallit [the wrapping of the prayer cloth]. I was thinking about the drinking of the wine and the shattering of the glass."

"Yes, that's wonderful. That's everything that I wanted to do with you guys. However, I don't want your pastor mentioning the name of Jesus," the cantor said.

"What?" I asked.

"If he's going to mention the name of Jesus, then we can't stand together on the same platform," he explained.

"Well, he's going to mention the name of Jesus," I said.

"Then we're not going to be doing it at the same time."

"Well. I guess we're not going to do it at the same time."

"Do you understand what you're doing?" the cantor asked me.

"I know exactly what I'm doing. And I am not going to not mention the name of Jesus."

"Well, we have to create a separate ceremony, so who's going to go first?"

"My pastor will go first, and you will go second."

Dana and I were looking at each other like *What in the world just happened?* We were really still only there for the sake of his mother, because when he asked for the tickets, Dana was already over it.

"How much is it going to be?" Dana asked.

"$1500."

That was crazy! Dr. Tigner was doing it for free. It was just weird. When we left the cantor's house, we were just looking at each other in disgust. We both knew we were just doing it for his mother. He called her when we were driving back.

"Why would he ask me for UCLA tickets? What kind of man is this? Why would you tell him that he can come to the foundation for free?" he yelled.

She started crying. "I just want him to do this part, honey!"

I stepped in. "Carole, don't worry about it. We're going to do it. We'll have two separate ceremonies in one, so everybody will be happy. It'll be a long wedding, but everybody will be happy."

Everyone agreed on it. The wedding was getting closer and closer.

A huge aspect of wedding planning is putting your lives together because you are going to be living together as one. Marriage is bridging the gaps between two lives and making them one. This is a part of the wedding planning as well because you have to join accounts, living arrangements, etc. Dana wanted to have a marriage counselor that neither of us knew so that they could be neutral.

David and his wife had been going to marriage counseling, so his wife gave us a good candidate to do our marriage counseling. It was in the Valley, and the counselor just so happened to be a Christian, so I was happy about that. He had also counseled families that came from different religious backgrounds. I was kind of leery about it because I didn't want Dr. Tigner to feel bad that I didn't use him as a counselor, but I think he understood that Dana wanted somebody neutral.

I had been married before, so I knew the things that we needed to talk about were family influence, money, and figuring out where we were going to live. So we did that in different sessions of our counseling, and it was great. Dana was very open. We talked about sex and how we had not had sex yet. We had been dating for over a year and wanted to wait until our wedding night to have sex. We talked about children, and how we definitely wanted to have children. We also talked about finances, and if we wanted to get a prenup or not. Dana did not want to.

"I love Leah. I want her to have access to everything that I have, and that's it," he stated.

I was good with that because that's what I believe as well. Whatever I have, you have, and whatever you have, I have. I had property and assets that I had in my possession, so I had no problem sharing that with him. He had assets in his possession that he wanted to freely share with me. He was 42 years old and had been single for a very long time. I think his family had gotten used to him being single, whereas David got married when he was 30 years old. His wife had seen the family business grow from nothing into something. I think that she had feelings of me possibly being a gold-digger or someone that was trying to take everything, so on several occasions, she was really adamant about Dana and me getting a prenup. She would even say it in front of my face, telling Dana that he needed to get a prenup because we didn't know what the relationship was going to become or if it would last. The family's money was all in one pot, and everyone got paid by that one pot.

I knew that the stereotype was that if you're African American, and your family doesn't have as much as the White family of the person you're dating, then you're a gold-digger, and that was not the narrative for me. I hadn't taken a dime from Dana. I was becoming his wife, so if he wanted to share his assets with me, then that's what he wanted to do.

Dana would be adamant every single time she would say to get a prenup.

"No. I'm not getting a prenup! Leah is going to have access to everything I have."

I was so happy that Dana stood up for me. His mother agreed because she didn't have a prenup with Dana's father. David and his wife did not have a prenup, so why would I come in and have one? It made no sense, and it made me feel really bad and insecure, and a bit distrustful. But I decided to be the bigger person and be friendly and loving even though I knew how she felt.

We successfully went through a few sessions of counseling, and then I would always go back and tell Dr. Tigner about different things that we talked about in the sessions. With the prenup situation, he thought it was ridiculous, and agreed that I shouldn't have one. But the one thing that he did not agree with was our living situation.

Dr. Tigner had advised me that if I moved into Dana's house it would be very hard to get him to move. He said that when you move into someone else's house no matter if you remodel or change it to fit you, it is still not yours. You will never feel like it is "yours" or "ours"; it will always be his. He went on to tell me that when he married Varie he had her pick out a house to purchase because he wanted to begin their marriage in a house they started in together. It just helps in a new marriage. For some reason I did not act on this piece of advice. I thought it was too late, and we had already changed everything. I would grow to regret that decision.

Now it was the countdown. Dana and I had begun to stay together and sleep together all night, even though we did not have sex. Dr. Tigner had advised me to start staying there a couple nights a week so that I could get used to being around him. On the nights that I wasn't staying with him, he stayed with me. It was fine. I noticed his sleeping habits. We slept on different sides of the bed, but we slept. I taught him about melatonin and all these things that I used to go to sleep. I got him on a vitamin regimen with green tea and antioxidants, and even anti-aging supplements. I was setting up our house with lots of water and healthy food because I was really into that. However, we did set up a candy bar in our kitchen with all of our favorite candies and snacks.

Emily, who was my matron of honor (along with my grandmother), planned my bachelorette party. It was at a winery in Temecula, and I don't understand why she did that because I don't drink, but I think she just wanted to do something different. Mostly all of the bridesmaids were able to make it. Some couldn't because they were out of town. We invited a couple of my friends like Cassie and some other ladies who wanted to join us.

Emily kept the whole thing a secret from me. She came that Saturday morning and brought me a cute velour sweatsuit. I put on my sandals, and she told me to have a change of clothes for later on. We were all ready and headed out to Temecula. We had a wine tasting, we got spa treatments, we hung out in the Jacuzzi, and then we had a sex toy introduction to make it fun. That night we had dinner, and we all just really enjoyed each other. We did games like *How well do you know Leah?* and we even made poems. We all bonded, and just talked and reminded each other about old memories. They paid for everything and didn't let me spend a dollar. We all drove back to LA that night. It was a quick trip. It was such a great, positive experience and such a difference from my first experience. They were just as excited for me as I was.

The weekend of the wedding had finally arrived. But first, we had to do Dana's 10th anniversary foundation event. He had worked so hard and raised so much money. He was going to be able to give the foundation over $300,000 that year. It was truly amazing. It was a sold-out event with 1,500 people in attendance.

From the year before, I had learned that I needed to look like the belle of the ball, so I had worked on my weight, and was really small and fit. I was working out 6-7 days a week, running 3-5 miles a day. I got a gown and had my makeup professionally done. Melissa did my hair, and it was perfect. I got to walk the red carpet, and once again, he was introducing me to all the reporters and the press as his fiancée, and that we were getting married in two days. It was just awesome.

Carole introduced Dana and David that night, and she wanted me and David's wife on stage with her as she presented the twins. She was ranting and raving about me, and how everyone was so excited for Sunday. Muhammad Ali, Denzel Washington, and Hank Aaron, who were the honorees of the night, were outstanding. Lonnie,

Muhammad Ali's wife, spoke and was so inspiring. It couldn't have been better. It was just wonderful!

Now we had to do the rehearsal, the rehearsal dinner, and the wedding. The rehearsal dinner was on a Saturday. I was starting to get nervous. I went for a really long run, and then decided that I wanted to go see Dr. Tigner. I had worked for him this whole time. I didn't neglect my assisting position, even though he hired someone else to pick up the slack if I had to go out of town or to an engagement with Dana. But I missed my talks with him. During this wedding planning, I was gone a lot. I just missed the counsel and the mentorship.

I drove to his house, and we sat down in his office.

"Well. Tomorrow's the day," he said.

"Yep! Tomorrow is the day," I agreed.

"How are you feeling?"

"A little scared," I admitted.

"Why?"

"It's just crazy how fast this was," I said.

"Leah, you see how when a man is ready, he's ready, and he'll do whatever it takes. When he loves you, he loves you. Isn't that amazing how the Lord works?"

"Yes. And I just have to thank you for everything. Your counsel and your coaching meant everything to me."

"Leah, you were the one who followed it to a T," he laughed.

"Well, I wanted to be blessed. I wanted to do right. I was so afraid of messing up and ending up like how I was with James."

"I know. But you did it! I'm so proud of you."

I started crying a little bit.

"Why are you crying?" he asked.

"I'm just scared…"

"No… just walk in this. Walk into your blessing. God is with you. Don't be afraid."

I could tell he was a little scared too. It was like a father losing his daughter. I could just tell. It was funny because I had my dad on one hand really excited for me, and Dr. Tigner on the other hand, who was pretty emotional about it. But he was playing it off really well.

I gave Dr. Tigner a big hug before leaving. He wasn't coming to the rehearsal dinner, but Varie and the kids were. My godson, Robert (Dr. Tigner and Varie's son) was one of my ring bearers, and their daughter, Denise, was one of my flower dancers.

"All right, well if you need me, call me!" Dr. Tigner said.

"Of course!"

It was time to get ready for the rehearsal dinner. We were moving into the presidential suite at The Four Seasons in Thousand Oaks that night. Since Thousand Oaks is so far from LA, we had a special deal with the hotel for our wedding party where anyone who wanted to stay for the weekend had a set rate. Pretty much everyone in the wedding party was getting rooms at The Four Seasons, and people who were just attending the weekend stayed as well.

I had to pack everything for the rehearsal dinner… everything! I had to pack the dress I was going to wear, my wedding dress, my shoes, my lingerie for our honeymoon night, my robe, I mean every single thing that I needed to have for the weekend, I needed to have packed. I also had to bring my grandmother's dress that she was going to wear, so I had to make sure that I had all of these things together.

I had bridal gifts for each of my bridesmaids: white robes with their names in a champagne monogram. I had made our makeup appointments so that everyone was going to get their makeup done in my presidential suite at different time slots. I had my masseuse,

Lana, come that morning to give me a massage before everything got too hectic.

My grandmother and I were going to stay in one room the night of the rehearsal dinner and then move into the presidential suite that day. I wanted my grandmother with me so she didn't have to worry about driving or anything. It was time...

I put everything in my car and drove to Sherwood Country Club in Thousand Oaks for the wedding rehearsal. I had everything in my car for that night. When I got to the wedding rehearsal, the kids were there first. Everybody was late because it was just so far.

I had this choreographed dance for the flower girls that I had in my first wedding. I wanted them to learn it and do it. So I taught them that. Then I had to create a dance really fast for the flower dancers. The flower dancers would start off the processional, and then the bridesmaids and groomsmen would come down. Then the flower girls would do their dance, and then the ring bearers would walk down. After the ring bearers I would walk down with both of my parents. I wanted both of my parents to escort me down the aisle.

And I had a very special surprise. Dana loves the way I sing. He heard me sing in church. Also, my dad made sure that I knew every genre of music. He would teach my brother and me all types of music. Our favorite song that my dad and I used to sing was *Whenever I See Your Smiling Face* by James Taylor.

One day, when Dana and I were going to opening day at Dodgers Stadium, we were listening to the radio when James Taylor came on. I got really excited and turned the music up.

"You know about James Taylor?" he asked me.

"Of course!"

An African American girl knowing about James Taylor was kind of strange. But I knew almost every song that he had ever written and performed. I knew the lyrics and everything.

"My dad and I would always sing *Whenever I See Your Smiling Face* on my way to school, every morning," I continued.

"Well, sing it!" he said.

And I sang it.

"Oh my gosh, Leah! That is amazing! Do you know The Carpenters?"

"Do I know The Carpenters? I love The Carpenters!"

And so I started singing that.

So my surprise was, as I walked down the aisle, instead of the traditional bridal march, I was going to sing The Carpenters' *Close To You.*

Our rehearsal was a bit disorganized. Think about it. Twenty-eight bridesmaids and groomsmen, four flower girls, three ring bearers, my mom, my dad, my grandmother, Carole, his brother, his wife… I mean sheesh! It was a circus! On top of that, the wedding planner had no plan as to how we were going down the aisle. Everybody was just looking at each other with confusion. I am not like that. I'm an administrator, a coordinator, a planner. So no. I stood in the middle of everyone and yelled, "OKAY, STOP!"

Everyone looked at me.

"This is a mess! We cannot have this tomorrow! This is what we're going to do. Everybody line up!"

So I put everyone in order and delegated the entire operation beat by beat. We practiced, we rehearsed, and it was still a mess, but it was getting late, and we had to go to the restaurant for the rehearsal dinner. I was just like *Whatever!*

Dana saw me really frustrated, and he ran from the other side of where I was standing, picked me up, and said, "Leah, everything's going to be all right! I love you! This is okay, it's going to be fine! We're getting married tomorrow!" And everybody saw it, but specifically my friends Natasha, Tia, and Emily couldn't help but comment how different this was than James.

Natasha came up to me and said, "Leah, I just have to say, this whole vibe is totally different than your last one! Oh my gosh! He really loves you, Leah. He really, really loves you."

"I know, right?"

"Ugh, I'm just so happy for you. God, what a difference!"

Now we were headed to the rehearsal dinner site. We held it at this Italian restaurant close to both the Sherwood Country Club and The Four Seasons hotel. Dana's family's favorite food was Italian. Dana's mom was paying for everyone. It's tradition for the groom's family to pay for the rehearsal dinner. It was a preset menu with pizza, lasagna, chicken parmesan, salads, and just more food than we could handle. We all crowded into a private dining room, and it was going to be a night of laughter where people shared embarrassing stories about us. We recorded the whole evening.

My dad was always the one to pray first, and even though Dana's mom wasn't really into that, it was still something that was very important to me, so of course I wanted my dad to pray.

"Hello! Hello! Could I have everybody's attention? Let's pray. You know tomorrow's a special occasion. Thank you for everyone coming out, thank you to Carole for hosting this dinner for us. Everyone, please bow your head, and hold hands with the person next to you. *Lord, we pray that tomorrow is* NOTHING *like the mess of today."*

Everyone started laughing because the rehearsal was such a mess, and so disorganized, and everyone knew it.

"Please bless the food, bless Dana and Leah, let us have fun tonight, in Jesus' name, everyone say Amen."

The entire night was a night of laughter and love. We heard embarrassing stories from Dana getting caught up at Final Four, and stories about David and Dana because they were so close. David told everyone how happy he was that Dana had finally found someone to put up with his shenanigans, craziness, aggressiveness, and ADD. My friends were talking about how proud they were of me, and how I was a true testament of how God can turn everything around. My grandmother got up next to give her speech. At first, it started off really good, then she went into this tangent about raising children and teaching kids how to read, and everybody was just looking at each other like *What on earth is she talking about?* It was still pretty funny, though. So there were tears, there was laughter, but most importantly, there was joy.

Dana and I gave everyone their gifts: we gave the shell-toe sneakers to all the groomsmen, and I gave my girls their robes. The dinner was over, and we were headed back to the hotel. Some people went back to LA, including my parents because my dad wanted to go to church on Sunday before the wedding.

That night my grandmother and I got back to the room. She looked at me and said, "Baby, did I talk too much?"

I didn't want to make her feel bad, so of course I said, "No, not at all!"

"Okay, because I feel like I talked too much."

"No, Mama, it was fine. It was beautiful!" I said.

I was so happy to be going to sleep the night before my wedding with my grandmother with me. The hotel was gorgeous; it was absolutely beautiful. She loved that part, because she always would say, "I've worked hard all my life. I deserve to stay in nice hotels!"

Dana and I had decided that before we got married, we were both going to write each other a letter. So that night before I went to bed, I wrote him a beautiful letter about our new life together, and how blessed I was that I had him in my life. I told him that the best was yet to come, that he was my love, my partner, my perfect match, and that I was so excited to be his wife.

I made sure my grandmother was good in her bed, and I was in my bed, and we both went to sleep.

The morning of my wedding day, Sunday, August 15th, 2010, I woke up, and it was a *beautiful* day. The sun was shining so brightly. Sunday was always my and Dana's favorite day. It was the perfect day to get married.

When my grandmother woke up, I told her that we were moving to the presidential suite. I knew my grandmother was a little nervous, too, because she was acting a little needy. She wanted to be with me so much, which I loved because I love her, but I could just feel her nerves.

We moved to the presidential suite and took all of our clothes. The presidential suite was so huge, it had at least four rooms with a huge living room, a huge den and dining room, and huge bathrooms with saunas. There was even a massage room. It was just amazingly stunning. I ordered us some pancakes, sausage, and fruit, and invited all the bridesmaids to come eat while they were getting ready. My masseuse, Lana, was on her way to come massage me.

As Lana was massaging me, the doorbell of the suite kept ringing. People just kept coming in. My grandmother was so nervous, she was acting like she forgot how to open up the door! She forgot where the front door of the suite was. I had to get up at least three times throughout my massage to open up the door.

The makeup artists were getting set up, the hairdressers were getting set up... so there was no peace. My grandmother, who before could coordinate things with her eyes closed and be like my assistant and make sure everything was running well, was forgetting everything. I was pretty much doing *everything!* But at the same time, I wanted my quiet time because I was getting married.

My wedding coordinator sent over California Chicken Cafe for lunch so that everyone could eat. Even though the wedding wasn't until 5 p.m., the setup had to start early, especially for 14 women to get dressed. Everyone was on a makeup and hair time schedule. The day was moving so fast, and I couldn't catch my breath. I decided to just kind of lock myself into the bedroom. I was so overwhelmed I began to cry, and I didn't even know why. I started questioning if I had made the right decision. Maybe I should call this off and not marry him. I mean, every thought in my brain was going crazy.

I looked at the time and saw that our church service was over. I called Dr. Tigner.

"Leah?"

"Yes?"

"Are you crying?" he asked.

"Yes."

"What is wrong?"

"I just want to make sure that I'm making the right decision."

"What? You're about to get married in a few hours, what do you mean did you make the right decision? WHAT DO YOU THINK? Leah, I'm worried! I'm really worried! You don't think you're making the right decision? Have you lost your mind? Do you know all the things that are in motion right now? Okay. I'm worried. Did some-thing happen?"

"No, nothing happened. I'm… I'm just scared!"

"Leah. You've got to get it together. You are getting married. Dana loves you. What are you worried about?"

"I guess I was just worried about everything happening the way it had happened before."

"This is not going to happen how it happened before, Leah. This is totally different. God is with you… This is your blessing. Walk into it. Stop crying."

Usually, it would be my dad telling me to stop crying, but I defi-nitely couldn't call my dad because he would have been going insane. Dr. Tigner prayed for me, we got off the phone, and I got in the shower. I was putting on all my perfume and undergarments so that I could just have my robe on as I got my hair and makeup done.

My friends could tell from my face that I was in my anxious mode. My friend Charlotte poured me a glass of wine, even though I don't drink wine, and she said, "Girl, I know you don't drink, but this is good stuff, and it'll relax you."

I drank it slowly as I got my makeup done. My bridesmaids were turning out to be so gorgeous. Our makeup artists, Angel and Lisa, were just fabulous. I had met Angel when I first started working out, and she worked in the Manhattan Beach MAC, and then Lisa worked there too. I just stayed with them throughout dating Dana and all his events. So it was only right to have them do the brides-maids' makeup because I wanted everyone to match.

Then the photographers arrived to start taking pictures. All of a sudden, my grandmother was putting on her dress and said, "Leah!"

"Yes?"

"Where's the jacket that goes to my dress?"

"What?" I asked.

"Where's the jacket that goes to my dress? Didn't you bring it?"

She had a three-piece outfit. It was a bustier, a long skirt, and a jacket that went around her shoulders. My grandmother was not going to walk down the aisle with her shoulders out. So I stopped getting my makeup done to find this jacket. It was nowhere to be found.

"Leah, I'm not walking down the aisle like this."

Lord have mercy... We tried to wrap a scarf around her shoulders, and it looked terrible.

So everything was being pushed back since my grandmother didn't have a coat. I called Dana's assistant and said, "You've got to go to the wedding store where we bought the dress and buy a jacket for my grandmother."

Next, I called the wedding place and told them that we were missing the jacket. They assured me that the jacket was in the bag when I left the store.

"No it wasn't! It's not in the bag! I need another jacket!"

"Well, you're going to have to pay for it."

"I'm not going to pay for another jacket. It wasn't in the bag!"

"Leah. It was definitely in the bag. If you want this jacket, you need to pay for it before we close in an hour."

That jacket was $300. I gave them my credit card so I could pay for it, then called Dana's assistant back to go pick it up from the store and bring it to Thousand Oaks. Can you imagine going to Beverly Hills and picking up this jacket, just to drive all the way back to Thousand Oaks? We took care of that, but it really pushed everything back for me: hair and makeup. Now getting dressed was backed up because we had to wait for an hour for Dana's assistant to bring the jacket to my grandmother.

All the bridesmaids got dressed and went downstairs. Now it was time for me to get dressed. So Melissa finished my hair, and then helped me put my dress and shoes on. The photographers got several shots of me getting dressed and adding finishing touches. They kept telling me how beautiful I was, and how they'd done so many brides' photoshoots, but they had never seen makeup on a bride as beautiful as mine. I didn't know if they were joking, but it made me feel good.

I asked Emily to give Dana the letter I had written for him the night prior. As she walked in the hallway to give it to Dana, Dana was in the hallway on his way to give his letter to me. They exchanged letters, and while I was finishing getting dressed, she brought me Dana's letter.

Leah, what an incredible journey. I can't wait to spend forever with you.

It was just confirmation that everything was working and going as planned. I put on the last finishing touches to my dress, then I fixed my hair and put my headpiece on. The photographer told me, "I want you to look out of the window and open up the window as the sun hits your face. We want this whole movement. We're going to take still shots, and a video of you opening up the drapes from the back, showing the silhouette of your dress."

We did this whole moment of me opening the drapes of the window and looking out the window with the sun shining on my face. Kind of like a new beginning. As I was doing this, I was thinking, *It's been seven years since I left James. It's been seven years...* The number of completion... It took me seven years to get ready for this moment. Seven years of heartache, seven years of reinventing myself, seven years of being broke, seven years of finding my way through different relationships—forming the LadyLike Foundation, becoming a principal, meeting Dana—seven years. It took seven years to get to the point of a new beginning. And my life, like the Lord said, had changed drastically. Now I was getting ready to walk down the aisle and become Mrs. Dana Pump. A sense of joy and overwhelming excitement filled my soul as I thought of the seven years that had created a new me.

Everyone was ready. My grandmother was good and had her jacket. The bridesmaids were dressed, my mom was ready with her beautiful dress on. My grandmother had a couple of her best friends with her by this point. She was just so proud and happy. We all got in the limousine and headed to Sherwood Country Club. My bridesmaids were a little annoyed with the fact that I was barely talking or socializing that much, but I didn't mean to be that way. I was just really going through a lot in my head with all the things that were happening and changing. The fact that my life had done a 180 was almost surreal.

While we were in the limo, Varie said, "Leah, are you okay? Dr. Tigner called me and said that you thought you weren't making the right decision."

"I know... I'm just really nervous," I admitted.

"I know. Well, I'm praying for you. You know you look beautiful, and everything is going to be perfect."

"Thank you... Thank you so much, Varie." I gave her a big hug.

We were already an hour late, and the sun was setting. We didn't want the sun to set on our ceremony. The wedding was getting ready to start, so Brian McKnight had been waiting for an hour to sing. The band had been playing for over an hour.

The wedding coordinator saw me and said, "You look beautiful. Are you ready?"

"Yes. I'm ready. Let's go."

They took my whole bridal party down to where they were supposed to walk in, and then they had me take some more pictures by myself. I got into the horse and carriage that drove me all the way to where the aisle was for me to walk down... As I was riding in the carriage, I could hear Brian McKnight singing *Never Felt This Way About Loving You.* I could see the bridal party, from a distance, going down the aisle. I was just so nervous that I was shaking. I was praying that I stopped shaking so that when I would sing, I didn't sound so nervous.

My uncle began playing the tune to the bridal march, because I didn't want to give away the surprise that I was singing. The processional with the bridesmaids and groomsmen began. The beautiful flower girls danced, then the ring bearers went down, and they were so cute, then Dana was walking down the aisle with his mom on one hand and his nephew, Cole, on the other hand, and mind you, I was still seeing all of this from a distance. They were walking down the aisle to the Final Four song, *One Shining Moment,* because you know everything had to be sports related. The funniest thing was that his mom was waving to everybody, Cole was smiling, and Dana was crying like a baby. I was surprised if he could even see, I mean he was sobbing down the aisle. Dr. Tigner reached over to him and said, "Dana, you've got to stop crying, man."

Now it was time for me to walk down the aisle. As the horse and carriage approached, my mom and dad were waiting at the end of the aisle. They were crying too. My mom told me that they were just so happy that the Lord gave them another chance to be a part of my wedding and be accepted this time. I mean, I'd put them through so much with James, this was a complete do-over.

Everybody was gasping at how beautiful the white horses and carriage were. It was like Cinderella. I got out of the horse and carriage, and my wedding coordinator was right there with the mic. I asked if the mic was on, and it was, so everyone heard me ask that. My uncle started playing, and I started singing. I walked down the aisle with the microphone behind my bouquet of flowers as I sang to Dana. *Why do birds suddenly appear every time you are near... just like me, they long to be close to you.... Why do stars fall down from the sky every time you walk by... just like me, they long to be close to you. On the day you were born, the angels got together and decided to create a dream come true, so they sprinkled moon dust in your hair, and golden starlight in your eyes so blue... That is why all the girls in town follow you all around. Just like me, they long to be close to you...*

People were in awe and were crying. It was just a breathtaking moment. Pastor Tigner said, "Who gives this bride away to this groom?"

"Lillian Walker and I," my dad said. He gave me a hug and sat down.

Then Pastor Tigner began to do this beautiful ceremony of the reason God created marriage. He talked about how I was his assistant for years. He talked about how I wanted so badly to be in a relationship and to be married again, and how God brought Dana into my life. He talked about Dana's foundation and his basketball camps, and how the Lord orchestrated our steps to meet and become partners in life. He expressed how beautiful the union was and how God had sanctioned it. It was just the most beautiful wedding ceremony I had ever heard in my life. Dr. Tigner went over and beyond to tell a story of our love, and intertwined the vows between it, with our rings.

After Dr. Tigner got up, he sat down, and the Jewish cantor got up and did all the ceremonial pieces: the prayer wrap, the wine, the breaking of the glass...

Dr. Tigner got back up again and said, "I now pronounce you husband and wife."

Dana kept saying, "Can I kiss her now, can I kiss her now?!"

We kissed, and everybody cheered and roared. We walked back down the aisle as husband and wife to The Black Eyed Peas' "I Gotta Feeling."

Everyone was dancing down the aisles and cheering and clapping. It was just perfect.

We were married!!! Let the reception begin!

The reception was simply gorgeous. The tennis court area of the Sherwood Country Club was completely draped with silk white drapes open so that the starlit sky was our ceiling. There were huge flower arrangements on each table which had champagne silk crinkled tablecloths. The lighting was spectacular, creating a romantic mood highlighting the dance floor with our initials in gobo lights in the center of the dance floor. The DJ was playing all of the hits which kept the party going.

Everyone was happy, dancing, the drinks were flowing from the bars, hors d'oeuvres were being passed to all of our guests. Everyone was waiting to go into the beautifully draped banquet area. They were being entertained by the DJ, food, and the photo booth, which was our gift to every guest. They would take pictures from the photo booth, and we would keep a copy to create a photo book for our memories. Dana and I were taking photos by ourselves, which was rushed because the reception had to start, the clock was moving fast, and we had to be finished with everything by a certain time.

It was time for everyone to go inside the reception area. As the curtains opened and people entered, you could see the excitement on everyone's faces. It was like they were anticipating even more excitement than they'd experienced in the ceremony. They were right; we had lots of surprises in store.

All of our guests were seated and all of the wedding party lined up to make their grand entrance. The DJ played "Bring 'em Out" by T.I. and Jay Z, and each wedding party couple made their entrance with a dance they created. It was so fun and funny. My parents walked in and danced, my grandma and Dana's mother entered and danced, it was wild! So much fun.

Now it was our time to make our entrance as Mr. and Mrs. Dana Pump. For the past five weeks, we'd hired a dance teacher to choreograph our first dance. Dana was very adamant about having a dance instructor and having a choreographed routine as our first dance. I got a little nervous because Dana was on the side of the entrance trying to remember the routine. He was going over and over it, and it was not what we'd rehearsed. I was very afraid.

The DJ told everyone to stand as Mr. and Mrs. Dana Pump made our official entrance as husband and wife. We walked in hand and hand and headed toward the dance floor. People were cheering and clapping. All of a sudden, our song came on. It was "You Are My Everything" by Andy Gibb. We were ready to showcase our routine. We walked to our respective corners and then...Dana turned bright red. He forgot everything! I was trying to coach him, but it failed— he had completely forgotten. All of the lessons, all of the money was a waste.

To save the moment, I motioned to the DJ to stop the music and called everyone on the dance floor to dance with us together. It was hilarious! People were so confused, and Dana was so embarrassed, and I just held him tight, swaying side to side and saying, "Babe, it's okay!" Everyone joined us on the dance floor, and we had a ball. Then all of a sudden Dana's Jewish friends started motioning for the

Jewish traditional dances where all the men surround the groom and all of the women surround the bride in circles. Then Dana and I were to dance by ourselves in the middle and the people around us danced in circles surrounding us. What a night! Then all of a sudden, two chairs were brought to the dance floor for the Hora dance with the song "Hava Nagila" playing in the background. Dana and I were hoisted up in the air on chairs and everyone danced around us. It was fun and scary because it felt like they were going to drop us. The night was amazing. So amazing one of the guests of my family from the church that I grew up in came up to my dad in the reception and said, "I have never seen Black people and White people having so much fun together!" It was truly one of the most beautiful weddings one could ever behold.

After the dancing, everyone took their seats, and the dinner began. We served only the best: Chilean sea bass and filet mignon. The food was delicious. While we ate to keep the time moving because the city of Thousand Oaks set a time limit for the reception, Dr. Tigner prayed, and many people made toasts—my parents, Dana's mother, and some of our friends.

Dana went around to everyone, thanking them for coming. He was in heaven, having the time of his life. So did I; I went around thanking everyone for coming. Even my school staff came. I was so happy to have them there. The surprises did not stop. All of a sudden, Jeffrey Osborne came on the dance floor and started singing "On the Wings of Love," the most loved wedding song, and then serenaded us with, "Can you Woo Woo Woo!" He also passed the mic around to people asking them if they could Woo Woo Woo, and they tried with all of their might. It was so exciting, amazing, and wonderful.

Finally, to end the night, I got to dance with my dad to our favorite song, "Whenever I See Your Smiling Face" by James Taylor, while a video montage of my life played on the large screens overlooking the reception. Then Dana and his brother David danced with their mother to Celine Dion's "Because you Loved Me," while a video montage of Dana's life showed on the screen. It was a beautiful moment. After the dance, Dana and I both spoke, thanking everyone for coming, thanking our parents for the gorgeous wedding, and then Dana had to tell everyone that we were excited to start our own family and have our own children. When I spoke I thanked my parents and my grandmother. As soon as I mentioned her name I started crying because I couldn't describe the love I had for her and how grateful I was to her for all that she had done and sacrificed for me.

We rushed to cut the cake, which was a beautiful champagne and silver six-tier cake that had different designs on each tier with bling inside every rosebud. Dana's mother insisted that we get the cake from the famous Rosebud Bakery, and she paid for it. It was marble cake with chocolate filling. Although I love Hansen's cakes, I agreed to let Carole have her way.

The night ended with everyone saying that it was the most beautiful wedding they had ever attended, and it was so fast! No one wanted to leave, especially my dad. He had the time of his life. God had completely let us have a do-over, and I think all of us were so happy.

That night, Dana and I went back to our presidential suite. We took a bath together. Our wedding coordinator put together this beautiful bath with rose petals and champagne, even though we don't drink. So we opted against the champagne.

I put on my bridal outfit for the night, and we consummated the marriage, and it was just perfect. It was worth the wait. He and I both agreed that waiting made everything better. We slept all night, woke up, ate breakfast, and packed our bags so that we could go back to our house and make our flight to Hawaii.

We were just in love. I was so happy. Everything I had ever wanted and dreamed of was happening right in front of me. It was a lot of work, a lot of pain and tears, and standing on my faith. I truly learned and understood the benefit of trusting God.

We got back to the house, got our honeymoon luggage, and were about to head out to the airport when Dana said, "Leah. I remember what you told me about your ex-husband and how he cursed out your dad on your way to your honeymoon. I want to change the narrative. I want to go by your parents' house and thank them so much for allowing me to marry you."

Wow... He had no idea how much that meant to me because that point of my life was so hurtful. So on our way to the airport, we stopped at my parents' house. We got out of the car and went inside the house together. My dad was so overjoyed. "Leah and Dana, last night was the best night of my life. I had so much fun." My mom agreed. My dad acted a crazy fool, dancing his little heart out, and was singing his heart out on the mic. But I wanted him to do that; I owed that to him.

To redo a wedding, and to give my parents the adoration, acceptance, and appreciation that they deserved was so fulfilling.

Dana told my dad, "I just wanted to stop by because Leah told me what happened the day that they left for their honeymoon. I just wanted to come by and tell you guys thank you, and redo it."

My dad looked like he was ready to cry. But he held it in and gave Dana a tight hug. "Man, I love you. I love you and Leah. Thank you so much for doing this."

We hugged my parents and thanked them for everything. We headed to the airport for our honeymoon in Hawaii. I just kept thinking about how God had blessed me to get married to the love of my life, my partner in life, who I loved, and that it was something God had for me all along. I just had to be open and receptive to what God had for me, even though it wasn't what I had planned in my mind. It wasn't my dream, but it was God's dream for me. I had to go through seven years of challenges like overcoming adversity, getting over disappointment, being brokenhearted, working hard, and being obedient to what God had called me to do for me to receive my biggest blessing.

My life had changed drastically, and I was so fulfilled. It was like we were walking into our destiny together.

Seven. The year of completion.

Seven. The number of perfection.

Seven. The moment that
God changed my life.

Seven.

Thank God for seven.

Leah Cher Pump

*L*eah Cher Pump is the president and CEO of the LadyLike
Foundation. After being an elementary school teacher
for 9 years and a principal for 2 years in the private school system in
Los Angeles, Leah's vision for starting this company began in 2004
when her pastor, Dr. R.A. Williams Jr., appointed her as the director of the Youth and Young Adult Ministry at the McCoy Memorial
Baptist Church in Los Angeles, California. As the Youth and Young
Adult director, Leah implemented many successful programs, one
of which was the "LadyLike" class. At her church, "LadyLike" was
designed to teach young women through the word of God, how to
be virtuous and well rounded.

In 2007, Leah decided to launch the LadyLike Foundation as a
non-profit 501c3 whose purpose is to educate, empower and inspire
young women living in underprivileged inner-city communities.
Through a cutting-edge academic curriculum, scholarships, life skill
lessons, mentorships, and experiences young ladies are challenged
to reach their highest potential and placed on a platform for success.

Currently, the LadyLike Foundation has completed its 12TH year
as a non-profit organization continuing its programs open to girls
ages 12 to 18. The foundation has also given away over $100,000.00
in college scholarships to college bound young ladies within the
community who have a 3.5 GPA or higher and are furthering their
education at Prestigious Universities such as Harvard, Stanford,

UC Berkeley, UCLA, USC, Howard, Vassar, UC Santa Barbara, Spellman, Prairie View A&M University, and NYU just to name a few.

Leah is a graduate of the University of California at Berkeley with a Bachelor of Arts Degree in Sociology and a Minor in Education. She received her Masters Degree in Education from Pepperdine University. Leah is a native of Los Angeles, California and has been married to her husband Dana Pump, President and CEO of the Harold and Carole Pump Foundation, Double Pump Inc., and The Pump Group for 10 years.

Leah has received several awards for her philanthropic work and contribution to young girls. Some of her awards include: The "Youth Champion" Award from the Wiley Speech and Therapy Center, and the "Spirit of Giving Award" with her husband from the Fonkoze Organization, and the "Inspiration Award" from AEG Women in Entertainment Luncheon.

Leah has a passion for young women. She dreams that all of the young women she encounters establishes a relationship with the Lord, realizes their value, reaches their full potential, and becomes socially, intellectually, and mentally prepared to compete in today's society. She truly believes that the LadyLike Foundation will be the organization that enables women of all cultures, ages, and socioeconomic backgrounds to becoming the virtuous, well-rounded "Lady" that God has created them to be.